ATTENDING

McGILL-QUEEN'S STUDIES IN THE HISTORY OF IDEAS
Series Editor: Philip J. Cercone

Attending

An Ethical Art

Warren Heiti

McGill-Queen's University Press
Montreal & Kingston · London · Chicago

ISBN 978-0-2280-0612-1 (cloth)
ISBN 978-0-2280-0613-8 (paper)
ISBN 978-0-2280-0739-5 (ePDF)
ISBN 978-0-2280-0740-1 (ePUB)

Legal deposit third quarter 2021
Bibliothèque nationale du Québec

Printed in Canada on acid-free paper that is 100% ancient forest free
(100% post-consumer recycled), processed chlorine free

This book has been published with the help of a grant from the Canadian
Federation for the Humanities and Social Sciences, through the Awards to
Scholarly Publications Program, using funds provided by the Social Sciences
and Humanities Research Council of Canada. Funding was also received from
Vancouver Island University.

Funded by the   Financé par le
Government   gouvernement
of Canada   du Canada

Canada Council   Conseil des arts
for the Arts   du Canada

We acknowledge the support of the Canada Council for the Arts.

Nous remercions le Conseil des arts du Canada de son soutien.

Library and Archives Canada Cataloguing in Publication

Title: Attending: an ethical art / Warren Heiti.

Names: Heiti, Warren, 1979– author.

Series: McGill-Queen's studies in the history of ideas; 82.

Description: Series statement: McGill-Queen's studies in the history of ideas;
82 | Includes bibliographical references and index.

Identifiers: Canadiana (print) 20210138971 | Canadiana (ebook)
20210139064 | ISBN 9780228006138 (paper) | ISBN 9780228006121
(cloth) | ISBN 9780228007395 (ePDF) | ISBN 9780228007401 (ePUB)

Subjects: LCSH: Ethics.

Classification: LCC BJ1012 .245 2021 | DDC 170—dc23

This book was typeset by Marquis Interscript in 10,5 / 13 New Baskerville.

To Bethany Hindmarsh

Contents

Figures

ATTENDING

L'éducation de l'attention est le principal.
Simone Weil, *Œuvres complètes*, VI.3.255

1

Introduction

§1.1. WE MAY DISCERN AT LEAST TWO GENEALOGIES in ethical psychology. One genealogy is nearly two thousand, five hundred years old: it starts with Plato; another goes back only seven hundred and fifty years or so to a scholastic interpretation of Aristotle. These genealogies offer different *images* of ethical psychology. The first was inherited, in the twentieth century, by Simone Weil, Iris Murdoch, John McDowell, and Jan Zwicky; let us call it the *Platonic ethical psychology*.[1] According to this psychology, the ethical agent is a *witness*: her primary responsibility is not to change the world but *to understand* it. Her fundamental temperament is *patience*. Her proper work is *attending*, and its ἀρετή (*aretē*) is *clarity*. Clear perception is a function of an *integrated* character. Insofar as this agent does act, her action is *responsive to* and *determined by* what she understands. In this image of agency, action is always interaction. The energy needed for action is not generated by the agent herself; she receives it, like light, from others.

Let us call the second image, which has been articulated for our time by Michael Smith, the *Humean moral psychology*.[2] According to this psychology, the ethical agent is an actor: his primary responsibility is *to change* the world. It is important that this image distinguishes between two psychological faculties: the "cognitive" faculty – call it *belief* – reflects the way the world is; and the "non-cognitive" faculty – call it *desire* –

---

1 See Weil, "Attention and Will" and "Reflections on the Right Use of School Studies"; Murdoch, *The Sovereignty of Good*; McDowell, "Virtue and Reason"; and Zwicky, "Imagination and the Good Life," and "Alcibiades' Love."

2 See Smith, "The Humean Theory of Motivation." The Humean theory might not be Hume's own theory, but it is Smith's name for a theory inspired by Hume.

represents some preferred and counterfactual state of the world. Insofar as these faculties operate independently, the agent's psychology is in a *disintegrative* state. His fundamental temperament, resulting from the discrepancy between the two representations, is one of *dissatisfaction.* His proper work is *problem-solving,* and its excellence is *prudence.* Crucially, the agent's action is not determined by anything external to him. According to this image of ethical psychology, freedom is unimpeded *self-determination.*

Together, the Platonic and Humean psychologies are encompassed by the *Aristotelian ethical psychology.*[3] Aristotle is pivotal to this story. According to Sokrates and Plato, virtue is knowledge, and no-one can both know what is good and fail to be moved by it. However, when we face the phenomena, it appears that there are plenty of counter-examples to this thought; that is, there are examples of agents who know that an action is wrong but commit it anyway. Aristotle reports the following apparent fact: "the incontinent man, knowing that what he does is bad, does it as a result of passion."[4] He observes that this view contradicts that of Sokrates: "for it would be strange—so Socrates thought—if when knowledge was in a man something else could master it and drag it around like a slave. For Socrates was entirely opposed to the view in question, holding that there is no such thing as incontinence."[5]

Aristotle does not wish to reject the Sokratic view but to finesse it so that it does justice to the relevant facts. He emphatically agrees with Sokrates that "*no one* would say that it is the part of a practically wise man to do willingly the basest acts."[6] And he introduces the character of the *incontinent,* or *akratic,* agent to explain the special sense in which one can know what is wrong and nevertheless do it. The akratic agent is one who experiences a disharmony between the reasoning and desiring components of his soul. This disharmony occludes his knowledge of what is good; Aristotle says that he has knowledge like someone who is "asleep, mad, or drunk."[7]

---

3 Technically, it should probably be called the *Aristotelico-Platonic ethical psychology.* But that name is a mouthful.

4 Aristotle, *Nicomachean Ethics,* VII.1.1145b12–13.

5 Ibid., VII.2.1145b23–6. Cf. Plato, *Protagoras,* 352b–c.

6 Ibid., VII.2.1146a6–7.

7 Ibid., VII.3.1147a13–14.

For our purposes, here is what is crucial about the *akratic* agent: he is in *agony*, in the etymological sense; a contest is taking place in his soul between what he knows and what he wants. The *continent*, or *enkratic*, agent is no less agonized; they both deliberate by weighing putatively competing considerations. Indeed, the psychological structure of the enkratic and akratic agents is the same. The main difference is that the enkratic agent manages, after struggling, to do what is good, while the akratic agent ultimately fails to do it.

In the face of some irresoluble ethical predicaments, such agony is appropriate. But there are arguably some other contexts, however rare, which invite an uncomplicated response. Weil offers an example: "There are cases where a thing is necessary from the mere fact that it is possible. Thus to eat when we are hungry, to give a wounded man, dying of thirst, something to drink when there is water quite near. Neither a ruffian nor a saint would refrain from doing so."[8] Weil suggests that clear perception of the relation between the thirsting man and the water – that is, the man's need for the water – is enough to move the agent to act.

While the Platonic virtuous soul is harmonized, or integrated,[9] it might appear that the Aristotelian soul is broken. The possibility of akrasia depends on a distinction between the reasoning and desiring components of the soul.[10] In drawing this distinction, and the correlative distinction between epistemic and characterological virtues, Aristotle might seem to introduce a hairline fracture into the centre of the soul. G.E.M. Anscombe is one interpreter who seems to glimpse in Aristotle a prototype for the Humean theory of motivation. According to this theory, motivation must be analysed into two "distinct existences": a *belief*, which is true when it fits the world, and a *desire*, which is satisfied when the world fits it. Ultimately, the desire is what motivates; insofar as the agent is dissatisfied with the way the world is, he is moved to change it. McDowell argues, however, that it is misguided to interpret

8 Weil, "Necessity and Obedience," *Gravity and Grace*, 44 / 55. Generally, references to Weil's work will follow this format – Weil, Title, # / # – where the first number refers to the English translation and the second refers to the French original. When the French title is not evident from the English, it will be specified. OC stands for *Œuvres complètes*.

9 See Plato, *Republic*, IV.443d–e; Aisara, "On Human Nature"; Kosman, "The Faces of Justice."

10 Aristotle, *Nicomachean Ethics*, I.13.1102b13ff.

Aristotle as a proto-Humean. But it is equally misguided to interpret him as a cognitivist, a theorist for whom beliefs alone are sufficient to motivate. For Aristotle, the reasoning and desiring aspects of the soul are *distinct* but *inseparable*, "like concave and convex in the circumference of a circle."[11] Similarly, practical wisdom and integrated character are interdependent.

The problem of akrasia is sometimes called the problem of "weakness of the will." But this phrase is anachronistic and deeply misleading. According to Charles H. Kahn, the first unified theory of the will and its weakness was not developed until Aquinas: "There is nothing remotely comparable in Aristotle's description of *akrasia*, for which the term 'weakness of will' is wholly inappropriate."[12] Hannah Arendt agrees: the faculty of the will, she says, is "a faculty of which ancient philosophy knew nothing and which was not discovered in its awesome complexities before Paul and Augustine."[13] According to Arendt, the Pauline soul is split into a conflict between its carnal and spiritual halves.[14] Into this conflict, the will is inserted as a third faculty; it appears "as a kind of *arbiter* ... between the mind that knows and the flesh that desires. In this role of arbiter, the will is free."[15] Let us call this doctrine *voluntarism*, the doctrine that *volition is free*; that is, the doctrine that volition is independent of, and unconstrained by, anything other than itself.

The agony of the Pauline soul might seem like the agony of the Aristotelian soul, but there is an important difference. For Aristotle, although the reasoning and desiring components may be in conflict, they are internally related. Insofar as the agent knows what is good, she desires it. For Aristotle, the agony of akrasia is the result of an epistemic obscurity, which can be dispelled. For the Pauline soul, however, the agony is ineradicable. The deliverances of the spirit and the flesh can never determine what the soul will do. This radical indeterminacy is inherited by the Humean moral psychology. As an "original existence," a Humean desire can never be determined by a belief.

---

11   Ibid., I.13.1102a31.

12   Kahn, "Discovering the will: From Aristotle to Augustine," 245.

13   Arendt, "Some Questions of Moral Philosophy," 72. For drawing my attention to this text, thanks to Bethany Hindmarsh.

14   Cf. Romans 7:13ff.

15   Arendt, "Some Questions of Moral Philosophy," 119. Cf. Nietzsche, *On the Genealogy of Morals*, §§I.13, II.2.

Here is the fundamental difference between the Humean psychology and the Platonic one: in the latter, the desiring component of the soul is capable of *listening to* and *harmonizing with* the reasoning component.[16] In other words, the Platonic psychology is *integrative*. By contrast, in the Humean psychology, desire and belief are "distinct existences"; they do not communicate: it is "impossible, that reason and passion can ever oppose each other, or dispute for the government of the will and actions."[17] In other words, the Humean psychology is *disintegrative*. Everything hangs on how we read the enkratic or akratic agent. Here is a suggestion: the agony of the enkratic agent is understandable only if we read it in relation to the Platonic ethical psychology. The enkratic agent is a character on a spectrum, a character who is aspiring toward the norm of integrative agency: a limiting case which he dimly intuits.

The success of the Humean theory in a large number of cases does not justify its universalization. That attempt at universalization is illicit and stimulated by a prejudice, which assumes that a thing's essence is hidden and revealed by analysis. Thus, when a Humean theorist encounters what appear to be cases of integrative agency, he assumes that analysis will reveal the essential (but hidden) constituents of belief and desire. But we can appeal to Walter Chatton's "anti-razor" in maintaining that *more than one kind of account* is necessary to explain polydimensional phenomena.[18] There is at least one dimension of action which is not best explained by the Humean theory, and which requires Weil's Platonic account. This dimension is *attending*. One form of attending, which is fairly common, is *listening*.

Consider the example of listening to someone who has been irreversibly hurt and who is inconsolable. By hypothesis, the situation cannot be changed, and thus it is distorting or idle to invoke a Humean desire. The Humean theory is unable accurately to explain either the motivation or the ethical significance of this kind of example. Furthermore, such ethical contexts, in their unchangeability, resemble some aesthetic contexts. Weil offers an example:

16 See Aristotle, *Nicomachean Ethics*, I.13.1102b30–2, III.12.1119b15–16.

17 Hume, *Treatise*, II.III.§III.¶7. Cf. ibid., Appendix; and Smith, *The Moral Problem*, 7.

18 See Maurer, "Ockham's Razor and Chatton's Anti-Razor," 464. For Ockham's and Chatton's principles, see Hyman and Walsh, eds., *Philosophy in the Middle Ages*, 431–2.

When we listen to Bach or to a Gregorian melody, all the faculties of the soul become tense and silent in order to apprehend this thing of perfect beauty—each after its own fashion—the intelligence among the rest. It finds nothing in this thing it hears to affirm or deny, but it feeds upon it.[19]

This kind of aesthetic appreciation – arguably a real case – is not goal-directed; it does not wish to alter anything in what it perceives; it affords no purchase for a world-changing desire. But it is responsive to the work of art. No less than ethical listening, it requires the Platonic psychology for its explanation.

We are not rejecting the Humean psychology. It correctly analyses cases of enkratic and akratic agency and is thus encompassed by the Aristotelian psychology. Furthermore, the Humean psychology is needed for the exercise of *elenctic attending* – a kind of attending that we use to criticize false beliefs and bad desires in others and ourselves. The enkratic (or akratic) agent inhabits the disintegrative perspective, whose perception approximates (and aspires to) that of the integrative perspective. Where the integrative agent perceives the one thing needed, the enkratic agent agonizes over several considerations even when some of them are irrelevant. The crucial distinction here is between attending to a unified focus, and dispersing attention across a multiplicity of potentially competing foci. But the disintegrative perspective remains indispensable even for the integrative agent; it is from that perspective that we can engage in moral critique and revision. In cultures organized by systemic oppression, attention may move along grooves toward unjustly privileged foci. Prejudice, no less than virtue, silences some aspects of a situation.[20] In order to free our perception from prejudice, we need to have periodic recourse to the disintegrative perspective. By performing the Humean analysis on ourselves (or by submitting ourselves to such analysis by others), we may be able to identify which of our beliefs are false, and which ones have been distorted by hatred or fear. But we also need the Platonic psychology – however rare and non-generalizable – as a paradigm to which we may aspire.

§1.2. One of the main proponents of the Humean theory is Michael Smith. He describes it as "the standard picture of human psychology." According to this picture, he says:

---

19 Weil, "Intelligence and Grace," *Gravity and Grace*, 129 / 147.
20 See Fricker, "Silence and Institutional Prejudice."

... there are two main kinds of psychological state. On the one hand there are beliefs, states that purport to represent the way the world is. Since our beliefs purport to represent the world, they are assessable in terms of truth and falsehood ... And on the other hand there are desires, states that represent how the world is to be. Desires are unlike beliefs in that they do not even purport to represent the way the world is. They are therefore not assessable in terms of truth and falsehood. Hume concludes that belief and desire are therefore distinct existences: that is, that we can always pull belief and desire apart, at least modally.[21]

In other words, the Humean theory is dualistic: its two basic constituents are belief and desire, and there is no necessary connection between them. The denial "that agents who are in belief-like states and desire-like states are ever in a *single, unitary, kind of state*" is the "cash value" of the Humean theory.[22] Depending on whether one emphasizes belief or desire in one's explanation of action, one may be categorized as a "cognitivist" or a "non-cognitivist." A cognitivist thinks that beliefs themselves can be motivating. A non-cognitivist does not deny that the agent has beliefs, but claims that the active ingredient in motivation is desire.

Smith distinguishes between two features of moral judgement: what he calls "the objectivity of moral judgement" and "the practicality of moral judgement." According to the first feature, its objectivity, "we seem to think moral questions have correct answers; that the correct answers are made correct by objective moral facts."[23] Metaphysically, this feature implies *realism*, the thesis that there are moral facts; and psychologically, it implies *cognitivism*, the thesis that moral judgements express beliefs about moral facts (which beliefs can be true or false). According to the second feature of moral judgement, its practicality, "moral judgements seem to be, or to imply, opinions about the reasons we have for believing in certain ways, and, other things being equal, having such opinions is a matter of finding ourselves with a corresponding motivation to act."[24] Psychologically, this feature implies *non-cognitivism* – the thesis that moral judgements express desires (which are not truth-apt); and metaphysically, this feature implies *irrealism* – the thesis that there are no moral facts.

21 Smith, *The Moral Problem*, 7.
22 Ibid., 119.
23 Ibid., 6.
24 Ibid., 7.

These features sound technical, but they are meant to reflect ordinary intuitions about moral judgements: when we speak or argue about moral questions, we often feel that there are correct or incorrect, better or worse responses to these questions (the objectivity feature); and when we make moral judgements, we expect those judgements to be accompanied by the appropriate motivation (the practicality feature). Suppose, for example, that Federico and Debbie are arguing about whether she should cut down the elderly western red cedars living in her yard; he is arguing that she should not, while she is arguing that she should. The disagreement is not arbitrary: by hypothesis, if one is defending one's position and trying to persuade one's interlocutor, one feels that one is right and one's interlocutor is wrong. Furthermore, suppose that Federico convinces Debbie that it is wrong to kill the trees. Normally, he would then expect her to be motivated according to her new judgement; she would put down the chainsaw. If she conceded that she should not kill the trees and then proceeded to kill them, the discrepancy between her judgement and her action would be perplexing; it would require special explanation.

The tension between the objectivity and the practicality of moral judgement is captured in what Smith calls "the moral problem." Following David McNaughton, Smith articulates this problem as an inconsistent triad of propositions. We may paraphrase them in the following way:

1 *Cognitivism and realism:* Moral judgements express truth-apt beliefs about apparent moral facts. (Objectivity.)
2 *Internalism about motivation:* There is a necessary or internal connection between a moral judgement and appropriate motivation. (Practicality.)
3 *The Humean theory:* The structure of the psyche is dualistic; its two basic constituents are belief (a truth-apt mental state that tries to represent the way the world is) and desire (a non-truth-apt mental state that represents a counterfactual state of the world).[25]

If one subscribes to the Humean theory, then one must choose to reject the objectivity feature or the practicality feature – one cannot consistently subscribe to all three propositions. Rejecting (1) cognitivism and

25 Cf. McNaughton, *Moral Vision*, 23; Smith, *The Moral Problem*, 12.

realism results in expressivism (the theory – in its crudest version – that moral judgements express emotive grunts of approval and disapproval), while rejecting (2) internalism results in externalism (the theory that there is no necessary connection between moral judgement and appropriate motivation).[26]

I would not describe things in this way, and it is as a gesture of respect toward the dominant discourse in anglophone philosophy that I offer this sketch of the landscape. But I shall argue that this way of articulating the problem rests on a mistaken assumption. If we can expose and criticize the assumption, then the problem may dissolve. The assumption is *psychological dualism*, the thesis that there are only two fundamentally different kinds of mental state. One might think that one could correct this mistake by rejecting the Humean theory. On that account, the theorist could remain committed to both cognitivism and internalism – and some of McDowell's interpreters adopt this tack. There is, however, a more subtle possibility: that what is accurate about the Humean theory may be saved by recontextualizing it. The Humean theory has a place in a polydimensional psychology. Such a psychology also enables us to save what is true about Plato's vision: that sometimes knowing is enough for virtue. Aristotle offers us the needed polydimensional account, one that includes *both* the Humean theory *and* the Platonic psychology. The Humean theory saves the phenomena of akrasia and *enkrateia* (continence), while the Platonic psychology saves the phenomenon of *aretē* (virtue).

The Humean theory by itself is inadequate. If we adhere exclusively to it, then we sacrifice some real and important phenomena to theoretical parsimony. Nor, with due respect to Smith, is it "the standard picture." Plato and Aristotle, Spinoza and Freud, Martha Nussbaum and Jan Zwicky all believe that the psyche is more complex.[27] In order to understand and do justice to its complexity, we need a complex philosophical psychology, as Anscombe and Murdoch have argued. Anscombe claims

26 On expressivism, see, for example, Ayer, "Critique of Ethics and Theology," *Language, Truth and Logic*, 136–58. On externalism, see, for example, Brink, "Externalist Moral Realism."

27 See, for example, Plato, *Republic*, IV, and *Phaidros*, 246a–257b; Aristotle, *Nicomachean Ethics*, I.13, and *On the Soul*, II.3; Spinoza, *Ethics*; Freud, *An Outline of Psychoanalysis* and *Civilization and Its Discontents*; Nussbaum, *Upheavals of Thought*; and Zwicky, *Alkibiades' Love*.

that moral philosophy should be laid aside "until we have an adequate philosophy of psychology, in which we are conspicuously lacking."[28] Following her, Murdoch writes: "A working philosophical psychology is needed which can at least attempt to connect modern psychological terminology with a terminology concerned with virtue."[29] These calls have been followed by a sub-discipline in philosophy called "moral psychology," which is further divisible into at least three different streams. (1) One stream plaits together cognitive science, empirical psychology, and philosophy of mind; in this area, Christopher Mole and Wayne Wu are doing pioneering research on attention. (2) Another stream maintains that ethics requires a careful study of the complex structure that Plato and Aristotle call ψυχή (*psychē*, or soul) and its excellences, which they call ἀρεταί (*aretai*, or virtues); in this area, some of the wiser minds are dead: in addition to Plato and Aristotle, they include Weil and Murdoch. (3) Yet a third stream overlaps with some aspects of the preceding two: namely, feminist moral psychology, an internally diverse field whose theorists include Sue Campbell, Audre Lorde, María Lugones, and Margaret Urban Walker, among many others.[30] This third stream draws on the empirical resources of the first stream while also examining the social dimensions of character traits and psychological states that may be shared with the second stream. To reflect the difference among the streams, we shall call the first *moral psychology* and the second *ethical psychology*;[31] and Walker calls the third stream "*social moral psychology*."[32] This book is primarily concerned with the second stream, but when appropriate it acknowledges intersections with the first and third streams.

§1.3. It is typical in professional anglophone philosophy to conceive of philosophy as the identification and solution of problems. Such philosophy is modelled on a picture of science and envisaged as

28 Anscombe, "Modern Moral Philosophy," 1.

29 Murdoch, "On 'God' and 'Good,'" *The Sovereignty of Good*, 46.

30 For one sample of the range, see DesAutels and Walker, eds., *Moral Psychology: Feminist Ethics and Social Theory*. See also Lorde, "The Uses of Anger"; and Lugones, "Playfulness, 'World'-Travelling, and Loving Perception." For drawing my attention to Lorde's essay, thanks to El Jones.

31 For the different emphases of the terms "moral" and "ethical," see Williams, *Ethics and the Limits of Philosophy*, 6.

32 Walker, "Moral Psychology," 104.

making linear progress over time; a researcher solves a problem, publishes the results of his research in a journal, and the field advances. The problems are often highly specialized, and their solutions require a technical and precise lexicon; they may be legible only to a handful of experts. Like theories of spontaneous generation or phlogiston, solved philosophical problems are rendered obsolete. The work of earlier philosophers is relegated to the shelves of libraries (themselves increasingly at risk of becoming obsolete) and regarded as merely of historical interest. One of the most brilliant philosophers I have had the fortune to meet told me that there is more wisdom in a single journal of contemporary philosophy than there is in all of philosophy before Descartes.[33] With due respect to that philosopher, this book takes a different view. It is based on the faith that the ancients still have something to teach us. It treats their works not as mere historical artifacts but as vital possibilities for thinking and doing – for ways of living. And for this reason, an approach that might at first glance appear anachronistic – claiming, for instance, that Smith's Humean theory is encompassed by Aristotle's psychology – is instead an attempt to treat their philosophies as contemporaneous.

Nor does this book seek to present solutions to "the moral problem." The idea that the job of moral philosophy is to solve problems is not self-evident or compulsory, and it has been challenged by Julia Annas and Peter Winch (among others).[34] It is a culturally specific idea, belonging to a very recent development in the history of Western philosophy and deriving from a specious aspiration to positivist science. It is also the signature mark of a theory of motivation whose monopoly this book resists. Some of the deepest problems are insoluble: consider, for instance, the problem of the relationship between parent and child; the problem of mortality (of ourselves and others); the problem of what to eat and what not to eat; the problem of partial and impartial responsibilities; the problem of the one and the many. But the fact that these problems are insoluble does not mean that philosophy has no work to do with respect to them. "The proper method of philosophy," Weil

33 Weil's evaluation is the opposite: "For my part, except for Racine, I don't value anything that came after 1660 (right down to our day) as much as that which dates from before it" (Weil, quoted in Pétrement, *Simone Weil: A Life*, 371).

34 See Annas, "Being Virtuous and Doing the Right Thing"; and Winch, "Moral Integrity."

writes, "consists in clearly conceiving the insoluble problems in all their insolubility and then in simply contemplating them, fixedly and tirelessly, year after year, without any hope, patiently waiting."[35]

Weil's ethics is essentially the practice of attending to particulars. It is radically unlike the moral theories of Hobbes, Kant, and Mill, and those of their descendants. Her ethics is not captured by a simple action-guiding principle or decision-making procedure; nor is it structured like a complicated system into which such principles are inserted and by which they are defended. For this reason, it might appear to belong to the camp of "moral particularism," whose proponents include, among others, Jonathan Dancy, David McNaughton, and Margaret Olivia Little.[36] That camp denies that morality requires general principles; it asserts, instead, that the variables in particular circumstances determine the right or wrong thing to do. As we shall see, however, Weil's work does not stake out a position in this territory of competing moral theories. Her closest philosophical relatives are not system-builders such as Kant or Dancy, but clarifiers such as Wittgenstein and Zwicky. Mario von der Ruhr claims that Weil, like her teacher Alain, is concerned with "the relation between *form* and *content*, with finding the right *voice* in the formulation of one's thoughts." While she does not adopt Alain's format (the *propos,* a kind of micro-essay) for her own reflections, Weil "sees her essays as similarly open-ended exercises in conceptual clarification, rather than as attempts at systematisation or theory-building."[37] Her ethics of attending is ultimately *not a theory but a method.*

To say that it is not a theory is not to say that it is not thoughtful; but that its way of thinking is like the older θεωρία (*theōria*) – contemplating with the eye of the soul. Like Wittgenstein's *Nachlaß,* Weil's œuvre is not systematic; and like his, much of hers was unpublished during her lifetime. While she was a prolific writer of essays (including the book-length essay *The Need for Roots,* which she wrote for the Free French in London), the style of her notebooks is often non-discursive, taking the form of discontinuous, aphoristic fragments, and has more in common with the meditations of Marcus Aurelius (a philosopher she admired) than it does with the theorizing of Aquinas or Locke.

35 Weil, *First and Last Notebooks,* 335 / *La connaissance surnaturelle,* 305.
36 For a sample, see Hooker and Little, eds., *Moral Particularism.*
37 Von der Ruhr, *Simone Weil: An Apprenticeship in Attention,* 51.

Here it may be helpful to enlist a distinction that Weil herself draws between two kinds of philosophers: those who use a Sokratic method of contemplating meaning and "those who construct a representation of the universe to their liking; the latter alone can be said, strictly speaking, to have systems."[38] This distinction resonates with some remarks by Wittgenstein. In the foreword to a manuscript that would be published posthumously as *Philosophical Remarks,* he draws a contrast between two spirits: the one that inspires his manuscript and "the one which informs the vast stream of European and American civilization in which all of us stand." The second, he says, "expresses itself in an onwards movement, in building ever larger and more complicated structures; the other in striving after clarity and perspicuity in no matter what structure."[39] Correspondingly, "true philosophy," Weil claims, "does not construct anything. Its object is given, namely, our thoughts. It only makes an inventory of them, as Plato said."[40] We should not overly stress this distinction, but it does convey a sense of how Weil wishes to address Sokrates's question "How should one live?"[41] Not by painstakingly constructing a linguistic replica of a corner of the cosmos and then running repeatable experiments and quantifying the results, but by carefully reflecting on what we are and what living well means for us.

Ethics, if it is anything, is a practical art, a way of living. Philosophizing about ethics is valueless unless it *means* something in practice. Weil claims that philosophy "does not consist in accumulating knowledge, as science does, but in changing the whole soul. Value is something which has a relation not only to knowledge, but also to sensibility and action; there isn't any philosophical reflection without an essential transformation in sensibility and in the practices of life."[42] Such a characterization of philosophy is reminiscent of Plato's image of education in the *Republic:* it consists not in pouring information into an empty vessel, like inserting sight into sightless eyes, but in turning around the already-seeing eye of the soul.[43] Doing philosophy is doing more than

---

38 Weil, "Philosophy," *Formative Writings,* 288 / 293.

39 Wittgenstein, "Foreword," *Philosophical Remarks,* 8. Cf. Wittgenstein, *Culture and Value,* 6–8.

40 Weil, "Some Reflections around the Concept of Value," 111 / 59.

41 Plato, *Republic,* I.344e and I.352d.

42 Weil, "Some Reflections around the Concept of Value," 109 / 57.

43 Plato, *Republic,* VII.518b–d.

merely processing information. "Philosophy (including problems of cognition, etc.)," writes Weil, "is *exclusively* an affair of action and practice. That is why it is so difficult to write about it. Difficult in the same way as a treatise on tennis or running, but much more so."[44]

What makes a treatise on tennis difficult? If the point of the treatise is to help someone to understand tennis, it will need to include not only an account of the rules, but also a description of the physical movements; and the best way to convey those movements is not to *describe* them but to *show* them. And for the aspiring tennis player, demonstrations by the instructor will not be enough; the apprentice will need to practise the movements with her own body. This brief metaphilosophical remark, written in Weil's last notebook, offers the key to appreciating her early dissertation on Descartes: in order to understand his meditations, she could not merely describe them: she had to execute her own meditations in the first person. And she discovers that the most clear and distinct truth is not "I am" but "I can." Activity is more axiomatic than mere existence. If philosophizing about ethics is meaningful, then it is not best represented by a body of doctrine or a tablet of commandments; it must instead set the soul in motion.

At the end of his "Lecture on Ethics," Wittgenstein makes a claim toward which Weil might feel sympathetic: "Ethics so far as it springs from the desire to say something about the ultimate meaning of life, the absolute good, the absolute valuable, can be no science."[45] Wittgenstein is not disparaging ethics – on the contrary, he says that he respects it deeply. He is trying to indicate the limits of science, defined as a systematic description of the world, the totality of true propositions picturing the totality of facts.[46] In conversation with Friedrich Waismann, he elaborates on his thinking from the "Lecture" and criticizes the very idea of moral theory: "Is value a particular state of mind? Or a form inhering in certain data of consciousness? My answer is: Whatever one said to me, I would reject it; not indeed because the explanation is false but because it is an *explanation*. // If anybody offers me a *theory*, I would

---

44 Weil, *First and Last Notebooks*, 362 / *La connaissance surnaturelle*, 335. Cf. Wittgenstein, *Tractatus Logico-Philosophicus*, prop. 4.112.

45 Wittgenstein, "Lecture on Ethics," 12.

46 See Wittgenstein, *Tractatus*, props. 1.1, 3.01, 4.01, 4.11.

say: No, no, that doesn't interest me. Even if the theory were true that would not interest me—it would not be *what* I seek."[47]

— "But what, exactly, is wrong with a theoretical explanation?" an interlocutor might ask. "Why would he reject it even if it were true?" — Because, he says, "the scientific way of looking at a fact is not the way to look at it as a miracle."[48] This idea of *a way of looking* is also important for Weil. A theory is one way of looking at a phenomenon. But an aphorism is another way of looking. If we assume that whatever is meaningful about an aphorism can be translated into a theory, then we are assuming that style is irrelevant to meaning. Moreover, we may be assuming that aphoristic insight is illegitimate unless it yields to theoretical reconstruction. Regarding analytic theories of metaphor, Zwicky writes: "developing an understanding of metaphor is taken to be tantamount to developing a *theory* of how metaphor manages to (appear to) mean. // What this highlights is the fact that systematic philosophy's notion of understanding is in fact a form of legitimation: a person cannot claim to have understood the meaning of a metaphor unless he or she can provide a 'rational reconstruction', *criteria*."[49] Similarly, some philosophers take ethical understanding to be tantamount to having a moral theory; but there is a significant difference between a phronetic approach to particular ethical contexts and a general moral theory (even a theory of "moral particularism").

§1.4. The preceding reflections have implications for method. What is at stake may be thrown into relief by assembling some of Aristotle's methodological remarks from the *Nicomachean Ethics*:

Our discussion will be adequate if it has as much clearness as the subject-matter admits of, for precision is not to be sought for alike in all discussions ... Now fine and just actions, which political science investigates, exhibit much variety and fluctuation ... And goods exhibit a similar fluctuation ...

47 Wittgenstein, quoted in Waismann, "Notes on Talks with Wittgenstein," 15–16.
48 Wittgenstein, "Lecture on Ethics," 11.
49 Zwicky, *Lyric Philosophy*, L83; for definitions of "criterion," see ibid., R41. Cf. Zwicky, "What Is Lyric Philosophy?," §26, and "Dream Logic," 141–2 / *AL*, 100. Whenever possible, the first printings of Zwicky's essays will be cross-referenced with their printings in *Alkibiades' Love* (*AL*). [N.b. While this book, *Attending: an ethical art*, engages with Zwicky's work, she did not see the manuscript prior to its publication. I am entirely responsible for any errors or misreadings in my presentation of her work.]

We must be content, then, in speaking of such subjects and with such prem-
isses to indicate the truth roughly and in outline ...

*

And we must also remember what has been said before, and not look for
precision in all things alike, but in each class of things such precision as accords with the subject-matter, and so much as is appropriate to the inquiry.

*

But this must be agreed upon beforehand, that the whole account of matters
of conduct must be given in outline and not precisely, as we said at the very
beginning that the accounts we demand must be in accordance with the
subject-matter; matters concerned with conduct and questions of what is
good for us have no fixity, any more than matters of health. The general account being of this nature, the account of particular cases is yet more lacking
in exactness; for they do not fall under any system or precept, but the agents
themselves must in each case consider what is appropriate to the occasion,
as happens also in medicine or navigation.[50]

Three times in the first two books, Aristotle emphasizes that the account
of ethics must fit the subject matter. Like matters of health, questions
of what is good for us exhibit variety and fluctuation. If we are committed to stylistic coherence, as Aristotle seems to be, then our account will
need to allow for that varied and fluctuating character. Truth-telling is
possible, but it must be done roughly and in outline. If we try to be
more precise than the subject matter permits, then we are likely to miss
the truth, or to misrepresent the phenomena.

    Beside Aristotle's methodological remarks, let us set Wittgenstein's
only explicitly ethical remark from his *Investigations*:

For imagine having to sketch a sharply defined picture 'corresponding' to a
blurred one. In the latter there is a blurred red rectangle: for it you put
down a sharply defined one. ... —But if the colours in the original merge
without a hint of any outline won't it become a hopeless task to draw a sharp
picture corresponding to the blurred one? Won't you then have to say: "Here
I might just as well draw a circle or heart as a rectangle, for all the colours

---

    50 Aristotle, *Nicomachean Ethics*, I.3.1094b11–21; I.7.1098a26–9; II.2.1103b34–
1104a10; translation altered.

merge. Anything—and nothing—is right."——And this is the position you are in if you look for definitions corresponding to our concepts in aesthetics or ethics.[51]

Since the sharp rectangle does not really correspond to the blurred one, one might as well draw a circle, and since it seems arbitrary, nothing is right. But the feigned despair is not justified; it is prompted by importing, into this "blurred" context, an inappropriately "sharp" standard of accuracy. If the subject matter of ethics is "blurred," then "sharp" definitions will be arbitrary. But why insist on what is arbitrary when it is not compulsory?

Aristotle recognizes that the sharp standard is inappropriate for this subject matter. Since the subject matter is varied and fluctuating, our account must be sensitive to those features. But they are not flaws or defects (unless judged by the inappropriate standard); they are simply what things are like here. If we find a more appropriate standard, then apparent defects may disappear. Instead of clinging, rigidly, to a sharp standard, we might defer to the discernment of the person of practical wisdom and the flexibility of the Lesbian rule, a malleable leaden rule used on the island of Lesbos to measure curved surfaces of stone.[52] Aristotle is not arguing for obscurity or imprecision; he is arguing for *context-sensitivity*. He is cautioning us that he will not be providing an instruction manual that tells us, in advance of all particular cases, how to solve moral problems. Like doctors and navigators, we ourselves will need to consider what is "appropriate to the occasion," and what is appropriate is not prescribed by "any system or precept."

Of course, good doctors and navigators do not merely ad-lib; but Aristotle's point is that experience matters. There is no harm in reading books, but "we ought to attend to the undemonstrated sayings and opinions of experienced and older people or of people of practical wisdom not less than to demonstrations; because experience has given them an eye they see aright."[53] If we are attempting to train an agent's

---

51 Wittgenstein, *Philosophical Investigations*, §77.

52 On the Lesbian rule, see Aristotle, *Nicomachean Ethics*, V.10.1137b29–32. Cf. this book, §3.3.

53 Aristotle, *Nicomachean Ethics*, VI.11.1143b11–14. Aristotle's respect here for the opinions of older people may be contrasted with Plato's depiction of the elderly Kephalos, whose experience has not made him wise (Plato, *Republic*, I.328c–331d).

sensitivity – rather than transmit a set of general principles or a decision procedure – then our approach might be other than theoretical (or might involve other-than-theoretical strategies). We might expose her to particular exemplars of the sort of sensitivity that we are trying to elicit; or we might expose her to particular contexts in which her own sensitivity is exercised. Both Roger Shiner and John McDowell compare Books 3 to 5 of the *Ethics* to a gallery of character sketches.[54] According to their reading, Aristotle is not building a system of virtue, but presenting a set of exemplars.

(Since we shall be exploring the suggestion that Aristotle's way of thinking about ethics resonates with Weil's, we must acknowledge that she calls him "the corrupt tree which bears only rotten fruit."[55] She has a powerful reason for denouncing him: Aristotle holds "the conviction that, for all who are slaves by nature, servitude is the condition which is at the same time happiest and most just," and this conviction, she says, inspires "his great argument in justification of slavery." Even if we reject his wrong conviction, "we are necessarily led in our ignorance to accept others which must have lain in him at the root of that one. A man who takes the trouble to draw up an apology for slavery cannot be a lover of justice."[56] There is a great deal to think about here – Aristotle's argument and Weil's critique of him, and also the question her critique raises concerning the coherence of a philosopher's thinking. It goes without saying that Aristotle's argument – including the fact that he not only thought it, but also made it public – is horrifying. For some, such as Weil, his offence against justice is sufficient reason to set the rest of his philosophy aside. I take this response seriously and respect it. Nor do I wish to minimize the offence. Still, there are other aspects of Aristotle's philosophy that are arguably distinct from his views on slavery, and if we can salvage those aspects – his particularist, context-sensitive approach; his account of practical wisdom and sound-mindedness; his insight into the interdependence of reason and passion; his emphasis on the importance of shaping character – then they may help us in thinking about Weil's ethical psychology.)

---

54 Cf. Shiner, "Ethical Perception in Aristotle," 80; and McDowell, "Some Issues in Aristotle's Moral Psychology," 28, n. 12.

55 Weil, *First and Last Notebooks*, 355 / *La connaissance surnaturelle*, 328. Cf. Matthew 7:17–18; and Luke 6:43.

56 Weil, *The Need for Roots*, 241 / 306–7. Cf. Aristotle, *Politics*, I.4–7.

In keeping with the spirit of an alternative conception of ethics, we need a method that does not aim exclusively at a theoretical construction of general principles prior to experience. We need, rather, a method that encourages the contemplation of particular cases, comparing them for similarities and dissimilarities. If, as Zwicky suggests, the experience of understanding is "the dawning of an aspect that is simultaneously a perception or reperception of a whole," then one way the facilitation of understanding may proceed "is by the judicious selection and arrangement of elements of that whole. Another is by the setting up of objects of comparison."[57] In accordance with a similar style of thinking and writing, Weil's pedagogy, as it matured, increasingly incorporated examples, as Simone Pétrement observes: "In the outlines of the courses that have been found, those that can be dated for the year at Bourges [1935–36] with certainty or great likelihood show that more than ever she offered her students the concrete, living examples to be found in literary works, novels, or poetry."[58]

Professional anglophone moral philosophers, by contrast, sometimes deploy "thought experiments" in which to test their theories. These thought experiments may resemble images, and because they are surrounded by the abstract landscapes of discursive prose, they are often more memorable than the essays in which they appear. However, they are typically highly schematic and prefabricated to prove the theorist's point. Complaints about the artificiality or implausibility of the parameters are dismissed as illegitimate; in discussing the Hobbesian "state of nature" or the Rawlsian "veil of ignorance," for example, it is illicit to dispute the foundational assumption that humans are basically self-interested and rational. Other thought experiments are deliberately farcical. Both sorts of thought experiments lack "the infinite specificity of truth."[59] In this book, we shall try to do things differently. Following the precedent of philosophers such as Weil and Winch, we shall draw on examples and images from literature, film, visual art, and newspapers, including Ansel Adams's *Aspens, Northern New Mexico,* Vittorio De Sica's *Bicycle Thieves,* Gerard Manley Hopkins's "As kingfishers catch fire," James Joyce's "The Dead," Ursula K. Le Guin's *The Dispossessed,* Madame

57 Zwicky, *Wisdom & Metaphor,* L2. Cf. Wittgenstein, *Philosophical Investigations,* §§122, 130.

58 Pétrement, *Simone Weil: A Life,* 250.

59 Zwicky, *Contemplation and Resistance,* 11 *verso.*

de Lafayette's *La Princesse de Clèves*, Édouard Manet's *Argenteuil, les canotiers*, Alan Paton's *Too Late the Phalarope*, Mary Pratt's *Dick Marrie's Moose*,
Sophokles's *Antigone*, John Steinbeck's *The Log from the Sea of Cortez*,
Souvankham Thammavongsa's "A Firefly," Leo Tolstoy's "Father Sergy,"
and Jan Zwicky's "History." Using examples from art or life is like taking
the inquiry out of the lab and into the field.

§1.5. We are living at the end of an era, and it is a time filled with
ignorance, complacency, greed, hatred, cruelty, injustice, violence,
affliction, and grief. Every day, more horrors are reported, and their
scale is staggering. It is hard not to despair. It can seem bourgeois,
even irresponsible, to be reading and writing while the world is burning. Attention may seem like a frail and insignificant thing at best, if
not a culpable indulgence. However, Weil believed in attending, and
she did not live in happier times than ours. She left Paris one day
before the German army entered that city. She witnessed the panzer
divisions go clanking through Nevers.[60] For most of her adult life, she
was passionately engaged in political activism on behalf of the disad-
vantaged members of her society, at home and abroad, advocating
for the working class and those trying to resist oppression in the
French colonies. A sympathetic yet critical reader of Marx, she had
no hope that a revolution would deliver us into a future utopia. From
her year of experience working in factories, she learned that she did
"not possess any right whatever, of any kind,"[61] and that an "obviously
inexorable and invincible form of oppression does not engender re-
volt as an immediate reaction, but submission."[62] She was familiar
with the πλεονεξία (*pleonexia*) and massive inertia that determine the
impulses of "the great beast,"[63] and the futility of individual defiance.
And yet she believed in attending.

In 1943, in the last year of her short life, in exile in London, she wrote
a "Draft for a Statement of Human Obligations." It opens with a profession of faith:

60 Pétrement, *Simone Weil: A Life*, 378–9.
61 Weil, "Factory Journal," *Formative Writings*, 225 / 170.
62 Ibid., 226 / 132.
63 πλεονεξία means greed, excess, wanting more than one needs. "The great
beast" is Plato's metaphor for society (*Republic*, VI.493a–c).

There is a reality outside the world, that is to say, outside space and time, outside man's mental universe, outside any sphere whatsoever that is accessible to human faculties. Corresponding to this reality, at the centre of the human heart, is the longing for an absolute good, a longing which is always there and is never appeased by any object in this world. ...

Just as the reality of this world is the sole foundation of facts, so that other reality is the sole foundation of good. ...

Although it is beyond the reach of any human faculties, man has the power of turning his attention and love towards it.

Nothing can ever justify the assumption that any man, whoever he may be, has been deprived of this power.[64]

Although Weil was at that time attracted to Christianity, this profession of faith is carefully ecumenical. Indeed, its roots are older than Christianity. The idea of a good beyond being that is the proper object of love is Platonic.[65] For the moment, let us set aside the metaphysical dimension of Weil's profession and focus on the last sentence of the quoted passage: "Nothing can ever justify the assumption that any man, *whoever he may be*, has been deprived of this power," that is, the power of turning attention and love toward the good. It is an astonishing declaration. At the time of Weil's writing, there was no shortage of empirical evidence against this thesis; and she was not unacquainted with this evidence. Surely, then, she must have been in the grip of an ideology insulating her from the facts. But she was no ideologue, as demonstrated by her critiques of Marxism and Catholicism, two movements to which she was strongly attracted.[66] Her faith was twofold: faith that each of us can attend to the good, and faith that, by attending to each other, we can recognize this capacity in others – including those who do evil. Such faith is far from easy.

64 Weil, "Draft for a Statement of Human Obligations," 221–2 / 74–5.

65 Cf. Plato, *Republic*, VI.509b.

66 For example, Weil criticizes Marxism for its unjustified belief in an oppression-free utopia at the end of history (see her "Critique of Marxism," *Oppression and Liberty*, 38–54, and "Is There a Marxist Doctrine?," ibid., 160–84), and Catholicism for the practice of anathema (see her "Spiritual Autobiography," *Waiting for God*, 21–38).

Two aphoristic passages by Weil serve as the central inspiration for this book. We have already encountered one of them, and we shall return to them more than once. These passages are written in notebooks that Weil gave to her friend Gustave Thibon before she left France in 1942. The first book of Weil's writings, *La pesanteur et la grâce*, a collection of aphorisms edited by Thibon from her notebooks, was published posthumously in 1947. The English translation, *Gravity and Grace*, appeared in 1952. The following two passages are drawn from the sections «La nécessité et l'obéissance» ("Necessity and Obedience") and «L'attention et la volonté» ("Attention and Will"), respectively:

Il y a des cas où une chose est nécessaire du seul fait qu'elle est possible. Ainsi manger quand on a faim, donner à boire à un blessé mourant de soif, l'eau étant tout près. Ni un bandit ne s'en abstiendrait ni un saint.

There are cases where a thing is necessary from the mere fact that it is possible. Thus to eat when we are hungry, to give a wounded man, dying of thirst, something to drink when there is water quite near. Neither a ruffian nor a saint would refrain from doing so.[67]

*

Le poète produit le beau par l'attention fixée sur du réel. De même l'acte d'amour. Savoir que cet homme, qui a faim et soif, existe vraiment autant que moi – cela suffit, le reste suit de lui-même.

The poet produces the beautiful by fixing his attention on something real. It is the same with the act of love. To know that this man who is hungry and thirsty really exists as much as I do—that is enough, the rest follows of itself.[68]

Both passages concern offering relief for a vital need: the need for water, the need for food. Both passages also involve analogies. The first suggests that relieving someone's thirst is analogous to eating when one is hungry. The second passage suggests that relieving someone's need for

67 Weil, *La pesanteur et la grâce*, 55; and *Gravity and Grace*, 44. Cf. Weil, *Notebooks*, I.224.
68 Weil, *La pesanteur et la grâce*, 137; and *Gravity and Grace*, 119. Cf. Weil, *Notebooks*, II.449.

sustenance is analogous to producing a beautiful poem. In both cases, the action follows from attending to reality. Attending is enough, and acting is necessitated. These are strong claims, and they attract objections, some of which we shall consider in due course. For the moment, however, let us regard these passages not as arguments designed to persuade us, but as testimonies. Can we recognize what Weil is witnessing? The familiar connection between feeling hungry and eating is natural; could there be a similarly natural connection between perceiving someone else's hunger and relieving it? If so, what conditions would be needed for us to experience that connection? What circumstances might interfere with perceiving someone else's vital needs as immediately as our own?

Suppose, furthermore, that the point of the analogy with poetry is not to aestheticize charity (in fact, Weil thinks that we moderns have wrongly distinguished charity from justice); suppose, instead, that she is trying to tell us something about a method for attending. There is "a way of waiting, when we are writing, for the right word to come of itself at the end of our pen, while we merely reject all inadequate words."[69] According to this method, writing is primarily a "negative operation": the writer is not creating *ex nihilo*, but is patiently clearing away.[70] What would it mean for an agent to practise this way of attending in relation to a particular being? Could we imagine our action as already given, like the poem that is revealed after the wrong words have been cleared away? This book tries to think through these and other questions that arise from these two aphorisms. It does so by revisiting the aphorisms and setting them beside the work of other thinkers (some more sympathetic, some less). Overall, it is a defence of an ethics of attending that originates in and is inspired by Weil's work and developed in the work of Iris Murdoch, John McDowell, and Jan Zwicky.

The following ten sections of the book are written in such a way that they may be read independently from each other. The book does make an overarching argument, and it may be read from start to finish. But there is more than one way of reading it. Rather than summarize the individual sections here, I shall let most of them speak for themselves. However, let me say a few words about Section 11. Etymologically, a

69 Weil, "Reflections on the Right Use of School Studies," 63 / 94.
70 Weil, *Notebooks*, I.29 / *OC*, VI.1.302. It is Pseudo-Dionysus who sets the precedent for such technique: see *Mystical Theology*, Chap. 2 (1025b).

conclusion is a "complete shutting." This book has no conclusion in that sense. If an introduction is a leading-into a book, the last section will be an ἔξοδος (*exodos*), a way out of the book. Rather than proceed in continuous, discursive prose, it takes an unorthodox form – a form that might allow it to make what Zwicky calls a "lyric argument": "The positioning of resonant particulars to facilitate perception of their attunement, the presentation of other texts or works or things for comparison, constitute lyric arguments."[71]

This last section revisits some of the themes and materials from the preceding sections, but follows them in a new direction. In particular, it thinks about what a Weilian ethics of attending would mean in the context of ecological ethics, and it suggests an alternative to the campaign of trying to solve what might be called "the problem of the criterion" – the problem of identifying the characteristic that makes a thing deserving of "moral consideration." As Thomas Birch argues, the history of ecological ethics shows that whenever we have fixed the criterion, we have been wrong: we have excluded some beings that ought to have been included. Birch makes a radical suggestion: instead of repeating our error, we should abandon the project of fixing a criterion and adopt a practice of what he calls "universal consideration." Since there is no thing that cannot be a focus of attention, the only coherent stance is to be open to attending to anything. This approach does not tell us who the moral patients are; nor does it tell us what acts are prescribed or forbidden. For those who are accustomed to moral theory, universal consideration may seem too indeterminate and too inclusive to be useful. But it is only by attending to the relevant particulars that we can learn what is required. Must an ethics of attending lead to an animistic ethics? I do not know. But I believe it does lead there.

---

71 Zwicky, "What Is Lyric Philosophy?," §34.

2

Reflections on an Ethics of Attending

§2.1. WHAT, EXACTLY, IS ATTENTION? Simone Weil writes:

To strike a cicada in full flight, it is enough to see it, and nothing else, in the entire universe; then you cannot miss it. To become an archer, lie for two years under a loom and do not blink your eyes when the shuttle passes; then for three years, facing toward the light, make a louse climb up a silk thread; when the louse appears to be larger than a wheel, larger than a mountain, when it hides the sun, when you see its heart, then you shoot: you will hit it in the heart.[1]

This passage is a distillation of a story in a Daoist text from the fourth century,[2] and it appears in the margins of one of Weil's notebooks. It seems to be about archery, but the art that it describes is not restricted to that practice. It tells us that the art of attending consists in focusing and waiting; and it tells us that focusing and waiting are enough for action. If there is such an art, and if it can be learned, then it is arguably an art of some significance for ethics.

While Weil's concept of attention has been little discussed in mainstream anglophone moral philosophy, Iris Murdoch thought it important enough to inspire a book-length triptych of essays. For Murdoch, an ethics of attending is an alternative to the class of moral theory that is transfixed by the idea of the agent as a decision-making, problem-solving doer. Since attending is less dramatic than deciding and doing, it is also less conspicuous. Indeed, it seems commonplace. In

---

1 Weil, *Notebooks*, I.30, n. 1 / *OC*, VI.1.279; translation altered.
2 Cf. Liezi, *The Book of Lieh-tzǔ*, 112–13.

philosophy-of-mind scholarship concerning attention, it has become customary to quote William James, who declares: "Every one knows what attention is. It is the taking possession by the mind, in clear and vivid form, of one out of what seem several simultaneously possible objects or trains of thought. Focalization, concentration, of consciousness are of its essence."[3] If James is right, and the essence of attention is evidently focalization, then why go to the trouble of investigating the concept? On this question, let us listen to Weil: "*Not to understand new things, but by strength of patience, effort and method to come to understand those truths which are evident with one's whole being.*"[4]

Weil would agree with James that attending is characterized by focusing. But while he claims that the opposite of attention is "the confused, dazed, scatterbrained state which the French call *distraction*,"[5] she claims that its opposite is "contempt."[6] This contrast reveals that, unlike James's concept of attention, Weil's concept is intrinsically ethical. For her, it is also characterized by patience and responsiveness, and contrasted with muscular efforts of will. We see these characteristics illustrated in the instructions for archery above. The archer focuses and waits and, eventually, the focusing and waiting produce a response. (If the will has a role in this process, it may be expressed in *refraining* from acting until the right moment.) This idea, that right acting follows from attending, is central to Weil's thinking about attention.

The poet produces the beautiful through attention focused on the real. Same with the act of love. Knowing that this man, who is hungry and thirsty, truly exists as much as I do—that's enough, the rest follows of itself.[7]

This aphorism is very dense, and it will be helpful to identify its themes. Weil is suggesting that there is an analogy between what we might initially call "aesthetic" and "ethical" attending. She implies, however, that both "kinds" of attending are the same.[8] In "aesthetic" and "ethical"

---

3 James, "Attention," 403–4.

4 Weil, *Notebooks*, I.144 / *OC*, VI.2.149. Cf. Pétrement, *Simone Weil: A Life*, 30–1; and Wittgenstein, *Philosophical Investigations*, §129.

5 James, "Attention," 404. Cf. Rozelle-Stone, "*Le Déracinement* of Attention," 101b.

6 Weil, "Forms of the Implicit Love of God," *Waiting for God*, 95 / 141.

7 Weil, "Attention and Will," *Gravity and Grace*, 119 / 137; translation altered.

8 Cf. Wittgenstein, *Tractatus*, prop. 6.421.

contexts, attending consists in focusing on something real. By so focusing, the attentive agent comes to know the reality of the focus, and in knowing, she produces a beautiful artwork or a good deed. Furthermore, says Weil, this knowing is "enough."

— "Enough for what?" a skeptical reader may interject. "If I don't know the context, how am I to interpret her conclusion? What is 'the rest,' and why does it follow?" — The aphorism does not elaborate a context for its insight. Weil expects the reader to recognize what she recognizes: in this situation, there is only one salient feature: the reality of this hungry and thirsty human being. — "But *what* follows from recognizing this feature?" — For Weil, this question makes no sense. Insofar as the question arises in us, we have not yet *read* the situation, we have not understood its meaning.[9]

Weil's concept of attention is rooted in the Platonic thesis that virtue is knowledge; and she is, in her distinctive way, adapting and developing that thesis. (In contrast with Plato, she expresses more respect for bodily needs, and for the possibility that humane manual labour and physical exercise are methods of learning virtue and coming into contact with reality.)[10] However, at least since David Hume asked his skeptical questions about moral judgement, the Platonic thesis has seemed dubious to many philosophers. And in the hands of some theorists inspired by the work of John McDowell – Jonathan Dancy, David McNaughton, and Margaret Olivia Little, for instance – the thesis seems to implicate a fraught complex of other theses: moral cognitivism, moral internalism, and moral realism, to name a few. Moral cognitivism is the claim that moral judgements articulate truth-apt beliefs; moral internalism is the claim that moral judgements are internally or necessarily related to appropriate motivation; and moral realism can be construed as the view that there are "mind-independent moral facts." If we assemble these claims, we may say that justified true belief about (or perhaps accurate perception of) moral facts motivates appropriate response; or as

9 Cf. Weil, "Essay on the Notion of Reading." See this book, §5.

10 This respect remains constant from her early dissertation to her late work. Physical exercise is included in the education of the guardians in Plato's *Republic*, but unlike Weil, Plato does not consider it equal to contemplation. Of Weil's marriage of materialism and Platonism, Chenavier writes, "To escape from its disarray, an epoch like ours requires both a Marx 'surpassed from the interior' by Plato, and a Plato who would have 'integrated' Marx" (*Simone Weil: Attention to the Real*, 80).

Murdoch says, "true vision occasions right conduct."[11] At the heart of this tripartite theory is a refusal, by Dancy and others, to accept Hume's metaphysical disintegration of facts and values.

But to other philosophers, that disintegration seems plausible, and perhaps even mandatory, to explain some phenomena: the existence of the amoralist, for example – someone who allegedly *understands* the content of morality, but experiences *no motivation* to act in accordance with it. (Or consider Dostoevsky's Underground Man, who wilfully defies the Platonic thesis and affirms his freedom by knowingly choosing to do what is bad.)[12] David Brink argues that moral externalism – the claim that moral beliefs are not intrinsically motivating – is capable of explaining the amoralist, and that this capability counts decisively in favour of externalism.[13] But it seems peculiar that a moral theory (assuming that one is in the business of theory-building) should be constructed with deference to a creature such as the amoralist. Plato arguably regards this creature as seriously as any twenty-first-century philosopher does – witness Thrasymakhos and Kallikles – but he does not adjust his philosophy to make the amoralist comfortable. That is, he does not construct a theory that deferentially accommodates the psychology of the amoralist at the expense of diminishing the explanatory power of the theory for other psychologies (those that are virtuous, for example).

§2.2. Both Weil and Murdoch offer an undramatic example of the exercise of attending and its relevance to ethics; its ordinariness makes it intriguing. Their example is school studies. Murdoch writes about learning the Russian language and claims that "studying is normally an exercise of virtue."[14] — "How so?" — Because there is something here – the Russian language – which is real, and to which the student must be responsible; and meeting that responsibility requires the exercise of (among other things) respect, patience, honesty or

---

11 Murdoch, "On 'God' and 'Good,'" 66. — "Who cares if internal moral realism is glimpsable in Murdoch? She's not the primary association for the idea in philosophy." — Correct: she is not the primary association; but she ought to be, because her work (following Weil's) is the unacknowledged origin of the idea. For this genealogy, see this book, §4.

12 Dostoevsky, *Notes from Underground*, I.VII (pp. 19ff.).

13 Brink, "Externalist Moral Realism," §3.2.

14 Murdoch, "The Sovereignty of Good Over Other Concepts," *The Sovereignty of Good*, 89.

accuracy, and courage. In order to learn that language, the student must acknowledge that it is possible for her to go wrong; and she must be prepared to check and to correct her work in the light of the language itself – that is, with her teacher, native speakers, dictionaries, textbooks, and so on. The accuracy of her translation can show, for instance, whether she has attended respectfully to the language (or to the poem, or to the poet). Weil makes the analogy acute: "The fulfilment of our strictly human duty is of the same order as correctness in the work of drafting, translating, calculating, etc. To be careless about this correctness shows a lack of respect for the object."[15] Such a stricture may seem too severe. The stakes don't seem comparable; why should we think that admitting a mere translation mistake, for example, requires courage? – Doesn't it, though? Don't students sometimes confess that they are afraid to ask a question in case it will show that they lack knowledge?

In a key text, "Reflections on the Right Use of School Studies with a View to the Love of God,"[16] Weil suggests that ordinary school studies educate the very attentional capacity that is relevant to ethics: "So it comes about that, paradoxical as it may seem, a Latin prose or a geometry problem, even if they are done wrong, may be of great service one day, provided we devote the right kind of effort to them. Should the occasion arise, they can one day make us better able to give someone in affliction exactly the help required to save him, at the supreme moment of his need."[17] This claim sounds incredible; but what if it were true? What if devoted study could improve our character? And what, exactly, is the nature of the alleged similarity between studying and attending to someone? Is it that both are forms of problem-solving? On the contrary: to conflate attending with problem-solving is to read the analogy in the wrong direction: rather than imagine suffering persons as problems needing to be solved, we should imagine school studies as things needing attention. A student's relation to her studies, like her relations with other persons, should not be antagonistic but responsive.

Weil suggests that attending to a geometry problem and attending to someone in affliction should both have at their centre a kind of

---

15 Weil, "Training," *Gravity and Grace*, 123 / 141.

16 Weil, "Reflections on the Right Use of School Studies," *Waiting for God*, 57–65 / 85–97.

17 Ibid., 65 / 97; translation altered.

patient receptivity or responsiveness. She warns that we must not confuse such attending with willing in accordance with a rule; nor should it be confused with warmth of heart, impulsiveness, or pity.[18] At the climax of her "Reflections," Weil writes:

The love of our neighbor in all its fullness simply means being able to ask him: "What are you going through?" It is knowing that the sufferer [*le mal-heureux*] exists, not as a unit in a collection, nor as a specimen from the social category labeled "unfortunate" [«*malheureux*»], but as a human being, exactly like us, who was one day stricken and marked with a special mark of affliction [*le malheur*]. For this reason, it is enough, but it is indispensable, to know how to look at him in a certain way.

This way of looking is first of all attentive. The soul empties itself of all its own contents in order to receive into itself the being it is looking at, just as he is, in all his truth.[19]

Attending, loving, and knowing – Weil does not discriminate among these three activities. Implicit in this passage is a version of the Platonic thesis that virtue is knowledge. However, what the attentive agent knows is neither a Platonic form nor a specimen from a category. Weil stresses, rather, the specificity of attending: when one knows how to attend, one is able to acknowledge the reality of *this* particular human being, a reality as palpable as one's own. As Jan Zwicky writes: "Ontological attention is a response to particularity: *this* porch, *this* laundry basket, *this* day. Its object cannot be substituted for, even when it is an object of considerable generality ('the country', 'cheese', 'garage sales')."[20] Let us call the "object" of attending its *focus*. Notice that Weil's characterization of attending above remains mostly indeterminate; insofar as attending is an art, it involves emptiness and receptivity. "Attention is an effort," she writes, "the greatest of all efforts perhaps, but it is a negative effort."[21] The oxymoron in the last phrase is deliberately torqued. True attending is, in fact, effortless – but in the way that skilful archery or adept dancing is effortless.

---

18 Ibid., 64 / 96.
19 Ibid., 64–5 / 96–7; translation altered.
20 Zwicky, *Wisdom & Metaphor*, L52. Cf. Zwicky, "Imagination and the Good Life," §II.33.
21 Weil, "Reflections on the Right Use of School Studies," 61 / 92.

Consider this passage from Zwicky's elegy for James Gray:

The difficult thing about such genius, especially if one is trying to write about it, is its invisibility. It seeks anonymity the way water seeks low places. It *makes* nothing. Rather, it unmakes trouble. And it does this not by direct application of effort, by "fixing" things, but by listening — without fear, without an agenda, the way a doctor might listen to a patient's heartbeat or breath. "What am I hearing here?" A completely open, unselfed attention. In the clear light of such attention, what is troubling can be, simply, what it is: an odd ambition, a constricted choice, a broken heart. The clench that makes such things *into* trouble evaporates. "Oh," one says, seeing the stick for a stick, the puddle for a puddle — or the ocean for the ocean — "this is just the world." The gift of such seeing, the ability to give such vision to another, even if only for a moment, is matchless in its efficacy. It can heal appalling wounds and relieve the deepest, most persistent pain. But, though its effects are often striking, the gift — like light itself — remains something we rarely see; we are aware, mostly, of what it illuminates.[22]

Weil would recognize this description of attending (even as the described phenomenon itself eludes the linguistic grasp). It rests on the contrast between wilful effort and effortless, fearless listening, a contrast we shall revisit (see Section 2.3). The metaphor of light is apt, since, as Zwicky observes, this attention is illuminating but invisible. And the illumination is not judgemental. In this respect, it is like the light in a biblical verse that Weil much admired: "for he makes his sun rise on the evil and the good, and sends rain on the just and the unjust."[23] Such indiscriminate attending is not easy to understand. How could one not judge the unjust? It seems inhuman.

History

—after Joseph Haydn, Op. 24, No. 2, Adagio

It's quiet now.
The nameless officers for State Security

---

22 Zwicky, "Just the World," 36. (The water metaphor is Daoist; cf. Laozi, *Daodejing*, §§8, 32.)
23 Matthew 5:45.

shrug on their overcoats
and head home through the pre-dawn streets.
Oiled locks turn,
then turn again.
The generals snore.
Now light comes.
You will think it cold,
the way it fingers
open eyes, the darkened cheekbones,
the blood between the legs.
You will think it deaf as generals
the way it stands beside the ones still dying
and moves on.
But see
how weightlessly it gathers them,
the gold curl and the ebony,
with what tenderness
the folded silence of the ribs.[24]

The poem is a single stanza with four movements: the setting of the pre-dawn scene, the entrance of light and the addressee's first judgement, the addressee's second judgement, and the revelation of light's non-judgemental attentiveness. There are no pyrotechnics in the poem. While some of the sentences do stretch over more than one line, the enjambements are not dramatic, and mostly the phrases and the lines coincide. "The nameless officers for State Security" and the snoring generals are as bland as types in an allegory. There is an almost complete abstention from metaphor, since the personification of light, fingering and standing as it does, is so plain as to escape notice (this plainness is key to its quiet power); and the one conspicuous metaphor – "deaf as generals" – signals an error on the part of the addressee. For light, even if it cannot hear, is not like the generals. Indeed, the fourth and final movement (beginning with "But see / how weightlessly ...") corrects the two judgements in the second and third movements ("You will think it cold ..." and "You will think it deaf as generals ..."). Why might we think it cold or deaf? Because

24 Zwicky, *Robinson's Crossing*, 49.

it seems unaffected by last night's bloodshed. In the wake of violence, we might feel that the world should join with us in grieving. The sun should hide its face in anguish, light should stay at the side of those still dying. The fourth movement offers a different way of thinking about the attentiveness of light: indifference as tenderness. Such attention is not susceptible to rational justification; it responds not to merit but to being. It excludes nothing.

§2.3. Weil's thinking about attending is closely aligned with her philosophy of education. Her "Reflections on the Right Use of School Studies" belongs to a collection of writings that she bestowed upon J.M. Perrin (the priest who tried, unsuccessfully and not entirely sympathetically, to persuade her to become baptized in the Catholic Church). This essay is ostensibly a meditation on the nature and purpose of education, but it is also one of the clearest expressions of Weil's ethics of attending. At the beginning of the essay, she throws down a gauntlet: "Although people seem to be unaware of it today, the development of the faculty of attention forms the real object and almost the sole interest of studies."[25] Elsewhere, in a set of complementary aphorisms edited by her friend Gustave Thibon and titled "Attention and Will,"[26] she repeats this thought: "Teaching should have no aim but to prepare, by training the attention, for the possibility of [a certain application of the full attention to the object]. ... // All the other advantages of instruction are without interest."[27]

What an astonishing claim. Some of us may think, not without reason, that we go to school to train for a *job* – that school is a kind of accreditation programme for participation in the workforce. Or perhaps we think that school is where we go to learn – and that learning is the accumulation of information or data; when we graduate, we will *know more* than when we started. Weil insists that these ideas of and approaches to education are *without interest.* — "But what, then, would be the point of education? Isn't it important that we know that *modus ponens* is a valid argument-form; that the square on the hypotenuse of a right-angled triangle is equal to the sum of the squares on the other two sides; that Odysseus blinded the Kyklops, and that Oidipous blinded himself with

25 Weil, "Reflections on the Right Use of School Studies," 57 / 85.
26 Weil, "Attention and Will," *Gravity and Grace*, 116–22 / 133–40.
27 Ibid., 120 / 137.

his wife's (his mother's) brooches; that the 'Indian Residential School' system is a great injustice; that anthropogenic climate change is actually happening; and so on? Are we not less ignorant for having learned these truths? (And having been rendered less ignorant, can we not improve the world?)"

— School can indeed be a delivery system for these and other truths. But Weil suggests that learning how to attend is fundamental, for if we lack that capacity, we will be incapable of understanding the truths that school offers. "Because the *fact* is nothing if it is not *understood*," writes Zwicky, "if we don't *see* it, grasp what *has* to be the case for it to be true and thereby take it into our souls."[28] We can memorize the formula "$a^2 + b^2 = c^2$," but unless we figure out, for ourselves, how it works, we will remain juvenile dogmatists, forever at the mercy of someone else's authority. And education is not only an instrument for enrooting our true beliefs; it is also an instrument for scouring our false beliefs, some of which are cataracts on the eyes of the soul.

The thoughts that motivate Weil's essay appear simple:

- Studying in the right way is a method of practising attending.
- By practising attending, one becomes more attentive.

At the end of her essay, she connects these thoughts with another one:

- Being attentive is crucial to being a responsible ethical agent.

Gathered together, these thoughts suggest that studying in the right way is a method of becoming a more responsible ethical agent. In the background of Weil's argument is the ancient Greek insight that learning virtue is like learning a trade or an art. As Aristotle says: "the virtues we get by first exercising them, as also happens in the case of the arts as well. For the things we have to learn before we can do them, we learn by doing them, e.g. men become builders by building and lyre-players by playing the lyre; so too we become just by doing just acts, temperate by doing temperate acts, brave by doing brave acts."[29] He is echoing Plato, who writes, "And don't just actions

---

28 Zwicky, *Plato as Artist*, 65 / AL, 187.
29 Aristotle, *Nicomachean Ethics*, II.1.1103a31–b3.

produce justice in the soul and unjust ones injustice?"[30] If learning virtue is like learning an art, then there will be different roles for apprentices and experts. At first, we are clumsy and we make mistakes. But, by offering tips and models to emulate, adepts and exemplars can help us improve.

Notice that Weil's ideas above lean on the undefined notion of studying "in the right way." But what *is* the right way? Weil claims that two conditions must be met in order to make right use of school studies. The first condition is to recognize the opportunity offered by school studies to train the attention, and to devote one's studies to this purpose. (We shall return to this condition.) "The second condition," Weil writes, "is to take great pains to examine squarely and to contemplate attentively and slowly each school task in which we have failed."[31] From such examination, we can acquire knowledge of our own fallibility, and this knowledge is what Weil calls the virtue of humility. As we shall see, this virtue is indispensable for tempering the impetuous will, thus affording enough scope for attention to achieve clear perception.

To satisfy the second condition for using school studies in the right way, it is enough to want to do so. But to satisfy the first condition, something more is needed: "There must be method in it. A certain way of doing a Latin prose, a certain way of tackling a problem in geometry (and not just any way) make up a system of gymnastics of the attention."[32] By analogy with the gym, where one's physical body is exercised, school is a place where one exercises one's attention, making it stronger and more flexible.[33] Let us look more closely at this method. As we saw above, attending is not merely a feeling of pity or charity. It is, as Weil repeatedly insists, "a certain way" of looking and waiting. "In every school exercise," she writes, "there is a special way of waiting upon truth ... There is a way of giving our attention to the data of a problem in geometry without trying to find the solution or to the words of a Latin or Greek text without trying to arrive at the meaning ... // Our first duty toward school children and students is to make known this method to them, not only in a general way but in the particular form that bears

30 Plato, *Republic*, IV.444d.
31 Weil, "Reflections on the Right Use of School Studies," 59 / 89.
32 Weil, "Attention and Will," 120 / 137–8.
33 Cf. Plato, *Gorgias*, 464a–c; and *Republic*, III.401d–e, VII.527d–e.

on each exercise."[34] Frustratingly, after having emphasized the importance of specific methodological forms – figuring out a geometry problem is different, she suggests, from translating a passage of Greek, for
instance – she does not disclose these forms.

She does, however, offer some helpful remarks about a general
method. She begins by drawing a contrast between attention and will:
"Most often attention is confused with a kind of muscular effort"; but
effort of that sort – exerting the will, gritting our teeth, contracting our
brows – "has practically no place in study."[35] Muscular effort does have
a role in another domain. Suppose that you are digging holes in which
to plant trees. It's hard work. After digging a number of holes, you get
tired. Then you will yourself to dig another hole. Over time, with practice, you get stronger and the digging gets easier. Here is an example
of a recognizable and legitimate use of will: it guides the body through
healthy tiredness to meet reasonable goals. But Weil claims that such a
use of the will is misapplied to school studies. – Those of us who have
stayed awake until four in the morning, reading the heaps of text needed
for the next day's classes, might disagree. It required a significant effort
of will, we might protest, to keep ourselves from losing consciousness.
But Weil would respond: perhaps will-power is needed to pass your eyes
across the text. But *understanding* is a different activity.[36]

"The intelligence can only be led by desire," she writes. "The joy of
learning is as indispensable in study as breathing is in running."[37] Weil
is not promoting the shallow idea that teaching can be "entertaining."
Joy, she suggests, is like oxygen. It is not frivolous; it is, quite literally,
necessary to the life of the mind. Will is what props our eyes open
when we are tired. But it is joy that lets us learn. (Interestingly, this
claim has received some empirical corroboration.)[38] Joy is the

---

34 Weil, "Reflections on the Right Use of School Studies," 63 / 94.

35 Ibid., 60–1 / 90–1.

36 Bourgault notes some moments of ambiguity in Weil's treatment of the will,
but concludes: "one thing is constantly clear in her oeuvre: the physical manifestations of our will—the tensing of muscles—cannot be regarded as manifestations of
the *purest* kind of attention" ("Weil and Rancière on Attention and Emancipation,"
227).

37 Weil, "Reflections on the Right Use of School Studies," 61 / 91. Cf. Weil,
"Attention and Will," 118, and *Intimations of Christianity*, 123.

38 See Shanker, "Emotion Regulation through the Ages," 108.

experience of becoming clearer in the presence of something beautiful.[39] This clarification occurs by itself, while the student maintains a stance of patient receptivity.

Having delimited the role of the will, Weil then offers a positive characterization of attending: "Attention consists of suspending our thought, leaving it detached, empty, and ready ... Above all our thought should be empty, waiting, not seeking anything, but ready to receive ..."[40] If we want to learn about something, we should try to empty our mind of preconceptions, turn our attention toward the focus, and wait until it becomes clear. This is not only a method for learning about "animate" interlocutors, who can actively teach us about themselves; it is also a way of attending to apparently "inanimate" things, such as a geometry problem, a Russian poem, or a hazelnut. If we are patient, then there is a sense in which the geometry problem will solve itself.

— "How can you call that a method?" an interlocutor might exclaim. "It's little more than an exhortation: 'Wait and see. And if you don't see, wait some more!' Contrast that with the Cartesian method: 'Analyse the thing into its simplest parts. Then reconstruct it, and if necessary make it conform to a linear order from simplest to most composite.'[41] Whatever you think of those rules, they at least have more content than Weil's maddeningly vague recommendation!" — Yes, but Weil's method can also be understood as a variation on Descartes's first and more fundamental rule: "carefully to avoid hasty judgment and prejudice; and to include nothing more in my judgments than what presented itself to my mind so clearly and distinctly that I had no occasion to call it in doubt."[42] In other words, yes: be patient. Wait, and see.

The relationship between attending and patience is even clearer in Weil's native French, because the relevant terms are cognate: *attendre* ("to wait"), *l'attente* ("waiting" or "the wait"), *l'attention*. Because attending is slow and focused, it is difficult to practise under conditions of acceleration and distraction. (In such contexts, the best that we can achieve might be an approximation.) The role of patience in Weil's method of attending is remarkably similar to its role in Richard Wollheim's method of aesthetic appreciation:

39 Cf. Spinoza, *Ethics*, IIIP11S.
40 Weil, "Reflections on the Right Use of School Studies," 62 / 92–3.
41 Cf. Descartes, *Discourse on Method*, AT VI.18–19.
42 Ibid., AT VI.18.

I evolved a way of looking at paintings which was massively time-consuming and deeply rewarding. For I came to recognize that it often took the first hour or so in front of a painting for stray associations or motivated misperceptions to settle down, and it was only then, with the same amount of time or more to spend looking at it, that the picture could be relied upon to disclose itself as it was.[43]

Notice how closely Wollheim's method resembles Weil's:

Method for understanding images, symbols, etc. Not to try to interpret them, but to look at them till the light suddenly dawns.

Generally speaking, a method for the exercise of the intelligence, which consists of looking.

Application of this method for the discrimination between the real and the illusory. In our sense perceptions, if we are not sure of what we see we change our position while looking, and the real appears. In the inner life, time takes the place of space. With time we are altered, and, if as we change we keep our gaze directed towards the same thing, in the end illusions are scattered and the real appears. This is on condition that the attention be a looking and not an attachment.[44]

Both Wollheim and Weil are suggesting that exercising patient receptivity in relation to some particular – to a painting, or to a problem, for example – is a method for coming to understand that particular on its own terms. The perceiver and the painting are, in a sense, synchronizing their rhythms;[45] the perceiver adjusts herself to the painting, analogously to the way a biologist in the field might adjust herself to the rhythms of the animals. Both Wollheim and Weil accept *accuracy* as a norm of perception, and they suggest that patient receptivity, governed by this norm, is a way of making contact with reality. Stray associations and motivated misperceptions should be allowed time to settle down; illusions, to scatter. Then the painting discloses itself as it is; the real becomes visible.

On the other hand, if we make an error, says Weil, then it is traceable to impatience on our part:

---

43 Wollheim, *Painting as an Art*, 8. Cf. Burns and MacLachlan, "Getting It," §I.
44 Weil, "Attention and Will," 120 / 138; translation altered.
45 Cf. Abram, *The Spell of the Sensuous*, 54.

All wrong translations, all absurdities in geometry problems, all clumsiness of style, and all faulty connection of ideas in compositions and essays, all such things are due to the fact that thought has seized upon some idea too hastily, and being thus prematurely blocked, is not open to the truth. The cause is always that we have wanted to be too active; we have wanted to carry out a search.[46]

Here Weil is adopting a theory of error that she borrows from Descartes (and the Stoics).[47] In Meditation Four ("Concerning the True and the False"), Descartes draws a distinction between the faculty of the intellect and that of the will, roughly analogous to Weil's distinction between attention and will. The two faculties have different functions. The intellect perceives; and when it perceives well, it perceives clearly. (The intellect's virtue is clarity.) The will, on the other hand, does something else: in the practical and theoretical realms, it says *yes* or *no*. For example, I am thirsty and perceive some water. My will says, "Yes, drink" or "No, don't." Or I perceive "$2 + 3 = 5$." My will says, "Yes, that's true" or "No, that's false." Error occurs when the will pre-empts the intellect. For example, I glimpse some liquid, and my will yanks on its leash and barks, "Yes, drink" – but the liquid is gasoline. Or: I see "$25^2 = 275$," and my will impulsively blurts out, "Yes, that's true" – but really it's false.

The contrast between will and attention may seem to correlate with a dichotomy between activity and passivity. But it is instructive to reflect on an analogy with sight. The extraocular muscles can position the eye, but they do not determine what is salient in the field of vision. Steven Burns and Alice MacLachlan offer another analogy: "We do not say 'passivity' ... there is activity in the preparations for receptivity. Remember the *time* that Wollheim takes in front of a painting. Similarly, one does not fall asleep by making an effort to fall asleep, but one does typically prepare mind and body for rest, putting aside the dirt and clothing and troubles of the day, finding a dark and quiet place to lie down, and so on."[48] One can no more force oneself to attend than one can will oneself to fall asleep. But it does not follow that one is powerless to facilitate attending. The right way of using these faculties is to wait

46 Weil, "Reflections on the Right Use of School Studies," 62 / 93.

47 For the Stoic sources of the theory, see "The criteria of truth" in Long and Sedley, eds., *The Hellenistic philosophers*, §40 (pp. 241–53).

48 Burns and MacLachlan, "Getting It," §I.

patiently until one perceives clearly, and to let that perception determine the will. The dynamic is exactly like the dynamic described in the Daoist instructions for archery. Most of the activity precedes the moment of action; that activity consists in watching and waiting until the target is unmistakable. Notice also the connection with the virtue of humility; if one is aware of one's own fallibility, then one should not be hasty in making judgements. To avoid error, one should keep one's will on a leash – or better yet, train one's will so that a leash is unnecessary. (We shall return to Weil's Cartesian theory in Section 3.5.)

At the climax of her essay, Weil makes explicit the ethical dimension of attending. Recall her suggestion: "The love of our neighbor in all its fullness simply means being able to say to him: 'What are you going through?'"[49] We ask this question almost every day – "How are you?" – but we tend to ask in a perfunctory way, as a routine tic in the social mechanism. Weil imagines us asking this question differently, leaving room for the other to respond truthfully. She does not pretend that such openness comes easily – on the contrary, she says, it is "a very rare and difficult thing."[50] Learning it is a life's work. For Weil, the attentiveness conveyed by this question is at the very root of ethical responsibility. Recall also her claim that studying trains the same aptitude for attending that may be exercised in ethical contexts: "a Latin prose or a geometry problem, even if they are done wrong, may be of great service one day ... they can one day make us better able to give someone in affliction exactly the help required to save him."[51] This claim is at least as astonishing as the essay's opening claim that accumulating truths is not the main purpose of education. Now Weil is claiming that doing one's geometry homework can save lives – even if one gets the answers wrong.

— "But," an interlocutor may interject, "there are at least four objections to this thesis. One objection is that, if you fail your geometry midterm, then maybe you're not very good at paying attention and shouldn't be trusted to take care of a suffering person. Another objection (probably not consistent with the first) is that a suffering person is nothing like a right-angled triangle, and so they require different kinds of attention. A third is that the way in which the relationship has been framed is wrong. Weil seems to imagine an asymmetrical structure

49 Weil, "Reflections on the Right Use of School Studies," 64 / 96–7.
50 Ibid., 64 / 96.
51 Ibid., 65 / 97; translation altered.

in which there is an agent and a patient: an active attender and a passive attendee; the attendee paralysed by affliction, and the attender the saviour. Surely such a framing overlooks the fact that suffering doesn't always destroy our agency. Can't we collaborate with others in addressing our needs? And can't the attender be the attendee of the other's attention? Why assume that attention is unilateral? Fourth, we may object that Weil is overestimating the value of attention. On the facing page, she writes: 'Those who are unhappy have no need for anything in this world but people capable of giving them their attention.'[52] But this claim is plainly false. People suffer in all sorts of ways for all sorts of reasons. If I need food and water, or shelter, or medical treatment, or assistive technology, or truth and reconciliation, or revenge, then mere attention will not be enough to meet these needs."

— Let us try to respond to these objections on Weil's behalf. The reply to the first objection is the most straightforward: Weil is not claiming that failed geometers make good paramedics. What she suggests is that success or failure in any single instance of attention is secondary to the overall practice of attending. As long as one is trying to develop good habits, it is forgivable to not be perfect during one's apprenticeship.

The other three objections are more daunting, but they are answerable. The second objection above seems to assume that attention is inflexibly uniform; but according to Weil, attending is initially a kind of emptiness; it is available to be determined by the focus. If the focus is a right-angled triangle, then attending will be determined in one way, and if the focus is an injured starling, then attending will be determined in another way.

In response to the third, we may draw on Lorraine Code's suggestion that an object of attention can also be a subject.[53] As a kind of emptiness, attending is the first move in a longer conversation or the first step in an improvised dance. The question "What are you going through?" is an invitation for one's interlocutor to lead. In other words, *pace* the third objection: attending *is* interactive, and neither party is exclusively active or exclusively passive; on the contrary, they may take turns.

52 Ibid., 64 / 96.
53 Cf. Code, "Taking Subjectivity into Account," §4 (pp. 32–9).

In response to the fourth objection, Weil could concede that attending alone may not be enough to meet some needs; but she could still insist that it is necessary. In order to learn what someone's needs are, we need first to listen.[54] Listening expresses respect but does not exhaust it. Our obligation to respect others, she says, "is only performed if the respect is effectively expressed in a real, not a fictitious way; and this can only be done through the medium of man's earthly needs. ... // So it is an eternal obligation towards the human being not to let him suffer from hunger when one has the chance of coming to his assistance."[55] Hunger is a concrete example of a need that we are obliged to relieve, but the obligation is general: we are bound, "both in public and private life, by the single and permanent obligation to remedy, according to one's responsibilities and to the extent of one's power, all the privations of soul and body which are liable to destroy or damage the earthly life of any human being whatsoever."[56] This is not the appropriate moment for examining Weil's argument for the ground of this obligation (that argument is basically a Platonic revision of the argument in Kant's *Grounding*). The purpose of citing these passages here is simply to demonstrate that Weil does not make the mistake of thinking that attending can be a substitute for food or water. As Sophie Bourgault writes, Weil's account of needs and justice "calls for both genuine concern for the plight of others *and* for concrete actions to address their needs."[57]

§2.4. As we observed above, Weil's concept of attention enters anglophone philosophy through Iris Murdoch's *The Sovereignty of Good*. In the three essays gathered into that book, Murdoch repeatedly acknowledges her "debt" to Weil,[58] a debt made explicit in "The Idea of Perfection," the first essay: "I have used the word 'attention', which I borrow from Simone Weil, to express the idea of a just and loving gaze directed upon an individual reality. I believe this to be the

---

54 Cf. Bourgault, "Attentive Listening and Care," 315.

55 Weil, *The Need for Roots*, 6 / 13.

56 Weil, "Draft for a Statement of Human Obligations," 225 / 78.

57 Bourgault, "Beyond the Saint and the Red Virgin," 13. Cf. ibid., 10, and Bourgault, "Attentive Listening and Care," 324.

58 Murdoch, "On 'God' and 'Good,'" 50.

characteristic and proper mark of the active moral agent."[59] In her defence of a Weilian ethics of attending, Murdoch provides a sustained criticism of a kind of morality that she believes to be prevalent and which she characterizes as "behaviourist, existentialist, and utilitarian." It is, she writes, "behaviourist in its connection of the meaning and being of action with the publicly observable ... existentialist in its elimination of the substantial self and its emphasis on the solitary omnipotent will, and ... utilitarian in its assumption that morality is and can only be concerned with public acts."[60] She diagnoses the behaviourist constituent as a misinterpretation and a misapplication, to the realm of moral theory, of certain strands of Wittgenstein's anti-private language arguments.[61] (Basically, if meaning is socially determined and morality is a social institution, then private mental events are morally irrelevant.) And she claims that moral theory "of an existentialist type is still Cartesian and egocentric."[62] There is thus a conceptual incoherence in the pairing of the public criteria of behaviourism with the quasi-Cartesian freedom of existentialism. But Murdoch's main concern is that this kind of moral theory mistakenly conflates the "inner" with the "private," and therefore eliminates an important dimension of the ethical life.

The related terminology – "inner," "interior," and so forth – may be misleading if it seems to conjure up a picture of nocturnally dark boxes, enclosing unshowable beetles. But there is nothing necessarily *private* about the psyche that Murdoch is defending. A psyche can be shared, but its sharing occurs in a space different from the space demarcated by behaviourism and logical positivism. Murdoch applauds Wittgenstein for dissolving the fiction of mental privacy (the theory that the contents of my mind are intrinsically and logically private); but she worries that a faction of moral theorists have misinterpreted the scope and import of Wittgenstein's critique. If public observability, according to a very narrow, positivistic standard of the observable, is the ultimate criterion for the morally real, then, according to Murdoch, we would sacrifice much that is central to ethics. In particular, we would become unable to explain or to recognize the ethical importance of contemplation or

---

59 Murodoch, "The Idea of Perfection," *The Sovereignty of Good*, 34.
60 Ibid., 8–9.
61 Ibid., 15; cf. Wittgenstein, *Philosophical Investigations*, §§304–8.
62 Murdoch, "On 'God' and 'Good,'" 47.

attention; and the psychological, characterological work that surrounds and grounds behaviour would become irrelevant.

Murdoch makes her case acute by offering an example of psychological work that does not produce observable behaviour and does not change the world. A mother (M) feels unjustified hostility toward her daughter-in-law (D). However, M "behaves beautifully" to D, "not allowing her real opinion to appear in any way"; and Murdoch underlines this aspect of her example "by supposing that the young couple [that is, M's son and his wife, D] have emigrated or that D is now dead." Murdoch tells us that M "is an intelligent and well-intentioned person, capable of self-criticism, capable of giving careful and just *attention* to an object which confronts her." And in the example, that is exactly what M does: she attends to D, "until gradually her vision of D alters."[63] D is discovered to be not reckless but spontaneous, not noisy but joyous, and so on.[64] It is important not to misinterpret this change in vision as arbitrarily subjective; Murdoch emphasizes that when M "is just and loving she sees D as she really is."[65]

The accurate perception is the just and careful one. That is, the affective charge is not synthetically added to the perception, and it would not be revelatory to analyse the perception into separate constituents of bare perception and affect. Ethical clarity requires emotional resonance. The proposal that one could have accurate perceptual access to another being, completely unmediated by emotion (a kind of arch-rationalism) is as unrealistic as the competing proposal that moral perception can be reduced, without remainder, to emotional impulses (emotivism). The fiction of dispassionate perception is deserving of something like Berkeley's critique of Locke's abstract idea: just try to imagine it.

The concept "reality," as Murdoch acknowledges, operates here as a normative concept, and she uses it to indicate that it is possible to perceive responsibly or wrongly. As Christopher Mole argues in his study of Murdoch: "Being loving and just, and possessing the other virtuous character traits, is not a matter of being in a particular sort of private,

---

63 Ibid., 17.

64 Such "secondary moral words" or "normative-descriptive words" (Murdoch, "The Idea of Perfection," 22, 31) are what Williams (inspired by Murdoch and Anscombe) will later call "thick" ethical concepts.

65 Murdoch, "The Idea of Perfection," 37.

inner state. It depends on our mode of engagement with the world."[66] We must understand attending not as a private mental state but as an orientation toward reality. M's initial perception, her hostility, is inaccurate or unclear, while her altered perception, her acceptance, is accurate or clear; and in both cases the norm of accuracy is defined by the focus, namely D. As Miranda Fricker suggests, M may be understood to exercise the virtue of testimonial justice, which involves critical reflection on her own prejudices as well as openness to reality.[67] By hypothesis, the alteration of M's vision has no correlate in her observable behaviour; and yet the alteration, Murdoch maintains (and expects her reader to agree), is an ethical improvement: in perceiving more justly, M has become more just. The idea is traceable back to Plato: how one knows is not ethically neutral; epistemic virtue is characterological. As Zwicky suggests, Plato's conception of justice as the right ordering of the soul "is an attempt to respond to a common intuition that moral gestures matter even if they do not have a noticeable impact on the state of the world."[68]

There is no need to deny that such an improvement *could* manifest in observable behaviour, and the aim of Murdoch's argument is not to detach attending from action. But she insists that "the idea which we are trying to make sense of is that M has in the interim been *active*, she has been *doing* something, something which we approve of, something which is somehow worth doing in itself."[69] Murdoch's point is that it is in the interims between the huge Broadway show-tunes of decisions, acts, and outcomes that the continuous, subtle humming of ethical psychology takes place. While this humming would be inaudible to card-carrying consequentialists or behaviourists, it is far from negligible; it can have integrity, or not. The dynamic might be imagined as a river that lives mostly under the earth, emerging only at disparate junctures along its course. While it is visible and drinkable at the exposed moments, the river continues running even when it is unseen. Indeed, Murdoch clarifies the interval between acts as well as the contemplative work that

---

66 Mole, "Attention, Self and *The Sovereignty of Good*," 82.

67 Fricker, "Silence and Institutional Prejudice," 295–6. However, Mullett suggests that Murdoch's picture of moral agency may be insufficiently relational ("Shifting Perspectives," 112–13). Cf. Bowden, "Ethical Attention," 71.

68 Zwicky, "A Ship from Delos," *Learning to Die*, 60.

69 Murdoch, "The Idea of Perfection," 19.

occurs in that interval. "The moral life," in her view, "is something that goes on continually, not something that is switched off in between the occurrence of explicit moral choices. What happens in between such choices is indeed what is crucial."[70] Along with Weil, she suggests that the *way* the agent attends (which is a function of how her capacity for attending has been cultivated)[71] can determine how she will act.

By isolating M's contemplation, Murdoch has controlled for certain variables in the interests of making her case. We intuitively recognize the ethical relevance of contemplative work, even in the limiting case in which that work occurs in solitude and results in no observable behaviour and no change in the world. Our lived exercises in contemplation are rarely, if ever, so isolated. Even in Murdoch's example, in which D has emigrated or died, M must nevertheless interact with her daughter-in-law's image. Nor is the image "private"; it is an image *of* D. Some readers might think that Murdoch's behaviourist-existentialist-utilitarian theorist is not worth critiquing, since it is at best a sort of generic caricature, and at worst a position that no theorist ever held because it cannot be taken seriously. (On the other hand, a moral psychologist as sophisticated as Sue Campbell can refer to behaviourism as if it were a *fait accompli*: "Most contemporary philosophers hold some version of the thesis that behavior is constitutive of the mental.")[72]

Murdoch identified a powerful and (at the time of her writing) largely unchallenged assumption in Western anglophone moral theory – theory that has been captivated by systematic principles and decision procedures, and the acts (or acts of will) that are supposed to issue from them, at the expense of a finely detailed investigation into ethical psychology and character. And her argument is directed at opening a space for investigation into this less recognized area. The work of attending is not private (in the sense of Cartesian privacy); nor is it unobservable (unless one adheres to the strictures of logical positivism). However, it is subtle, context-sensitive, and unsystematizable. For these reasons, it is difficult to talk about, and, since theory consists in talking, difficult to theorize.

70 Ibid., 37.

71 It is important to note that an agent's capacity to attend can also be cultivated in ways over which she has no personal control; and that some kinds of cultivation, voluntary or not, can result in distortions, perversions, or vices of inattentiveness.

72 Campbell, *Interpreting the Personal*, 61.

3

Further Reflections on an Ethics of Attending

§3.1. WE HAVE SEEN THAT ATTENTIVENESS is a cardinal virtue, and that it is connected to the virtue of humility. Like virtue in general, attentiveness can be cultivated through practice. According to Simone Weil, one way of training the attention is the right use of school studies, and she sketches a general method for this training; it involves a stance of emptiness, patience, and receptivity. She makes the striking claim that an aptitude for attending is crucial for ethical agency. We have also reflected on Iris Murdoch's defence of a Weilian ethical psychology. This psychology is not primarily concerned with acts of will or consequences, and it might not produce observable behaviour. Nevertheless, it is needed in order to account for certain kinds of ethical improvement, and in particular for the judicious attempt to perceive reality clearly. Such clear perception, Murdoch argues, can determine right action. Having been introduced to Weil's and Murdoch's conception of attention, we now turn to considering some neighbouring conceptions drawn from contemporary moral psychology, philosophy of mind, aesthetics, and the history of European philosophy.

In a useful review of research in philosophy of mind, Sebastian Watzl distinguishes between two general approaches to theories of attention: reductionist and anti-reductionist. As its name suggests, the reductionist approach tries to reduce attention to "a fairly specific type of neuronal or computational process or mechanism."[1] If such a reduction were successful, it would either eliminate the "intuitive" picture of attention attributed to William James, or relegate it to a "crude" folk psychology.

---

1 Watzl, "The Nature of Attention," 845.

It is clear that Weil and Murdoch are not pursuing the reductionist research programme.

For the anti-reductionist approach, Watzl provides a comprehensive taxonomy of twelve or thirteen different forms of attention. (At least two of these forms overlap with some of James's six varieties of attention.)[2] These forms include "*focal* vs. *global* or distributed attention, where the first is narrowly directed at a particular object or event, while the second spreads over a scene as a whole"; and "*Voluntary* vs. *involuntary* attention, where the first, roughly, is controlled by the subject's intentions or goals (and in this sense an intentional action), whereas the second occurs without such intentional or voluntary control (e.g. when attention is grabbed by a salient stimulus)."[3] These contrasting forms may not be unrelated. Suppose, for example, that Watzl's global attention corresponds to Weil's state of patient receptivity; when presented with a stimulus, that state could transform into focal attention. Furthermore, both Weil and Murdoch suggest that repeated intentional exercise of attention produces an aptitude for attending that is action-determining; in terms of Watzl's taxonomy, repeated voluntary attention could produce a disposition for involuntary attention. But the fit is not perfect, since Weil and Murdoch challenge the dichotomy between the voluntary and the involuntary.

We might complexify Watzl's taxonomy by thinking about where attending would fit into ethical psychology. If attentiveness is a virtue, then, by Aristotle's account, it would be a mean between vices of excess and deficiency.[4] Like courage, it would be a complex virtue involving more than one axis. Along a social-epistemic axis, we may find vices of hostile ignorance and surveillance; along a cultural axis, vices of distraction and idolatry;[5] along an individual imaginative axis, vices of fancying and skepticism. We must also reserve a space for contempt, which Weil defines as "the contrary of attention."[6] One might have thought that

2 Cf. James, "Attention," 416.

3 Watzl, "The Nature of Attention," 846.

4 Cf. Aristotle, *Nicomachean Ethics*, II.6.

5 For a discussion of hostile ignorance, see Mills, "White Ignorance"; for a discussion of distraction, see Rozelle-Stone, "*Le Déracinement* of Attention." Concerning surveillance as a vice or distortion of attention, I have learned a great deal from discussions with Bethany Hindmarsh concerning her research for "Surveillance: A Study in Moral Psychology."

6 Weil, *Waiting for God*, 95 / 141. Cf. this book, §2.1.

contempt was a kind of attention infused with negative affect. Weil suggests, however, that it is anti-attentive. If she is right, then her suggestion tells us something important about the nature of attending and its relationship to foci. Note that these several vices are not *kinds* of attention; they are distortions. This list is incomplete and merely provisional; it may be discarded or revised in light of clearer intuitions and case studies.[7]

Of these multiple axes, deficiencies, and excesses, we shall sample only one extreme of one axis. Fancying is the opposite of skepticism in the following sense: while the skeptic doubts the independent existence of other minds, or the "external" world, and might be described as excessively scrupulous about reality, the fancier is entirely unscrupulous and moved by personal whim.[8] Fancy may be illustrated with a literary example. In James Joyce's short story "The Dead," Gabriel and Gretta Conroy are at a Christmas-time gathering at the home of Gabriel's aunts. The evening is coming to an end and some of the guests are departing. Gabriel pauses in a dark part of the hall; he sees Gretta near the top of a flight of stairs, listening to a singing voice accompanied by piano.

He stood still in the gloom of the hall, trying to catch the air that the voice was singing and gazing up at his wife. There was grace and mystery in her attitude as if she were a symbol of something. He asked himself what is a woman standing on the stairs in the shadow, listening to distant music, a symbol of. If he were a painter he would paint her in that attitude. Her blue felt hat would show off the bronze of her hair against the darkness and the dark panels of her skirt would show off the light ones. *Distant Music* he would call the picture if he were a painter.[9]

The example is complex: Gabriel appears to be attending to his wife, Gretta, who is attending to Bartell D'Arcy as he sings "The Lass of Aughrim." Gabriel is both right and wrong. He is right to notice that there is "grace and mystery" in her attitude. But he is wrong to use her attitude as a symbol for something that it is not. The symbol is Wife,

---

7 For example, Jenni describes a "pervasive and routine," "unmotivated lack of focus" which she calls "'simple' inattention" (Jenni, "Vices of Inattention," 279). Such inattention is not exactly distraction.

8 Coleridge distinguishes fancy from imagination (*Biographia Literaria*, 205–6).

9 Joyce, "The Dead," 221.

and what it symbolizes, for him, is their shared and tender past; however distant it may be, it remains perceptible, and Gabriel turns away from Gretta herself and toward moments "of their secret life together [that] burst like stars upon his memory."[10] However, his remembering is not collaborative but introspective, and that is its error. As we learn near the end of the story, Gretta, too, has turned away and is looking into her own secret life – a life before she met the man who would become her husband. She is thinking of the young man Michael Furey, who died from love of her.

The structure of Gabriel's turn is analogous to a turn described by J. Baird Callicott in his critique of the Western aesthetics of nature. He argues that European popular appreciation for natural "landscapes" was stimulated in the seventeenth century by the painting and exhibition of artificial ones:

People saw landscape paintings in galleries, enjoyed an aesthetic experience, and so turned to the painters' motifs for a similar gratification. Natural beauty thus shone forth in the West, but, like the moon, by a borrowed light.

A device of the period, the Claude glass, named for the 17th-century French landscape artist, Claude Lorraine, tells the whole story. The new natural aesthetes carried the rectangular, slightly concave, tinted mirror with them into the countryside. Upon finding a suitably picturesque prospect, they turned their backs to it and rear-viewed its image in the Claude glass. Thus framed, the natural landscape looked almost (but of course not quite) as pretty as a picture.[11]

In the Uffizi Gallery in Florence, one can see a twenty-first-century version of the Claude glass in action. Dressed up for the occasion, and finding Botticelli's *Birth of Venus* (for example), gallery-goers will stand in front of the painting, turn their backs to it, and use their smartphones to take "selfies" with the painting as backdrop. While the gesture of turning one's back is emblematic of not attending, that gesture itself is not the primary failure of attention in these cases. Indeed, Gabriel fancies that he is turned toward (memories of) his wife; the fact that he is nevertheless inattentive shows that merely having an object in the spotlight of consciousness is not enough to constitute attending. What makes

10 Ibid., 224.
11 Callicott, "The Land Aesthetic," 171.

the user of the Claude glass and the selfie-taker inattentive is the way they use the natural landscape or the Botticelli. They use the landscape or the painting in the same way that Gabriel uses the symbol Wife. True attending is interactive. But Gabriel, the user of the Claude glass, and the selfie-taker all foreclose on the possibility of resonance. Gretta herself does not participate in Gabriel's fantasy; in his personal, introspective drama, there is no role for her. Similarly, the natural landscape or the Uffizi painting are treated as inanimate, as inert material for illusion, or as flattering backgrounds for the ego.

When Gabriel learns the truth, he feels humiliated: "While he had been full of memories of their secret life together, full of tenderness and joy and desire, she had been comparing him in her mind with another."[12] But his articulation of that truth is distorted, because he wrongly interpolates himself into her memory of her lover: in truth, she had been remembering Michael and not thinking of Gabriel at all. The whole story is composed for the final paragraph, which sides with neither the perspective of Gretta nor that of Gabriel, with their particular foci, but instead withdraws to an impersonal, synoptic perspective:

A few light taps upon the pane made him turn to the window. It had begun to snow again. He watched sleepily the flakes, silver and dark, falling oblique-ly against the lamplight. The time had come for him to set out on his journey westward. Yes, the newspapers were right: snow was general all over Ireland. It was falling on every part of the dark central plain, on the treeless hills, fall-ing softly upon the Bog of Allen and, farther westward, softly falling into the dark mutinous Shannon waves. It was falling, too, upon every part of the lonely churchyard on the hill where Michael Furey lay buried. It lay thickly drifted on the crooked crosses and headstones, on the spears of the little gate, on the barren thorns. His soul swooned slowly as he heard the snow falling faintly through the universe and faintly falling, like the descent of their last end, upon all the living and the dead.[13]

The falling snow echoes the rain falling in the lyrics of "The Lass of Aughrim": "*O, the rain falls on my heavy locks / And the dew wets my skin, / My babe lies cold.*"[14] It also echoes the rain falling in some of Weil's

12 Joyce, "The Dead," 231.
13 Ibid., 235–6.
14 Ibid., 221.

favourite verses from the Book of Matthew (which we considered in Section 2.2): "You have heard that it was said, 'You shall love your neighbor and hate your enemy.' But I say to you, Love your enemies and pray for those who persecute you, so that you may be sons of your Father who is in heaven; for he makes his sun rise on the evil and the good, and sends rain on the just and on the unjust."[15] Like the light in Zwicky's "History," like the sun and the rain in Matthew, the snow falls indifferently. As the sun does not discriminate between the good and the evil, and as the rain does not discriminate between the just and the unjust, so the snow falls equally on the living and the dead. It encompasses Gretta and Gabriel and Michael as contemporaries. Like the sun and the rain, the snow is an image of completely impersonal attending. But the landscape that it blankets is forlorn: the plain is dark, the hills treeless, the churchyard lonely, the thorns barren; in the inanimate waste, only the snow and the dark mutinous Shannon waves are moving. Yet the desolate imagery is overlaid with the almost inaudible music of the chiasmus – falling softly and softly falling, falling faintly and faintly falling – and enclosed by the tetrameter couplet at the end.

This impersonal perspective is anticipated by a glimpse earlier in the story. Gabriel stands at the table, prepared to give a speech, and the conversation falls silent:

The piano was playing a waltz tune and he could hear the skirts sweeping against the drawing-room door. People, perhaps, were standing in the snow on the quay outside, gazing up at the lighted windows and listening to the waltz music. The air was pure there. In the distance lay the park where the trees were weighted with snow.[16]

One is simultaneously at the table with Gabriel, in the drawing-room with the waltzers, on the quay with the listeners, and in the park with the trees. Such imaginative perception is not fancy. Nor is it attention rapt by the particular (as the archer's attention was rapt by the cicada in Section 2.1, and as Murdoch's will be rapt by the kestrel in Section 3.7). If we were doing a Platonic dialectic, we would make a division here between two forms of attending. On the one hand, there is an

---

15 Matthew 5:43–5. Cf. Weil, "Human Personality," 98; *Notebooks*, I.106, I.210, I.221, I.232, I.272, I.277; *The Need for Roots*, 259–60; and *Waiting for God*, 101, 135.
16 Joyce, "The Dead," 212.

impersonal, empty, *day-like* attending, which can be in many places at once without being broken into parts; and on the other hand, there is a *ray-like* attending, which focuses on one particular, precious and losable, unique in the universe. Perhaps these forms of attending are species of the genera that Lucy Alford calls "transitive" and "intransitive" attention; namely, forms of attention that do and do not take an object, respectively.[17] In Weil's work, we find both forms of attention, although she does not draw an explicit distinction between them; indeed, the first form of attention can become the second. Attention that is empty, patient, and receptive can become particularized and focused; the agent waiting for an animal to emerge from the forest can become transfixed by the epiphany of a deer.[18]

§3.2. As we continue to investigate Weil's concept of attention, it will be useful to compare it with two anti-reductionist accounts of attention that might appear to parallel hers: Mihaly Csikszentmihalyi's theory of flow and Christopher Mole's theory of attention as cognitive unison. An important similarity among these three accounts of attention is that they all understand attention to be a function of an *integrative* perspective. They agree that attention is not merely some epiphenomenon that can be analytically reduced to elements of a neurological substratum. Csikszentmihalyi likens his approach to a biological approach that "looks at the animal as a whole system interacting with other systems in its environment."[19] While he advocates for a holistic approach, he does not argue that it should replace an analytic one; he argues that both approaches are necessary for a complete understanding. (We shall find this crucial insight echoed by John Steinbeck in Section 6.5.)

17 Alford, "Out of Nothing: Imagination as a Mode of Poetic Attention." A more comprehensive and detailed study of the distinction between transitive and intransitive attention should be found in Alford, *Forms of Poetic Attention* (Columbia University Press, forthcoming). Regarding intransitive attention, cf. Alford's discussion of what she calls "vigilance" in her "Problems in Post-Foundational Ethics" (esp. chap. 5, "The Problem of Ethics as a Problem of Attention," 217ff).

18 Cf. Lilburn, "Poetry's Practice of Philosophy," 39; Williams and Penman, *Mindfulness*, 103.

19 Csikszentmihalyi, "Attention and the Holistic Approach to Behavior," 6. For drawing my attention to Csikszentmihalyi's work, thanks to an anonymous reader.

In Csikszentmihalyi's holistic approach, attention plays a decisive role in what he calls "optimal experience" or "flow": "Optimal experiences occur when a person *voluntarily* focusses his attention on a limited stimulus field."[20] The stimulus itself might be unpleasant or even threatening, but the agent who succeeds in voluntarily investing his attention enters a "flow" state, in which he is unselfconsciously absorbed in his activity. Csikszentmihalyi identifies eight major components of a successful investment of attention. Of these, the second, fifth, and seventh components might also feature in Weilian attending: (2) one must be able to concentrate, (5) one acts "with deep but effortless involvement," and (7) "concern for the self disappears."[21]

Csikszentmihalyi characterizes the fifth component of his theory of flow as "one of the most universal and distinctive features of optimal experience": "people become so involved in what they are doing that the activity becomes spontaneous, almost automatic; they stop being aware of themselves as separate from the actions they are performing."[22] Closely connected with such spontaneity is his seventh component: a dissolving of self-consciousness. In this respect, Julia Annas argues that the phenomenology of flow aligns with the phenomenology of virtue. She suggests that these two features of Csikszentmihalyi's account fit with features of an Aristotelian account of virtue: "Firstly, the virtuous activity is experienced as intrinsically worthwhile and enjoyable ... Secondly ... it is a mark of the mature virtuous person that her actions are not motivated by thoughts that are routed through thoughts of the self."[23] Indeed, these features distinguish the phenomenology of virtue from the effortful and self-controlled phenomenology of apprenticeship, as we shall see. In acting virtuously, the agent acts in a way that is effortlessly involved and unselfconscious; but it does not follow that she is immersed in a passive and mindless stream of feelings. Annas emphasizes that Aristotelian virtue should be understood by analogy with practical skill. It is because the expert has repeatedly practised carefully and thoughtfully that she is able to respond spontaneously when required.

20　Ibid., 7.

21　Csikszentmihalyi, *Flow*, 49.

22　Ibid., 53.

23　Annas, "The phenomenology of virtue," 30. Cf. Williams, "Utilitarianism and moral self-indulgence," 48; and Zwicky, "Alcibiades' Love," 91 / *AL*, 291. Cf. this book, §9.

At least three significant dissonances can be discerned between Csikszentmihalyi's phenomenology of flow and Weil's account of attending. One, as Csikszentmihalyi himself acknowledges, is that flow is amoral; what he calls the "autotelic personality" may elect to pursue goals that harm others – a scientist, for instance, may be moved by contemplating images of his country's enemies dying agonized deaths to enter a state of flow while manufacturing sarin.[24] Weil, on the other hand, because she has faith in the Platonic thesis that virtue is knowledge, maintains that truly attending cannot lead to cruelly harmful action. Indeed, her view is that it is impossible to derive motivation from the attentive contemplation of an evil act; and that a good act, contemplated attentively, is necessarily motivating. This, she says, is the "definition" of the good.[25] Anne Colby and William Damon, in their study of the psychology of moral exemplars, criticize the theory of flow for its ambivalence about appropriate goals.[26] While moral exemplars may enter states of "unself-conscious immersion," their "goals" are neither arbitrary nor discretionary. On the contrary, they say, such exemplars repeatedly testify that they feel compelled, by "moral necessity," to make their commitments to noble causes such as racial equality or the alleviation of poverty. As we shall see, Weil regards this sense of necessity as a characteristic entailment of clear attentiveness.

By contrast (and here is the second dissonance), Csikszentmihalyi's "state of flow" is both voluntary and self-controlled. In one of his examples, a US Air Force pilot keeps his sanity in a North Vietnam prison by deciding to play golf in his mind. "When adversity threatens to paralyze us," writes Csikszentmihalyi, "we need to reassert control by finding a new direction ... a meaningful goal around which to organize the self. Then, even though that person is objectively a slave, subjectively he is free."[27] Here, existentialism sounds almost like Stoicism; and yet their images of freedom are different. For the existentialist, the will at every

---

24 See Csikszentmihalyi, *Flow*, 69–70. Annas recognizes this feature of Csikszentmihalyi's account – "flow can be available even to someone as unvirtuous as Eichmann" ("The phenomenology of virtue," 30) – but does not seem to think that it renders the account unfitting for virtue.

25 Weil, *Gravity and Grace*, 48, 119 / 59, 136.

26 Colby and Damon, *Some Do Care*, 83–5. For drawing my attention to Colby and Damon's book, thanks to an anonymous reader.

27 Csikszentmihalyi, *Flow*, 91–2.

moment transcends whatever material or historical conditions the agent finds himself in.[28] In defending Weil's ethics of attending, Murdoch at the same time criticizes what she calls the "empty lonely freedom" of this existentialist will, which is undetermined by reasons.[29] For the Stoic, by contrast, the will is no less determined than anything else in the cosmos; the Stoic achieves freedom insofar as she is able to understand how and why things are determined.

A third dissonance between Weil's and Csikszentmihalyi's accounts of attention is that the latter accepts prevailing economic metaphors ("paying" attention, for example) and claims that attention, defined as psychic energy, is a limited resource possessed by the perceiver.[30] If the perceiver invests his attention prudently, then he will be rewarded with enjoyable experiences. Under capitalism, he writes, attention can be bought: "A wage earner exchanges psychic energy for money by investing his attention in goals determined for him by someone else ... In contemporary societies, control over money directly translates into control over other people's attention."[31] In Csikszentmihalyi's analysis, what distinguishes alienated from non-alienated consciousness is that the former is the *involuntary* sale of attention.[32] The wage-labourer's attention to the matter on the assembly line is purchased along with his labour. Nicholas Carr correspondingly suggests that the Taylorization of factory labour was an attempt to quantify and mechanize attention.[33]

It is not surprising that Weil is no proponent of Taylor's system: "The base kind of attention demanded by Taylorized work is incompatible with any other form of attention, because it empties the soul of everything but the concern for speed. This kind of work cannot be transformed—it must be abolished."[34] If there is a moral problem in the worldview of the market, it is this: how to coordinate private spending

28 Rousseau may be the origin of this existentialist thesis: see *Discourse on the Origin of Inequality*, 32–3.

29 Murdoch, "The Idea of Perfection," 27; cf. ibid., 36.

30 Similarly, in Yves Citton's cultural study of collective attention, he formulates a "POSTULATE OF LIMITED RESOURCE: *the total quantity of attention available to humans is limited at any given time*" (Citton, *The Ecology of Attention*, 31). For drawing my attention to Citton's book, thanks to an anonymous reader.

31 Csikszentmihalyi, "Attention and the Holistic Approach to Behavior," 16.

32 Ibid., 12.

33 Carr, "Is Google Making Us Stupid?"

34 Weil, quoted in Pétrement, *Simone Weil: A Life*, 461; cf. ibid., 291–2.

with the public good?[35] But the economic model for attention is not peculiar to Csikszentmihalyi; it is a dominant mainstream model for theorizing attention.[36] Weil's model for attending, on the other hand, is not economic but ecological. To perceive the economy as animate is mere fetishism; an ecological cosmos, by contrast, is truly animate and self-moving. For Weil, the energy needed for ethical action does not come from the agent's finite and private reserve; she receives it, exactly as she receives physical nourishment, from external sources.

Like Csikszentmihalyi, Mole understands attention as an integrative activity. He returns to James, and problematizes the frequently quoted claim that everyone knows what attention is. In James's own work, Mole identifies at least two distinct notions of attention: "In one strand of James's thinking ... attention was associated with perception, with phenomena of 'sensory clearness,' and with processes on what we might think of as the input side of the cognitive economy. In another strand of James's thinking, attention was associated with willed action, volition, and so with processes on what we might think of as the output side of the cognitive economy."[37] To these notions, Mole adds the activity of attending in the process of thinking, and argues that the relevant phenomena are "too many and too various" to be covered by a single causal mechanism. Therefore, he claims, "the explanation of attention must take a form other than the process-specifying form that is the favorite of cognitive psychologists." Mole's own explanation is that attention is cognitive unison. He exploits an analogy with musical unison: "If we have a group of musicians and we wish to know whether they are playing in unison, we don't need to know which of them is playing, which instruments are being played, how loudly they are playing, or how many of them are playing. All we need to know is, of those who are playing, whether anyone is playing anything other than the melody."[38]

The analogy seems elegant. But closer inspection reveals that Mole's notion of attention is not entirely analogous to the kind of musical unison he defines here. According to the *Oxford Dictionary of Music*, melody is a "succession of notes, varying in pitch, which have an

---

35 Cf. Csikszentmihalyi, "Attention and the Holistic Approach to Behavior," 18.

36 Cf. Citton, "Attentional Capitalism," *The Ecology of Attention*, 44–62.

37 Mole, "The Metaphysics of Attention," 62. Cf. Mole, *Attention Is Cognitive Unison*, 5.

38 Mole, "The Metaphysics of Attention," 66–7.

organized and recognizable shape," and unison is the sounding "of the same note by all performers."[39] In Mole's notion of musical unison, unison is sameness of content; all performing musicians are performing the same succession of notes. By analogy, in attending, all operating cognitive processes should be processing the same content. But Mole's notion of attention is adverbial, and what is essential to an adverbial phenomenon is "not *what* happens to what but *how* the things that happen happen."[40] Attending is not reducible to any particular cognitive process; it is, rather, a *way* of processing. An adverbial theory of attending is promising insofar as it offers resources for making sense of Weil's repeated claim that attending is, at least initially, empty or contentless. Similarly, an adverbial theory might help to make sense of her emphasis on the importance of a *method* or *way* of attending. Furthermore, virtues in general are understandable as adverbial phenomena. A courageous person does not possess some thing called "courage"; instead, when she finds herself in situations requiring courage, she acts courageously. Similarly, an attentive person does not possess a thing (or process) called "attention"; she looks and listens attentively.

But Mole's approach and Weil's approach differ in three significant respects. Weil's account of attending cannot be classified as cognitive because she does not subscribe to *cognitive/non-cognitive* dualism. For Weil, attending is not only an act of the mind, brain, consciousness, reason, belief, or perception; nor is it only a set of cognitive processes operating in unison; it is an act of the whole agent, in which her passions and body are integrated with her intellect. Indeed, as we shall see, for Weil an important characteristic of attending is the seizure of the agent as an ensouled body. A second difference in approach follows from the first: because Weil does not subscribe to dualism, she does not face the same explanatory problem that motivates Mole. Recall that Mole identifies two different sorts of process in James's "cognitive economy": perceptual clearness and willed action. These processes both seem to play a role in attending, and yet they are, by hypothesis, different; seen that way, attention cannot therefore be reduced to a single process, and we

---

39 Entries for "melody" and "unison" in *Oxford Dictionary of Music*, 6th ed., ed. Joyce Kennedy, Michael Kennedy, and Tim Rutherford-Johnson (Oxford: Oxford University Press, 2012).

40 Mole, "The Metaphysics of Attention," 70; emphasis added. Cf. Mole, *Attention Is Cognitive Unison*, 28–9.

must seek an explanation of attention at a higher level. Weil's account, on the other hand, integrates the two aspects that James identifies. For Weil, perceptual clarity *is* free action. There is a sense in which the particular circumstances, clearly perceived, act through the agent.

A third disparity between Mole's and Weil's approaches is connected with Mole's analytic definition of attention in terms of necessary and sufficient conditions:

A person is paying attention if and only if, among the set of resources that that person could bring to bear in performing whatever task he is engaged with, there are no resources that are doing anything other than serving that particular task. More precisely, the agent performs τ attentively just in case there is some task υ that the agent understands to be a way of performing τ, and just in case the agent is performing υ on the basis of that understanding, and performing υ in such a way that the set of cognitive resources that the agent can, with understanding, bring to bear in the service of υ does not contain resources that are occupied with activity that doesn't serve τ.[41]

As we have already noted, since Weil does not subscribe to *cognitive/ non-cognitive* dualism, she would not accept the emphasis here on attention as a primarily cognitive phenomenon. Because, for Weil, attentiveness is a cardinal virtue, and because habit has a role in the development of virtue, being attentive will involve habitual ("non-cognitive") acts. The expert cyclist attends with her body no less than with her mind, and her expertise includes trained sensitivities that do not rise into consciousness. Indeed, their not rising into consciousness is a measure of the cyclist's expertise. Unlike the apprentice, she does not need to deliberate and make decisions in order to avoid obstacles; she simply avoids them. (Recall that Weil agrees with Csikszentmihalyi that unselfconsciousness is a feature of attending.) So there are at least some "tasks" that the attentive cyclist performs which play a role in constituting her cycling attentively – and which are not "cognitive" in a narrow sense. Would Weil then accept a revision of Mole's definition that included "non-cognitive" resources or activities? (Notice that the first sentence of Mole's definition is general enough to accommodate such an expansion.) No,

41 Mole, "The Metaphysics of Attention," 67. Cf. Mole, *Attention Is Cognitive Unison*, 51.

she would not accept such a revision. The disparity between Mole and Weil here constitutes a difference of philosophical style.

§3.3. A difference between philosophical styles is not insignificant. Weil does make some general remarks about her concept of attention and a method for practising attentiveness. But she declines to provide an analytic definition in terms of necessary and sufficient conditions. She offers instead what might be called a *characterization* of the concept. By analogy with offering a character sketch of a person, a characterization of a concept should enable us to recognize it in the field, without foreclosing on its capacity to surprise us. Furthermore, Weil's refusal to analyse the concept is connected with the particularist angle of her ethics. Unlike Kantian or utilitarian moral theory, Weil's ethics of attending is not governed by general criteria.[42]

— "Wait! Either the concept of attention is generically categorizable or it isn't. If it is, then we should be able to fix its extension by articulating its necessary and sufficient conditions (however general). Once articulated, these conditions should supply a discriminatory mechanism, a means for correctly applying the concept and for criticizing incorrect applications. Look, if we can't say what classes of things would fall outside the concept, then the concept is vacuous. Furthermore, if the concept is ungeneralizable, then how can we use it?"

— In response, while this objection is important, it conflates modest generalizations with analyses of concepts. A generalization is like the direction "Stand roughly there."[43] The direction is not precise, but it is usable (that is, it is meaningful and understandable); there are ways of following it and ways of getting it wrong. But someone who drew a chalk circle around an area, and insisted that "there" was circumscribed by the drawing, would have *interpreted* the direction; and that interpretation is not equivalent to the original. There is a way of understanding a generalization that is not an interpretation.[44] Weil does offer some general remarks about what attention is and about a method for its exercise, but she does not offer an analysis of the concept.

---

42 For my use of the term "criteria," see Zwicky, *Lyric Philosophy*, §§41ff.
43 Cf. Wittgenstein, *Philosophical Investigations*, §§71, 88.
44 Cf. ibid., §201.

Were the distinction not so fraught, we might try to explain the difficulty of specifying attention in terms of form and content. If form follows content, then the form of attending must follow the content of the focus. Abigail Lipson and Michael Lipson, in their discussion of a Weilian ethics of attention, draw a comparison between attention and "Aristotle's *epistemikon*, the organelle within the psyche that can perceive Forms, and as to which Aristotle says that it is itself formless."[45] It is not entirely clear whether they are alluding to the noetic power, "the place of forms," in general, or to the νοῦς παθητικός (*nous pathētikos*), the "passive intellect," in particular. But the point seems to be that attention, like formless matter, is primed to receive the form of its focus.[46]

— "But surely the valorization of psychological formlessness is politically dangerous; an asymmetrical relation in which the attender is so deferential that her interests are defined by those of the attendee is prone to exploitation. Hilde Nelson, Peta Bowden, and Jan Zwicky, in their respective discussions of Weil's work,[47] have warned of the oppressive potential of an ethics that endorses self-denying deference to others." — We shall return to this objection. For the moment, a more promising analogy than the passive intellect may be the Aristotelian virtue of φρόνησις (*phronēsis*),[48] with its sensitivity to particulars. And a different Aristotelian metaphor may be more appropriate: the metaphor of the flexible lead ruler used by the architects of Lesbos. Aristotle writes:

---

45 Lipson and Lipson, "Psychotherapy and the Ethics of Attention," 19. Lipson and Lipson refer to all of *De Anima*, but the relevant passages occur at III.4.429a10ff.

46 Lévinas finds the receptivity of the Aristotelian intellect more sympathetic than Platonic maeiutics (see *Totality and Infinity*, §A.5 [p. 51]). As an anonymous reader for the Press rightly observed, there is a significant resonance between Weil's ethics of attending and Lévinas's conviction that ethics is listening to the other. An exploration of the resonance, with attention to these philosophers' different styles of philosophizing and to Lévinas's perplexing excoriation of Weil, is deserving of a separate study.

47 Cf. Nelson, "Against Caring"; Bowden, "Ethical Attention"; Zwicky, *Contemplation and Resistance*.

48 Henceforth transliterated and anglicized as "phronesis." A note on terms: since *akrasia, phronesis*, and *sophrosyne* have found their way into the OED, they will be set in roman type, as will *enkrateia* (to match akrasia).

In fact this is the reason why all things are not determined by law, namely, that about some things it is impossible to lay down a law, so that a decree is needed. For when the thing is indefinite the rule also is indefinite, like the leaden rule used in making the Lesbian moulding; the rule adapts itself to the shape of the stone and is not rigid, and so too the decree is adapted to the facts.[49]

Commenting on this passage, Martha Nussbaum elaborates:

Aristotle tells us that a person who attempts to make every decision by appeal to some antecedent general principle held firm and inflexible for the occasion is like an architect who tries to use a straight ruler on the intricate curves of a fluted column. Instead, the good architect will, like the builders of Lesbos, measure with a flexible strip of metal that 'bends round to fit the shape of the stone and is not fixed' (1137b30–32). Good deliberation, like this ruler, accommodates itself to what it finds, responsively and with respect for complexity. It does not assume that the form of the rule *governs* the appearances; it allows the appearances to govern themselves and to be normative for correctness of rule.[50]

Notice that the Lesbian rule is context-sensitive but not relativistic. There are facts to which the rule must adapt, and these facts include the spatial dimensions of the column. While those dimensions cannot be measured accurately by an inflexible ruler, it does not follow that they are relative to the mind of the perceiver. In this respect, the Lesbian rule is like the Aristotelian mean. The mean is relative to the agent, but objective facts about the agent and her context play a role in determining the mean. As an example, suppose that Niko and Milo are both participating in a hunger strike, but Niko has extensive training in such strikes and Milo does not. What counts as sound-minded and courageous for Niko will be different from what counts as such for Milo.

To suggest that attending must be as pliant as phronesis is not to claim that one must escape one's own perspective or one's character; nor is it to claim that one must unquestioningly conform to the perspective of the focus. "To be wise," writes Jan Zwicky, "is to be able to grasp another form of life without abandoning one's own; to be able to

49 Aristotle, *Nicomachean Ethics*, V.10.1137b27–32.
50 Nussbaum, *The Fragility of Goodness*, 301.

translate experience into and out of two original tongues. To resist, then, the translation that is a form of reduction."[51] Attending to another's experience need not – indeed, cannot – involve a reductive translation of one's own, or the other's, experience. A responsible translation must respond, without prejudice, to what, specifically, is offered. Recall that both Weil and Murdoch cite translating as an exercise in virtue. Fidelity to reality is the norm governing that exercise. The Lesbian rule, as a metaphor for phronesis, and translating, as an illustration of attending, are images for thinking about a kind of context-sensitivity that is not shallowly relativistic.[52]

§3.4. — "ok," an interlocutor might chime in, "so you're not going to offer an analytic definition of attention. And you're claiming that you can't offer one because the form of attention is specified by the so-called focus? But Weilian attention is not unique in this respect. Listen to Kant: 'Act only according to that maxim whereby you can at the same time will that it should become a universal law.'[53] A general formula still requires the input of particulars. One merit of mainstream theories is that their application is straightforward. They offer us explicit, actionable guidance toward solving moral problems. Take a look at Philippa Foot's sensational example: you're the driver of the runaway subway, there's a fork in the tracks; to the left, where the subway is headed, five workers are on the track; to the right, there's one worker, what do you do?[54] The utilitarian says: 'The right thing to do is to maximize expected aggregate pleasure and minimize pain: so act to kill fewer people: turn right.' The deontologist says: 'Never treat another person merely as a means: if you turned right, you'd be treating that person as a means, so you must refrain from acting.' Cartoonish as it is, this is an archetype of some real moral dilemmas, and for that reason it has gripped the imaginations of undergrads and cognitive scientists alike. And we can tell that these theories aren't vacuous because they deliver different, and mutually exclusive, solutions. So how, may I ask, does your theory solve this problem or others like it?"

---

51 Zwicky, *Wisdom & Metaphor*, L94.
52 Cf. Code on "mitigated relativism" ("Taking Subjectivity into Account," 40).
53 Kant, *Grounding for the Metaphysics of Morals*, Ak. 421.
54 Foot, "The Problem of Abortion and the Doctrine of the Double Effect," 8.

— A moral theory that pretends to "solve" such a problem has forfeited its claim to ethics. Bernard Williams suggests in his critique of utilitarianism that "there are certain situations so monstrous that the idea that the processes of moral rationality could yield an answer in them is insane."[55] In Foot's thought experiment, the utilitarian theory delivers the required direction, as it does in the case when one is harbouring a fugitive and the murderer is banging at the door (that is, it says that we should lie to the murderer).[56] But in neither case is the prescribed action the *right* one. By the time we arrive on the scene in such cases, the time for right action, if there was such a time, has already passed. In Kant's view, it is not permissible to lie to the murderer because, as he correctly tells us, "truth is not a possession the right to which can be granted to one person but refused to another."[57] Furthermore, as Weil urges, the need for truth is a sacred need and a lie lacerates the soul.[58] But, as utilitarianism also correctly tells us, if forced to choose, we should lacerate the murderer's soul rather than betray the fugitive's life, because, forced to quantify, we must say that the laceration is less harmful than the killing – but quantification is a sign that we have left the space of ethics.

Seven years after Foot published her thought experiment, Ursula K. Le Guin published a version of the same problem. Unlike Foot, Le Guin acknowledges that the problem is tragic. In this passage, the speaker is the driver of a truck train carrying ore; he is speaking to his passenger, a hitchhiker riding with him in the cab. There has been a long drought and famine in the land. The driver wonders what he would do if he were driving a provisions train that was mobbed, en route, by people desperate for food. Would he run them down to get the food to its destination? "'But hell, you going to run down kids, old men? They're doing wrong but you going to *kill* 'em for it? I don't know!'"

The straight shining rails ran under the wheels. Clouds in the west laid great shivering mirages on the plain, the shadows of dreams of lakes gone dry ten million years ago.

55 Williams, "A critique of utilitarianism," 92.

56 Contrast Kant, "On a Supposed Right to Lie," Ak. 425–30; and Mill, *Utilitarianism*, 32.

57 Kant, "On a Supposed Right to Lie," Ak. 428.

58 Weil, *The Need for Roots*, 36 / 53. Cf. Kant, "On a Supposed Right to Lie," Ak. 426.

"A syndic, fellow I've known for years, he did just that, north of here, in '66. They tried to take a grain truck off his train. He backed the train, killed a couple of them before they cleared the track, they were like worms in rotten fish, thick, he said. He said, there's eight hundred people waiting for the grain truck, and how many of them might die if they don't get it? More than a couple, a lot more. So it looks like he was right. But by damn! I can't add up figures like that. I don't know if it's right to count people like you count numbers. But then, what do you do? Which ones do you kill?"[59]

If one weighs eight hundred lives in the balance against two, as the utilitarian calculus tells us to do, then sacrificing two to save eight hundred looks like the right thing to do. But, as the driver worries, what if it is not right "to count people like you count numbers"? What if each person is a world, and the weight of each world is infinite? What if the arithmetical way of looking at the problem is mistaken? What if one and one are not greater than one? And what if the messy circumstances also make it impossible to accord respect to each and every person? What if the problem is not soluble?

I suspect that a great many moral problems – perhaps most of them – leave no room for the exercise of virtue. In confronting such problems, we may be forced to resort to moral theory. But it would be a mistake to conclude that theory is thereby vindicated and attending is valueless. Nelson suggests that attention is necessary but not sufficient for morality; in this suggestion, she is in agreement with Nussbaum. Meanwhile, Lipson and Lipson claim that "the capacity to attend can be exercised in the service of all the major theories of ethics as they currently exist"; and that "an interest in attentional style may be held in common by adherents of otherwise divergent systems (consequentialist or deontological)."[60] By contrast, we are here considering the suggestion that, in some cases, attending is enough for right action; and, in other cases, it is incompatible with the major systematic moral theories. Weil's notion of attention is not an additional theory, to be tacked onto the end of the ever-lengthening list that includes deontology, consequentialism (both act and rule versions), contractarianism, virtue ethics

59 Le Guin, *The Dispossessed*, 311–12.

60 Nelson, "Against Caring," 13; Nussbaum, "'Finely Aware and Richly Responsible,'" 524 (cf. Nussbaum, "Why Practice Needs Ethical Theory," 227–55); Lipson and Lipson, "Psychotherapy and the Ethics of Attention," 17, 21.

(theoretical versions), land ethics, feminist moral theories, moral particularism, and so forth.

Margaret Urban Walker is right to call into question the monopoly of the "theoretical-juridical model" of moral theory: "a *codifiable* (and usually compact) set of moral *formulas* (or procedures for selecting formulas) that can be applied by *any* agent to a situation to yield a justified and determinate *action-guiding* judgment."[61] Julia Annas calls this model "the *computer manual model*":[62]

If we need a decision procedure, a systematic and theorizable way of telling us what to do, then it will seem reasonable to think of the major aim of moral theory as being that of producing a *theory of right action*. This will be a theory which will produce, and defend theoretically, some decision procedure for telling us what to do, where "telling us what to do" means: giving specific instructions for how to act which are applicable to everyone in the same way.[63]

If that is what moral philosophy is, then Weil's notion of attention does not belong in the same category. But what if the purpose of moral philosophy is not to formulate a theory telling us what to do? As Peter Winch suggests, what if "philosophy can no more show a man what he should attach importance to than geometry can show a man where he should stand"?[64] Indeed, on a case-by-case basis, Weil's notion of attention might very well undermine the computer manual model, because, when we exercise our attention, sometimes what we perceive is that the "justified and determinate *action-guiding* judgment" is not right – that all the available choices involve some kind of violence and injustice. When we attend to each of the particulars on its own terms, we may perceive indefeasible and incommensurable needs: the need for truth, the need for life. Such perception could result in paralysis.

61 Walker, "Feminism, Ethics, and the Question of Theory," 28.

62 Annas, "Being Virtuous and Doing the Right Thing," reprinted in Shafer-Landau, ed., *Ethical Theory*, 737a. In the original printing (in *Proceedings and Addresses of the American Philosophical Association*), this phrase is "the *technical manual model*" (63). Because "technical" is cognate with τέχνη (*tekhnē*), which has different connotations for Aristotle, I think that "computer" better captures the aspect of moral theory under discussion.

63 Annas, "Being Virtuous and Doing the Right Thing," *American Philosophical Association*, 63.

64 Winch, "Moral Integrity," 191.

More radically, even in more fortunate circumstances in which it is possible to discern a right action, there will be cases in which the prescriptions and justifications of moral theory distort the real reason for acting.[65] Furthermore, there will be cases in which a formula or decision procedure is useless and inappropriate because there is no decision to be made. (We shall discuss such issues in Section 4.) If our goal is to provide a final general definition of what is good and what is right, to ascertain whether these types are instantiated in a given context, and to prescribe and justify action, then we are bound to regard Weil's remarks as distracting. If, on the other hand, we believe that living ethically is an ongoing practice that requires openness to revising or even abandoning our assumptions in the face of unanticipated facts,[66] and which demands sensitivity to problems that cannot be solved in advance of examining their details – including problems for which there is no solution – then Weil may offer some insight.

§3.5. Foot has offered us the image of a lonely moral agent driving a subway train, facing a grim dilemma between killing one and letting five die. Unlike the driver in Le Guin's novel, Foot is not conflicted about what one ought to do. "If the choice is between inflicting injury on one or many," she writes, "there seems only one rational course of action."[67] Enshrined in the juridical-theoretical model is the picture of the moral agent as a decision-maker and problem-solver. When faced with a moral problem, he applies his theory and it tells him how to solve the problem. The theory also supplies the rationalization or justification for the solution. It is unlikely, however, that the bereaved family in this case will be consoled by the claim that the killer acted rationally. And it is surely a distortion to claim that "Kill one innocent" is a *solution* to the problem "Kill one innocent or many innocents?" As G.E.M. Anscombe suggests, a theory that purports to justify such a "solution" is corrupt.[68] Beside the theoretical-juridical or computer manual model, let us set the model defended by Weil and Murdoch. According to their model, an agent can be moved to

65 On such distortions, see Dworkin, "Unprincipled Ethics," §10 (pp. 236–8).
66 Cf. Colby and Damon, *Some Do Care*, 168, 184.
67 Foot, "The Problem of Abortion," 12.
68 Cf. Anscombe, "Modern Moral Philosophy," 17.

action directly by the focus of attending, without the mediation of theory or decision-making procedure.

Recall Descartes's Stoic theory of error, which Weil borrows to explain that error is the result of an impatient will – a voluntary wandering away from the truth. Clear perception of truth or goodness, on the other hand, says Descartes, leaves no room for choice. This way of thinking radically challenges our conventional notions of freedom, agency, and action. We might assume that freedom is freedom to choose; the greater the number of options and the fewer the constraints, the greater our freedom. Under that assumption, Descartes's claim sounds paradoxical: "In order to be free I need not be capable of being moved in each direction; on the contrary, the more I am inclined toward one direction … because I clearly understand that there is in it an aspect of the good and the true … the more freely do I choose that direction."[69] He is claiming that *freedom* consists in having one's thinking *determined* by the truth or in having one's action *determined* by the good.

Such an experience is the experience of necessary truth, and it will govern the practical syllogism no less than the deductive argument. It is this idea that Weil develops in greater detail in the set of aphorisms titled "Necessity and Obedience."[70] Most of us take for granted that we are agents or doers; that we cause our actions, which effect changes in the world. Weil's conception of agency is different. When one understands, one is not a doer, but a *medium*. Ideally, one should be like an arrow – "impelled": "To be only an intermediary between the uncultivated ground and the ploughed field, between the data of a problem and the solution, between the blank page and the poem, between the starving beggar and the beggar who has been fed."[71] Consider Steven Burns's discussion of Weil's example of a child attending to a mathematical problem: "In Weil's eyes, the real accomplishment of the child is a negative one; he has lost sight of his own ability and of the challenges and rewards of arithmetic, and has concentrated his attention purely

69 Descartes, *Meditations*, AT VII.57–8. Descartes's philosophical ancestors here are the Stoics: cf. Cicero, *Academica*, 2.37–8, in Long and Sedley, eds., *The Hellenistic philosophers*, §40.O.

70 Weil, "Necessity and Obedience," *Gravity and Grace*, 43–50 / 54–61. For a detailed study of Weil's conception of necessity, see Burns, "Virtue and Necessity."

71 Weil, "Necessity and Obedience," 46 / 57. (N.b. "beggar" translates «*malheureux.*») Cf. Weil, *Notebooks*, I.126.

on the numbers. If the sum is correctly done, then the sum itself is the reason for this."[72] Notice where Burns locates the reason: neither in the child's mind nor in the abstract laws of mathematics, but in the sum itself. According to this ideal, our primary ethical responsibility, odd as it may sound, is *not* to rush around manipulating the world and making it better; our primary responsibility is witnessing – perceiving the world as clearly as we can.

Following Weil, Murdoch also understands that making room for the role of attending in ethics requires a re-imagining of agency. She writes: "Moral change and moral achievement are slow; we are not free in the sense of being able suddenly to alter ourselves since we cannot suddenly alter what we can see and ergo what we desire and are compelled by. In a way, explicit choice seems now less important: less decisive (since much of the 'decision' lies elsewhere) and less obviously something to be 'cultivated'. If I attend properly I will have no choices and this is the ultimate condition to be aimed at."[73] This view is compatibilist – a view that free action follows from the interaction of character and circumstance.[74] Like Weil, Murdoch suggests that the agent's freedom is located less in the critical instants of decision than in the agent's education prior to those decisions. To the extent that she cannot clearly perceive the contexts in which she will be required to act, an agent is less free. Thus the concept of freedom is re-imagined: according to Murdoch, it is not the absence of impediments in the pursuit of our personal desires; it is a scouring away of our intellectual and perceptual prejudices, and the facilitating of clearer perception. Nor, she adds, is freedom undetermined willing. It is, rather, "a function of the progressive attempt to see a particular object clearly"; it is "the experience of accurate vision which, when this becomes appropriate, occasions action."[75]

---

72 Burns, "Justice and Impersonality," §1 (p. 479). Cf. Weil, *Notebooks*, I.29.

73 Murdoch, "The Idea of Perfection," 39–40. In her review of Weil's *Notebooks*, Murdoch quotes Weil with approval: "We should pay attention to such a point that we no longer have the choice" (Weil, *Notebooks*, I.205 / *OC*, VI.2.297, quoted in Murdoch, "Knowing the Void," 613).

74 Cf. Aristotle, *Nicomachean Ethics*, III.4–5; and Hume, "Of Liberty and Necessity," *An Enquiry Concerning Human Understanding*, 53–69.

75 Murdoch, *The Sovereignty of Good*, 23, 67.

§3.6. As we saw in Section 3.3, some commentators have expressed concern that an ethics of emptied attention can degenerate into politically dangerous self-abnegation. Recall this important passage from Weil's "Reflections," in which she describes some characteristics of attending: "our thought should be empty, waiting, not seeking anything, but ready to receive."[76] Commenting on this passage, Nelson writes, "Neither Weil nor Murdoch seem to have devoted much thought to the political consequences for women of a morality that promotes receptivity and submission."[77] Peta Bowden has also criticized the narrowness of Weil's focus and its dangerous political implications. Of Weil and Murdoch, she writes:

... the accounts of attention described thus far are severely flawed by their own inattention to the socio-political impacts on personal capacities for responsive attentiveness in particular situations and the general perspectives persons bring into play to inform and illuminate that attention. ... For example, many writers have pointed out how, under western social norms governing gender, women often define their self-interests and desires almost entirely in terms of the interests of their family members. As a result attention to others is burdened not so much by the impositions of self-centred aims and images but by those of self-denial.[78]

Zwicky makes a more nuanced criticism, suggesting that Weil suffered from insufficient compassion for the self; furthermore, under patriarchy, self-denial is culturally reinforced in women.[79]

Weil and Murdoch both seem to assume that the self necessarily interferes with receptivity. Murdoch writes: "In the moral life the enemy is the fat relentless ego. Moral philosophy is properly ... the discussion of this ego and of the techniques (if any) for its defeat."[80] Her thinking here is consonant with Weil's. For Weil, the existence of the self is a major obstacle to ethical integration; and her technique for the defeat of the egoistic self is called "decreation" (what Murdoch calls

76 Weil, "Reflections on the Right Use of School Studies," 62 / 93.
77 Nelson, "Against Caring," 13.
78 Bowden, "Ethical Attention," 70.
79 See Zwicky, *Contemplation and Resistance*, 8–11.
80 Murdoch, "On 'God' and 'Good,'" 52.

"unselfing").[81] However, Weil and Murdoch's assumption is questionable: namely, the assumption that concern for the self is always a vice, and that attending to others is universally virtuous. If Bowden is right, then there can be pathologies and excesses of the attention, resulting from systemically unjust socio-political conditions. Weil and Murdoch's assumption of default egoism,[82] and their prescription that it should be corrected through dedicated, other-directed attention, seem similarly questionable, especially in cultures where the responsibility of attending has not been fairly distributed. It does not follow that other-directed attention is not ethically appropriate; but, under oppressive conditions, such attention is susceptible to exploitation. And so the universality of the prescription to be attentive might be withdrawn in favour of a context-sensitive study of particular cases.

Sophie Bourgault, on the other hand, defends Weil's work as a resource for feminist theorists of care. And she suggests that the universality of Weil's thinking about needs is especially relevant: "By attaching so much importance to the existence of *universal* and concrete *political* obligations to care for all those who suffer or who have needs in a community, Weil offered a theory that is, in my view, feminist."[83] By locating needs, rather than rights, at the foundation of her politics, Weil resists the schism between an ethics of justice and an ethics of care. In her view, caring for the vital needs of others does not fall into a supererogatory domain of charity or benevolence; it is a requirement of justice. She believes that this requirement was widely recognized in antiquity: "The Gospel makes no distinction between the love of our neighbor and justice. In the eyes of the Greeks also, a respect for Zeus the suppliant was the first duty of justice. We have invented the distinction between justice and charity. It is easy to understand why. Our notion of justice dispenses him who possesses from the obligation of giving."[84] As Bourgault observes, Weil in her late work asks us "to discard for good the untenable (and modern) distinction between love and justice. Weil

---

81 See, for example, the sections on "The Self," "Decreation," and "Self-Effacement" in *Gravity and Grace*, 26–42.

82 For an incisive critique of default egoism, see Campbell, "Empathy and Egoism."

83 Bourgault, "Beyond the Saint and the Red Virgin," 20.

84 Weil, "Forms of the Implicit Love of God," *Waiting for God*, 85 / 125. Cf. Singer, "Famine, Affluence, and Morality," 235.

was convinced that if we could somehow overcome that problematic split, the receiving" – and giving – "of assistance and care from the state or from fellow human beings would no longer be regarded as humiliating or discretionary – it would, rather, become obligatory."[85] By dissolving the assumed dichotomy between justice and care, this tack affords an indirect response to Nelson's and Bowden's objections. Nelson's argument is not necessarily opposed to this tack, since she claims that an ethics of attention can avoid the shortcomings of an ethics of justice or care. There is another tack, which attempts to redistribute the responsibility for attending.

Supposing that Weilian attention might be generally characterized as *patient receptivity* or *responsivity*, is it possible to distinguish this receptivity from politically questionable forms of *subordination?* Laurence Thomas's account of "moral deference" might be helpful for thinking about this question. "Moral deference," he writes, "is the act of listening involved in bearing witness to another's moral pain, but without bearing witness to it."[86] Such listening is needed to compensate for epistemic deficits and distortions that result from socialization in a systemically unjust culture. To emphasize the structural nature of oppression, Thomas writes of the "emotional category configuration" of those who have been "upwardly" or "downwardly socially constituted." In his view, this configuration serves as a kind of lens for experience. As a result of a process of social constitution, members of privileged groups and those of oppressed groups have different emotional configurations, and thus differently refracted experiences. For this reason, a member of a privileged group might lack direct access to the experience of a member of an oppressed group, especially when it is experience of what Thomas calls "hostile misfortune" – misfortune that is specific to an oppressed group.

Nor is ratiocination sufficient to cross the epistemic gap. As Thomas writes, "If one encountered a Holocaust survivor, it would be moral hubris of the worst sort — unless one is also such a survivor — to assume that by way of rational imaginative role-taking ... one could even begin to grasp the depth of that person's experiences."[87] Similarly, he claims, it would be hubris for a heterosexual man who has not been raped to assume that he can imagine (or rationally reconstruct?) the experience

85 Bourgault, "Beyond the Saint and the Red Virgin," 13.
86 Thomas, "Moral Deference," 377.
87 Ibid., 360.

of a woman survivor of rape.[88] (It is not entirely clear whether Thomas is referring to the limits of reason or of the imagination.)

But Thomas is not a skeptic about other minds; on the contrary, he has faith in the possibility of trans-category communication. It is possible, he says, for a privileged person *to learn about* the experiences of an oppressed person, if the privileged person is willing to listen and the oppressed person is willing to communicate. The listener must have the humility to recognize his own epistemic limits. Furthermore, members of privileged groups owe deference to members of oppressed groups: "Moral deference is owed to persons of good will when they speak in an informed way regarding experiences specific to their diminished social category from the standpoint of an emotional category configuration to which others do not have access."[89] If we think of attention moving in this direction, then it might circumvent some of the criticisms made by Nelson and Bowden. In the dynamic described by Thomas, the oppressed woman is not obliged to deny herself in order to defer to the privileged man.

Weil would agree with Thomas that deference is owed to those who endure oppression (in her terms, attention is owed to those who endure affliction). Bourgault argues that Weilian attending may be thought of as a political act. Like Thomas, she suggests that attentive listening may be especially important in cases that resist empathy: "we ought not to insist on strong empathy *as a necessary requirement to listening.* ... For one thing, most socio-political situations entail listening to others with whom we have fairly little in common—and at times, with people we do not like very much. And it is precisely in these tough cases that listening is of utmost importance."[90] Even without answering the question of whether empathy is possible or appropriate, we can recognize that listening is indispensable for social justice. (And yet, as Karen Houle suggests, one unsettling possibility is that one may offer to listen, and the other may refuse to communicate; and the refusal may be justified.)[91]

---

88 Ibid., 361.

89 Ibid., 373–4. Thomas acknowledges that moral deference is not limited to "persons of good will" and that anger, pain, and anguish are appropriate responses to injustice.

90 Bourgault, "Attentive Listening and Care," 327.

91 See Houle, "Making Strange," 181–3.

§3.7. Despite legitimate misgivings on the part of Nelson and Bowden about the dangers of self-abnegation, there remains something compelling about Murdoch's example of aesthetic attending:

I am looking out of my window in an anxious and resentful state of mind, oblivious to my surroundings, brooding perhaps on some damage done to my prestige. Then suddenly I observe a hovering kestrel. In a moment every-thing is altered. The brooding self with its hurt vanity has disappeared. There is nothing now but kestrel.[92]

The illustrated change in perception is arguably an improvement; the hovering kestrel is an epiphany of beauty that calls the perceiver out of her "brooding self." Notice some of the features of this epiphany: it does not result from a conscious decision; the kestrel presents itself and seizes the attention of the perceiver. The epiphany also displaces or decentres the self. As Weil writes, "Perfect joy excludes even the very feeling of joy, for in the soul filled by the object no corner is left for saying 'I'."[93] While anxiety and resentment and hurt vanity were momen-tarily dominant, they were also transient and insubstantial, like clouds crossing the sky of the psyche. The epiphany enables Murdoch to shift her perspective: "And when I return to thinking of the other matter" – the hurt vanity and so on – "it seems less important." It seems so because it is.

Furthermore, there is a difference between *self-abnegation* (which can indeed be a vehicle for oppressive violence) and something like *self-moderation* or *self-regulation*. Self-control is similar to abnegation in its attitude to the self. Both abnegation and wilful control assume that the self is a threat and must be either eliminated or muzzled. Moderation, on the other hand, assumes that the self, as self, is a neutral medium of relation that can be in or out of tune. The confusion between control and moderation is exemplified in English translations of the Greek virtue σωφροσύνη (*sōphrosynē*),[94] which is rendered as "moderation,"

92 Murdoch, "The Sovereignty of Good Over Other Concepts," 84.
93 Weil, "The Self," *Gravity and Grace*, 31 / 41.
94 Henceforth transliterated and anglicized as "sophrosyne."

"temperance," and "self-control."[95] At its extreme, the virtue begins to look like steely vigilance, a muscular policing of monstrous impulses. But this picture is a misinterpretation of the virtue: it confuses ἐγκράτεια (*enkrateia*),[96] which is not a virtue, with sophrosyne, which is. (In later sections, we shall elaborate on this distinction.) A better translation than "self-control," and one that recognizes the epistemic dimension of the virtue and its relation to phronesis, is "sound-mindedness." Again, the Aristotelian idea of the mean is helpful. The self and its energies are not essentially vicious or essentially in need of suppression. It is more appropriate to see the self as a phenomenon susceptible to deficiencies, excesses, and a eudaemonic mean. An agent with sophrosyne is someone who has tempered her self and its energies, and is free to experience them in beneficial ways.[97]

Let us consider the suggestion that the virtue of sophrosyne is needed for the exercise of attention, and that one can tell a virtue-ethical developmental story about its cultivation. Stuart Shanker's research into the psychology of self-regulation is relevant here. He defines self-regulation "as the ability to stay calmly focused and alert, which often involves — but cannot be reduced to — self-control."[98] He traces the conflation of self-regulation and self-control to Plato's reading of Homer.[99] It is true that Plato uses violent imagery to portray the controlling of the so-called bad horse (appetite) by the charioteer (the philosophical component of the soul): the charioteer "violently yanks the bit back out of the teeth of the insolent horse, only harder this time, so that he

---

95 In retranslating passages from Euripides's *Bakkhai*, students in Tim Casey's seminar at Bard College in the summer of 2015 suggested that an agent with sophrosyne may be described as "chill," or as exhibiting the virtue of "chillness." In my view, their suggestion, while amusing, is not off-target; indeed, it identifies an aspect of the virtue that is missed by the standard English translations.

96 Henceforth transliterated and anglicized as "enkrateia."

97 Cf. Zwicky, "Alcibiades' Love," 88–90 / *AL*, 287–9. For an articulation of the distinction between sophrosyne and enkrateia, cf. Kosman, "Self-Knowledge and Self-Control in the *Charmides*," §4.

98 Shanker, "Self-Regulation," 4.

99 See Shanker, "Emotion Regulation through the Ages," §§2–4. Shanker is ambivalent about whether Platonic emotions should be classed as "cognitive" or "non-cognitive" phenomena (ibid., 115) – for Plato, as for Aristotle, emotions must be capable of communicating with reason – but he stresses that reason is cast in the role of controller.

bloodies its foul-speaking tongue and jaws, sets its legs and haunches firmly on the ground, and 'gives it over to pain.'"[100] Weil herself resorts to similar imagery when she discusses a circumscribed role for the will, which may be used for "training the animal within us": "Of course if this violence we do ourselves is really to be of use in our training it must only be a means. When a man trains a dog to perform tricks he does not beat it for the sake of beating it, but in order to train it, and with this in view he only hits it when it fails to carry out a trick."[101]

Contra Plato and Weil, Shanker suggests that violent training, or wilful control, is in fact ineffective: "we know from abundant data that the overuse of punitive measures to elicit compliance is a predictor of externalizing problems."[102] Furthermore, Plato's and Weil's interest in wilful control is inconsistent with wiser and more prominent emphases elsewhere in their thinking. When Plato defines the virtue of sophrosyne in the *Republic*, he stresses that it is an *agreement* – "a kind of consonance and harmony" – among the components of the soul.[103] A non-consensual subordination of the appetitive to the philosophical component (as in the case of the abused horse) would *not* exemplify the virtue. He also declares that "nothing taught by force stays in the soul," and recommends that "play" be used to teach the future rulers of the *kallipolis*.[104] And Weil repeatedly insists that the interference of the will is counterproductive to the discipline and the exercise of the attention.

The ideal of self-regulation, as Shanker makes clear, is not abnegation or control, but balance. And this balance will be achieved, not through the repression of emotions, but through the collaborative expression

---

100 Plato, *Phaidros*, 254e.

101 Weil, "Training," *Gravity and Grace*, 124–5 / 142–3.

102 Shanker, "Self-Regulation," 6.

103 Plato, *Republic*, IV.430e, 431e–432a. It is common for scholars to assign sophrosyne specifically to the working class and the appetitive part of the soul (to complete the pattern begun by wisdom and courage). But that is not what Plato's text says: "*unlike* courage and wisdom, each of which resides in one part ... moderation spreads *throughout the whole*" (emphasis added). As North insightfully observes, sophrosyne, like justice, is a holistic virtue (rather than one that is class- or part-specific); see her *Sophrosyne*, 172–3, and 199, n. 6. Kosman agrees ("The Faces of Justice," 157, 161).

104 Plato, *Republic*, VII.536e.

of them.[105] Self-regulation, he argues, is learned through *co*-regulation: that is, it is learned both by imitating self-regulators and by collaborating with them in the process of understanding one's own responses to environmental stimuli. Weil's major insights are conceptually independent of the rhetoric of self-abnegation into which she occasionally drifts. To summarize some of these insights: disciplined attending is enough for appropriate response in particular contexts, from school studies to the appreciation of art to more obviously ethical situations; attention is educated or disciplined or regulated through its repeated exercise in these contexts; and the focus will communicate with what is attending; in short, attending is interactive. Although it is not often discussed in anglophone moral philosophy, this kind of attention is needed for any liveable ethics.

---

105 Shanker, "Self-Regulation," 7. On collaborative expression, see Zwicky, *Lyric Philosophy*, L250; and Campbell, "Expression and the Individuation of Feeling," *Interpreting the Personal*, 47–67.

4

Attending

Each single grain of this rock, each mineral splinter of this mountain filled with night, in itself forms a world.

– Albert Camus[1]

§4.1. WE HAVE CONSIDERED AN OVERVIEW of the concept of attention as that concept is defined by Simone Weil and then adopted by Iris Murdoch. In their work, attention is patient receptivity determined by its focus. Due to its emptiness and pliancy, this attention seems, at first glance, similar to Aristotle's passive intellect. But we found that valorizing passivity can be politically dangerous, and also that attending does not fit into the dichotomy of passivity and activity. A more promising comparison, suggested by Nussbaum, is that between attention and the virtue of phronesis, or practical wisdom. In Aristotle's ethics, phronesis is characterized by the same kind of receptivity that characterizes Weilian attending. And since phronesis responds to particulars, it is difficult to construct a general theory that does justice to it (as Aristotle repeatedly emphasizes).[2] As we shall see in this section, the Weilian torch is passed from Murdoch to John McDowell: what Weil and Murdoch call *attention* is what McDowell calls *sensitivity*; and he explicitly connects sensitivity with *phronesis*. Aristotle's definition of phronesis and his insight that it is *structurally* different from enkrateia and akrasia are his refinements to the Platonic thesis that virtue is knowledge. Crucially, phronesis is an amphibious virtue; like attention, it cannot be reduced to a mental act or a bodily motion; it is neither exclusively "cognitive" nor exclusively "non-cognitive." Indeed, seen from a characterological angle, it may be understood as sophrosyne, the virtue concerned with embodied animal

---

1 Camus, *Le mythe de Sisyphe*, 168.
2 Cf. Aristotle, *Nicomachean Ethics*, I.3.1094b10–25, II.2.1103b25–1104a10.

pleasures and pains, because clear phronetic perception is made possible by passionate equanimity.

In this section, we reflect on the role of attending in ethical psychology. According to Weil, attending is enough for action (including overtly ethical action). If we attend and perceive clearly and accurately, then we will be relieved of the agony of choosing; the appropriate response will follow autonomically. Recall her suggestion quoted in Section 2.1: "Knowing that this man, who is hungry and thirsty, truly exists as much as I do—that's enough, the rest follows of itself."[3] By implication, neither a general moral theory nor an altruistic inclination is necessary. Knowing is enough. Weil agrees with Plato: virtue is knowledge. The reference to knowledge might seem to make her suggestion "cognitivist" but, as we shall see, her conception of knowing will not conform to the cognitivist model. In the case before us, what one knows is not the principle that one should respect other persons as ends; nor is it the principle that one should maximize expected aggregate utility. What one knows is that *this* human being needs food and water.

Purely Platonic epistemology and metaphysics, with their commitment to the ultimate reality of the abstract forms, cannot do justice to such knowledge. Insofar as Weilian attention is knowledge of a particular, it involves a revision of Platonism. Platonic theatre, however, with its vividly realized particular characters, does offer a way forward. While Aristotle is no playwright, he saves the insight of Platonic theatre in his ethics: both the agent and the focus of phronesis – the knower and what she knows – are particulars, each one unique in the universe. If we assumed, with much analytic epistemology, that knowledge is some kind of justified true belief, then we might wonder how belief, however true and justified, could move us. But Weil's knowing of the need of *this* human being is not reducible to the formula "S knows that p" (where "S" is a subject and "p" is a proposition).[4] For Weil, believing is not merely assenting to a proposition. It is responding to the call of reality. And, as we shall see in Section 8, reality is vibrantly alive; the foci of attention are not inert objects of knowledge but full participants in what Weil calls "the dance of perception."

3 Weil, "Attention and Will," 119 / 137; translation altered.
4 Cf. Code's critique of this narrow and formulaic approach to epistemology in her "Taking Subjectivity into Account."

But how does one move from knowing to acting? "There are cases where a thing is necessary," writes Weil, "from the mere fact that it is possible."[5] Elaborating on what she means by "necessary," she writes: "Seeing the relations among things, and oneself, including the ends that one carries within, as one of the terms. Action follows naturally." Furthermore, if we "fix attention on the relations among things, a necessity appears that we cannot *not* obey."[6] She gives the following example of this triangulated relationship: here is a person dying of thirst, and there is a glass of water; the third point of the triangle is our perspective on the dying person and the water. What appears in that perspective is the relationship between the need of the dying person and the water. Weil analogizes that case to the case in which we have a need of our own: "Thus to eat when we are hungry, to give a wounded man, dying of thirst, something to drink when there is water quite near." Simply having a need is enough to move us to relieve it. Weil is suggesting that this natural connection between having and relieving a need also obtains between perceiving someone else's need and relieving it. Furthermore, she suggests that this connection is pan-psychologically compelling: "Neither a ruffian nor a saint would refrain" from giving water to the dying man.[7]

— "There are so many flaws with the example that I don't know where to start," an interlocutor might at this point object. "First, you've been stressing the importance of specificity, but the situation is terrifically under-described. I definitely don't have enough information to know how to act, even granting, for the sake of argument, that barefaced facts alone could move me. (And they can't.) A novelist might be able to supply enough sordid details to make the situation persuasive; but details could also backfire, defeating whatever alleged reason I had for acting. Suppose I learn that the water was gathered from the well by Rhea, a young woman with opalescent eyes and no living relatives, recovering from acute cholera in the next bed? Or suppose I learn that the man, a hijacker by the name of Wallach, has just been admitted to the field hospital after having wandered for days in a state of severe dehydration, and his rehydration must be administered gingerly by professionals? I could go on. Furthermore, Weil's final remark is so wilfully naive that

---

5   Weil, "Necessity and Obedience," 44 / 55.
6   Ibid., 48 / 60; translation altered. Cf. Weil, *Notebooks*, I.156 / *OC*, VI.2.201.
7   Weil, "Necessity and Obedience," 44 / 55.

it's almost laughable. The counter-examples are legion: we can easily imagine a ruffian, or an amoralist, or a run-of-the-mill depressive, who sees whatever it is that Weil sees but refrains from doing what she prescribes. And what about the soldiers who mocked Christ on the cross, who saw his thirsting and suffering body and offered him vinegar?[8] Like Weil, they perceived his need, but instead of relieving that need, they used it to torment him. The simplest explanation for such cases of weakness of will and viciousness," our interlocutor might conclude, "is that the agents don't share her do-good desires. Which just goes to show that Weil's Neoplatonic internalist cognitivism – the position that a moral judgement is necessarily motivating, and that a moral judgement just is a sort of belief – is wrong, and that the Humean theory is right: every complete motivating state has got to be a belief-desire combo."

— But are we obliged to universalize whatever explanatory apparatus is applicable in these cases? Let's say, for the sake of argument, that the behaviour of the amoralist (or the akratic or vicious agent) is best explained by analysing his motivation into two distinct mental states, a belief and a desire (or the absence of a desire). Then let us *look and see* whether or not this analytical picture is universally applicable; and let us investigate by studying particular examples. In what follows, we shall do four things: in Sections 4.2, 4.3, 4.5, and 4.6, we set Weil's example beside some other examples (of virtue, continence, reading, and aesthetic appreciation). In Sections 4.2 and 4.3, we discuss McDowell's account of virtue, which accommodates these examples; it is an account that flowers out of the work of Murdoch and Weil, with its roots in the ethical psychology of Aristotle and Plato. The χριστός (*khristos*) himself offers a Platonic explanation for the behaviour of those who crucify and torment him: "they know not what they do."[9] If virtue is knowledge, as Plato argues, then a deficiency in virtue may be explained by a deficiency in knowledge. In Section 4.4, we see why one interpretation of McDowell's account, the "cognitivist" interpretation, is ultimately unsatisfactory. It is unsatisfactory because it is constructed by *contrast* with the Humean theory – whereas we are seeking an account that can dissolve the dualism assumed both by this interpretation and by the Humean

---

8 Luke 23:36. There is scholarly debate about whether the vinegar is vinegar, and whether the offering is cruel or compassionate. But the objection above assumes the simplest interpretation of the English translation.

9 Luke 23:34.

theory. Finally, in Section 4.7, we consider one last example that cannot
be explained by the Humean theory without distortion. This example
is listening to a testimony concerning irreversible harm. Listening is an
ordinary but ethically significant phenomenon, and to save it, we require
the Platonic psychology.

§4.2. Consider the following case: Lora K. Shrake, a college student,
was driving along a country road in Illinois when she saw a woman in
a fenced pasture being mauled and gored by a huge bull. Shrake
quickly parked, climbed through the electrified fence, and struck the
bull repeatedly with a two-foot length of rubber tubing, enabling the
injured woman to crawl to safety.[10] For the purposes of our investigation, what interests us is Shrake's own account of her action:

INTERVIEWER: When you were there at that fence, and you had the choice
to either stay put or to go through it, what was going through your mind?
Was there a calculation there?
SHRAKE: No, I can't really say that. I mean ...
INTERVIEWER: Weighing your options or anything like that?
SHRAKE: I did not. No. It was just, here's the problem, here's what I need to
do, and something needed to happen.[11]

The case of Shrake is sensational and individualistic: we see a single
agent acting in a super-heroic way. As a picture of virtue, however, it
could be misleading, especially if we believe that it is typical and use
it as a yardstick. Most virtue will be much less visible than this instance. And in some cases, the agent will act as an expression of her
community rather than as an autonomous moral star. Furthermore,
as we shall see, continence will be far more prevalent than virtue.
Most of us would be bystanders who hesitated before offering help.
The reason we are starting with the case of Shrake is that it is a limiting case. As such, it allows us to isolate and reflect on three features
that are characteristic of virtue: (1) The protagonist perceives an

---

10 Citation for Lora K. Shrake, *Carnegie Hero Fund Commission*, mychfc.org/
Awardee.aspx?hero=69979. For drawing my attention to this example, thanks to
Carolyn Richardson.

11 Shrake interviewed in "The Good Show," hosted by Jad Abumrad and Robert
Krulwich, *Radiolab*, WNYC, New York Public Radio, 15 December 2010.

aspect of the situation as *salient*: "She was clearly struggling";[12] (2) Other aspects of the situation, which might otherwise be countervailing reasons, are *silent*: "I didn't think of what [the bull] could have done to me;"[13] (3) Perception of the salient aspect *necessitates* action: "here's what I need to do."

Let us elaborate on the third feature, the idea that perception of a salient aspect can necessitate action. Compare Weil's account: "The words of the Breton ship's apprentice to the journalist who asked him how he had been able to act as he did: 'Had to.'"[14] Or take the case of Suzie Valadez, "a single mother of four young children with no money at all, not even a car, a tenth-grade education, only slight knowledge of Spanish, and almost no work experience,"[15] who was moved by a vision to minister to the basic spiritual and bodily needs of the poor of Juarez, Mexico; of her calling, she says: "I didn't know how I was doing it or why, but I know the Holy Spirit was leading me, saying, 'You *have* to help them, you *have* to help them.'"[16] Similar examples could be multiplied indefinitely.

On the basis of their empirical research on moral exemplars, Anne Colby and William Damon argue that this sense of necessitation is a defining feature of the psychology of exemplars:

There is a sense of great certainty, and a conspicuous absence of doubt, in their moral conduct. We saw this in Susie Valadez's conviction that she "had to help the poor," and we will see it again in others—for example, Virginia Durr, who felt that "there were no choices to make" when she confronted the issues of racial segregation in Alabama. ...

Their feelings of moral necessity had given them their great sense of certainty, and this in turn had relieved them of their fears and doubts. Courage became irrelevant, an unexercised affective appendage.[17]

---

12 Ibid.

13 Shrake, quoted in Kevin O'Neal, "Hometown hero helped battle a bull to save woman's life," *The Indianapolis Star* (4 May 1996), C2.

14 Weil, "Necessity and Obedience," 49 / 60; translation altered. Cf. Weil, *Notebooks*, I.155 / *OC*, VI.2.201. In her notes from a course that she taught at Auxerre (1932–33), Weil writes, "Story of the little ship's apprentice from Concarneau [in Brittany] who held the tiller forty-eight hours" (*OC*, I.378).

15 Colby and Damon, *Some Do Care*, 43.

16 Valadez, quoted in Colby and Damon, ibid., 46.

17 Colby and Damon, ibid., 70–1.

The last statement is motivated in part by the exemplars' disavowal that they had acted courageously. But there is a better explanation of this disavowal. Recall Julia Annas's claim that the phenomenology of virtuous activity is characterized by effortlessness and unselfconsciousness. She also argues that the thinking of a virtuous person does not include thoughts about virtue: they are "self-effacing in the virtuous person, as thoughts about skill are in the skilled person."[18] The deliberations of the apprentice in virtue might include thoughts such as "What would a brave person do here?" or "What would be the courageous thing to do in this context?" By contrast, it is a mark of expertise in virtue that the expert's thinking does not include such thoughts: "People who perform brave actions often say afterwards that they simply registered that the person needed to be rescued, so they rescued them; even when prodded to come up further with reasons why they did the brave thing, they often do not mention virtue, or bravery."[19]

We also have McDowell's claim that the virtuous person need not possess an articulate concept of the virtue according to which he acts; and if he does possess such a concept, it need not enter his reason for acting virtuously: "It is enough if he thinks of what he does, when—as we put it—he shows himself to be kind [that is, virtuous], under some such description as 'the thing to do.'"[20] Rather than conclude, with Colby and Damon, that courage is irrelevant, we may say that the expert is freed from self-regarding thoughts about her own virtue, and this freedom is itself a function of her expertise. Paradoxically, the expert is both free and determined. "The belief in moral certainty," write Colby and Damon, "precluded a sense of behavorial choice (much as would a belief in logical necessity preclude a sense of intellectual choice)."[21]

In his essay "Virtue and Reason," McDowell offers an account of virtue that can accommodate the examples above. This account is the Platonic ethical psychology, which is preserved and recontextualized as one branch in the Aristotelian ethical psychology.[22] While McDowell does

---

18 Annas, "The phenomenology of virtue," 24.
19 Ibid., 22.
20 McDowell, "Virtue and Reason," §2 (p. 332).
21 Colby and Damon, *Some Do Care*, 79.
22 One could equally say that the Aristotelian ethical psychology is the Platonic ethical psychology revised.

not mention Weil, he does acknowledge his debt to Murdoch,[23] and the genealogy of his account is traceable through Murdoch to Weil.[24] The grounding of McDowell's virtue ethics in Murdoch's has been documented by Justin Broackes, and Sabina Lovibond has written an unsympathetic chapter on Murdoch's debt to Weil;[25] it remains for us only to notice that what McDowell borrows from Murdoch is what she borrows from Weil.

The benefits of recognizing this family tree are significant. First, since McDowell's ethical psychology is also Aristotelian, the genealogy serves to justify a rapprochement between Weil and Aristotle (despite Weil's antipathy to Aristotle). Second, it has implications for moral particularism (a theory that claims that general principles are not necessary for moral judgement). Moral particularism, a major theory in analytic anglophone moral philosophy, owes its central characteristics to a thinker from outside that discipline. However, the theoretical articulation of particularism is alien to the spirit of Weil's attending to particulars, and that means that we can appeal to her work for resources that are not on McDowell's radar. In this respect, Weil's different philosophical orientation is an advantage; by adopting that orientation, we can circumvent some of the objections attracted by McDowell's account and recover the pre-theoretical urgency of Weilian attending.

McDowell suggests that ἀρετή (*aretē*) is a *sensitivity*, an aptitude for perceiving the needs displayed by a particular situation; virtue, in general, he says, is "an ability to recognize requirements which situations impose on one's behaviour."[26] And what, exactly, is a requirement? It is not a thing like an individual participant in the situation; if we enumerate the participants, the requirement is not among them. A requirement must, rather, be a structural aspect of the situation; "this person needs that water," for instance, where the thirsting person stands in relation both to the water and to the agent witnessing the situation. It is the polydimensional set of relations that displays the situation's

---

23 See McDowell, "Virtue and Reason," 350, nn. 35–7.

24 See Murdoch, *The Sovereignty of Good*, 34, 40, 50, 104.

25 See Broackes, "Introduction," *Iris Murdoch, Philosopher*, 8–18; and Lovibond, "The Simone Weil factor," *Iris Murdoch, Gender and Philosophy*, 28–46.

26 McDowell, "Virtue and Reason," §2 (p. 333).

requirement. A requirement is a *gestalt*: a coherent whole that is different from a sum of parts.[27]

McDowell further argues for the Platonic claim that this sensitivity (that is, virtue) is knowledge. For the purposes of his case, McDowell focuses on the particular virtue of kindness. "A kind person," he writes, "can be relied on to behave kindly when that is what the situation requires. Moreover ... that the situation requires a certain sort of behaviour is (one way of formulating) his reason for behaving in that way, on each of the relevant occasions." The requirement may be cited as a reason for the agent's action only if she perceives it; McDowell thus suggests that the perception of the requirement is a necessary condition for the behaviour to qualify as a kind (that is, virtuous) action. He further suggests that the perception is a sufficient condition: "the requirement imposed by the situation, and detected by the agent's sensitivity to such requirements, must exhaust his reason for acting as he does."[28]

The reasons for virtuous action, according to McDowell, are what may be called *silencing* reasons; they focus the agent's attention such that the pull of what would otherwise be competing reasons is not felt. "The view of a situation which he arrives at by exercising his sensitivity is one in which some aspect of the situation is seen as constituting a reason for acting in some way; this reason is apprehended, not as outweighing or overriding any reasons for acting in other ways which would otherwise be constituted by other aspects of the situation ... but as silencing them."[29] Here, the proper state to contrast with virtue is enkrateia, or mere continence: an enkratic or continent person, however commendable, does not perceive an aspect of a situation as imposing a singular requirement, but as overpowering the competing demands of other aspects.[30] Recall the contrast that we drew in Section 3.7 between (1) sophrosyne, understood as the virtue of sound-mindedness,

27 Cf. Zwicky, "The Experience of Meaning," 88.
28 McDowell, "Virtue and Reason," §2 (p. 331–2).
29 Ibid., §3 (p. 335).
30 Cf. Von der Ruhr's contrast between Luke's Samaritan, who helps without hesitating, and another Samaritan, who also decides to help but only after weighing the inconvenience. Of this enkratic Samaritan, Von der Ruhr writes that he "would still have done the right thing, but he clearly wouldn't have served Luke's purpose, which was to show that a genuine love of the neighbour silences such deliberations" (*Simone Weil: An Apprenticeship in Attention*, 45).

and (2) less-than-fully-virtuous, effortful self-control. The same contrast shows up here between aretaic sensitivity and enkrateia.[31]

§4.3. The contrast between *aretē* and enkrateia may be illustrated by the disagreement between Antigone and Ismene in Sophokles's *Antigone*. The tragedy opens with a conversation between the two sisters. Yesterday their brothers Polyneikes and Eteokles killed each other, Polyneikes attacking Thebes and Eteokles defending it. Their uncle Kreon, now ruler of Thebes, has buried Eteokles but has forbidden the burial of Polyneikes, on pain of death by stoning. Should Polyneikes be buried? There are reasons on both sides: according to Antigone, it would be noble to bury Polyneikes, and doing so would "be good to those / Who are below."[32] (Later in the play, she will explicitly articulate her reverence for the gods' unwritten laws, even in defiance of the human-made laws of the polis.)[33] According to Ismene, the decree of Kreon and the penalty for disobedience are too heavy. Like Antigone, she recognizes "those beneath the earth," but for her, human force has more authority than divine law.[34] We could say that her fear outweighs her sense of obligation to her dead brother.

Here is the key difference in psychological structure between the two sisters: while Ismene experiences a conflict, Antigone does not. As Weil explains: "Between two loyalties, the loyalty to her vanquished brother and the loyalty to her victorious country, she does not hesitate an instant."[35] She does not recognize the legitimacy of Kreon's decree – "He has no right to keep me from my own"[36] – nor is she dissuaded by the threat of death. After Antigone has been caught burying Polyneikes, Ismene manages to overcome her fear and offers to share her sister's suffering;[37] ultimately, we could say, she tries to do the right thing. We may say that Antigone's act is aretaic, while Ismene vacillates between akrasia and enkrateia. McDowell could account for the contrast

---

31 Annas observes the same contrast ("The phenomenology of virtue," 27).

32 Sophokles, *Antigone*, ll. 74–5.

33 Ibid., ll. 456–60.

34 Ibid., ll. 65–6.

35 Weil, "Antigone," *Intimations of Christianity*, 20 / *OC*, II.2.334. There are numerous interpretations of the ethical conflict in *Antigone*. For the sake of simplicity, this discussion assumes Weil's reading.

36 Sophokles, *Antigone*, l. 48. Cf. ibid., ll. 450–7.

37 Ibid., ll. 536ff.

in the following way: for Antigone, the fact that her brother is left unburied is enough to move her; it is a requirement, or a silencing reason, beside which Kreon's decree and the threat of death are irrelevant. Ismene, on the other hand, is torn between fidelity to her family and obligation to the polis, between love and fear; she experiences a conflict of reasons.

McDowell's contrast between the structures of virtue (*aretē*) and continence (enkrateia) is designed to circumvent an objection. According to the objection, sensitivity to a situational requirement cannot be sufficient for virtue, since "a person's perception of a situation may precisely match what a virtuous person's perception of it would be, although he does not act as the virtuous person would."[38] Indeed, as we have acknowledged, it seems that there are plenty of counter-examples of persons who allegedly understand what they ought to do, but who are unmoved, or paralysed, or who act contrary to the allegedly perceived requirement. And, as McDowell admits, such counter-examples would seem to demand an extra, motivational component in the explanation of the virtuous person's action. McDowell's response to this objection is that the virtuous person's perception is *not* precisely matched by that of the continent (or incontinent) person: to exercise the sensitivity which is virtue, the agent must perceive an aspect of a situation as a *requirement*.

Ismene perceives the aspect that moves Antigone, but not in exactly the same way. Her appreciation of what she perceives is "clouded, or unfocused, by the impact of a desire to do otherwise."[39] We might say that she perceives that she has an obligation to bury her brother; but in addition, she feels afraid for her life, and her fear conditions and mitigates her sense of obligation. She both has and does not have knowledge of what she should do, like someone "asleep, mad, or drunk."[40] The virtuous agent perceives clearly what the continent agent perceives unclearly; the virtuous agent perceives a silencing reason, while the continent agent perceives that reason in conflict with other apparent reasons. On the other hand, if we find ourselves facing a fraught and complicated situation in which there is a real conflict among equally serious reasons, then enkratic perception of the conflict might be the

38 McDowell, "Virtue and Reason," §3 (p. 333).
39 Ibid., §3 (p. 334).
40 Aristotle, *Nicomachean Ethics*, VII.3.1147a13–14.

best that we can manage.[41] The cost of admitting this possibility is that a large portion of our right actions will turn out to be merely enkratic, not aretaic; they will be performed under conditions where clear perception is not realizable and where spontaneous response would be reckless. True virtue will turn out to be very rare.

Before turning to a number of other objections, let us consider a couple of portraits of enkratic and akratic characters. Madame de Lafayette's *La Princesse de Clèves* is the narrative of an enkratic hero and her exacting askesis. Mlle de Chartres marries the decent, courageous, and generous Prince de Clèves, only to fall in love with the rakish Duc de Nemours, "nature's masterpiece."[42] While ambition and love affairs are "the life-blood of the court,"[43] the Princesse de Clèves has been painstakingly trained in "virtue" by her mother. Mme de Chartres spoke to her daughter of "men's insincerity, of their deceptions and infidelity, of the disastrous effect of love affairs on conjugal life ... she also taught her how difficult it is to preserve virtue except by an extreme mistrust of one's own powers."[44] She indoctrinates her daughter into a sociology and a morality of suspicion and constraint. (This suspicion is well justified by the patriarchal social context.) On her deathbed, and recognizing her daughter's inclination for M. de Nemours, Mme de Chartres warns: "you are on the edge of a precipice. You will have to make great efforts and do yourself great violence to hold yourself back."[45] (Notice that this instruction, like Mme de Chartres's earlier training of her daughter, shares the assumption of Platonic and Aristotelian psychology that the soul is complex: that its multiple parts are the precondition of the possibility of inner conflict and harmony.)

The prohibition of the parent is introjected and becomes the moral law, and the rest of the novel details Mme de Clèves's psychological agony as she struggles to enforce that law. The spectacle consists in the conflict between Mme de Clèves's will and her passion, and indeed she

41 Cf. McDowell, "Virtue and Reason," 348, n. 5; and Stohr, "Moral Cacophony." Stohr's elevation of enkratic agony to the status of virtue is not dissimilar to Weiss's contention that the best we can achieve is not knowledge but merely true belief; for a discussion of why such views are mistaken, see this book, §7.

42 Lafayette, *The Princesse de Clèves*, 5.

43 Ibid., 14. In this respect, the society of the novel is similar to that of Beaumarchais's *Le Mariage de Figaro* or Renoir's *La Règle du jeu*.

44 Lafayette, *The Princesse de Clèves*, 10.

45 Ibid., 39–40.

magnificently exemplifies Kant's test case for moral agency: someone whose will cleaves to duty against inclination.[46] By resorting to the great effort and violence prescribed by her mother, she succeeds in remaining faithful – in deed, if not in feeling – to her husband. As she declares, "The most austere virtue could not have dictated conduct more correct than mine."[47] But he knows that she loves another and he dies of a broken heart.

Finally free, she is propositioned by M. de Nemours: "your virtue is no longer opposed to your feelings and it is my hope that you will follow those feelings in spite of yourself." When she remains steadfast in her refusal, he complains: "you alone have made for yourself a law that virtue and reason could never impose."[48] The muscularity of her askesis and her adherence to her self-legislated law are impressive. In the dénouement of the novel, she retreats to an estate, where she becomes ill, but she uses her illness to meditate on death and to detach herself from the world. "None the less, when she recovered a little, she found that M. de Nemours had not been erased from her heart; she summoned to her aid, in order to defend herself against him, all the reasons she had marshalled for never marrying him." These reasons include her widow's duty to her dead husband's memory and her peace of mind (the inevitable cooling of Nemours's passion and the ills of jealousy, she reasons, would make her miserable). "A great combat took place within her. At last she overcame the remains of a passion already weakened by the sentiments her illness had inspired."[49] She retires for part of each year to a house of religion and lives a short and saintly life.

We may refrain from approving or disapproving of the Princesse's end. Instead, let us focus on the psychological dynamic. It is difficult not to admire the Princesse's severity. Her psyche is the site of ferocious combat between passion and a powerful rational will. Assisted by her illness, she succeeds in wrenching herself from Nemours and achieving detached autonomy. Had she been untroubled by temptation or permitted her passion to direct her will, the narrative would have been unrecognizable, for the novel is, primarily, the drama of her psychological agony. As it is, we are presented with the victory of an enkratic hero.

---

46 Kant, *Grounding for the Metaphysics of Morals*, Ak. 398.
47 Lafayette, *The Princesse de Clèves*, 137.
48 Ibid., 150–1.
49 Ibid., 154.

Despite its violence, there is something magnificent about the strength of her will. We shall see a similar strength in Section 9, when we discuss the story of Father Sergy, who succeeds in resisting temptation by chopping off his own finger. (Spinoza would say that it is not the will that is victorious in these cases, since there is no such faculty; he would say, rather, that a stronger image overpowers a weaker one.) The agony experienced both by the Princesse and by Father Sergy is a symptom that each of their souls is in a disintegrative state.

Alan Paton's *Too Late the Phalarope* approaches the same psychological structure from the other direction. It is a tragedy, narrated by Sophie, the aunt of the protagonist, Pieter van Vlaanderen. Like the Princesse de Clèves, Pieter is married but faces temptation.[50] His susceptibility to temptation has historical roots. Since he was a child, Pieter's soul has been dual: "For the truth was he [Pieter's father Jakob] had fathered a strange son, who had all his father's will and strength, and could outstride and outshoot them all, yet had all the gentleness of a girl, and strange unusual thoughts in his mind, and a passion for books and learning, and a passion for flowers of veld and kloof, so that he would bring them into the house and hold them in his hands, as though there were some deep meaning that he was finding in them."[51] The gender dualism and the psychological dualism are conceptually independent, and we may remain agnostic about the former in order to focus on the latter: in Pieter's soul there are, on the one hand, will and strength and, on the other, gentleness and passion. These aspects might have been integrated, but Pieter's stern and judgemental father is hostile toward his gentleness and passion. As Mme de Chartres introjects her voice of criticism into her daughter's psyche, so Pieter's father does to Pieter.

The result is that Pieter's soul is fractured into a state of disintegration and agony. Whether he succeeds in resisting temptation becomes a

50 The temptation is too complex to discuss in detail here, since it transgresses not only his marital commitment to his wife, but also the apartheid system of South Africa. Pieter, a white man, is attracted to a Black woman, Stephanie. While the temptation to be unfaithful to his wife may be wrong, it cannot be wrong to disobey the so-called Immorality Act of a racist system. However, to complicate things even more, there is a further power imbalance between Pieter and Stephanie: while he is a police lieutenant, she is a young single mother and bootlegger, who is desperate not to lose custody of her child.

51 Paton, *Too Late the Phalarope*, 8. For introducing me to this work, thanks to Bethany Hindmarsh.

contingent matter. The first evening that he is unfaithful, when his wife, Nella, and their children are out of town, he acts in a premeditative way: he pours himself an extra brandy, calls a friend to cancel an appointment, and takes off his uniform and puts on old clothes. One detail is especially telling: "But he did not look at the beds, his or Nella's, nor even the beds of the children."[52] It is telling because it suggests both shame and weakness. Had Pieter looked at the beds and imagined his family, he might have gathered from them the strength that he needed. Later, when reflecting on his infidelity, he himself thinks a similar thought:

That I could not understand, that I could so endanger them [his children]; *therefore I knew the power of my enemy. For had an angel said to me, you may buy this victory, with an eye or a hand, or with both hands and eyes, I would have said, I buy it. Even had the mad sickness been upon me, and an angel had come there with my son, and said, go on and the child will die, I would at once have desisted.*[53]

This passage is important for a couple of reasons. To protect his children, Pieter would have sacrificed his eyes and hands; and yet, even though he could have protected them simply by refraining from committing this act of infidelity, he committed it. That is irrational. The passage also suggests that akrasia is less a "weakness of the will" than *a failure of imagination.* Had Pieter been able to call upon an image of his son, that image would have cancelled the image that was tempting him; it would have constituted a silencing reason. Failing that virtuous imagining, Pieter could have acted enkratically: like the Princesse, he could have defeated temptation by wilfully doing violence to himself.

Virtue involves both having the right images and not having the wrong ones. One must have the right images not merely potentially (in one's unconscious, for instance), but in a way that is readily actualizable; one must be able to call on them in moments of need. Images can be made actualizable through practice, which might involve repeatedly meditating on them. Concerning the importance of not having the wrong images, Weil makes some helpful remarks:

Even to allow one's imagination to dwell on certain things as being possible (which is quite a different thing from forming a clear conception of their

52 Ibid., 116.
53 Ibid., 120. Italics in original.

possibility, an essential element in the case of virtue) is to have pledged one-self already. Curiosity is the cause of this. We should refuse to allow ourselves [not to conceive, but to dwell on] certain thoughts; we should not think *about*. People suppose that thinking does not pledge them, but it alone pledges us, and licence of thought contains every form of licence. Not to think *about*—supreme faculty. Purity, a negative virtue.

She adds, "(There is also the fact that not to think *about* is an *art*, and one that is very little known)."[54] One mark of the virtuous agent is that she will clearly perceive silencing reasons that necessitate right action. Recall the thought that opens this section: with suitable training, from the perception of a possibility follows the appropriate response, as naturally as eating follows from feeling hungry. But another mark of the virtuous agent is that possibilities for wrong action will not occur to her. Weil calls this mark "purity"; it is the negative aspect of virtue. (Virtue's positive aspect is the clear perceiving of silencing reasons.) Bernard Williams agrees: "It could be a feature of a man's moral outlook that he regarded certain courses of action unthinkable, in the sense that he would not entertain the idea of doing them: and the witness to that might, in many cases, be that they simply would not come into his head."[55] And just as there is an art of making the right images readily actualizable, so there is an art of not thinking the wrong images. (We return to the role of the imagination in ethical psychology in Sections 8 and 11.)

The key point of this discussion is that, while the outcomes are different, the psychological structures of Mme de Clèves and Pieter van Vlaanderen are the same. Both are tempted and both perceive reasons for resisting that temptation; each one's psyche is the theatre for the conflict between temptation and reason. The relevant difference is that Mme de Clèves succeeds in overcoming temptation, while Pieter fails. In other words, she exemplifies enkrateia, while Pieter exemplifies akrasia. Perhaps Mme de Clèves's success can be ascribed to the exceptional power of her will. But I suspect that the difference has more to do with chance. By chance, Mme de Clèves falls ill, and it gives her time to reflect and detach herself. By chance, Pieter is in a bad mood one

54 Weil, *Notebooks*, I.110 / *OC*, VI.2.104–5; square brackets in original.
55 Williams, "A critique of utilitarianism," 92. Cf. Annas, "The phenomenology of virtue," 27; and Winch, "Moral Integrity," 178, 189.

evening when his family is out of town, and he runs into his cousin, they have several brandies together, and he becomes drunk;[56] against that backdrop he begins his preparations for committing infidelity. If enkrateia and akrasia are structurally identical, then enkrateia, however widespread and admirable it may be, is fundamentally insecure: it is always open to the possibility of conflict and the risk of being converted into akrasia. By contrast, virtue is sure: Antigone is invulnerable to Ismene's fears and Kreon's threats. She *knows* what she needs to do. The psychology of enkrateia and akrasia, in its susceptibility to internal conflict, is *disintegrative*, whereas the psychology of *aretē*, in its tendency to harmony, is *integrative*. The enkratic agent has merely a true opinion of the right thing to do, whereas the virtuous agent has knowledge – a distinction we shall discuss further in Section 7. The enkratic agent's true opinion is always open to rational reconsideration; whereas the virtuous agent's knowledge, grounded in the experience of necessary truth, is unshakeable.[57]

§4.4. The major objection to McDowell's argument, which he himself notes,[58] is that it confuses "facts" and "values" (or "cognition" and "appetite"); and this objection threatens to deprive McDowell's account of virtue of its aspirations to objectivity. According to the objection, which issues from the camp that credits Hume as its progenitor, a "cognitive" description of the facts cannot, on its own, motivate action; one must add a "non-cognitive" appetitive element. To the belief, for example, that one's friend is in trouble and open to being comforted must be added the desire to attend to the needs of one's friends. It is not difficult to imagine how such beliefs and desires might combine to motivate someone to comfort a friend. But the addition of the desire does not explain how the salient fact *silences* other considerations. A given agent may have any number of contingent desires capable of tugging him in any number of directions. According to one story, the agent might weigh these various desires, and a

56 But if he has "the power of not getting drunk," as Aristotle suggests (*Nicomachean Ethics*, III.5.1113b32–3), then the role of chance in Pieter's transgression may be diminished.

57 On this distinction between true opinion and knowledge, see Zwicky, *Plato as Artist*, 84–5 / AL, 202–3.

58 McDowell, "Virtue and Reason," §3 and §6.

"second-order" desire might perhaps help him to select a "first-order" desire upon which to act; if his overall preference is to be a kind person, then perhaps he decides to comfort his troubled friend instead of going to a pleasant party.

According to McDowell's account, there is at least another possibility. In this other case, it is not accurate to say that one acts on the most preferred option: because *there are no other options.* The case of spontaneous response – in which calculative deliberation does not occur – is a limiting case, but we can also imagine a less urgent case where one contemplates a situation and gradually comes to understand that only one action is available. That is, sometimes acting *is* the result of having weighed our preferences; but sometimes it is *not.* In some cases, when an agent is asked to explain her actions, she will say (along with the Breton ship's apprentice), "I had to do it." This testimony cannot be explained by the Humean theory in a way that does justice to the agent's perspective. And to refuse to countenance the testimony because we have a prior and exclusive commitment to the Humean theory is to reason in a circle. Instead, we could expand our explanatory repertoire and try to exercise some contextualist flexibility.

While McDowell's account is sympathetic to a Weilian ethical psychology, his interpreters (Jonathan Dancy, David McNaughton, Margaret Olivia Little, et alia) make a number of mistakes. One of the most serious mistakes is their moral cognitivism, understood as the reduction of desires to beliefs. Some might feel that moral cognitivism and non-cognitivism are like the mythical Skylla and Kharybdis, the extremes of the only available strait, and that one can only choose to steer close to one or the other. The metaphor is so trite that we may have forgotten that there was originally a third way. In Book Twelve of the *Odyssey*, the goddess Kirke tells Odysseus what to expect on his voyage home: You can attempt the πλαγκταὶ πέτραι, the "crazy rocks," against which all but one ship have been wrecked; or you can brave the dangerous strait between Skylla and Kharybdis.[59] Odysseus, transfixed by the monsters, does not even consider the crazy rocks, and instead asks, But can't I

59 If one steers close to Skylla, one will sacrifice six sailors, one for each of her heads; but if one steers close to Kharybdis, the entire ship will perish. So described, the dilemma seems to invite a consequentialist solution; and Odysseus's refusal to listen to Kirke could also be understood as a refusal of consequentialist reasoning.

defeat Skylla, and sail past untouched? And Kirke admonishes him, saying, "Must you have battle in your heart forever?"[60]

When we are transfixed by the debate between cognitivists and noncognitivists, what, exactly, is transfixing us? What is the picture that holds us captive? The first step, the decisive movement in the conjuring trick,[61] is the one that commits us exclusively to a Humean theory of motivation, a picture of two radically distinct mental states, with, it is said, distinct "directions of fit." This figurative distinction has been attributed to G.E.M. Anscombe, who draws a contrast between two lists: the one in the shopper's hand, and the one in the hand of the detective following the shopper. The shopper's list is like desire: it is satisfied when the world fits it; the detective's list is like belief: it is true when it fits the world.[62] (Anscombe alleges that this distinction is traceable back to Aristotle; but that is a different story, which we shall address in Section 6.)

Even McDowell's interpreters, who want to free us from the hegemony of such a picture, make the mistake of Odysseus. To save the Platonic thesis that virtue is knowledge, with appropriate Aristotelian revisions, McDowell's interpreters effectively reduce what a Humean would call "desires" to what a Humean would call "beliefs."[63] That is, they start with a nice, dualistic theory of motivation, and compress it into a monistic one. And then they try to defend this position by arguing that some beliefs can have two directions of fit. However well intentioned these tactics, some of us might see this picture as a palimpsest on a Humean original and feel that an entire dimension of psychology has been submerged or obscured. And, faced with Kirke's choice, we might feel tempted to lower one of the rowboats and try our luck at the crazy rocks.

Let us be clear: we are not challenging the legitimacy of the Humean theory. On the contrary, it is correctly applied in explaining cases of enkrateia and akrasia; furthermore, the analytic psychology pictured by that theory is needed for the exercise of *elenctic attention*, or moral

---

60 Homer, *Odyssey*, XII.116; Fitzgerald's translation.
61 Wittgenstein, *Philosophical Investigations*, §§115, 308.
62 Anscombe, *Intention*, §32.
63 E.g., McNaughton, *Moral Vision*, 109ff; and Little, "Seeing and Caring," 132.

critique.[64] That is, in order to criticize ourselves and others, we may need to analyse agency into belief and desire; and from this disintegrative perspective, we may be in a position to identify and discard false beliefs or eradicate rotten desires. As Miranda Fricker suggests, a virtue of epistemic justice requires us to reflect critically on our own beliefs and to correct those which have been distorted by prejudice.[65] But despite the ongoing need for such analysis, it does not follow that agency is always originally dualistic in structure.

In the following three sections, we contemplate some examples of aesthetic and ethical contexts. While ethical contexts are practical ones, what is remarkable about these particular contexts is that *there is nothing to be done*; there is no problem to be solved, or there is no solution to the problem. The examples that we consider are examples of attending, or listening, or witnessing.

§4.5. I hesitate to call them examples of "action." It would be better to call them examples of "reaction," or "response," or what Jan Zwicky would call "gesture": "the immediate, untutored response of a human being to meaning."[66] Relatively sophisticated and complicated actions, the kind that might be analysable by a theory of practical reasoning, spring from a deeper root. Consider Wittgenstein's remark: "The origin and primitive form of the language game is a reaction; only from this can more complicated forms develop. // Language—

---

64 From the Greek ἔλεγχος (*elenkhos*): "argument of disproof or refutation ... generally, cross-examining, testing, scrutiny, esp. for purposes of refutation" (LSJ). In Plato's dialogues, Sokrates is a master of the elenctic method. Cf. Zwicky, "Alcibiades' Love," 92ff / *AL*, 291ff; and this book, §§6.4, 7.1, 7.6, 9.4. For helping me to understand this important point about moral critique, thanks to Michael Doan and Meredith Schwartz.

65 Fricker, "Epistemic Injustice," §3 (pp. 161–4).

66 Zwicky, *Lyric Philosophy*, L242. For Zwicky, meaning and understanding are both gestural. To mean is to make a gesture (L241), and understanding is the experience of meaning; to understand is to extend one's hand, to gesture in response to a gesture (L250). Meaning and understanding stand to one another in the structure of call and response, or, more appropriately, response and co-response (L181). Humans, like many other things in the world, are resonance bodies; and a thing that is capable of receiving resonance is also capable of transmitting it. While the terms "untutored" and "human" are euphonious in Zwicky's definition, there is nothing uniquely human about gesturing.

I want to say—is a refinement. 'In the beginning was the deed.'"[67] Adapting this remark, we may say that the origin and primitive form of action is a *reaction,* a gesture. (We shall discuss reactions in greater detail in Sections 5 and 8.)

And while a gesture is immediate, and in a sense reflexive, it cannot be reduced to a mechanism. On the contrary, as familiar and even instinctive as many gestures seem to be, they often require a polydimensional context for their appreciation. Consider another remark by Wittgenstein: "Two people are laughing together, say at a joke. One of them has used certain somewhat unusual words and now they both break out into a sort of bleating. That might appear *very* extraordinary to a visitor coming from quite a different environment. Whereas we find it completely *reasonable.*"[68] The practice of joke-telling and laughing, call and response, finds its place in the midst of a terrifically complex, but fundamentally animal, form of life. And much training and acculturation precede, and are compressed into, the single gesture of laughing at a joke.

Consider too an activity as ordinary as reading the newspaper; perhaps one reads some sad news and weeps. But what an astonishing event! Just how astonishing is illustrated by Weil in her "Essay on the Notion of Reading":

Black marks on a piece of white paper are quite different from a punch in the stomach. But sometimes the effect is the same. ... Two women each receive a letter, announcing to each that her son is dead. The first, upon just glancing at the paper, faints, and until her death, her eyes, her mouth, her movements will never again be as they were. The second woman remains the same: her expression, her attitude do not change; she doesn't know how to read. It's not the sensation but the meaning which has seized the first woman, reaching [*atteignant*] immediately, brutally into her mind.[69]

The response of the first, literate woman – her fainting – is completely natural, appropriate, and understandable; it is only by contrast with the non-response of the second, illiterate woman that it begins to seem

---

67 Wittgenstein (quoting Goethe), "Cause and Effect: Intuitive Awareness," 21.10.

68 Wittgenstein, *Culture and Value,* 78e.

69 Weil, "Essay on the Notion of Reading," 297–8 / 13–14; translation altered. Cf. Weil's sketch of this example (*Notebooks,* I.22 / *OC,* VI.1.294).

astonishing. And what is astonishing about it is not that she responds to the death of her son by fainting. No: what is astonishing is that an extremely complex training has prepared her to understand what is communicated by the letter – a training in the practice of literacy; for a fluent practitioner, it is possible for black marks on a piece of paper to be immediately transparent to their meaning. And an explanation of the woman's response can be complete without including mention of this extremely complex practice – because this practice finds its place in a shared form of life.

Suppose that the woman's daughter enters the room, and, finding her mother lifting herself from the floor, bends to offer her hand, asking, "What's wrong? Why have you fallen?" In response, the mother may say any number of things: "Because your brother has died"; or, "Because I have just heard some very sad news"; or, "Here, see for yourself." At no point is she obliged to mention that she has just deciphered some arcane hieroglyphics. And her not mentioning them is not an omission. No interpreting has taken place.[70] The gesture of the letter, its meaning, and the woman's gesture of understanding, her fainting, together constitute a complete arc, a complete structure of call and response. In giving her reason for what she did, the woman is not culpable for not mentioning the practice of literacy that enabled her to understand the letter. It would be wrong to say that the practice is even assumed; it is much deeper than that; it is rather embossed in the background of a form of life in which such calls and such responses are possible.

And while the woman's fainting is non-arbitrarily connected with the letter – while it is a gesture of understanding – that understanding could be manifested in different ways.[71] Suppose that the woman gives the letter to her daughter, and, instead of fainting, the daughter crumples the paper; or she cries out; or she places the paper carefully on a table and walks over to the window and stares out at the blowing snow. Wittgenstein offers examples of comparable gestural responses: "Recall

70 Cf. Wittgenstein, *Philosophical Investigations*, §201; and Zwicky, *Lyric Philosophy*, L245–L246.

71 One might object that fainting cannot be a "gesture of understanding" because it – like laughter – is an involuntary "non-cognitive" reflex. But laughter is the *best* gesture of understanding a good joke – much better than a "cognitive" explanation of what makes the joke funny. So why can't fainting be a gesture of understanding the death of one's child?

that after Schubert's death his brother cut some of Schubert's scores into small pieces and gave such pieces, consisting of a few bars, to his favorite pupils. This act, as a sign of piety, is *just as* understandable to us as the different one of keeping the scores untouched, accessible to no one. And if Schubert's brother had burned the scores, that too would be understandable as a sign of piety."[72] There is a diverse range of gestures that we are prepared to call (or at least that I am prepared to call) understanding the letter or being pious. And we will seek in vain for some common feature that runs, like a fibre,[73] through each and every one.

§4.6. Let us turn now to another example: a work of art – Vittorio De Sica's film *Bicycle Thieves*, and particularly a gesture that occurs at the end. If you have not seen this film, I would apologize for spoiling it, but it is an interesting fact about certain works of art that they cannot be spoiled by disclosure of the plot. Indeed, if you have not seen the film, we will not be able to explore enough context to communicate the meaning of the final gesture; but let us sketch some of it. In poverty-stricken postwar Rome, Antonio Ricci is hoping to support his family with a new job. To do this job, he depends on his bicycle, which the family has pawned its bed-sheets to acquire. On Antonio's first day at work, his bicycle is stolen. With his son, Bruno, he sets off the next morning to track down the thief. At the end of the long day, having failed to recover his own bicycle, he tries to steal another. That's it; the plot could fit on the back of an envelope, in the palm of your hand. André Bazin writes, "[The film's] social message is not detached, it remains immanent in the event, but it is so clear that nobody can overlook it, still less take exception to it, since it is never made explicitly a message. The thesis implied is wondrously, outrageously simple: in the world where this workman lives, the poor must steal from each other in order to survive."[74]

When we finally meet the thief, near the end of the film, he is shown with sympathy; that is, although he is not particularly likeable, we see that he is, if possible, even more destitute than Antonio, that he lives

72 Wittgenstein, "Remarks on Frazer's *Golden Bough*," 127.

73 Like the red thread of the British Navy. Cf. Wittgenstein, *Philosophical Investigations*, §67.

74 Bazin, *"Bicycle Thief," What Is Cinema?*, 51.

in one room with his mother and two siblings, possibly contending with epilepsy, and, it seems, is trying to assist an elderly man financially. Most of the film occurs in the space between the two symmetrical thefts. And what happens in that space is nothing more than the camera witnessing a relatively uneventful, undramatic day: the father and son shelter under some eaves during a rainstorm, they stop at a restaurant and share mozzarella sandwiches and a bottle of wine, which their family cannot afford, and so on. Bazin writes, "It would be no exaggeration to say that *Ladri di Biciclette* is the story of a walk through Rome by a father and his son."[75] Another such example is a neo-realist scenario described by De Sica's collaborator and screenwriter Cesare Zavattini:

A woman is going to buy a pair of shoes. Upon this elementary situation it is possible to build a film. All we have to do is to discover and then show all the elements that go to create this adventure, in all their banal 'dailiness,' and it will become worthy of attention, it will even become 'spectacular.' But it will become spectacular not through its exceptional, but through its *normal* qualities; it will astonish us by showing so many things that happen every day under our eyes, things we have never noticed before.[76]

Finally, consider a scene in De Sica and Zavattini's *Umberto D*, the scene in which the maid gets up and makes the morning coffee:

The camera confines itself to watching her doing her little chores: moving around the kitchen still half asleep, drowning the ants that have invaded the sink, grinding the coffee. ... We see how the grinding of the coffee is divided in turn into a series of independent moments; for example, when she shuts the door with the tip of her outstretched foot. As it goes in on her the camera follows the movement of her leg so that the image finally concentrates on her toes feeling the surface of the door.[77]

The final image of the maid's toes is a *lyric detail,* as that concept will be defined in Section 10. Here let us just say that such a detail is what one perceives when one is attentive; and in a coherent work of art, details

75 Ibid., 55.
76 Zavattini, "Some Ideas on the Cinema," §5.
77 Bazin, "*Umberto D:* A Great Work," *What Is Cinema?*, 81–2.

are like clues to the meaning of the whole.[78] Zavattini's love of ordinary reality, and his critique of the consolations of fantasy, is reminiscent of Weil. "The keenest necessity of our time is 'social attention,'" he writes. "Attention, though, to what is there, *directly*."[79] A walk through Rome by a father and his son. A woman going to buy a pair of shoes. A maid weeping quietly while she grinds coffee. The point of these films is not the excitement of plot; the camera concentrates on the "concrete instants of life," bearing witness to "their ontological equality."[80]

Let us focus, now, on the final gesture of *Bicycle Thieves*, the detail that holds all the others in the balance. Antonio has attempted to steal an unwatched bicycle, but he has been chased and caught. While he has been pardoned by the owner of the bicycle, he is ashamed in front of his son. Antonio and Bruno are dissolving into the crowd, and Antonio begins publicly to weep. Bruno reaches up and takes his father's hand. Different film critics have championed competing analyses of the symbolic significance of this gesture. But the gesture need not be a symbol for something other than itself, and such analyses are exactly as helpful as explanations of a joke. There is something deep about the gesture, something that cannot be reproduced here, which requires the context of the complete film for its full appreciation. One understandable audience response to the gesture would be to weep. Of course, one might not weep. We can imagine a range of audience gestures, which we needn't specify in advance, which would express an understanding of the gesture on the screen. Furthermore, reasons can be offered for these gestures, and the reasons needn't be analyses of symbols.

Suppose that someone, let us call her Larisa, has just watched the film, and is weeping. Her friend Andrei comes into the room and asks her, "What's wrong, why are you weeping?" She points to the screen and says, "Look!"; or, "Look, Bruno is holding Antonio's hand." Here are some possibilities: Andrei has previously seen the film, and when he recognizes its final image, her weeping makes sense to him. Or: he has not seen the film. The image on the screen, deprived of context, strikes him as maudlin, and her behaviour seems overly sentimental. She promptly shows him the whole film, and then he understands. (In other words, she introduces him to these characters, their world,

78 Cf. Zwicky, *Lyric Philosophy*, L111.
79 Zavattini, "Some Ideas on the Cinema," §3.
80 Bazin, "*Umberto D*: A Great Work," 81.

their form of life, in which this gesture has its place.) Or: she shows him the whole film, and the final gesture still fails to make an impression on him.

At this point, someone might despair: "Well, that's the end of it! The impossibility of agreeing on a single best interpretation of a work of art just shows that infinitely many interpretations are equal." But such despair would be premature. Larisa has other techniques for reorienting Andrei's vision. She might say: "Reflect on the film: throughout their day together, the father has not once touched the son with tenderness; in fact, on two previous occasions, when the son stumbled and fell in the rain and when he was nearly run over by a car, the father was oblivious. You must see Bruno's gesture against that background." Or: she might read Bazin's observation aloud: "Before choosing this particular child, De Sica did not ask him to perform, just to walk. He wanted to play off the striding gait of the man against the short trotting steps of the child, the harmony of this discord being for him of capital importance for the understanding of the film as a whole."[81] Or she might ask: "Do you remember when we read Pasternak's *Doctor Zhivago*? How astonished you were by the end of the fifth chapter, the deaf hunter standing in the train compartment as it is plunged into darkness, holding out in his hand the gift of the wild duck, how that gesture held the rest of the chapter in the balance?[82] *That* gesture is like *this* one." And so on. These are the sorts of reasons that we can offer to facilitate appreciation of a work of art. One emphasizes other features of the work that are salient in relation to this feature; or one sets up objects of comparison. And so on.

What we have seen here is an example of the form of reason-giving – with Zwicky, we might call it *lyric argument*[83] – that Wittgenstein sketches in a lecture recorded by G.E. Moore:

Reasons, [Wittgenstein] said, in Aesthetics, are 'of the nature of further descriptions'; *e.g.* you can make a person see what Brahms was driving at by showing him lots of different pieces by Brahms, or by comparing him with a contemporary author; and all that Aesthetics does is 'to draw your attention

---

81 Bazin, "*Bicycle Thief*," 54–5.

82 See Pasternak, *Doctor Zhivago*, 165. For the structure of lyric closure, see Zwicky, *Lyric Philosophy*, §§211–12.

83 Zwicky, "What Is Lyric Philosophy?," §34.

to a thing', to 'place things side by side'. He said ... that what he, Wittgenstein, had 'at the back of his mind' was 'the idea that aesthetic discussions were like discussions in a court of law', where you try to 'clear up the circumstances' of the action which is being tried, hoping that in the end what you say will 'appeal to the judge'. And he said that the same sort of 'reasons' were given, not only in Ethics, but also in Philosophy.[84]

Following Wittgenstein, McDowell defends this form of reason-giving. When one gives reasons in ethics, he writes, "one exploits contrivances similar to those one exploits in other areas where the task is to back up the injunction 'See it like this': helpful juxtapositions of cases, descriptions with carefully chosen terms and carefully placed emphasis, and the like. (Compare, for instance, what one might do and say to someone who says 'Jazz sounds to me like a mess, a mere welter of uncoordinated noise'.)"[85] As both Wittgenstein and McDowell acknowledge, such reason-giving is normative but not foolproof. One presents one's case to the judge. And it is possible that the case won't secure the judge's assent, even if one has all the relevant facts and the case is well assembled.

§4.7. Let us conclude our illustrations of Weil's ethics of attending, listening, and witnessing with one more example. Imagine that you are a volunteer for an emergency telephone service. It might be similar to the Samaritans, a service founded in 1953 by Chad Varah, and initially designed to respond to calls from suicidal people. At first he answered the calls himself, but in less than a year he was able to transfer that responsibility to a staff of volunteers. Here is how he characterizes them:

There are in this world, in every country, people who seem to be 'ordinary', but who, when meeting a suicidal person, turn out to be extraordinary. They can usually save lives. How? They give the sad person their total attention. They completely forget themselves. They listen and listen and listen, without

---

84 Moore, "Wittgenstein's Lectures in 1930–33," 106. On this methodology, cf. Wittgenstein, *Philosophical Investigations*, §§122, 127, 130; Zwicky, *Wisdom & Metaphor*, L2; Shiner, "On Giving Works of Art a Face"; and Burns, "The Place of Art in a Reasonable Education." Kosman argues that this method plays an indispensable role in Platonic dialectic ("The Faces of Justice," §III [pp. 163–6]).

85 McDowell, "Are Moral Requirements Hypothetical Imperatives?," §6 (p. 21).

interrupting. They have no message. They do not preach. They have nothing to sell. We call them 'Samaritans'.[86]

We can recognize this giving of attention. Like Weil, Murdoch, and Zwicky, Varah emphasizes its unselfconsciousness and its empty receptivity. Elsewhere, he emphasizes an aspect of listening that is almost Daoist: "What *did* the volunteers do when they came to take their turn on duty? The answer seemed clear: A great deal of nothing."[87] Varah is not criticizing the listeners; on the contrary, he is commending non-doing as an excellence.

I learned of the Samaritans from Alice MacLachlan, who worked for them at end of the nineties. Here is her account of a crucial aspect of her training:

The line that the man and woman who trained me used, and which I have never forgotten, was this: when someone is in terrible distress, it's as if they are in a deep pit or a hole. There are individuals or organizations out there who will throw down a rope, or try to assist them in getting out (of course they have to take the rope). What the samaritans do is crawl down into the pit to sit with them so that they are not alone.

This image was intended to offer us a framework for thinking about what it was to be on the other end of the phone, and how to engage with the person to whom we were listening. Crucially, it was about how to listen and not how to talk/*help*.

It remains one of the most powerful pieces of moral advice anyone has ever given me.[88]

The image of the pit illustrates a defining characteristic of this method of listening, a characteristic that differentiates it from what we might call an *instrumentalist* method of listening. An example of instrumentalist listening is the diagnostic kind: the doctor asks you about your symptoms and listens while you recount them. In such a case, listening serves some external purpose: to gather data for the diagnosis of your condition. (Diagnosis, in its turn, serves a further purpose in treatment.) According

86 Varah, quoted in "Obituary: Chad Varah," *The Economist*, 21 November 2007, www.economist.com/obituary/2007/11/21/chad-varah.

87 Varah, "The Samaritans: Befriending the Suicidal," 175–6.

88 MacLachlan, email communication, 23 July 2019.

to the instrumentalist method, listening is a means to achieving some end that is external to the activity of listening. There is nothing wrong with this kind of listening; it has important work to do in its appropriate domain. Still, it is distinct from another kind of listening that is the focus of our investigation; to indicate the distinctness of the instrumentalist kind, let us call it *auditing*.

The listener who descends into the pit to be with the one who suffers is not listening for some external purpose (she is not auditing). Even the purpose of preventing suicide is bracketed and set aside; if suicide prevention happens, it is a happy by-product.[89] What, then, *is* the goal of this kind of listening? There is no goal. This listening is a counter-example to the assumption that all meaningful activity is teleological. The instrumentalist auditor reasons in the following way (where α is the activity of listening and τ is some goal, e.g., *the relief of suffering*):

I believe that α is a means to achieving τ.
If I want τ, then I should do α.
I do want τ.
Therefore, I should do α.

Notice that the instrumentalist auditor is amenable to the Humean theory. In this example of reasoning, we can discern a distinct belief and a distinct desire, which, when combined, motivate action. The Weilian listener, by contrast, does not reason in that way. If she reasons, she reasons in this way:

This caller is suffering.
So I listen.

In this couplet, the first premise is a fact, and the conclusion is an action. What is at stake here is the question of whether all practical reasoning, and in particular the reasoning conducted by phronesis, is assimilable to the Humean model. Prima facie, the reasoning of the Weilian listener here is not Humean. The theorist committed to the Humean model will reply that the couplet is enthymematic: analysis will reveal the hidden elements. But let us wait and see.

---

89 N.b. These remarks are not meant to be a description of the actual Samaritan method.

Imagine, then, that you are a volunteer for an emergency telephone service similar to the Samaritans. You have been screened and have been acquainted, through basic training, with accounts of the service like those of Varah and MacLachlan above, but you have not yet completed the more advanced training. However, several other volunteers have called in sick, and you have been asked to substitute. Your supervisor has given you this instruction: "Don't judge; don't give advice. If the caller is at risk, refer the call to me. Otherwise, just listen." It's after midnight. You sit in a windowless cubicle in the basement of a school. You can hear the faint buzzing of the fluorescent tubes, and the murmuring of other listeners from the neighbouring cubicles. Your phone rings, and you answer. A stranger's voice appears on the line. After some initial questions, you ascertain that the caller is not at risk. But something terrible has happened to her. And it is irreversible. What can you do? Here is the analogy with attending to a work of art: you are witnessing something that you cannot change. So, you listen. And keep listening.

Can the listening be forced into the Humean frame? Let's try: you desire that the caller's distress be lessened, and while you accept that you cannot change the event that caused the distress, you believe that listening to her will lessen her distress. Perhaps some people would reason in this way, peering over the shoulder of the distressed person at some goal in the middle distance. But such a reasoner is not really listening *to his interlocutor;* he is comparing her with someone else, a less distressed person he wants her to become. And he is trying to use listening behaviour as a tool to change her into that less distressed person. Significantly, his reason for "listening" is not one that he can share with his interlocutor without sounding tactless and mechanically clinical. Furthermore, notice what happens if we adjust the example in the following way: suppose that you know, in this particular context, that listening will *not* lessen the caller's sadness; she is, we can imagine, inconsolable, or perhaps her distress is wholly appropriate to her circumstances. In that case, listening is useless for altering the world. And yet you are not excused from listening. So, even if the Humean auditor is a real kind, one whose motivation can be analysed into fact-reflecting beliefs and world-changing desires, it is not the only kind, nor the kind that drives this investigation.

There is at least one other kind of listener, who listens for a different reason. It is possible to listen to the caller for her own sake. In giving the reason for such listening, we do not need to scrutinize the mind of the listener. Instead, we may gesture directly toward that feature of the world that moves us. Suppose that, by the time you hang up the phone, you are late to meet your friends at a bar downtown; when you arrive, a friend asks why you are late. And you say, "Because I received a call from someone in distress." No mention need be made of mental states. Everything is open to view. It would be natural to say that what moved you was the caller herself. If she were present, you could gesture toward her. Only if we have a prior commitment to the Humean picture are we obliged to suspect that this gesture is an enthymeme, in need of further analysis. Ordinarily such a gesture is enough to render one's action understandable.

We have found at least one kind of ethically meaningful activity – listening, a form of attending – that is not best explained by the Humean theory. At stake here is what counts as a reason and what work practical reasoning can do (in particular, the reasoning conducted by phronesis). Not all practical reasoning is instrumentalist, and not all meaningful activity is teleological. When asked why he is "listening," the Humean auditor introspects and cites his own mental states. When asked why she is listening, the Weilian listener gestures toward things in the world. The Humean auditor tries to be autonomous: all his energy comes from inside his self. The Weilian listener, by contrast, acknowledges that she depends on sources of energy that are outside her self. This difference is not insignificant. If the Weilian listener is a real kind – and she is – then it means that we can be motivated by a wider range of things than the Humean theory permits, and our repertoire for reason-giving is also deepened. And it means that we need to appeal to the Platonic ethical psychology to explain the motivational structure of the Weilian listener. Action is always interactive. The energy that we need for acting is not our private property; we receive it, like light, from others.

5

Reading and Character

"The bee sees ultraviolet."——Does this mean that the rose isn't red, after all?
                                                                    – Jan Zwicky[1]

§5.1. WE HAVE REVIEWED SOME of the characteristics of a Weilian ethics of attending. We have seen that John McDowell is the Anglo-American inheritor, via Iris Murdoch, of that ethics: what Simone Weil and Murdoch call *attention* is what McDowell calls *sensitivity*. Attention, or sensitivity, is immediately responsive to the requirements of a particular situation. The Weilian ethical psychology can be contrasted with the Humean moral psychology with its dualistic belief-desire structure. While the Humean agent weighs the pros and cons before making a prudential decision, the Weilian agent *sees*. In the limiting case, such seeing flows immediately into acting. We have witnessed the Weilian ethics in action in a number of particular cases, and we have seen that it is needed to explain at least two species of action: appreciating a work of art and listening to someone's suffering. Both of these species of action belong to the genus *attending*. Nor are they negligible: appreciating art and listening to suffering are integral to our form of life. So any ethical psychology that failed to save these phenomena would be flawed.

But the Humean theory does fail to save them. It fails because, by hypothesis, in the limiting cases, the relevant situation is unchangeable, and goal-directed reasoning of the Humean sort is inappropriate. So our ethical psychology needs to be more complex than the Humean theory; minimally, it needs to be more than two-dimensional – in other words, polydimensional. One of those dimensions, the Weilian one, consists in the clear and accurate perception of what is salient in a particular context. Paradigm cases include the flash of understanding in

---

1 Zwicky, *Lyric Philosophy*, L224.

the face of meaning: the meaning of an artwork or a living being's vital need. In these cases, understanding does not consist in inference; it is not the application of a general principle or rule to a particular case. It is epiphanic. And the epiphany is enough for appropriate motivation.

We turn now to study a form of attention that Weil calls *lecture* ("reading"). In her "Essay on the Notion of Reading" (which we encountered in Section 4.5), she investigates the phenomenon of meaning. Perceiving meaning in the world is as immediate, she suggests, as perceiving linguistic meaning in a text. There is some resemblance between her approach and an approach by McDowell in which he claims that aesthetic and ethical values might be analogized to "secondary qualities."[2] Like Weil, McDowell suggests that the apprehension of value is akin to sensory perception. Furthermore, both Weil and McDowell think that our capacity to perceive value or meaning[3] can be educated; with training, we can become more literate, and we can transition from an inadequate reading to one that is more adequate. Let us set these approaches side by side, and ask whether both are vulnerable to the same objection.

If meaning or value is relativized to special perceptual apparatuses, then a skeptic might complain that meaning is not really there, objectively, in "the fabric of the world."[4] On the contrary, according to this line of thinking, David Hume is right when he warns of the mind's "propensity to spread itself on external objects," "gilding or staining [them] with the colours, borrowed from internal sentiment." Virtue and vice, he claims, "may be compar'd to sounds, colours, heat and cold, which, according to modern philosophy, are not qualities in objects, but perceptions in the mind."[5] Weil, McDowell, and Hume all agree that value or meaning may be compared to colour; what is in question is whether this comparison, if apt, renders value unregenerately and merely subjective. This question is the focus of the first half of this

2 See McDowell, "Aesthetic Value, Objectivity, and the Fabric of the World" and "Values and Secondary Qualities."

3 Throughout this section, I use the terms "meaning" and "value" roughly synonymously. Following Weil and Zwicky, I understand meaning to be much broader in scope than linguistic meaning. Cf. Zwicky, "What Is Lyric Philosophy?," §§2–4.

4 Mackie, *Ethics: Inventing Right and Wrong*, §1.1 (p. 15).

5 Hume, *A Treatise of Human Nature*, I.III.§XIV.¶25, quoted in McDowell, "Values and Secondary Qualities," §4 (p. 143); Hume, *An Enquiry Concerning the Principles of Morals*, Appendix I.§V.¶21; and Hume, *Treatise*, III.I.§I.¶26.

section. In the second half, we turn to Weil's and McDowell's accounts of character. Both understand virtuous character as the actualization of a second nature. For Weil, that second nature (or second literacy) is a refinement of a first nature: our physical reactions to positive and negative affordances in the environment.

Weil begins her investigation into meaning by isolating some of the defining features of sensation, and by considering the examples of pain and heat:

We all know that sensation is immediate, brutal and grabs us by surprise. Without warning, a man is punched in the stomach; everything has changed for him before he knows what has happened. I touch something hot; I feel myself jump before realizing that I am being burned. Something seizes me. That is how the world treats me and it is through such treatment that I recognize it.[6]

Let us notice two defining features of sensation, as described by Weil: (1) our *physical reactions* to what we sense are sometimes prior to consciousness; and (2) sensation happens to us *involuntarily*. Weil is here borrowing from Descartes and his argument for the existence of material things in Meditation Six: "This [active] faculty [of producing ideas of sensible things] surely cannot be in me," he writes, "since it clearly presupposes [1] *no act of understanding*, and these ideas are produced [2] *without my cooperation* and often even *against my will*."[7] According to Descartes, these features imply that the mind is associated, somehow, with a body surrounded by an external world. And Weil draws the Cartesian conclusion: "We are not surprised by the power that blows, burns, sudden noises possess to seize us; because we know, or believe we know, that they come to us from outside, from matter."[8] The physicality of the verb is important: pain and heat *seize* us. Here it might be helpful to ask whether one can seize oneself. Can one grab oneself by the collar? What about the punch to the stomach: can one punch oneself? Involuntarily? For Weil, the preconscious and involuntary features of sensation are clues; they suggest that one is reacting to a stimulus that is not reducible to one's mind.

---

6 Weil, "Essay on the Notion of Reading," 297 / 13; translation altered.
7 Descartes, *Meditations*, AT VII.79; emphases added. Cf. ibid., AT VII.38.
8 Weil, "Essay on the Notion of Reading," 297 / 13; translation altered.

Having sketched these features of sensation, Weil turns to the investigation of meaning. "The mystery," she writes, "is that some sensations in themselves nearly indifferent seize us in the same way through their meaning. Black marks on a piece of white paper are quite different from a punch in the stomach. But sometimes the effect is the same."[9] The experience of meaning can be as powerful as a punch: it can seize us preconsciously, involuntarily, physically. These features, shared by sensation and meaning, suggest that we are no more the authors of meaning than we are of sensation. And meaning can seize us through phenomena that, read from a different angle, might seem innocuous. Weil proceeds to flesh out her analogy by discussing an example of literal reading:

Everyone has experienced to some degree the effect of reading bad news in a letter or newspaper; one feels seized, bowled over, as if by a blow, before realizing what it's all about, and even later the very sight of the letter remains painful. Sometimes, when time has somewhat dulled the pain, if, among the papers one is handling, the letter suddenly appears, a more vivid pain surges up, sudden and piercing as a physical pain, it seizes one as if it came from outside, as if it resided in this piece of paper in the same way burning resides in fire.[10]

But does burning reside in fire? Doesn't the analogy undermine Weil's argument?

Having been through the wringer of early modern epistemology – like Weil herself – we might recall that John Locke uses exactly the same analogy to argue for an opposite conclusion:

And yet he, that will consider, that *the same fire*, that at one distance *produces* in us the sensation of *warmth*, does at a nearer approach, produce in us the far different sensation of *pain*, ought to bethink himself, what reason he has to say, that his *idea* of *warmth*, which was produced in him by the fire, is actually *in the fire*, and his *idea* of *pain*, which the same fire produced in him in the same way, is *not* in the *fire*.[11]

---

9 Ibid.; translation altered.
10 Ibid.; translation altered.
11 Locke, *An Essay Concerning Human Understanding*, II.viii.16. (Italics in the original.)

Locke takes it to be obvious that burning (or pain) does *not* reside in fire; and he argues, by analogy, that the sensation of warmth is not in the fire either. This small argument is part of a larger argument toward the distinction between primary and secondary qualities. That distinction (allegedly) goes back to Demokritos and was consolidated in the early modern period by Galileo; but it is Robert Boyle's jargon that is popularized by Locke.[12] Here is Locke's definition of secondary (or "sensible") qualities: "Such *qualities*, which in truth are nothing in the objects themselves, but powers to produce various sensations in us by their *primary qualities*, *i.e.* by the bulk, figure, texture, and motion of their insensible parts, as colors, sounds, tastes, *&c.*"[13]

One might articulate the distinction in this way: there are objective, mind-independent properties, and then there are subjective, mind-dependent ones. Primary qualities – like bare extension – really reside in the object; but secondary qualities – like pain or colour – are effects of the object upon our sense organs and nervous system. The real world, fully analysed, is not the one that is phenomenologically present. It is, rather, colourless, soundless, tasteless, and so forth.[14] With McDowell, let us call this metaphysics "neo-Humean naturalism": the theory that the world is reducible to a collection of scientifically describable and value-free facts. According to McDowell, modern science "has given us a disenchanted conception of the natural world. A proper appreciation of science makes it impossible to retain, except perhaps in some symbolic guise, the common mediaeval conception of nature as filled with meaning, like a book containing messages and lessons for us."[15]

And yet Weil is working explicitly with a version of this allegedly obsolete conception: "The world is a text," she writes, "containing several meanings."[16] Elaborating her central metaphor, she observes: "What is remarkable is that we are not given sensations and meanings" – that is, we are not given two separate things, sensations on the one hand and meanings on the other – "we are given only what we read; we do not

12 Cf. Demokritos, DK 68B9; and Locke, *Essay*, II.viii.

13 Locke, *Essay*, II.viii.10. (Italics in the original.)

14 Cf. Descartes, *Principles of Philosophy*, §IV, art. 198.

15 McDowell, "Two Sorts of Naturalism," §5 (p. 174). Cf. Weber, "Science as a Vocation," 13.

16 Weil, *Notebooks*, I.23 / OC, VI.1.295. Cf. Allen, "The concept of reading and 'The Book of Nature.'"

see the letters."[17] Meaning is not *added* to sensations; on the contrary, sensations are *immediately meaningful* (they are "replete with meaning");[18] they do not *intervene* between the reader and what is read. Weil writes, "The blind man's stick, an example introduced by Descartes, provides an image analogous to that of reading. Everyone can have the conviction in using a pen that their sense of touch is conveyed into the pen's nib. If a flaw in the paper interferes with the pen, this resistance to the pen is given *immediately*, and the sensations in our fingers, in our hand, through which we read it, do not even appear."[19] Again, what is important is that the paper's flaw is presented to us immediately: the pen does not intervene between the flaw and the writer. Rather, the pen, becoming transparent, serves *to extend* the sense of touch. In Weil's terminology, sensation is perhaps a μεταξύ (*metaxu*) between meaning and reader: a medium that is the condition of direct contact. Consider her example: "Two prisoners whose cells adjoin communicate with each other by knocking on the wall. The wall is the thing which separates them but it is also their means of communication."[20]

Nor is reading (in the broad or metaphorical sense) the same as *interpreting* an appearance. Weil challenges an analytic epistemology in which our "cognitive" and "non-cognitive" equipment are imagined to make separate contributions that are added together in experience and can be separated again by analysis. She protests: "There is not an appearance and an interpretation … If I hate someone, there is not him on one side, my hatred on the other; when he approaches me something hateful approaches me."[21] The epistemology that Weil is defending is a gestalt epistemology.[22] Unlike the constructions of an analytic epistemology, gestalts are integrated wholes that are different from the sums

17 Weil, "Essay on the Notion of Reading," 298 / 14.

18 The phrase is from Zwicky, *Lyric Philosophy*, L241.

19 Weil, "Essay on the Notion of Reading," 298 / 14–15; emphasis added. Cf. Descartes, *Optics*, AT VI.84.

20 Weil, "Metaxu," *Gravity and Grace*, 145 / 164.

21 Weil, "Essay on the Notion of Reading," 299 / 15. Cf. Zwicky, *Lyric Philosophy*, L245.

22 Cf. Zwicky: "what Weil terms 'les significations', Max Wertheimer calls *Gestalten*" ("What Is Ineffable?," §1 [p. 200 / AL, 242]). Weil herself explicitly references gestalt psychology in connection with her theory of embodied reflexes (*Lectures on Philosophy*, 30–3).

of their parts.[23] Facial recognition is a good example of how we apprehend gestalts. For Weil, meaning "is to the appearances what a sentence is to the letters."[24] And yet the letters dissolve in the solvent of a sentence. It is for this reason that proofreading is difficult: "because more often than not while reading one sees the letters which the typographers have omitted as much as those they included; one has to force oneself to read a different meaning, not that of the words or sentences, but that of the letters of the alphabet."[25] Similarly, appearances are always already permeated with meaning. The readable unit is not the sense-datum, but the gestalt. What is intriguing about the analogy is that reading never ceases. Weil's proofreader switches from one reading to another, from reading at the sentential level to reading at the level of letters. Similarly, one might switch from reading meaning to reading "brute" sensations: but it is illicit to pretend that the second reading is somehow neutral or meaning-free.

§5.2. For twenty-first-century anglophone philosophers, this view must seem piteously naïve. Following Hume, we are accustomed to distinguishing between facts and values. If we find some fact meaningful or valuable, that is to be explained by the contribution made to perception by our non-cognitive equipment. The schism between facts and values is straightforwardly evident in cases of moral disagreement. Consider the following factual statement: during the 2009 garbage strike in Toronto, Lawrence Solomon wrote: "Toronto's unionized work force averages more than $30 per hour in wages and benefits, fully 50% higher than the private sector average. More important than the compensation, however, is the productivity of the workers. Private sector workers handle a staggering two-and-a-half to three times more waste per hour than Toronto's union workers."[26] In other words, non-unionized garbage collectors work harder and earn less than unionized collectors. According to one reading (mine, I confess), if any fact is a reason for the formation of unions, this is it. According to Solomon's reading, on the other hand, this same fact is a reason to fire the striking collectors and to privatize garbage collection.

23 See Zwicky, "The Experience of Meaning," 88.
24 Weil, "Essay on the Notion of Reading," 299 / 15.
25 Ibid., 298 / 14.
26 Solomon, "Bring back garbage's glory days," *National Post*, 25 July 2009.

As J.L. Mackie argued,[27] this disagreement is best explained by the hypothesis that the fact itself is morally blank: it does not make any particular reading compulsory. And recall Mackie's second and stronger argument, his "argument from queerness":[28] "If there were objective values," he writes, "then they would need to be entities or qualities or relations of a very strange sort, utterly different from anything else in the universe. Correspondingly, if we were aware of them, it would have to be by some special faculty of moral perception or intuition, utterly different from our ordinary ways of knowing everything else."[29] A moral fact is supposed to be a very peculiar thing, and to require a very peculiar epistemic faculty for its detection. But Mackie's caricature of the Platonic epistemology is spurious; according to Julia Annas, "The notion of a peculiar intuition is a construct of the empiricist assumption we saw at work in Mackie's interpretation, and does not correspond to anything in Plato."[30] A virtue – such as bravery, et cetera – is a *skill* (or art or expertise), and it is no more strange than other skills such as carpentry or playing the clarinet. Nor are its objects any more peculiar than dovetail joints or musical scales.

Furthermore, it is worth noticing that both Hume and Mackie make an undefended assumption. Famously reflecting on the derivation of *ought* from *is*, Hume writes: "For as this *ought*, or *ought not*, expresses some new relation or affirmation, 'tis necessary that it shou'd be observ'd and explain'd; and at the same time that a reason shou'd be given, for what seems altogether inconceivable, how this new relation can be a deduction from others, which are <u>entirely different</u> from it."[31] Mackie similarly asks: "What is the <u>connection</u> between the natural fact that an action is a piece of deliberate cruelty — say, causing pain just for fun — and the moral fact that it is wrong?"[32] To rephrase: What is the *connection* between a description and an *entirely different* proscription? What is the

---

27 Mackie, *Ethics*, §1.8 (pp. 36–8).

28 Ibid., §1.9 (pp. 38–42). (The argument requires either a rechristening or a critique by queer theory.)

29 Ibid., §1.9 (p. 38).

30 Annas, "Moral Knowledge as Practical Knowledge," 243. Of the three assumptions identified by Annas, the crucial one is that "our epistemological access to values is 'utterly different from our ordinary ways of knowing everything else'" (ibid., 238).

31 Hume, *Treatise*, III.I.§I.¶27; underlining added.

32 Mackie, *Ethics*, §1.9 (p. 41); underlining added.

connection between the "natural fact" and the *utterly different* "moral fact"? This ostensible coordination problem is an invention of moral theory. Mackie's example is self-undermining: there is no inferential connection between the "natural fact" and the "moral fact" because they are aspects of the same fact. If we are puzzled that an instance of deliberate cruelty is wrong, then we have not yet understood how these concepts are internally related. That is, we are not hard-boiled realists: we are instead suffering from a kind of illiteracy. If we follow Weil, then Mackie's thesis is backward. It is not value or meaning which is peculiar; on the contrary, it is the allegedly value-free fact that is "utterly different" from anything else in the universe.

In a couple of essays, McDowell confronts Mackie's thesis directly. McDowell argues against Mackie and against projectivism (the thesis that values are subjective and projected onto facts); and he draws an analogy between secondary qualities and ethical or aesthetic values. Recall Locke's theoretical framework: primary qualities really reside in objects, while secondary qualities are effects of those objects on our sense organs, and so on. In his discussion of Locke, Mackie writes: "The principle of this primary/secondary distinction is that the ideas of primary qualities resemble the grounds of the powers to produce them while the ideas of secondary qualities do not." And Mackie maintains that there is "a systematic error in our ordinary thinking": "we ascribe colours as we see them, tastes as we taste them, and so on to material things, in effect … we mistake secondary qualities for primary ones."[33] When we purport to discover objective values out there, in the world, we wrongly treat secondary qualities as if they were primary. The phenomenology of secondary qualities is mind-*in*dependent (that is, it feels as if we are *finding* something); but the metaphysics is mind-dependent: what we seem to find has in fact been *projected* by us.

McDowell's main charge is that Mackie illicitly conflates a couple of distinctions that should be kept apart. Let us distinguish between two senses of objectivity and two corresponding senses of subjectivity. On the one hand, something is *objective in the first sense* (o1) when it subsists independently of any perceiver, and *subjective in the first sense* (s1) when it is essentially phenomenal. On the other hand, something is *objective in the second sense* (o2) when it is part of "the fabric of the world," and

33 Mackie, *Problems from Locke*, §I.1 (pp. 15–16).

subjective in the second sense (s2) when it is projected onto that fabric. For an example of elision between the two senses of subjectivity, it is instructive to consult Galileo. Here he is, talking about subjectivity in the second sense (s2): "But just because we have given special names to these [secondary] qualities [these tastes, odors, colors, etc.], different from the names we have given to the primary and real properties, we are tempted into believing that the former really and truly exist as well as the latter." And here he is, talking about subjectivity in the first sense (s1): "And I again judge that heat is altogether subjective, so that if the living, sensitive body is removed, what we call heat would be nothing but a simple word."[34] To say (s1) that something is *essentially phenomenal* – that is, to say that it is disposed to be perceived only by a "living, sensitive body" – is not obviously equivalent to saying (o2) that it is an *unreal projection*. McDowell, for his part, wants to say that something can be subjective in the first sense (s1) while being objective in the second sense (o2); in other words, that something can be essentially phenomenal while nevertheless belonging, objectively, to the fabric of the world.

The analogy between values and secondary qualities is meant to do this work. McDowell defines a secondary property as "a property the ascription of which to an object is not adequately understood except as true, if it is true, in virtue of the object's disposition to present a certain sort of perceptual appearance; specifically, an appearance characterizable by using a word for the property itself to say how the object perceptually appears."[35] Like redness, or amusingness, or danger,[36] value is not understandable except in terms of how it would appear to a perceiving agent. Consider McDowell's example of danger or the fearful. The concept of the fearful is not understandable independently of the experience of fear; but that experience is best explained not as the result of an erroneous projection of fearfulness, but as a *response* to some aspect of the world: "we make sense of fear," McDowell claims, "by seeing it as a response to objects that *merit* such a response ... For an object to merit fear just is for it to be fearful."[37]

34 Galileo, *Assayer*, 9a and 11a.

35 McDowell, "Values and Secondary Qualities," §3 (p. 133).

36 McDowell, "Aesthetic Value," §2 (pp. 113–17), and "Values and Secondary Qualities," §3 (pp. 133–4), §4 (pp. 143–4).

37 McDowell, "Values and Secondary Qualities," §4 (p. 144).

Weil agrees: "It's not correct to say that we believe ourselves to be in danger because we are afraid; on the contrary, we are afraid due to the presence of danger; the danger is what frightens us; but danger is something I read."[38] Perhaps, if we subtracted from the world every being capable of feeling fear, then nothing would be fearful (in both senses). But that seems like an unduly ruthless test for objectivity. McDowell's argument is condensed into one sentence: "Values are not brutely there—not there independently of our sensibility—any more than colours are; though, as with colours, this does not prevent us from supposing that they are there independently of any particular apparent experience of them."[39]

§5.3. Now let us ask: is McDowell's analogy a good analogy? Are values *like* secondary qualities? There are historical reasons for McDowell's argument: Mackie wrote a monograph on Locke, and McDowell is turning Mackie's materials against him. But Weil's analogy is more coherent than McDowell's; and it is more coherent for the same reason that makes it seem naïve. In constructing his internal critique, McDowell concedes to Mackie's and Locke's dualism: there are primary qualities and there are secondary qualities, and in principle they can be pried apart. Primary qualities are "brutely there," while secondary qualities are essentially phenomenal. Even if we accept that a thing's phenomenal character does not prevent it from being objective, we nevertheless inherit the coordination problem: how, exactly, are these categorically different qualities related to each other? How can we be sure that secondary qualities track primary ones? The metaphysics remains two-tiered. And the skeptic can always wedge his crowbar into the gap. Weil's approach, by contrast, is non-dualistic. When she analogizes meaning to heat, she does not place it in a category separate from the substantial body to which qualities supposedly attach; on the contrary, meaning, heat, pain, and so forth are on the same ontological plane as bodies.

— "Hold on a second! You're claiming that Weil's approach is better than McDowell's because it's more naïve than his. But how is that an advantage? Suppose that she does avoid the skeptical attack on value and meaning, as you claim; her victory comes at the cost of adopting

38 Weil, "Essay on the Notion of Reading," 300 / 16.
39 McDowell, "Values and Secondary Qualities," §5 (p. 146).

an enchanted pre-modern metaphysics. Who can take that tactic seriously? At least McDowell's attempt to preserve the objectivity of value takes place within a worldview that is conscious of the advent of modern science! Even though it isn't guarded by cherubim and a flaming sword, we can't go back to the garden."[40] — To say that Weil's approach is naïve is not to say that it is shallow or immature. If we trace the etymology of the word "naïve," we find that it derives from Latin *nativus*: native, natural. Weil's approach is naïve in the sense that it accepts what is naturally afforded to the perceiving animal. There need not be anything unnatural in the hypothesis that value can be directly perceived. It has been defended by James J. Gibson in his ecological approach to visual perception (which is explicitly indebted to gestalt psychology). What Gibson calls an "affordance" is what an animal reads: "The *affordances* of the environment are what it *offers* the animal, what it *provides* or *furnishes*, either for good or ill."[41]

Here is an example: Water "affords drinking. Being fluid, it affords pouring from a container. Being a solvent, it affords washing and bathing." And another example: "An elongated object of moderate size and weight affords wielding. If used to hit or strike, it is a *club* or *hammer*. If used by a chimpanzee behind bars to pull in a banana beyond its reach, it is a sort of *rake*. In either case, it is an extension of the arm."[42] We might think that a tool is a very different kind of thing from a natural substance such as water, but on this point Gibson follows Aristotle: "It is a mistake to separate the natural from the artificial as if there were two environments; artifacts have to be manufactured from natural substances. It is also a mistake to separate the cultural environment from the natural environment, as if there were a world of mental products distinct from the world of material products. There is only one world, however diverse, and all animals live in it."[43]

---

40 For a version of this objection, thanks to Carolyn Richardson. Chenavier might reply: "It is not a question of 're-enchanting' the world by a return to a pre-modern unification or to an artisanal mode of production" (*Simone Weil: Attention to the Real*, 77). He suggests that rooted human cultures afford a way of coming into contact with meaning in the world. In the main text above, we pursue a different lead.

41 Gibson, "The Theory of Affordances," 127.

42 Ibid., 131 and 133.

43 Ibid., 130. Cf. Aristotle, *Physics*, II.1.

An affordance does fit the needs of animals, but it is not mind-dependent: "An affordance is not bestowed upon an object by a need of an observer and his act of perceiving it. The object offers what it does because it is what it is."[44] Like Weil's approach, Gibson's is resolutely non-dualistic, and for this reason it circumvents the coordination problem: "The theory of affordances is a radical departure from existing theories of value and meaning. It begins with a new definition of what value and meaning *are*. The perceiving of an affordance is not a process of perceiving a value-free physical object to which meaning is somehow added in a way that no one has been able to agree upon; it is a process of perceiving a value-rich ecological object."[45] Instead of speculating that there is some machinery whirring backstage, combining facts with values, sensations with concepts, Weil and Gibson accept the integrity of the world as it appears to living animals.

Gibson does not deny that some perceptions are not veridical. But like Weil, he insists that clear perceiving is a learnable art: "If the affordances of a thing are perceived correctly, we say that it looks like what it *is*. But we must, of course, *learn* to see what things really are—for example, that the innocent-looking leaf is really a nettle or that the helpful-sounding politician is really a demagogue. And this can be very difficult."[46] In connection with this idea that it can be difficult to discriminate between an accurate perception and an inaccurate one, Weil identifies two problems for her account of reading: "the problem of inquiring into what criterion allows us to make a decision" about whether one reading is better than another, and "what technique enables us to pass from one reading to another."[47] Misled by some of what they find on the internet, undergraduates sometimes assume that Weil is a poststructuralist about meaning – but nothing could be further from the truth. Weil is a *realist*, but her realism is an achieved second literacy (as we shall see). Her first problem above – of asking whether one reading is better than another – may be addressed by contemplating the particular cases that she offers.

Her example of the two mothers with their respective letters (which we studied in Section 4.5) illustrates a contrast between success and

44 Gibson, "The Theory of Affordances," 139.
45 Ibid., 140.
46 Ibid., 142.
47 Weil, "Essay on the Notion of Reading," 302–3 / 19.

failure at reading. As a matter of objective fact, the meaning of the first letter is that first woman's son is dead, and the meaning of the second letter is that the second woman's son is dead. The point of the example is *not* that each woman interprets her letter "subjectively." The point is that the second woman *fails* to perceive the objectively real meaning of her letter, and the reason is that she is illiterate. Since reading the letters is an analogy for reading appearances, the more general point is that perceiving some real meanings requires training.

Another of Weil's examples illustrates the contrast between worse and better readings: "For the sailor, the experienced captain, whose ship has in a sense become like an extension of his body, the ship is a tool for reading the storm, and he reads it quite differently than the passenger. Where the passenger reads chaos, unlimited danger, fear, the captain reads necessities, limited dangers, the means of escape from the storm, a duty to act courageously and honourably."[48] The passenger and the captain perceive different aspects of the same storm; the passenger reads the storm as dangerous, while the captain reads it as navigable. It does not follow that meaning is "subjective." The captain has more expertise – is more literate – with storms than the passenger. For the inexperienced passenger, the storm really is dangerous, and so he is afraid; for the captain, it really is navigable, and so she is calm.[49] It is for this reason that we want the captain, and not the passenger, to steer the ship. Similarly, we want our political leaders to be familiar with climate science.

Turning to Weil's second problem, let us ask, what technique will enable us to transition from worse to better readings? Her response, sketched in the "Essay on Reading" and elaborated in her lectures and notebooks, is Aristotelian. One repeatedly practises a given reading until it becomes internal to one's character. We might distinguish between *first* and *second literacy*: what Weil calls "congenital" and "conditioned" reflexes, or "spontaneous language" and "language proper."[50] Examples of first literacy include salivating at the appearance of food, crumpling over a punch to the stomach, flinching from having touched

48 Ibid., 301–2 / 18.

49 Aristotle's point about the "intermediate relatively to us" is relevant here (*Nicomachean Ethics*, II.6.1106a28).

50 Weil, *Lectures on Philosophy*, 30–1, 65 / 21–2, 66. Cf. Winch, *Simone Weil: "The Just Balance,"* 34–5.

a hot stove. The complex set of such gestures "is something *animal* (and so human too). It is what conveys affections. It is natural in the sense that it is made up of natural reactions of muscles, glands and lungs."[51] Second literacy is a refinement of first literacy,[52] and it is only because the world is readable by the body at the first level that we are able to develop the second. The body is radically naïve: it does not have any doubt about what happens to it. Nor does it discriminate between primary and secondary qualities. It responds directly, and in a way that orders experience.

"Our *perception* of the external world," says Weil, "constitutes the essential relation between us and what is outside us, a relation which consists in a *reaction*, a reflex. The elementary perception of nature is a sort of dance; this dance is the source of our perceiving."[53] Learning how to dance – becoming more fully literate – is a process of repeating a set of reflexes until they become autonomic. We shape the meaning of our perceptions, and hence our responses to them, not instantaneously but through a long apprenticeship in which "the body always participates."[54] (We return to the metaphor of the dance and its epistemological implications in Section 8.)

§5.4. In an important draft of an essay, which her editors have called «Notes sur le caractère,» Weil tells an Aristotelian story about the nature and formation of character.[55] An agent reads the meaning of given facts according to her character. "The notion of character," Weil writes, "belongs to a category of notions which one can never grasp nor define and yet which one cannot do without."[56] According to her, character is analogous to a literary style or a musical theme: like them, it is "an invariant that is found through varied manifestations."[57] In the case of character, these manifestations include "acts, gestures,

51 Weil, *Lectures on Philosophy*, 65 / 66.

52 Cf. Wittgenstein, "Cause and Effect: Intuitive Awareness," 381–3.

53 Weil, *Lectures on Philosophy*, 52 / 50, but trans. Winch, *Simone Weil: "The Just Balance,"* 41.

54 Weil, *Notebooks*, I.23 / *OC*, VI.1.295.

55 Weil, «Notes sur le caractère,» *Œuvres complètes*, tome IV, vol. 1, 80–9, 529–31. The translation is mine. An excerpt of Weil's essay is translated by Eric O. Springsted: "Notes on the Concept of Character," *Late Philosophical Writings*, 97–102.

56 Weil, «Notes sur le caractère,» 477.

57 Ibid., 87.

attitudes, words." Despite the difficulty of defining this invariant, it is indispensable because "one cannot pose a moral problem without putting the notion of character at the centre." And the moral problem, according to Weil, is "the problem of developing character."[58]

In what follows, we shall reflect on Weil's theory of character and set it beside some more recent theories in anglophone meta-ethics. As we saw above, for Weil, the development of character is the actualization of a second nature (or second literacy), and such actualization occurs through a process of habituation. The body plays a central role in this process. When confronted with a particular set of circumstances, an agent with an appropriately formed character is freed from deliberating, in a way that is analogous to the freedom of the expert musician or athlete. The practising apprentice must deliberate before acting; but the expert responds spontaneously. What the expert perceives is really there, but training is needed to perceive it. Accordingly, there is more than one kind of story that can be told to explain action: and the story that we tell about the apprentice's action, if misapplied to the action of the expert, will distort our understanding of that action.

In addressing the problem of developing character, Weil proposes three hypotheses. Her first hypothesis concerns the interaction of circumstances and character in the determination of action. She shares with Aristotle the view that action follows from character; furthermore, she believes that our ethical agency is exercised at a point upstream from the moment in which we act. An action is a function of an invariant and a variable (character and circumstances):

1° The reaction of a human being with regard to determinate circumstances at a determinate instant depends on circumstances and character; the possibility of choice is illusory. When we have to choose, the choice is already made.[59]

This hypothesis is echoed in the following remarks from Weil's notebooks:

---

58 Ibid., 83.
59 Ibid., 88.

Illusory choice. When we think that we have the choice, it is because we are unconscious, compassed about by illusion, and we are then but toys. We cease to be toys when we lift ourselves above illusion right up to necessity, but then there is no longer any choice; a certain action is imposed by the situation itself, clearly perceived.[60]

Recall Murdoch's claim from Section 3.5: "If I attend properly I will have no choices and this is the ultimate condition to be aimed at."[61] This picture sounds deterministic, and one might wonder where in it there is conceptual space for the vital notion of responsibility. While Weil is not insensitive to the need for such a notion, she distinguishes herself from her existentialist contemporaries. According to her account, responsibility or agency is not exercised in the moment of action; as Weil says, in that moment, the choice is "already made." It is already made in this sense: character is not alterable instantaneously, nor can we always instantaneously extricate ourselves from the circumstances in which we find or place ourselves. And yet action is a function of character and circumstances.

Nevertheless, we are not powerless. Character is invariant across a selected set of actions – it is both the limit and the condition of possibility of those actions – but it is not invari*able*. Indeed, the essay's key question is: how, exactly, does one modify one's character? "Our own power (i.e. the power of that which is free in us) to modify our character is indirect," claims Weil, "exactly as our power over matter, defined by work, is indirect."[62] But what does she mean in calling this exercise of power *indirect?* A passage from her "Essay on the Notion of Reading" connects this conception of work with her notion of reading. Recall that, for Weil, "reading" is a term of art: to read a fact is to perceive its meaning. She writes: "Perhaps I also possess a power to change the meanings which I read in appearances and which impose themselves on me; but this power too is limited, indirect and exercised through work. Work in the ordinary sense of the term is one example of it,

60 Weil, *Notebooks*, I.57 / *OC*, VI.1.335–6.
61 Murdoch, "The Idea of Perfection," 40.
62 Weil, «Notes sur le caractère,» 84.

because every tool is a blind man's stick, an instrument for reading, and every apprenticeship is learning to read in a certain way."[63]

The power is indirect in two senses: (1) confronted with a particular lump of matter, the apprentice craftsperson cannot just choose, in that moment, to transform that matter into whatever product she might wish. Similarly with the ethical agent: confronted with a particular set of circumstances, the agent cannot just choose, in that moment, to read these circumstances however she might wish. But in both cases, they can, in the present, prepare themselves for future confrontations. Furthermore, (2) both the apprentice craftsperson and the ethical agent prepare themselves by modifying the medium through which they read: the apprentice craftsperson repeatedly uses her tool (even when this tool is her own hand) until it becomes a transparent extension of herself, while the ethical agent repeatedly practises virtue in circumstances that will encourage the right sort of character.

The usefulness of circumstances in the training of the apprentice is intimated in Weil's second hypothesis:

2° Exterior circumstances continually exert an action more or less modifying on character — our past actions being included among these circumstances. This [modifying] action is now passing, now durable.[64]

In this view of action, circumstances play a dual role: they both modify character and interact with character to determine action. The "fragility" of character with regard to circumstances is ineradicable, according to Weil. She cites examples of Corneille's plays to illustrate the fantastical and vain effort to reject this fragility: "In the most extreme situations, in misery, exile, captivity, before death, etc., his personages still conserve their character."[65] If we are proud of our character, we want to believe that it is "unshakeable,"[66] immune to circumstances; at the same time, we want to believe that we can "in a certain measure voluntarily transform our own character."[67] But we are doubly mistaken. Character is subject to natural laws as rigorous and merciless as those which govern

---

63 Weil, "Essay on the Notion of Reading," 301 / 17–18.
64 Weil, «Notes sur le caractère,» 88.
65 Ibid., 529.
66 Ibid., 86.
67 Ibid., 88.

matter, and no mere act of will can shield it from unfavourable circumstances. However, the pliability of character and the muscle of circumstances can be harnessed; and there is a sense in which we can "voluntarily" transform our character – but only indirectly.

If we wish to modify our character, to "mould it and surpass it in the direction of a higher value,"[68] then we must identify the appropriate circumstances and seek out opportunities for placing ourselves in them. This potential is the second of two powers that Weil identifies in her third hypothesis:

3° Our own power ... over character ... is exercised in part by the orientation we give to our attention in moments of our life apparently indifferent and insignificant, moments which apparently do not engage us, when circumstances do not solicit any choice from us. On the other hand [our power is exercised] by the possibility we have of voluntarily placing ourselves in this or that set of circumstances which then act from outside to modify our character.[69]

Concerning the first power, the power of orienting our attention, Weil alludes to "a regime of attention which renders a human being impenetrable to certain things, very penetrable to others."[70] Character is *continuously* modified by circumstances, including during the intervals when we are not confronted with "moral" dilemmas. As Diogenes Laertios reports in an apocryphal story: "Plato once saw someone playing at dice and rebuked him. And, upon his protesting that he played for a trifle only, 'But the habit,' rejoined Plato, 'is not a trifle.'"[71] And Aristotle tells us that character comes from habit.[72] Hence, the way we orient our attention is never neutral: the orientation of our attention now, while standing in a queue for the theatre, will partly determine what orientation is available to us later, when we are called upon to help someone in need. (It is in this sense that our own past actions are included in the exterior circumstances which modify character.) Action is not the sudden effect of a free choice; instead, a particular action

68 Ibid., 86.
69 Ibid., 88.
70 Ibid., 83.
71 Diogenes Laertios, *Lives of Eminent Philosophers*, III.38.
72 Aristotle, *Nicomachean Ethics*, II.1.1103a17.

follows from a particular way of reading. Character is a way of reading circumstances which is developed by a gradual process. And this process consists in practising repeatedly in particular circumstances.

§5.5. Another way of understanding Weil's notion of character is to connect it with her notion of habit. This notion is discussed in her notebooks and in a fragment of an essay which her editors have called «L'habitude.»[73] In her notebooks, she writes:

Habit, second nature: better than first nature. …

What happens in the case of those who have acquired the necessary habit, work well, and are not of a high spiritual level?

They have been *trained*. Training, in the case of animals, only produces conditional reflexes (although, perhaps …); in man's case it can produce habits. What takes place then in the soul?

Taoists; and the louse. A certain quality of attention is linked with effective movements, without effort or desire.[74]

In referring to "Taoists; and the louse," Weil is referring to the instructions for becoming an archer that we read in Section 2.1. The archer's skill is a result of a long discipline of attending: for five years, she stares at the louse, until she can see its heart. Her training consists in doing the very thing – attending – that will be required of her when she acts expertly. And the action does not depend on effort or desire: attending itself is enough.

Weil's notion of second nature is not dissimilar to McDowell's; indeed, their shared ancestor is the Aristotelian notion. McDowell's account of second nature is designed to make sense of "virtue's demands on reason" without constructing a foundationalist justification for those demands. In "Two Sorts of Naturalism," he asks us to imagine a rational wolf who momentarily steps back from her nature and asks, reflectively, "What

73 Weil, «L'habitude,» *Œuvres complètes*, tome I, 275–7.

74 Weil, *Notebooks*, I.170 / *OC*, VI.2.237–8. Both Weil and McDowell seem to think of second nature as a specifically anthropocentric achievement (cf. McDowell, "Rational and Other Animals," *Mind and World*, §VI [pp. 108–26]); although notice that Weil hesitates. In my view, they are wrong; but I do not argue the case here.

should I do?"[75] Suppose that the virtuous answer is: act cooperatively with your fellows in the pack. It is vain to fantasize that this answer could be presented in such a way that it would be compulsory for someone who did not already find herself living a virtuous form of life. Neither the dictates of pure reason nor general facts about the nature of wolves can provide this answer with a foundation. As part of a larger argument (which doesn't concern us here), McDowell sketches a dilemma, which he then endeavours to dissolve: on the one hand, there is Kantian transcendental supernaturalism;[76] on the other, there is neo-Humean naturalism. This dilemma is a version of the one invoked by Mackie: spooked by the prospect of intrinsically normative facts that make an immediate and motivating appeal to reason (the first horn of the dilemma), the moral theorist recoils into a "disenchanted" picture of nature, a picture in which the mind projects meaning onto a meaningless world (the second horn).[77] But, according to McDowell, these extremes do not exhaust the options.

A third possibility would be to enlarge our sense of what we countenance as "natural." Suppose, for instance, that nature is not reducible to the totality of facts describable by positivist science; but that nature includes things that are there anyway, independent of any perceiver, but are perceptible only by a certain faculty in its developed state. Very broadly, we might call that developed state "phronesis." McDowell asks us to reflect on "the concept of second nature, which is all but explicit in Aristotle's account of the acquisition of virtue of character."[78] What Aristotle himself says is: "Neither by nature, then, nor contrary to nature do the virtues arise in us; rather we are adapted by nature to receive them, and are made perfect by habit."[79] There is nothing occult about this notion of actualizing a naturally occurring potentiality. "Virtue of character properly so called," writes McDowell, "includes a specifically shaped state of the practical intellect: 'practical wisdom', in the standard English translation. This is a responsiveness to some of the demands of reason ... The picture is that ethics involves requirements of reason

---

75 McDowell "Two Sorts of Naturalism"; cf. McDowell, "Reason and Nature," *Mind and World*, §IV.7 (pp. 78–86).

76 What McDowell also calls "rampant platonism" (*Mind and World*, §IV.6 [p. 77]).

77 Cf. McDowell, "Two Sorts of Naturalism," §7 (p. 179).

78 Ibid., §8 (p. 184); cf. McDowell, *Mind and World*, §IV.7 (p. 84).

79 Aristotle, *Nicomachean Ethics*, II.1.1103a23–6.

that are there whether we know it or not, and our eyes are opened to them by the acquisition of 'practical wisdom'."[80]

McDowell's metaphor is not quite felicitous: Aristotle claims that sensing – here, seeing – is disanalogous to virtue; while both are naturally occurring, virtue, unlike sight, is acquired through activity.[81] For a closer analogy, consider music appreciation: the sonata form is really there, but training is needed to hear it. (Or, if the artificiality of the sonata form is problematic, consider specific patterns of bird song or the signature whistles of dolphins.) Nor is there anything occult about the relevant faculty – namely, appreciative listening – which makes use of naturally occurring organs (the ear and brain). Experts perceive things that apprentices don't; and the fact that expertise is an intelligible concept, that we recognize the distinction between expert and apprentice, suggests that we – unlike some meta-ethical theorists – are not ordinarily alarmed by the idea of actualized second-natural perception. The important point, for our purposes, is that there are some real things which, while not obvious to an untrained eye or ear, are nevertheless perceivable after a process of training or habituation.

Both Aristotle's and McDowell's accounts of the development of second nature remain abstract. What is unique to Weil's thinking is her account of the role of the body in habituation. "The essential character of habit," she writes, "is liberty of soul regarding the parts of the body."[82] This liberty consists in parts of the body becoming transparent to the world, and the agent becoming unselfconscious. One could say that the agent develops a repertoire of reflexive gestures. She is then able to act – her body is able to move – spontaneously, without the intervention of a rational decision procedure. "The effect of habit," Weil claims, "is that true attention is rendered possible."

Attention is not the state of the bird fascinated by the snake or the apprentice cyclist fascinated by the obstacle. That is rather the contrary of attention. Attention is a manner of being active, a grip found by thought on things. It's the good cyclist who pays attention. He does not think of the movements of his arms that hold the handlebars, of his bust which leans; he thinks of the

80 McDowell, *Mind and World*, §IV.7 (p. 79); cf. McDowell, "Two Sorts of Naturalism," §8 (p. 185).

81 Cf. Aristotle, *Nicomachean Ethics*, II.1.1103a26–32.

82 Weil, «L'habitude,» 275.

actions possible by means of these instruments. He is conscious of his own limbs exactly like the blind man who feels with his stick. Similarly the reaper does not take detailed notice of the gestures that he makes to reap; he takes possession of the plain.[83]

Attention is not *fascination*, which is a state of passivity and fixation in relation to its object; attention, by contrast, is active and indifferent (non-attached) to its focus.

The apprentice does not have liberty regarding the parts of his body: he "acts as if the will had to push each muscle separately."[84] Consequently, the apprentice is doubly distracted: by the object of his fascination, and by the individual parts of his body; and he goes straight toward the obstacle that he wants to avoid. The expert's attention, on the other hand, is extended through the transparent medium of her body to the focus; she perceives the obstacle and steers clear.[85] It is similar with the expert musician: "When one sight-reads the piano, one is not (if one is skilful) more disposed to this note than to that one; but the nude note on paper immediately transforms itself, through the intermediary of the body rendered fluid, into note produced."[86] According to this reconception of action, the agent is not a doer but a medium through which the circumstances, clearly perceived, express themselves in action.

§5.6. The ideal interaction of circumstance and character is reflected in these remarks from Weil's notebooks:

The true difficulty, not to do what is good when one has seen it, but to see it so intensely that the thought passes into action, as when one reads a piece of music, and the notes which enter through the eyes leave as sound at the tips of one's fingers—as when one sees a Rugby football, and there it is in one's arms.[87]

83 Ibid.

84 Ibid., 276.

85 Cf. Janiaud, *Simone Weil: L'attention et l'action*, 18–22. For Janiaud's book, thanks to Stefano Mingarelli.

86 Weil, «L'habitude,» 276.

87 Weil, *Notebooks*, I.56 / *oc*, VI.1.334; translation altered. Cf. Zwicky, "Conversation," *Chamber Music*, 69.

In these remarks, Weil challenges and revises our conventional sense
of the role of choice in action. She decouples action from an effort of
will and fuses it with attending. In an image reminiscent of the one we
encountered in Section 3.5, she also imagines the agent as a medium:
the notes enter the eyes and emerge from the fingers as music; the fact
enters perception and emerges as action. One way of thinking about
what Weil is doing here is to see an analogy with an argument made by
Arthur Collins and Jonathan Dancy.[88] Briefly, Dancy, following Collins,
seeks to intervene in a story that is told about action, and to excise a
step. This step, he suggests, might feel mandatory, but properly understood, it renders action incoherent. According to "the three-part story,"
which he disputes, the human mind is a functional mechanism; it is the
intermediate step which takes facts as inputs and produces actions as
outputs. But the story is more elegant and more coherent when we omit
this step.

According to the three-part story, an explanation that does not cite
a mental state must be susceptible to psychologizing restatement: properly analysed, it will reveal the intermediate step. The restatement is
motivated by the possibility of different truth-values for these two putative explanations of action: if an agent is asked why he is doing some
action, he might respond: (1) "Because p," or (2) "Because I believe
that p." According to this line of thinking, even when it is not the case
that p (that is, when p is false), the second explanation can continue to
be true (in such a case, the agent's belief would not correspond to what
is the case, but it would be true that he had that belief);[89] and the second
explanation can continue to do explanatory work. The first explanation,
(1) "Because p," must be shorthand: fully analysed, the real explanation
is (2), "Because I believe that p."[90] What is needed to explain action are
mental events, not facts. As Collins writes, "Strictly speaking, reason-
giving explanations adduce psychological items such as beliefs and
desires in explaining actions."[91] (Such a criterion is arguably applicable
both to "non-cognitive" and "cognitive" theories.) Objective circumstances or facts can only play a role in the motivation or explanation of

---

88 See Collins, "The Psychological Reality of Reasons"; and Dancy, *Practical
Reality*, §§5–6 (pp. 98–137).

89 Cf. Dancy, *Practical Reality*, §5.2 (p. 110) and §6.3 (p. 131).

90 Cf. ibid., §5.2 (pp. 102–3).

91 Collins, "The Psychological Reality of Reasons," 109.

action if they are mediated by a "cognitive link";[92] the resulting complicated structure is what Dancy calls "the three-part story":[93]

The two stages in the three-part story may be understood as two parts of a complex explanation. First there is the 'proximal' explanation of the action, given by specifying the psychological state of the agent. Then there is the 'distal' explanation of the action, given by specifying what is responsible for the agent getting into that state. The distal explanation of the action is the proximal explanation of the psychological state.[94]

There is an analogy between this three-part story and a three-part story that Wayne Wu tells about attention. Like Christopher Mole's theory of attention, Wu's theory is anti-reductionist (although unlike Mole, Wu believes that attention is a process).[95] In his view, attention is the process of selecting for action. This selection solves what Wu calls the "Many-Many Problem": "the challenge of sifting through many 'inputs' and many potential 'outputs' to generate coherent behavior."[96] The inputs are physical or mental objects, the outputs are potential behaviours; altogether, the many inputs, the many outputs, and the possible links among them constitute a behavioural space. Attention solves the Many-Many Problem by selecting and correlating one input and one output, and thus generating behaviour. For the behaviour to count as intentional action, the correlation must be "regulated by the agent's motivational states."[97] Here is Wu's analytic definition of attention: "For all subjects S, appropriate item (objects, properties, spaces, etc.) X, and time period t:"

(SfA) S's attention to X at t is S's selection of X so as to solve the Many-Many Problem present to S at t—namely, selection of X inherent in S's traversing a specific path in the available behavioral space at t (i.e., at t, S selects X for action).[98]

92 Ibid., 110–11.
93 Cf. Dancy, *Practical Reality*, §5.1 (pp. 98–101).
94 Ibid., §5.2 (p. 109).
95 Wu, "Attention as Selection for Action," 103.
96 Ibid., 98. Cf. Wu, *Attention*, §3.3 (pp. 79–83).
97 Wu, "Attention as Selection for Action," 101.
98 Ibid., 109. Cf. Wu, *Attention*, §3.8 (pp. 95–9).

There are at least two reasons why Wu's theory cannot capture what Weil means by attention. First, Wu theorizes attention as the solution to a problem. But as we have seen, Weil believes that we may be called upon to be attentive in situations in which there is no problem to solve, or in which the problem is insoluble (recall the examples of attending to a work of art, or attending to a distressed caller). And Murdoch has argued that there can be meaningful attending in the absence of behaviour: recall her case of the mother and daughter-in-law, M and D. Wu could reply that attending itself is among the behaviours that can be selected: one may correlate an input with the output of attending-behaviour.[99] But this reply makes Wu's account of attention subject either to regress or to equivocation. Furthermore, McDowell has argued that, in the limiting case, the virtue of attentiveness does not face the Many-Many Problem. When the attentive agent clearly perceives the salient feature of a situation, she does not need to select among many "inputs" and many "outputs." By contrast, an agent who does confront a version of the Many-Many problem, who must weigh alternatives before deciding to select a path through "behavioural space," is at best enkratic.

A second reason that Wu does not capture Weil is that, when Weilian attending does issue in action, it does not do so as an intermediate functional mechanism. It is instead transparent to the fact that motivates the action. To understand this point, let us return to Collins and Dancy's objection to the three-part story. At the limit, according to Dancy, the three-part story is incoherent: "the three-part story is committed to the paradoxical claim that it is impossible to do an action for the reason that makes it right."[100] It is impossible, because what motivate us must be psychological items (beliefs, or pairs of beliefs and desires), while what make an action right or wrong are "not normally psychological states of the agent" but objective circumstances or facts; for example, "What makes my action wrong is that she badly needed help and I just walked away from her."[101]

Collins and Dancy suggest, however, that it is the conventional picture of reason-giving that is wrong. To make his case, Collins draws a distinction between reporting and endorsing beliefs as representations. When an agent asserts, "I believe that *p*," he both reports that he has that

99 Wu, "Attention as Selection for Action," 105.
100 Dancy, *Practical Reality*, §5.2 (p. 105).
101 Ibid., §5.2 (p. 104).

psychological item (that is, the belief that p) in his "belief box," and he endorses it. If this assertion is to explain action, then "the business-end of the assertion is the endorsement"; and what the agent endorses is not the mere existence of the belief but what it represents: that p.[102] In other words, both explanations – "Because p" and "Because I believe that p" – properly understood, are about the same subject matter: not the psychological item "belief," but, rather, the objective circumstances. The second explanation does qualify the assertion that p, "but does not withdraw it in favour of a different assertion." In other words, the explanation "Because I believe that p," no less than the explanation "Because p," makes a commitment to the obtaining of the objective circumstances represented by p.

For our purposes, Collins's crucial point is this:

The perspective of the agent, when rightly interpreted, is not a call for intro-spectible determinants of action. It is a reminder that it is objective circum-stances *as apprehended by the agent* that are relevant. The perspective is not the subject matter. An agent makes statements about the objective circumstanc-es as he understands them. This qualification: 'as he understands them' is not a shift to the mental realm.[103]

We might hear an echo of Gibson's insistence that affordances fit the needs of animals but are real independently of experience: "Note that all these benefits and injuries, these safeties and dangers, these positive and negative affordances are properties of things *taken with reference to an observer* but not properties of the *experiences of the observer*."[104] All representations have some form (they assume some perspective), but that form is not among the represented things (the subject matter). An agent's character is her perspective – her way of reading objective cir-cumstances – but that perspective is not reducible to an inventory of beliefs (or pairs of beliefs and desires). And if we wish to understand the agent's action, we need not peer inside her mind, searching for discrete and idiosyncratic desires and beliefs; we should try to read the facts as she reads them. Thinking about action in this way allows us to restore facts to their pre-theoretical status as reasons.

102 Collins, "The Psychological Reality of Reasons," 116.
103 Ibid., 120.
104 Gibson, "The Theory of Affordances," 137.

Let us make explicit the relevance of Collins and Dancy's argument to Weil's account of character. The three-part story is useful for explaining the behaviour of the apprentice: an agent whose character has not yet formed, who must deliberate, at each moment, about where to place his fingers on the fretboard or about how to respond to someone's need. Such an agent will make mistakes, and we will be able to tell a story, citing his beliefs, that will render those mistakes understandable. The expert whose character is well formed, on the other hand, will be primed to respond to particular situations. When her fellow musician plays a certain set of notes, she responds with an improvised riff. When an acquaintance is under threat, she does not hesitate to provide support. Her action will not be best explained by the three-part story, because her action is not the result of deliberation; it is the result of the interaction between her character and the circumstances. And her character, in turn, is the result of a long process of practice and habituation: the actualization of a second nature or a second literacy. Even that is saying too much. If asked to explain her action, the agent may simply point to the facts that moved her. Our capacity to accept such pointing as explanation will be proportional to our capacity to share her characterological perspective. That is, our understanding of virtuous action, and of the circumstances which motivate it, will be a function of our literacy.

6

Prudence or Phronesis

To be a poet is to have a soul so quick to discern, that no shade of quality escapes it, and so quick to feel, that discernment is but a hand playing with finely-ordered variety on the chords of emotion – a soul in which knowledge passes instantaneously into feeling, and feeling flashes back as a new organ of knowledge.

– George Eliot[1]

§6.1. AS WE HAVE SEEN, Simone Weil and John McDowell both analogize meaning or value to (what early modern philosophers would call) "secondary qualities" such as colour or heat. And for both of them, this analogy is a strategy for avoiding anti-realism. According to Weil, we are always reading the meaning of appearances; and our problem is not how to explain the "projection" of meaning onto allegedly meaning-free facts, but how to transition from a less accurate reading to a more accurate one. Like McDowell, she argues that character is the actualization, through habituation, of a second nature. Second-natural perception or literacy gives us access to meanings that are real but cannot be read by first-natural perception.

What is unique to Weil's thinking on this matter is her account of the role of the body in this process. Once fully trained, the agent's body is a transparent medium through which she reads circumstances – and through which circumstances, clearly perceived, express themselves in action. Weil's psychology is non-dualistic: in its grasp of a sufficient reason in the real world, it integrates thinking and desiring. We can trace Weil's and McDowell's psychologies back to a common ancestor in Aristotle, whose psychology is in turn a revision of Plato's. Perplexingly, there is also a genealogy that seems to trace the dualistic Humean theory to Aristotle. But on closer inspection, it turns out to be a scholastic

---

1 Eliot, *Middlemarch*, II.xxii.202–3.

interpretation of Aristotle. G.E.M. Anscombe, one of the founders of the modern sub-discipline of ethical psychology, is responsible for making an important contribution to this interpretation. So we shall need to set some of her work beside some of his.

Aristotle introduces the concepts of enkrateia and akrasia at the end of the first book of the *Nicomachean Ethics*. He connects recognition of these concepts with a division in the psychological structure between a desiring component and a reasoning component. This division is evident in the characters of the enkratic and akratic agents: "there is found in them also another natural element beside reason, which fights against and resists it."[2] Aristotle is assuming a general principle – what Julia Annas calls "the Principle of Conflict"[3] – articulated by Plato in the course of his own psychological dialectic: "the same thing will not be willing to do or undergo opposites in the same part of itself, in relation to the same thing, at the same time."[4]

Indeed, Aristotle's discussion of enkrateia can be understood as an elaboration of Plato's suggestion that the notion of self-control is absurd unless it implies an internal complexity.[5] Aristotle distinguishes enkrateia from the virtue of sound-mindedness, or sophrosyne; in the sound-minded person, the desiring component "listens still better to reason, since there it agrees with reason in everything."[6] The virtue is pictured as a kind of harmony, in contrast to the dissonance experienced in enkrateia. Enkrateia belongs to the same domain as the virtue of sophrosyne – which is concerned with pleasures and pains (particularly the tactile pleasures of eating, drinking, and sex)[7] – but enkrateia is not itself a virtue; nor is akrasia a vice. They are intermediate states in the continuum between virtue and vice.

As McDowell observes, enkrateia and akrasia are *structurally similar* states. Enkratic and akratic agents are both effortful, wilful decision-makers for whom moral situations are a special sort of *agony*. Homer shows Odysseus struggling mightily to control himself: "Knocking his breast he muttered to himself: / 'Down; be steady. You've seen

---

2 Aristotle, *Nicomachean Ethics*, I.13.1102b16–18.
3 Annas, *An Introduction to Plato's "Republic,"* 137.
4 Plato, *Republic*, IV.436b.
5 Ibid., IV.431a; cf. Annas, *Plato's "Republic,"* 117.
6 Aristotle (trans. Irwin), *Nicomachean Ethics*, I.13.1102b27–8.
7 Aristotle, *Nicomachean Ethics*, II.7.1107b4–6, and III.10.1118a23–32.

worse ...' / His rage / held hard in leash, submitted to his mind / while he himself rocked, rolling from side to side, / as a cook turns a sausage, big with blood / and fat, at a scorching blaze, without a pause, / to broil it quick."[8] This agony is characteristic of the disintegrative perspective. In the enkratic person, reason ultimately succeeds in controlling desire; in the akratic person, it does not. By contrast, consider the integrative perspective: when everything is harmoniously aligned, we do not characterize the act as effortful. The needed action issues spontaneously – like an arrow passing through the sockets of twelve axes in a row[9] – without the will having to yank the leash.

Aristotle's analysis will ultimately uncover four distinct components. Referring to (1) the non-reasoning component and (2) the reasoning component, he considers two different kinds of distinction between them: "Whether these [A] are separated as the parts of the body or of anything divisible are, or [B] are distinct by definition but by nature inseparable, like convex and concave in the circumference of a circle." Are the non-reasoning and reasoning components (A) metaphysically separable *parts*, or are they (B) distinct but inseparable, internally related *aspects* of a shared structure? Aristotle says this distinction "does not affect the present question."[10] But it does matter, greatly, and the various points of intersection with *On the Soul* do not help to resolve the question.[11] It matters for present purposes because the initial division undergirds the division between virtues of character and those of thought.[12] Since virtues of character pertain to the desiring component, and those of thought to the reasoning component, the status of the distinction between components bears directly on the question of unity: are the virtues unified or not? Moreover, if virtue *is* knowledge, does knowledge need character or not? What is at stake, ultimately, is whether the Aristotelian ethical psychology is exchangeable with some sort of Humean moral psychology. We shall return to this difficult question

---

8 Homer, *Odyssey*, XX.17-18, 22–7; Fitzgerald's translation. Cf. Plato, *Republic*, III.390d, IV.441b.

9 The image is from Homer, *Odyssey*, XXI.419–23.

10 Aristotle, *Nicomachean Ethics*, I.13.1102a28–32.

11 See Aristotle, *On the Soul*, II.2.413b13–32, III.9.432a15–b7, III.10.433a31–b13. Cf. ibid., III.10.433b21–7, where the *convex/concave* metaphor is used to explain the relationship of the body to the animal soul in the production of movement.

12 Cf. Aristotle, *Nicomachean Ethics*, I.13.1103a3–10.

when we consider the special relation between sophrosyne and phronesis (in Section 9.5). We shall see that the most apt metaphor for the relation among the psychological components (and thus among the virtues) is not anatomical dissection, but *convexity/concavity*. And we shall see that Aristotle is not an antiquated Humean.

§6.2. Aristotle subdivides his initial division, revealing: (1.a) a non-reasoning, *nourishing* component, shared by all living things, including plants (which component he dismisses as irrelevant to human ethics);[13] (1.b) a *desiring* component, which "shares in reason in a way," "by listening to reason as to a father";[14] (2.a) a *deliberative* reasoning component, whose function is pursuit of what is good, or "truth in agreement with right desire";[15] and (2.b) a *scientific* reasoning component, whose function is contemplative study of necessary truth.[16] Whereas the Principle of Conflict supported the initial division between (1) and (2), a different principle, which we may call the Principle of the Target (after the image at the beginning of Book VI), serves to individuate (2.a) practical and (2.b) theoretical reason. Aristotle articulates the principle: "where objects differ in kind the part of the soul answering to each of the two is different in kind."[17]

So there are two reasoning aspects, the scientific and the deliberative, which correlate with epistemic virtues of wisdom (σοφία/*sophia*) and phronesis, and correspond to different domains: the domain of invariable things and the domain of variable things. It is in the latter domain that an agent makes changes to the world. According to Michael Pakaluk, Aristotle appeals to "two sorts of kinship between the rational soul and the world. As regards things that cannot be otherwise, the soul cognizes and reliably attains truth by the soul's *becoming like them*; but as regards things that can be otherwise, the soul cognizes and reliably attains truth by making it so that *they become like the soul*. Take truth to be a correspondence between what the soul says and how the world is: one sort of truth results from the soul's coming into correspondence with the world;

---

13 Ibid., I.13.1102a32–b12. In my view, Aristotle is wrong to dismiss it. But that is a different story.

14 Aristotle (trans. Irwin), *Nicomachean Ethics*, I.13.1102b13–14, 1103a3.

15 Aristotle (trans. Ross), *Nicomachean Ethics*, VI.2.1139a30–1.

16 Ibid., VI.1.1139a6–8, 1139a27–8.

17 Ibid., VI.1.1139a8–10.

another kind of truth results from the world's coming into correspondence with the soul."[18] It is no accident that this gloss sounds like an echo of Anscombe's distinction between *observation* and *intention*.[19] Pakaluk explicitly references Anscombe's essay "Thought and Action in Aristotle: What Is Practical Truth?," which is an elaboration of a view sketched in her book *Intention*.

Recall Anscombe's allegory from Section 4.4: a man is grocery shopping, and he has a list of groceries. A detective is following the shopper, and keeping a record of the groceries that he places in the basket. The shopper's grocery list and the detective's record stand in different relations to the groceries in the basket: the groceries should match the shopper's list, and a discrepancy is a mistake in his performance; but the detective's record should match the groceries, and a discrepancy is a mistake in her record. The shopper with the grocery list is a personification of *intention*, and the detective with the record, of *observation*. Mark Platts famously develops Anscombe's distinction in the following way (while apologizing for its "picturesque idiom"): beliefs and desires have different "directions of fit": in aiming at truth, beliefs should be changed to fit the world; desires, on the other hand, aim at satisfaction, and the world should be changed to fit them.[20] Picturesque or not, the metaphor has stuck, and both Humeans and anti-Humeans have deferred to and struggled with it.[21]

In the same section in which she draws her distinction between intending and observing, Anscombe identifies a darkness:

Can it be there is something that modern philosophy has blankly misunderstood: namely what ancient and medieval philosophers meant by *practical knowledge?* Certainly in modern philosophy we have an incorrigibly contemplative conception of knowledge. Knowledge must be something that is judged as such by being in accordance with the facts. The facts, reality, are prior, and dictate what is to be said, if it is knowledge. And this is the explanation of the utter darkness in which we found ourselves.[22]

18 Pakaluk, *Aristotle's "Nicomachean Ethics,"* 219.
19 Anscombe, *Intention*, §32.
20 Platts, *Ways of Meaning*, §X.3 (pp. 256–7).
21 See, for example, Smith, "The Humean Theory of Motivation," §§6ff; McNaughton, *Moral Vision*, §7.1; Dancy, *Moral Reasons*, §2.3.
22 Anscombe, *Intention*, §32 (p. 57).

But it is illicit to lump ancient and medieval philosophers together in a single category, as Anscombe does here. Her conception of practical knowledge is not Aristotelian, but Thomistic.[23] In her effort to dispel the darkness, she explicitly invokes Aquinas: "the account given by Aquinas of the nature of practical knowledge holds: Practical knowledge is 'the cause of what it understands', unlike 'speculative' knowledge, which 'is derived from the objects known'."[24] Anscombe seems to be using her own translation; but if we turn to the relevant article – "Whether happiness is an operation of the speculative, or of the practical intellect?" – we find the fuller context for Aquinas's thought:

It would seem that happiness is an operation of the practical intellect. For the end of every creature consists in becoming like God. *But man is like God, by his practical intellect,* which is the cause of things understood, rather than by his speculative intellect, which derives its knowledge from things.[25]

What is the meaning of this bizarre phrase, "the cause of things understood," or "the cause of what it understands"? And how exactly is it Godlike? According to Richard Moran, *what* practical knowledge understands, that of which it is the formal or constitutive cause, is a special subclass of facts called *intentional action.*[26] In this respect, it is different from theoretical knowledge, which is passive or receptive in relation to the facts that it knows.[27] On a different interpretation, practical knowledge is a representation of another, more desirable world, combined with beliefs about how to change this world into that one. In its creativity, practical knowledge is Godlike.

Let us make note of two key points: intention is *independent* of observing; and intention is *unconstrained* by the observable facts. (Of course facts can interfere with intentions; but we are currently discussing not

23 For a study of Aquinas's influence on Anscombe's conception of practical knowledge, see Schwenkler, "Understanding 'Practical Knowledge,'" §3 (pp. 10–17).

24 Anscombe, *Intention*, §48 (p. 87).

25 Aquinas, *Summa Theologica*, II.i., Q3, Art. 5, Obj. 1; emphasis added. This passage is an objection, to which Aquinas has a reply. The dispute, however, is irrelevant to what concerns us: the idea that the practical intellect is Godlike. Both objection and reply accept some version of this idea.

26 See Moran, "Anscombe on 'Practical Knowledge,'" §3 (pp. 54–5).

27 Cf. ibid., §1.C (p. 47).

the satisfaction of intention but its conceptual outline.) Recall Michael Smith's claim about the "cash value" of the Humean theory: it denies "that agents who are in belief-like states and desire-like states are ever in a *single, unitary, kind of state*."[28] Anscombe's distinction between intention and observation fits the bill. She emphasizes the independence of intention by sketching a paradigm of practical knowledge: an engineer who gives orders for the construction of a building that he cannot see.[29] It is a limiting case: most practical knowledge will in fact involve some observing. But the two mental states are categorically distinct. Anscombe's engineer is more free than Aristotle's artist, whose work is constrained by matter (among other things), and Plato's δημιουργός (*dēmiourgos*), whose work must defer to the forms.[30] The engineer's "imagination" is unmoored from reality, and for this reason, it is not really imagination, but fancy.

§6.3. Anscombe writes that "the term 'intentional' has reference to a *form* of description of events";[31] and this form is revealed by asking the question, "Why?" When the relevant event is an intentional action, the answer should give a *reason*.[32] Typically, the reason will cite a goal external to the action itself. To borrow Anscombe's example: – "Why are you pumping poison into the cistern?" – "Because I am trying to kill the inhabitants of the house." Here the agent explains his action by referring to his intended goal. Fully analysed, the reason would need also to include a means-end belief: – "Why are you X-ing?" – "Because I want to Y, and I believe that X-ing is a means to Y." Anscombe claims that the mark of practical reasoning is "that the thing wanted is *at a distance* from the immediate action, and the immediate action is calculated as the way of getting or doing or securing the thing wanted."[33] Notice that this conception of practical rationality is essentially instrumental. Hence, it cannot be an account of the reasoning whose excellence is phronesis.

---

28 Smith, *The Moral Problem*, §4.7 (p. 119).
29 Anscombe, *Intention*, §45.
30 Cf. Aristotle, *Physics*, II.3ff; and Plato, *Timaios*, 28a–29a.
31 Anscombe, *Intention*, §47 (p. 84).
32 Ibid., §5.
33 Ibid., §41 (p. 79).

It is, however, consistent with Smith's analysis of a Humean motivating reason: "R at t constitutes a motivating reason of agent A to φ if there is some ψ such that R at t consists of an appropriately related desire of A to ψ and a belief that were she to φ she would ψ."[34] According to this account, desire and means-end belief are necessary and sufficient for a motivating reason. Furthermore, what is necessary to desire is not phenomenological content, but functional role; desiring to φ is "having a certain set of dispositions, the disposition to ψ in conditions C, the disposition to χ in conditions C´, and so on."[35] It's pleasingly simple: the desire to φ is a device for correlating input C with output ψ. Platts's metaphor of direction of fit can then be "cashed" in "non-metaphorical" terms of the counterfactual dependence of a belief or a desire that p on a perception that not p: the belief is extinguished while the desire persists. Finally, Smith assumes that reason explanations are teleological explanations. To ascribe a motivating reason to someone is to ascribe a goal to him, which is to ascribe a mental state with a world-to-mind direction of fit, which is to ascribe a desire, which is a functional device that takes C and spits out ψ.[36] So, if we want to explain why you were late to meet your friends at the bar – to return to the example from Section 4.7 – then we need to tell a story about how your long-term goal is to minimize suffering in the world and how you believed that listening to the caller would minimize her suffering.

Let's look also at Pakaluk's example: "Sound practical reason is *for* something ... // This qualification makes sense, because it often happens that what we regard as appropriate in an action depends upon the 'context' of that action, which in turn is affected by some kind of long-range goal or purpose; for instance: you are at a friend's house for dinner and usually you would have two or so glasses of wine with dinner, but a good friend of yours has just died in a car accident, and consistent with your sorrow, you decline to drink. Certainly having two drinks, you think, would display a kind of frivolity or thoughtlessness inappropriate

---

34 Smith, *The Moral Problem*, §4.1 (p. 92); cf. Smith, "The Humean Theory," §1 (p. 36).

35 Smith, *The Moral Problem*, §4.6 (p. 113); cf. Smith, "The Humean Theory," §6 (p. 52).

36 Smith, *The Moral Problem*, §4.7 (p. 116); cf. Smith, "The Humean Theory," §7 (p. 55).

to the circumstances."[37] — But who reasons in this way? This action (or abstention) is understandable. But understanding it doesn't require us to grasp a goal. What would the goal of the abstention be? "I want to grieve my dead friend, and I believe that not drinking two glasses of wine is a means of realizing this goal"? As soon as the action is rationalized in this way, it appears robotic and incomprehensible. Grieving is an activity, but it is not goal-directed. There is no such thing as "success" at grieving. The answer to the question "Why haven't you touched the wine?" is not "My goal is to grieve my friend" (a mental state) but "My friend is dead" (a fact). Similarly with listening. Some listening might be goal-directed; we have called it *auditing*. But some listening is *not* goal-directed. The explanation of this latter kind of listening is that someone needs to be listened to.

The idea that practical knowledge is teleological is connected with the idea that belief and desire, reason and passion, are independent of each other. The Humean theorist thinks that the structure of practical rationality can be neutrally described: desire sets the goal and thus the problem; then reason, indifferent to the nature of the goal, is relegated to figuring out how to attain it. In this picture, rationality is a kind of ethically agnostic mercenary that we employ to solve our problems, whatever they happen to be. Recall Anscombe's formula: – "Why are you X-ing?" – "Because I want to Y, and I believe that X-ing is a means to Y." The fact that the formula involves variables is significant: it implies that this form of reasoning is compatible with whatever goal you like: Y could be shopping, torturing infant monkeys, studying biodiversity in a rainforest, or defending one's native ground. But Aristotle's notion of practical wisdom is *not* compatible with all these different ends. Phronesis thinks about "what sorts of things conduce to the good life,"[38] and the good life is not a variable awaiting specification by my arbitrary preferences. It thus places a substantial constraint on the form of reasoning.

Aristotle does have a term for the Humean technique of problem-solving, but it isn't practical wisdom; it is *cleverness*: "There is a faculty which is called cleverness; and this is such as to be able to do the things that tend towards the mark we have set before ourselves, and to hit it."[39]

---

37 Pakaluk, *Aristotle's "Nicomachean Ethics,"* 213.
38 Aristotle, *Nicomachean Ethics*, VI.5.1140a28.
39 Ibid., VI.12.1144a23–6. Cf. Anscombe, "Thought and Action in Aristotle," 145.

This capacity, which seems to be a kind of knack (rather than an art), is necessary for practical wisdom, but can occur without it; and unvarnished cleverness is equally effective at pursuing good or bad goals. What this picture fails to appreciate is that reason might have a role in determining what one should desire; that there could be a dialectic between reason and desire. For Aristotle, deliberating cannot count as an exercise of excellent practical reasoning – the epistemic virtue called phronesis – unless what one desires is in accordance with characterological virtue. And phronesis is not reducible to amoral cleverness, as he makes clear: "Practical wisdom is not the faculty [of cleverness], but it does not exist without this faculty. And this eye of the soul acquires its formed state not without the aid of virtue." He concludes: "it is impossible to be practically wise without being good."[40]

Practical wisdom is unlike theoretical wisdom in that it is concerned with the domain of variable things. It is unlike craft (τέχνη/ *tekhnē*) in not having a goal in some product external to acting. It is tempting to draw the requisite distinction by claiming that some activities (virtuous ones) are purely "for their own sake" – but as Peter Winch cautions, the trouble with this locution is that "it makes [the agent's] behaviour *too like* that in which a man does what he does for the sake of something else."[41] Aristotelian practical wisdom is neither the Thomistic "knowledge of the artificer" nor its divine version, "*knowledge of approbation.*" Aquinas's account of the mechanism of this knowledge is proto-Humean: "the intelligible form does not denote a principle of action in so far as it resides in the one who understands unless there is *added to it* the inclination to an effect, which inclination is through the will."[42] In Humean terms, belief alone is insufficient to motivate. By this account, practical knowledge, divine or human, is causally efficacious (that is, world-changing); and its proper analysis will reveal at least two discrete constituents: a cognition plus a volition.

The volition is a novel entity; as Anscombe concedes, there is nothing in Aristotle's work that answers to this idea.[43] Hannah Arendt plausibly

---

40   Aristotle, *Nicomachean Ethics*, VI.12.1144a28–b1.
41   Winch, "Moral Integrity," 183.
42   Aquinas, *Summa Theologica*, I, q. 14, art. 8; emphasis added.
43   Anscombe, "Thought and Action in Aristotle," 146–7.

locates the advent of the will in Paul.[44] But as Charles H. Kahn argues, it is in the work of Augustine and ultimately that of Aquinas that Paul's dualistic moral psychology is systematized.[45] The bifurcation of the faculties of reason and passion, intellect and will, consolidated by Aquinas, reaches its acme in the Humean theory of motivation. Indeed, the Humean theory depends on the doctrine of voluntarism: "The term *voluntarism* (from the Latin *voluntas*, 'will') applies to any philosophical theory according to which the will is prior to or superior to the intellect or reason."[46] The will's independence from intellect or reason is needed to guarantee its freedom. But this theory of motivation is connected with a picture of the world as not only inert, but desolate. It is as though the agent is abandoned in a barren land that offers him nothing – except information – and he must search inside himself for the hidden springs of action, starting, each time, from scratch. Other beings cannot *give* him reasons to act; if he were dependent on their handouts, he would be unfree, and so he himself must construct reasons, from his own inner resources, relying especially on the batteries of potential energy called *volitions*. It is a picture of the lonely deity in the lightless waste, before the creation of the world.

§6.4. The dualistic scholastic interpretation of Aristotle is reflected in Terence Irwin's translation of a crucial definition in Book VI, Chapter 2 of the *Nicomachean Ethics*: "decision is either understanding combined with desire or desire combined with thought."[47] Aristotle's Greek statement is ambiguous, and it is not obvious how it should be translated into English. But the Greek lacks an exact counterpart for Irwin's phrase "combined with." The interpolation is an interpretive decision. It is not an accident that Irwin translates φρόνησις as "prudence." The tendency to interpret Aristotle in this way is traceable at least as far back as Aquinas:

---

44 See Arendt, *Willing*, §II.8 (pp. 63–73); and Arendt, "Some Questions of Moral Philosophy," esp. §III (pp. 97–122). Like Arendt, Nietszche suggests that the will is a Judaeo-Christian invention (*On the Genealogy of Morals*, §I.13).

45 Kahn, "Discovering the will," 238.

46 Taylor, "Voluntarism," *Encyclopedia of Philosophy*, vol. 9, p. 714.

47 Irwin translating Aristotle, *Nicomachean Ethics*, VI.2.1139b4–5. In the third edition of Irwin's translation, this clause remains unchanged, but an endnote is added: "Lit. 'either desiderative understanding or thinking desire'" (Irwin, "Notes," 278).

I answer that, The proper act of free choice is election, for we say that we have a free choice because we can take one thing while refusing another; and this is to elect. ... Now two things concur in the election: one on the part of the cognitive power, the other on the part of the appetitive power. ... Aristotle leaves it in doubt whether election belongs principally to the appetitive or the cognitive power: since he says that election is either *an appetitive intellect* or *an intellectual appetite.* But he inclines to its being an intellectual appetite when he describes election as *a desire proceeding from counsel.* And the reason of this is because the proper object of election is the means to the end. Now the means, as such, has the nature of that good which is called *useful;* and since the good, as such, is the object of the appetite, it follows that election is principally an act of an appetitive power.[48]

The view that Aquinas imputes to Aristotle is recognizable as a version of the Humean theory of motivation: belief, by itself, is inert; it must combine with ("concur" with) desire, and it is "principally" desire which does the motivating work. The mistake consists in Aquinas's illicit decision to resolve Aristotle's nice ambiguity. But here is an alternative reading of Aristotle: he does *not* leave it in doubt "whether election belongs principally to the appetitive or the cognitive power." Instead, he deliberately resists the schematic ranking that Aquinas seeks. Aristotelian decision (what Aquinas calls "election") is *neither* principally an act of the appetitive power *nor* principally an act of the cognitive power.

This might seem like a minor detail, but it matters. What Aristotle himself actually says is:

διὸ ἢ ὀρεκτικὸς νοῦς ἡ προαίρεσις ἢ ὄρεξις διανοητική ...
dio ē orektikos nous hē prohairesis ē orexis dianoētikē ...[49]

In David Ross's translation, this definition is rendered: "Hence choice is either desiderative reason or ratiocinative desire"; or, less idiomatically, "either desireful reason or reasonable desire."[50] The difference

---

48 Aquinas, *Summa Theologica,* I, q. 83, art. 3. Cf. ibid., II.i, q. 13, art. 1, and q. 14, art. 1.

49 Aristotle, *Nicomachean Ethics,* VI.2.1139b4–5; see Rackham, trans., *Nicomachean Ethics,* 330. For discussion of this clause, thanks to Eli Diamond.

50 Aristotle (trans. Ross), *Nicomachean Ethics,* VI.2.1139b4–5; and Ross, *Aristotle,* 207.

between Ross's translation and Irwin's is fine but significant. Irwin substantivizes what, in Aristotle's own words, are adjectives, and thus multiplies entities. According to this interpretation, reason and desire are two separate faculties that combine in choice. But it is arguable that Aristotle is using a felicitously ambiguous phrasing carefully to point at an ambiguous phenomenon. The idea that desire might be reasonable or that reason might be desireful is disorienting, since these two aspects of the soul are conventionally understood to be distinct. But in the virtuous person, according to Aristotle, they are integrated. By having listened to reason, the virtuous person's desire has become reasonable; by having been preserved by the right temperament, her reason has become desireful of the good. While we can find instances of reason without desire (and vice versa) in other contexts, in *prohairesis* (choice) they are so fully integrated – so harmonized – that we cannot say which is substance and which is mode. As Ross says, *prohairesis* is "not merely desire + reason."[51] Instead, "desireful reason" *is* "reasonable desire."

To be fair to Irwin, he has Greenwood and Rackham (among others) on his side.[52] He also acknowledges that Aristotle "does not commit himself to a Humean view of the relation between reason and desire."[53] However, the problem is that Irwin's translation, unlike Ross's, lends itself to a Humean interpretation that separates out two distinct faculties which we must then attempt to recombine, only to despair at their recalcitrance. (It is analogous to bisecting an organism, worrying about how to get the two pieces back together, and inferring – from the inevitable failure to reanimate the sutured corpse – that each piece is really a discrete and independent body.) If we approach Aristotle with this assumption (that is, this assumed separation of faculties), his ethics could look like a botched and clumsy attempt to solve a combinatory problem.

But that problem is *our* problem, not his, and what is distinctive about his position – what we miss if we don't approach it on its own terms – is that our problem does not arise within its parameters. Roger Shiner diagnoses the issue here: "It has not occurred to them [three twentieth-century scholars] that perhaps the categories of contemporary

---

51 Ross, *Aristotle*, 207.

52 Cf. Greenwood, *Nicomachean Ethics: Book Six*, 93; Rackham, trans., *Nicomachean Ethics*, 331. For drawing my attention to Greenwood, thanks to Gordon Shrimpton.

53 Irwin, "Notes," *Nicomachean Ethics*, 240.

meta-ethics are not the only ones at hand for ethical theory; that Aristotle, so far from being confused, is in fact being quite clear, and simply has a radically different approach to the whole business."[54] Similarly, McDowell has argued that Aristotle is "healthily innocent" of modern anxiety regarding morality's foundations (or lack thereof).[55] Let us consider the suggestion that he is also innocent of our anxiety regarding the moral coordination of reason and desire.

Shiner identifies two features which he finds characteristic of most contemporary meta-ethical theory: "Firstly, it is obsessed by moral epistemology. The great bogeyman is the moral sceptic, the man who denies the existence of moral knowledge. The sceptic effectively controls the course and aims of the game. He has laid down that values and facts are radically distinct, and that facts do not on the face of it entail values. … The second characteristic feature is the assumption of total incompatibility of Reason and Sentiment in moral judgement. Either Reason is the slave of the Passions, and moral judgement is essentially the work of the heart; or moral judgement is essentially cognitive, and feelings are but 'mists on the mental windscreen.'"[56] We may call these features "two dogmas of meta-ethics." Like W.V. Quine's two dogmas, they are at root the same. While they have gone through many sophisticated permutations and complications in the twentieth- and twenty-first centuries, and while Shiner's gloss is relatively rudimentary, the *fact/value* an d *reason/sentiment* dualisms are readily recognizable. They have their source in the faculty psychology of the eighteenth century[57] and are given their definitive articulation, as we know, in Hume's *Treatise*.[58] But according to Shiner, Aristotle "is not playing *this* game at all. … Aristotle's concern is simply … to *show* us the nature of practical wisdom and of moral virtue. … As part of this strategy, Aristotle expresses the fundamental insight that the distinction between Reason and Sentiment in moral judgement is an artificial one. If one looks at the φρόνιμος, what

---

54 Shiner, "Ethical Perception in Aristotle," 83.

55 Cf. McDowell, "Some Issues in Aristotle's Moral Psychology," §10; and McDowell, "Two Sorts of Naturalism," §§4, 10–11.

56 Shiner, "Ethical Perception," 83. Shiner credits the phrase about mist to R.S. Peters.

57 Cf. Lovibond, *Realism and Imagination in Ethics*, §6.

58 See Hume, *Treatise*, Book II, Part III, Section III ("Of the influencing motives of the will"), and Book III, Part I, Section I ("Moral distinctions not deriv'd from reason").

one sees is *both* a man whose reason is mature, acute and sensitive about moral matters, *and* a man whose feelings and emotions are *naturally* for good and wholesome things."[59]

If we subscribe to a progress ideology of philosophy, we might believe that Hume discovered something Aristotle had missed. But even if we are persuaded by Hume's arguments (or those of A.J. Ayer, or J.L. Mackie, among others), we are not forced either to salvage their prototypes from the *rigor mortis* of Aristotelian philosophy or to consign that philosophy to a daily-increasing heap of obsolete artifacts. There is no substitute for looking at the texts themselves to see whether they have anything to offer. And there is room in Aristotelian ethical psychology for the Humean view: that latter view is accommodated by the disintegrative perspective of enkrateia and akrasia. *Pace* Jonathan Dancy, Humeanism can be right some of the time.[60] Indeed, the Humean analysis is indispensable for the exercise of what we have called *elenctic attention*,[61] that is, the work of ethical criticism. When things go wrong, we need to be able to analyse the psyche, to check whether the error belongs to a false belief, a bad desire, a misshapen emotion, a rigid perspective, and so on.

— "Not so fast. According to Aristotle, 'enkrateia' is a conflict between reason and passion. But such a conflict can't happen for Hume, who is the source of the non-cognitivist doctrine referenced by Shiner: 'We speak not strictly and philosophically when we talk of the combat of passion and reason. Reason is, and ought only to be the slave of the passions.'[62] If Aristotle is right, then Hume is wrong." — But Hume can make sense of enkratic conflict by re-describing Aristotelian reason as a "calm passion."[63] And Smith is "less interested in *Hume*'s view than in a *Humean* view."[64] What defines the Humean view is a dualistic system with two incommensurable mental states. We are considering the suggestion that when the Aristotelian psyche disintegrates, it is correctly analysable by the Humean theory.

---

59 Shiner, "Ethical Perception," 83–4. On aretaic second nature, cf. McDowell, "Two Sorts of Naturalism," §8 (esp. 184–5), §10; and this book, §§5.4ff.
60 Cf. Dancy, *Moral Reasons*, §2.1 (p. 21).
61 Cf. this book, §4.4.
62 Hume, *Treatise*, II.III.§III.¶4.
63 Ibid., II.III.§III.¶8.
64 Smith, "The Humean Theory," §6 (p. 52).

But a phenomenon that Humeanism fails to save is the integrative ethical agency of the *phronimos*, the one with practical wisdom. To paraphrase Wittgenstein:

Hume, we might say, does describe a system of motivation; only not everything that we call acting is this system. And one has to say this in many cases where the question arises "Is this an appropriate description or not?" The answer is: "Yes, it is appropriate, but only for this narrowly circumscribed region, not for the whole of what you were claiming to describe."[65]

The phenomenon of integrative agency is excluded a priori, on the basis of a conceptual analysis that purports to uncover these separate, structurally incompatible, propositional attitudes b and d, where b is a propositional attitude with "a mind-to-world direction of fit" and d has "a world-to-mind direction of fit." But Platts's direction-of-fit metaphor cannot accurately capture Hume's own view. Both John McDowell and David McNaughton call Hume's theory "hydraulic,"[66] and that metaphor comes closer to Hume's characterization of passion as a non-representational "impulse" (and reason as an inert faculty for the "discovery" of truth and falsity). Indeed, Hume characterizes passion as an impulse to justify his claim that reason cannot argue with passion. But notice that the hydraulic theory does not illuminate action: conceived according to this absolute partition, the coincidence of an impulse with a discovery must always be fortuitous, which is to say that the picture ultimately describes a random mechanism. – "Why are these crocuses wet?" – "Because pressurized water coincided with rubber tubing pointed in their direction." – "Why has this car arrived at the Kitchener train station?" – "Because its motor coincided with a GPS that provided directions to this location." We can say such things; but in each case, there may be further questions. That is, one might want to know, for example, why these two things coincided; and to this question, the hydraulic theory can offer no answer that does not cite some antecedent coincidence.

§6.5. We need not object to the Humean analysis per se; in certain contexts, it can be useful. The objection concerns the move from the

---

65 Cf. Wittgenstein, *Philosophical Investigations*, §3.

66 McDowell, "Non-Cognitivism and Rule-Following," §4 (p. 13); and McNaughton, *Moral Vision*, §2.3 (p. 21).

possibility of deploying the analysis in *some* cases to the obligation to deploy it in *every* case. It is reductive to require all action to conform to a single dualistic model. Suppose that we concede that it is always possible, strictly speaking, to analyse these propositional attitudes; it is also possible to describe Ansel Adams's photograph of Mount Williamson in terms of pixels, or to switch to the dialect of subatomic particles. What is at stake here is not just the risk of talking oddly. What is at stake is the risk of sacrificing (our capacity to appreciate) some phenomena to excessive theoretical parsimony and inflexibility.

— "So, when Wittgenstein says, 'The visual table is not composed of electrons,'[67] what does he mean?" — Suppose that we have at least two different "systems of representation": on the one hand, "ordinary perception talk," which includes talk of visible things like tables, and on the other hand, "physics talk," which mentions subatomic things like electrons.[68] Depending on the context, one or other system of representation might be more appropriate. When a friend asks where we have left her cup of coffee, it makes little sense to direct her to the collection of electrons in the kitchen. But when we are conducting an experiment and looking through an electron microscope, the more finely grained "physics talk" might be exactly what we need.

Wittgenstein's remark about the "visual table" is, among other things, a critical reaction to his own early analytic theory of linguistic meaning, which posits "objects" (the referents of names) at the foundation of the system. When, despite solid appearances, we assume that something *must* be composite, *must* ultimately be constructed on simpler, more fundamental things – this compulsive "must" could be an occasion for some wariness. Why *must* it be so? Do we believe that we have grasped the essence of human moral psychology: the general form of motivation is $(b \cdot d)$? Why? And if an action does not appear to manifest these two propositional attitudes, what justifies our confidence that they must nevertheless be there, hidden in the tar sands of the mind? The essentialist approach is anti-contextualist; a single theory – a single system of representation – is supposed to explain all phenomena (even at the cost of sacrificing some of them). By contrast, we are considering the suggestion that more than one perspective is needed. There is room

---

67 Wittgenstein, *Philosophical Remarks*, §III.36. Cf. Wittgenstein: "Does my visual image of this tree, of this chair, consist of parts?" (*Philosophical Investigations*, §47).

68 For this suggestion, thanks to Michael Hymers.

for the Humean theory of motivation in our philosophy of action just as there is room for the specific gesture of referring in a more general view of meaning as use: it takes its place as one among many neighbourhoods in an ancient and maze-like city.[69]

Beside the fiction of a final analysis, let us set what might be called *Ricketts's rule of thumb:*

... the Mexican sierra has "XVII-15-IX" spines on the dorsal fin. These can easily be counted. But if the sierra strikes hard on the line so that our hands are burned, if the fish sounds and nearly escapes and finally comes in over the rail, his colors pulsing and his tail beating the air, a whole new relational externality has come into being—an entity which is more than the sum of the fish plus the fisherman. The only way to count the spines of the sierra unaffected by the second relational reality is to sit in a laboratory, open an evil-smelling jar, remove a stiff colorless fish from formalin solution, count the spines, and write the truth "D.XVII-15-IX." ...

It is good to know what you are doing. The man with his pickled fish has set down one truth and has recorded in his experience many lies. The fish is not that color, that texture, that dead, nor does he smell that way. ...

We determined to go doubly open so that in the end we could, if we wished, describe the sierra thus: "D.XVII-15-IX; A.II-15-IX," but also we could see the fish alive and swimming, feel it plunge against the lines, drag it threshing over the rail, and even finally eat it. And there is no reason why either approach should be inaccurate. Spine-count description need not suffer because another approach is also used. Perhaps out of the two approaches, we thought, there might emerge a picture more complete and even more accurate than either alone could produce.[70]

Despite the heightened Romantic rhetoric in which these remarks are cast, they are insightful. We might remember that, before he began publishing fiction, John Steinbeck was trained as a marine biologist at Stanford University. And he makes these remarks, not only as a novelist, but also as a student of biology.

---

69 Cf. Wittgenstein, *Philosophical Investigations*, §18.

70 Steinbeck, *The Log from the Sea of Cortez*, 2–4. The rule is named after Steinbeck's companion on the expedition, the scientist Ed Ricketts. For introducing me to Steinbeck's book, thanks to Amy Bespflug.

As Louis Groarke observes, the application of Ockham's razor is enshrined in the methodology of positivist science: "A plurality is not to be posited without necessity."[71] So we might tend toward parsimony, restricting ourselves to the Humean theory unless required by the phenomena to have recourse to further theories. But Groarke reminds us that Ockham's principle is countered by the principle of another fourteenth-century Franciscan, Walter of Chatton: "In the economy of philosophy, the razor may be minted coin, but as Chatton points out, the verso of the medal bears an inscription too. ... 'My rule is that if three things are not enough to verify an affirmative proposition about things, a fourth must be added, and so on.'"[72] Ricketts's rule of thumb, like Chatton's anti-razor, offers a wider context in which to situate unidimensional analyses. Such analyses might be appropriate for particular purposes – we might learn something by counting the spines of the sierra. But when we want to learn about a polydimensional phenomenon, the unidimensional analysis will be inadequate; it will need to be complemented by more angles of study.

§6.6. There is a psychological model that fits Smith's Humean theory. It is worth glancing at this model and contrasting it with a different model that fits some of Weil's characterizations of attending. Mark Williams summarizes some of the research in this area: "Miller et al. (1960) had suggested that the basic unit of behaviour was not stimulus–response (S–R). Instead, they suggested that behaviour was fundamentally about the pursuit of goals (and the avoidance of punishment or anti-goals), for which the format was *Test-Operate-Test-Exit* (TOTE). In such goal-directed systems, the fundamental unit of analysis is not a pair (S–R), but a triple: the current state, the goal (or desired) state, and actions to diminish the difference between the two."[73] This mode of processing may be called "discrepancy-based processing" because there is a discrepancy between the current state

---

71 Ockham, quoted in Groarke, "Following in the Footsteps of Aristotle," 195; cf. Maurer, "Ockham's Razor and Chatton's Anti-Razor," 463.

72 Chatton, quoted in Groarke, "Following in the Footsteps of Aristotle," 195–6; cf. Maurer, "Ockham's Razor and Chatton's Anti-Razor," 464. For the primary sources of Ockham's and Chatton's principles, see Hyman and Walsh, eds., *Philosophy in the Middle Ages*, 431–2.

73 Williams, "Mindfulness, Depression and Modes of Mind," 726a.

and the desired state. Insofar as attention is theorized as a mechanism for selection (and here we might recall Wu's theory from Section 5.6), it operates in this model by weighing and then selecting goals and actions to reduce the discrepancy between the desired state and the current state. We can see how this model maps neatly onto the Humean model: the agent's desire represents a counterfactual state of the world, and the agent is motivated by that desire (in combination with suitable beliefs) to change the current state into the desired state. The motivation is fundamentally dissatisfied: the agent desires what is not the case.

This model is a default model in daily life: "attention directed in this way, as part of a mode of mind that is designed to problem solve, is effective most of the time."[74] There is nothing wrong with goal-directed problem-solving, in appropriate contexts. However, it can backfire when it is used in situations for which it is ill-suited: for example, when the agent is sad, and his goal is "to be happy." As Williams and Danny Penman observe, sadness or unhappiness "aren't 'problems' that can be solved. They are emotions."[75] When discrepancy-based processing tries to solve sadness, it can trigger strategies such as ruminating or avoiding that are ineffective in this context, and can worsen the sadness, since the *Test* function keeps finding that the discrepancy has not been lessened (the *Operate* function has failed, and so the mind cannot *Exit* the processing): the result is a negative feedback loop.

Williams calls discrepancy-based processing the *Doing mode of mind* "because it performs well in solving problems and getting things done."[76] He contrasts Doing mode with what he calls *Being mode.*[77] This second mode is associated with *mindfulness,* a style of attending, with a long and complex history, that can be cultivated through meditation practices. In his comparative study of Greek and Indian philosophies, Thomas McEvilley observes that *phronēsis* is frequently translated as "wisdom." "But in Greek ethical thought from Plato to Epicurus," he writes, "it is closer to the more specific term, 'mindfulness' (Skt. *smṛti,* Pali *sati*)."[78]

---

74 Ibid., 726b.

75 Williams and Penman, *Mindfulness,* 28.

76 Ibid.

77 Williams credits Jon Kabat-Zinn with having made the distinction, but it is clearer in Williams's own work.

78 McEvilley, "The Ethics of Imperturbability," 609.

According to Williams, in Being mode, instead of trying to solve the "problem" of sadness, the mind is able to observe the emotion, as though it were a weather pattern momentarily passing through the psyche.

Williams draws six or seven contrasts between the Doing and Being modes.[79] Of these, let us note two: Doing mode is characterized by (1) *striving* and (2) *indirect, conceptual experience.* (1) In Doing mode, attention is transfixed by the gap between the desired state and the undesired current state, and the mind strives, by cogitating, to close the gap. Such striving is essentially wilful and effortful. However, if the undesired current state is an emotion, the striving will be futile, since emotions cannot be manipulated instantaneously by will. The *Test* function will keep reporting failure. (2) Doing mode is also "conceptual, language-based, verbal and analytic."[80] Instead of experiencing the world directly, the mind recoils into commentary. It describes a counterfactual, and judges the current state defective by contrast. Again, there is nothing intrinsically wrong with this mode of mind. For example, if we are trying to make the world more just, it will be indispensable. Unjust social structures *are* defective, and should be changed, and the Doing mode can help us to analyse the defects and to make the needed changes. From the angle of social justice, the Being mode might look complacent and blameworthy.

But again, it is context that will determine whether a given mode of mind is appropriate or not. (1) When world-change is not an option, the Being mode allows the mind to disengage from vain striving. For example, in the notorious Stoic image of the dog chained to the wagon, the dog will be dragged; striving not to be dragged will only strangle the dog.[81] (This image is surely more grim than what Williams has in mind, but it is useful as a limiting case.) (2) Instead of neurotically ruminating and adding a propositional narrative to the current state – "Why am I sad? What is wrong with me?" – the Being mode allows the agent to be present to the emotion or sensation, without comparing it with a more desired state, and without judging it as defective.

It is the Being mode, I believe, that Jan Zwicky praises in her elegy for James Gray: "In the clear light of such attention, what is troubling

79 See Williams, "Mindfulness, Depression and Modes of Mind," 729; and Williams and Penman, *Mindfulness*, 37–43.

80 Williams, "Mindfulness, Depression and Modes of Mind," 729.

81 SVF 2.975 (Long and Sedley, eds., *The Hellenistic philosophers*, §62.A).

can be, simply, what it is: an odd ambition, a constricted choice, a broken heart. The clench that makes such things *into* trouble evaporates. 'Oh,' one says, seeing the stick for the stick, the puddle for a puddle — or the ocean for the ocean — 'this is just the world.'" Notice that this mode is not compassionate at the expense of honesty: "what is troubling" might actually be troubling. It might really be an ocean and not a puddle: "sometimes what the doctor hears is that the patient will die."[82] Is Being mode the same as Weilian attending? It seems to be a *form* of attending. While Weil herself does not explicitly taxonomize different forms of attending, we may perceive in her work an implicit distinction between a non-particularized, impersonal day-like attending, and a particularized, focused ray-like attending.[83]

There is a great temptation to see the Doing mode as more responsible, since it is practically minded and concerned to ameliorate undesirable states of the world. This tendency is ancient, and one classic statement of the schism between the practical and contemplative is the parable of Mary and Martha in the Book of Luke. In that parable, Martha, an embodiment of the Doing mode, complains about her sister Mary, an embodiment of the Being mode who sits and listens to the Khristos while Martha is "distracted with much serving."[84] The Khristos chastises Martha, and perhaps we should read the chastisement as an attempt to redress an imbalance. One of the conventional textual cruxes of the *Nicomachean Ethics* concerns this same dichotomy between Doing and Being. What is happiness? Is it activity according to ethical virtue, as most of the book seems to testify, or is it contemplation according to epistemic virtue, as the tenth book suddenly declares? (Ibn Tufayl's *Hayy ibn Yaqzān* may be read as a meditation on this question, with the emphases reversed.) If we see the modes of mind not as permanent orientations, however, but as perspectives between which one may alternate as the situation requires, then the dilemma evaporates.

§6.7. If we focus on the possibility to which Shiner's remarks are pointing, we find an answer to the question dismissed by Aristotle near the beginning of his investigation: are the desiring and reasoning components of the soul "separated as the parts of the body or of anything divisible are, or are [they] distinct by definition but by nature

---

82 Zwicky, "Just the World," 36–7.
83 For this distinction, cf. this book, §3.1.
84 Luke 10:40.

inseparable, like convex and concave in the circumference of a circle"?[85] The components are not metaphysically separable *parts*, but inseparable, internally related *aspects* of a shared structure. Aristotle's metaphor is key to understanding the subtlety of this latter possibility: the distinction between convexity and concavity is meaningful (if one is trying to catch a baseball, for example, it makes a difference); but one cannot draw a convex curve without also, simultaneously, drawing a concave one. If this metaphor is apt, then Aristotelian psychology is structured analogously to the familiar gestalt figures of the Necker cube or Jastrow's duck-rabbit.[86] McDowell remarks on this "double aspect of practical wisdom, as correctness of motivational orientation and as cognitive capacity." He compares "the orectic state and the doxastic state" (what Humeans would call the "desire" and the "belief") to "interlocking elements in a mechanism, like the ball and socket of a joint." And, he claims, they "cannot be separated."[87] This general point is sympathetic to our investigation, but the metaphor is not accurate: *unlike* the *geometrical curves* inscribed by the ball or the socket, *the ball and socket themselves* can, of course, be separated (when this happens, we speak of a dislocated limb).[88]

It is a small point, but it shows that our usage of philosophical imagery matters: here, it determines what kind of structure is under discussion. Suppose we imagine that the desiring component (to which characterological virtues attach) is *separate* from the reasoning component (to which epistemic virtues attach); then we might imagine that "practical wisdom, the intellectual excellence operative in virtuous behaviour, serves merely as handmaiden to a separate motivational propensity, which exerts its influence from outside the intellect. ... On this interpretation, Aristotle's view is quasi-Humean: the relevant intellectual excellence is the slave, not indeed of the passions, but at any rate of a non-intellectual motivational directedness."[89] Both the motivational and the intellectual items can be regulated (via their respective virtues), but on this interpretation the partition is absolute.

85 Aristotle, *Nicomachean Ethics*, I.13.1102a28–32. We introduced this metaphor in §6.1.

86 Cf. Zwicky, "Lyric and Ecology," §VII.2, and *Wisdom & Metaphor*, §§56, 80.

87 McDowell, "Aristotle's Moral Psychology," §6 (p. 30).

88 To be fair to McDowell, he is probably thinking of Aristotle's own use of this metaphor in *On the Soul*, III.10.433b21–7.

89 McDowell, "Aristotle's Moral Psychology," §6 (p. 31).

Having assumed this partition, one is forced to choose between a Humean interpretation (like the one outlined above) or a "cognitivist" one: in this polar interpretation, "there is still a relation of subservience, but in an opposite direction. On this view, it is an exercise of the intellect that determines a fully virtuous person's motivational orientation." The content of an action's end "is autonomously fixed by the intellectual element," and the non-intellectual, characterological element, virtuously calibrated, merely "ensures the agent's obedience."[90] This picture, in which the intellect operates autonomously, looks, as McDowell says elsewhere, "like a supposed exercise of that bloodless or dispassionate Reason that stands opposed to Passion in a familiar and unprepossessing genre of moral psychology, one that Hume made it difficult to take seriously."[91] The choice is sufficiently stark to make one wonder whether the positions have been fairly reconstructed.

But we are not concerned, here, with the niceties of the species and subspecies of Humeanism and cognitivism; we are concerned with the alternative envisioned by McDowell, who urges that we do not need to choose between these two genera of interpretation: "Aristotle does not attribute dominance in the genesis of virtuous behaviour either to the practical intellect, conceived as operating autonomously, or to a wholly non-intellectual desiderative state."[92] The key to understanding this alternative is the Aristotelian *aretē* of phronesis, which is located exactly at the waist of the hourglass whose hemispheres are the reasoning and desiring components of the soul. "A virtue of character, strictly so-called," writes McDowell, "involves [an intimate] harmony of intellect and motivation … Practical wisdom *is* the properly moulded state of the motivational propensities, in a reflectively adjusted form; the sense in which it is a state of the intellect does not interfere with its also being a state of the desiderative element."[93] To appreciate this claim – that, in some sense, a cardinal virtue of thought is *identical* with a virtue of character – we need to focus more closely on the Platonic thesis that virtue is knowledge.

90 Ibid., §11 (p. 38–9).
91 McDowell, "Might There Be External Reasons?," §7 (p. 111).
92 McDowell, "Aristotle's Moral Psychology," §11 (p. 39).
93 Ibid., §11 (p. 40).

7

Virtue Is Knowledge, Character Is Fate

ἦθος ἀνθρώπῳ δαίμων.[1]
– Herakleitos

§7.1. WEIL'S AND MURDOCH'S *attention* and McDowell's *sensitivity* are traceable to the Platonic thesis that virtue is knowledge. Aristotle fine-tunes that thesis in order to make space for the psychology of enkratic and akratic agents. While he does agree with Plato that virtue is knowledge, he makes a distinction between characterological and epistemic virtue, and he suggests that there is an excellence that traces the edge between the two domains: this excellence is phronesis. We are not obliged to read Aristotle as a rebel, however; we may read him as articulating contours that are already intimated in Plato's thinking. Plato, no less than Aristotle, believes that character is crucially implicated in epistemology; but Plato's way of expressing this thought is different from Aristotle's, as different as his way of doing philosophy.

Aristotle's lecture notes are terse and stilted (although, if one reads carefully, also flecked with metaphors), and he builds his arguments in the same way that he recommends tragedians should build their plots: in sequential order, with a beginning, middle, and end.[2] By contrast, rather than theorizing about drama, Plato does philosophy in dramatic form.[3] His characters are not merely mouthpieces for Platonic doctrine; they are lively thinkers who both investigate and challenge theses. The emotions and habits of these thinkers affect how they think and argue,

---

1 Herakleitos, DK 22B119. In a draft, Weil translates: «*L'habitude est le génie* |des hommes| *de l'homme*» (*OC*, IV.2.143).

2 Aristotle, *Poetics*, 7.1450b25–30.

3 As Nussbaum has argued, Plato is both adopting the ancestral Greek way of doing philosophy and also revolutionizing it. See Nussbaum, "Plato's anti-tragic theater," *The Fragility of Goodness*, 122–35.

and also how they interact with their fellows. If their thinking is obscured with prejudice or false belief, then they may take wrong turns and reach distorted conclusions. Plato's dialogue *Meno* ends with a claim that seems to clash with Platonic doctrine: virtue is not knowledge nor is it teachable, says Sokrates; "but *if* we were right in the way in which we spoke and investigated in this whole discussion," then virtue is merely true belief, "a gift from the gods which is not accompanied by understanding."[4] How are we to read this conclusion? And if they were *not* right in the way in which they investigated, then where, exactly, did they go wrong?

There are at least two general ways of interpreting the dialogue (and addressing these questions), and in what follows, we shall consider both of them. According to one line of interpretation, the conclusion should be read straightforwardly: Plato is advancing the thesis that virtue is merely true belief. According to another line of interpretation, the conclusion should be read ironically: Plato is committed to the Platonic thesis that virtue is knowledge, but the interlocutors have reached a wrong conclusion because they took a wrong turn. While the second interpretive strategy coheres better with the rest of the Platonic corpus, it raises a puzzle: *why* did Plato craft the dialogue to end with a wrong conclusion? To address that question, we need to consider a third interpretive strategy, which reads *Meno* as a philosophical work of art. To read it as an artwork is to think not only about what it says, but also about what it shows; to regard the characters not as neutral vehicles for the author's arguments, but as complex, living organisms.

Meno is structured in three acts and revolves around four central questions: (1) "Can virtue be taught?" (2) "What is virtue?" (3) "How can one learn what one does not already know?" The fourth question is masked, but crucially important: (4) "What is teaching?" In the first act, Meno asks (1) the first question, and Sokrates insists that (2) the second one is prior. So they embark on the project of defining virtue. Meno is confident that he can say what it is, but fails three times and becomes dumbfounded; he then asks (3) the third question, which marks the start of the second act. In response, Sokrates offers a myth and a demonstration. According to the myth, before we were born, our

4 Plato, *Meno*, 99e–100a; emphasis added. Technically, to be consistent with the other transliterations, it should be "Platon, *Menon*," but in some cases I have let stand the spellings that are more familiar to the English reader.

souls knew virtue, and we can learn by recollecting. In the demonstration of this thesis, Sokrates guides an uneducated slave through the geometrical problem of doubling the square. On his third try, the slave succeeds in recollecting the solution. At this point, they are poised to address (2) the second question, but Meno, lacking courage, regresses to (1) the first. This moment is the decisive wrong turn and the start of the third act. Meno's Athenian host, Anytos, joins the conversation, and the interlocutors consider an empirical argument to the conclusion that virtue is not knowledge; Meno and Sokrates go on to discuss the distinction between knowledge and true belief; and the dialogue ends with its incredible conclusion.

The dialogue's four questions are interconnected. Sokrates's failure to teach Meno, his interlocutor, is explained by the latter's less-than-virtuous *character*. Furthermore, the role of character here affects our conceptualization of what virtue is: it is not the sort of thing that one can learn, independently of one's character, through "pure reason." Thus Plato's *Meno* anticipates the interdependence of Aristotle's characterological and epistemic virtues. In the dialogue, this interdependence is not stated discursively, but shown dramatically; and Plato's use of this method – showing – has implications for our own study of virtue. If we want to learn what virtue is, then we cannot be inert recipients of transmitted data. We must participate in our education and think our way through the gaps between what is said.

The drama begins abruptly, *in medias res*, with the first question. "Can virtue be taught?" On a visit to Athens, a young Thessalian aristocrat named Meno asks this question of Sokrates. Meno starts with some confident beliefs about virtue; but Sokrates subjects him to the questioning of the ἔλεγχος (*elenkhos*), and, roughly one-third into the dialogue, brings him to an ἀπορία (*aporia*). Meno is shocked, and says so: "Socrates ... you seem ... to be like [the stingray], for it too makes anyone who comes close and touches it feel numb, and you now seem to have had that kind of effect on me, for both my mind and my tongue are numb, and I have no answer to give you."[5] Later in the dialogue, Sokrates also manages to sting Anytos, who responds less politely than Meno. In this way Plato suggests one of the illicit motives for the accusers of Sokrates: they have been humiliated by Sokrates's exposure of their intellectual

5 Plato, *Meno*, 80a–b.

hypocrisy, and they retaliate by killing him. This understanding of the trial might offer a fresh angle on our original question, "Can virtue be taught?" Suppose for the sake of argument that the answer is "yes." Sokrates is portrayed by Plato as consistently courageous, moderate, and just; he denies that he is wise, but, unlike his fellow citizens, he knows when he does not know, and that negative knowledge is a kind of wisdom. In short, by classical Greek standards, Sokrates is a virtuous human being. Why then is he unjustly executed? If virtue can be taught, and if Sokrates is virtuous, why do his interlocutors turn out to be perpetrators of injustice?

Dominic Scott argues that Meno improves ethically over the course of the dialogue,[6] but the textual evidence counts against this claim. Meno is recalcitrant material; he is also conceited and overconfident. (According to Aristotle, an excess of confidence is a vice.)[7] He is accustomed to making "many speeches about virtue before large audiences on a thousand occasions, very good speeches," as he thought.[8] When Sokrates asks him what virtue is, he brags that it is "not hard" to tell; he then proceeds to repeat an unimaginative platitude deriving from conventional morality: virtue is helping friends and harming enemies.[9]

Meno's second definition – ruling over people[10] – expresses his desire for power. Throughout the project of attempting to define virtue, he likes to watch idly while Sokrates labours.[11] Like a "clever and disputatious" debater, he tries to score cheap points by rudely complaining about undefined terms in Sokrates's model definition of shape ("But that is foolish, Socrates"), instead of grappling with the substance of the definition itself.[12] He has trouble perceiving relevance and easily slides off topic.[13] He prefers the flourish of a "theatrical" answer in the style of his teacher Gorgias, even though that definition is inferior to the formal one offered by Sokrates.[14] He most admires in Gorgias that

6 Scott, *Plato's "Meno,"* 6, 209–13.

7 Aristotle, *Nicomachean Ethics*, III.7.1115b28–9. Sokrates gently teases Meno about his overconfidence at *Meno*, 84b–c.

8 Plato, *Meno*, 80b.

9 Cf. Polemarkhos's definition of justice in Plato, *Republic*, I.332d.

10 Plato, *Meno*, 73d.

11 Ibid., 75b.

12 Ibid., 75c.

13 Ibid., 76a.

14 Ibid., 76e.

he never promises to make his students good people, but only clever speakers.[15] His conception of what is "good" is materialistic rather than ethical: wealth, honour, and offices. As Sokrates says (with ironic pomp), "According to Meno, the hereditary guest friend of the Great King, virtue is the acquisition of gold and silver."[16] Xenophon's characterization reinforces this impression: "Menon the Thessalian was manifestly eager for enormous wealth—eager for command in order to get more wealth and eager for honour in order to increase his gains; and he desired to be a friend to the men who possessed greatest power in order that he might commit unjust deeds without suffering the penalty."[17]

Meno's reaction to discovering that, despite his previous confidence, he does not know what virtue is, is knee-jerk skepticism.[18] Indeed, he suffers from both epistemic and ethical skepticism,[19] not philosophically, but casually (that is, he has not thought his way through skepticism as a philosophical position, but merely entertains it as a fallback in the face of epistemic difficulty). When Sokrates repeatedly offers him second chances to retract false claims,[20] he is too dense to take the hint. But Meno's most important characteristics, for our purposes, are his cowardice and lack of discipline. At the climax of the dialogue, these characteristics are responsible for the disastrous turn in the conversation. (We shall return to this point in Section 7.3.)

§7.2. Can virtue be taught? The question is not without urgency; but it is inseparable from the prior, Sokratic question: What *is* virtue? Let us remember that the word "virtue" translates ἀρετή (*aretē*). The Greek word has a wider range than the English one; an alternative translation, "excellence," suggests some of that range. To be virtuous is to excel at being whatever it is that one really is. Gerard Manley Hopkins's sonnet illustrates the Platonic thought:

---

15 Ibid., 95c.
16 Ibid., 78d.
17 Xenophon, *Anabasis*, 2.6.21.
18 Plato, *Meno*, 80d.
19 Ibid., 96d.
20 Ibid., 78c–d, 96b–c, 98d.

As kingfishers catch fire, dragonflies draw flame;
As tumbled over rim in roundy wells
Stones ring; like each tucked string tells, each hung bell's
Bow swung finds tongue to fling out broad its name;
Each mortal thing does one thing and the same:
Deals out that being indoors each one dwells;
Selves — goes itself; *myself* it speaks and spells,
Crying *Whát I dó is me: for that I came. ...*[21]

Virtuous character seems not uncommon. I have observed displays of courage and integrity, self-discipline and sympathetic understanding, patience and kindness, and other, subtler virtues for which there are no conventional names. I seem to be able to recognize instances of virtue, but what is it, exactly, that I am recognizing? – And what if I am mistaken? Since I myself am not yet virtuous, how could I recognize virtue in others? Take courage, for example. When a knife-fight breaks out in the street and my friend intervenes and breaks up the fight, that seems courageous to me; but what if my friend's act is reckless? How can I tell? The questions transmit energy to one another, like boxcars banging along the tracks: the initial question, "Can I learn virtue?," unearths a deeper question, "What is virtue?," and that question, in its turn, provokes a skeptical question, "If I do not know what something is, then how can I learn about it?" This last question is known as "Meno's paradox," and it is what Meno asks from out of the core of his *aporia*.

Some might feel impatient with the question: if you don't know what something is, then you grope around until you stumble upon it; or you have a hunch, and, luckily, the hunch turns out to be right. — "But if you do not know what something is, then how can you know when you have stumbled upon it; how can you know whether your hunch is actually confirmed?" — OK, then you find someone who *does* know, and they teach you. — "But if you don't know what you are looking for, then how can you know whom to trust to teach you?" — At first glance, there appear to be various ways of escaping from the skeptical question: trial and error, a lucky hunch, appeal to authority, for instance; but the profound feature of the question is its repeatability.[22] It is not unlike

---

21 Hopkins, "As kingfishers catch fire," *Poems and Prose*, 51. Cf. Plato, *Republic*, I.352d ff.

22 For helping me to see this feature, thanks to Steven Burns.

your shadow: you can change the angle of your body or your relation-ship to the source of light, but your shadow inexorably copies whatever posture you have assumed. And, as it repeats itself, the skeptical question seems to scorch the very possibility of ever knowing anything.

Let us notice an analogy between Meno's paradox and a paradox about the acquisition of virtue from the *Nicomachean Ethics*.[23] Recall that Aristotle compares the learning of virtue to an apprenticeship in art: "the virtues we get by first exercising them, as also happens in the case of the arts as well. For the things we have to learn before we can do them, we learn by doing them."[24] According to this account, one becomes a good carpenter by practising carpentry, a good saxophonist by practising the saxophone, and a just person by practising just actions. The paradox is acknowledged in Book II, Chapter 4: an action is just, for example, if it is the sort of action that would be produced by a just character. But if I am not yet just, how can I produce the appropriate action? And if I cannot produce the appropriate action, how can I ever become just? Julia Annas addresses a version of this paradox: if right action is defined as what a virtuous person would characteristically do, how do we identify a virtuous person in a non-circular way?[25] And if we cannot identify a virtuous person, how can we know which actions are right?

Annas proposes a "developmental account," which attempts to break the binary of virtuous person and right action by interposing a third term, the developmental process.[26] In this account, there is an appren-tice, who is not yet expertly virtuous, and an expert: thus, "right action" has at least two different connotations, relative to the apprentice and the expert respectively. According to Annas, we can supply independent characterizations of the virtuous person and right action only if we confine ourselves to the perspective of the apprentice: right action is what the virtuous person would do, and the virtuous person around here is, let's say, *this* person. When one is an apprentice, one does the right thing if and only if one does what the virtuous person would do.

---

23 *Pace* Scott (*Plato's "Meno,"* 17–18), Aristotle is clearly alluding to Meno's initial question ("Can virtue be taught?") when he contemplates a puzzle about the acquisi-tion of happiness (*Nicomachean Ethics*, I.9.1099b9–11).

24 Aristotle, *Nicomachean Ethics*, II.1.1103a31–3.

25 Annas, "Being Virtuous and Doing the Right Thing," 67.

26 Ibid., 68.

But for an expert, virtue is not defined according to this external criterion; the expert does not merely emulate a model. The expert does
something else, something that is difficult to formulate definitively and
without seemingly circular reference to the expert. Annas admits that
the apprentice's identification of the virtuous person is not without risk:
"How do we identify the virtuous people? We do so in the way that we
identify good builders and pianists — that is, in a way which is initially
hostage to our own lack of expertise."[27] For Sokrates, the gap between
the not-yet-aretaic apprentice and the expert is crossable through trust.

§7.3. As we have discussed, *Meno* concerns itself with these three questions: "Can virtue be taught? What is virtue? How can I learn what I do
not already know?" The ostensible answers to the first two questions
– virtue cannot be taught, and virtue is reducible to true belief – seem
to stand in some tension with what will be Sokrates's answer to the
third question: namely, we already know (in a latent way) what virtue
is, and need only recollect this knowledge. There has been some disagreement among commentators about how to interpret the third act
and conclusion of the dialogue. As one commentator, Jane M. Day,
observes, these interpretations tend to fall into two kinds:

(a) Plato is here abandoning the uncompromising Socratic view that virtue
must always be knowledge, and while holding to the *ideal* that virtue should
be knowledge he now recognizes a second legitimate form of virtue consisting in 'right opinion' (*orthē doxa*).
(b) The true conclusion of the *Meno* is that virtue is knowledge and comes
from teaching, as argued at 87-9, while the whole subsequent argument is
ironical and consciously fallacious.[28]

In other words, the first kind of interpretation (a) accepts the ostensible
conclusion of the *Meno*, while the second kind of interpretation
(b) argues that the ostensible conclusion is ironic, and that it conceals
a true conclusion sequestered earlier in the dialogue.

One commentator, Roslyn Weiss, in her *Virtue in the Cave*, adopts (a)
the first kind of interpretation. Her title alludes to the Allegory of the
Cave from *Republic*, Book VII. Drawing on Sokrates's assessment of

27 Ibid., 73.
28 Day, "Introduction," *Plato's "Meno" in Focus*, 28.

himself and his fellow citizens in *Apology*, Weiss contends that humans are condemned to a "moral Cave, that is, to the realm of moral *opinion*."[29] She argues that the myth of recollection is a self-conscious fiction, deployed for merely pragmatic motives. Furthermore, she argues that the demonstration that allegedly supports the myth is really a farce: contrary to his disavowals, Sokrates is straightforwardly teaching geometry to the slave. But this instance of teaching has no bearing on the question of the teachability of virtue, Weiss claims, because geometry and virtue are utterly dis-analogous. The myth and its alleged demonstration do respond to Meno's skeptical question, but the strategy of response is not argumentative. According to Weiss, the myth and the demonstration together are a sophisticated and deceptive piece of theatre, designed to trick Meno into continuing with the inquiry. Weiss thus endorses the ostensible conclusion of the dialogue: virtue cannot be taught. Unlike geometry, horseback-riding, javelin-throwing, and so forth, virtue is not a kind of knowledge.

Other commentators have suggested that the empirical argument from the absence of teachers, which delivers the ostensible conclusion that virtue cannot be taught, is actually irrelevant, because it fails to attend to Sokrates's redefinition of learning as recollection. One of the first such commentators is F.M. Cornford, and his footnote is worth reproducing in full, because it identifies and condenses the central issue so deftly:

The ostensible conclusion of the *Meno* (98D–E) disguises this result [i.e., the result that virtue cannot be 'taught' in the ordinary sense], by resuming the argument that virtue cannot be knowledge, because, if it were, it must be 'teachable' (διδακτόν), and there are in fact no teachers of it (i.e., the Sophists who profess to teach virtue cannot do so). This argument deliberately ignored the distinction between 'teachable' (διδακτόν) and 'recoverable by recollection' (ἀναμνηστόν) which Socrates had just established (87B–C). The fact that the Sophists cannot 'teach' virtue does not prove that virtue is not knowledge of the sort that is recollected under Socratic questioning. As in other early dialogues the true conclusion is masked.[30]

29 Weiss, *Virtue in the Cave*, 4.
30 Cornford, "*Anamnesis*," 60, n. 1.

According to Sokrates, here and in *Phaidros* and *Phaidon*, the soul learns virtue by recollecting its pre-incarnate experience of the forms. But Sokrates does not *tell* us to believe this metaphysical doctrine; indeed, he suggests that the doctrine is less important than the Sokratic method. The method is displayed in the geometrical demonstration. What we need to trust is only that the method can be effective for ethical education too; that, despite the failure of the sophists to transmit virtue, nevertheless, virtue can be elicited by apt questions and clear paradigms.

However, the truth that *virtue is knowledge* is not itself explicitly transmitted by the dialogue. It is there; it is even articulated and considered. Near the beginning of the third and final act of the dialogue, Sokrates says: "Virtue ... is wisdom?" And Meno assents: "What you say ... seems to me quite right."[31] Jan Zwicky asks, "Why isn't this the high point of the dialogue, then, its rhetorical peak? Because the *fact* is nothing if it is not *understood*, if we don't *see* it, grasp what *has* to be the case for it to be true and thereby take it into our souls."[32] And it is clear that Meno does not understand.

But if we accept something like Cornford's interpretation (b), and resist Weiss's interpretation (a), then we face a difficulty. For Weiss's interpretation has the advantage that it explains the third act of the dialogue. If the third act is ironic, as interpretation (b) claims, then why is it written? If Plato means us to accept the thesis that virtue is knowledge, and therefore teachable, why does he not end the dialogue there, with the affirmation of that thesis, instead of proceeding to the contradictory conclusion? If the true conclusion is masked, as Cornford claims, then why is it masked?

In order to respond to these questions, and to appreciate the deep unity of the dialogue, we need to approach it as a philosophical work of art. This approach is developed by Zwicky. She calls the dialogue "a philosophical jewel":[33] "a complex ecology of argumentation, a survey

---

31 Plato, *Meno*, 89a.

32 Zwicky, *Plato as Artist*, 65 / *AL*, 187. Cf. Zwicky, *Wisdom & Metaphor*, L90–L91.

33 Zwicky, *Plato as Artist*, 13 / *AL*, 144; intentionally echoing J.S. Mill? "It [the famous doctrine of Reminiscence] is shown to us in the *Menon*, in which more that is characteristic of Plato is brought together in a smaller space than in any other dialogues: if the *Phaedon* and the *Gorgias* are noble statues, the *Menon* is a gem" (Mill, *Essays on Philosophy and the Classics* [Toronto: University of Toronto Press, 1978], 422).

of Plato's central views in a very small compass, an exquisitely nuanced report of both his idealism and his despair."[34] Central to her study of the dialogue is its dramatic form, and the importance of character (in this case, Meno's and Sokrates's characters) to philosophical investigation.[35] Her interpretation of the third act of the dialogue does not fit neatly into either of the two contrasting kinds of interpretation ([a] and [b]) sketched by Day above, but offers a third way.

"Virtue is knowledge," writes Zwicky, "*and* it is not transmissible ..."[36] That virtue is not transmissible is the lesson of the third act of the dialogue. If we assume, with Meno, *that teaching reduces to transmission*,[37] then citing the absence of transmitters will be persuasive. Scott nicely summarizes Meno's attitude to education: "The assumption that underlies Meno's abruptness in asking his [initial] question betrays an approach to education that will be opposed throughout the work: equipped with a collection of speeches, the teacher acts as informant; the learner in turn memorises whatever the teacher has to say. Education is a straightforward process of transmission. The other side of that contrast is the Socratic approach to education, where learning takes the form of a dialogue in which the 'teacher' asks questions, and the learner responds."[38] When Meno asks, "Can you tell me, Sokrates, can virtue be taught?" he is saying, "Just tell me, Sokrates. If you have a speech on the teachability of virtue, let's hear it. (Maybe I'll add it to my repertoire of impressive speeches.)" But what if transmission is not the only kind of teaching? Even if it cannot be *transmitted*, virtue can be *learned*, that is, *recollected*. This truth, however, as Cornford observes, is masked. And it is masked *for characterological reasons*. Meno is not the most promising student. His major errors (two of several) are (1) that he lacks the *courage* and *discipline* required to engage in the project of dialectic (which centrally features Sokratic definition); and (2) that he presumptuously conflates all *teaching* with *transmission*.

Consider (1) the first major error. At the climax of the dialogue, Meno's cowardice and lack of discipline are responsible for the wrong

---

34 Zwicky, *Plato as Artist*, 13 / AL, 144.

35 Ibid., 18 / AL, 148.

36 Ibid., 63 / AL, 186.

37 Weiss argues a different but related point that Meno assimilates all learning to that which comes from teaching ("Learning without Teaching," 5–6).

38 Scott, *Plato's "Meno*," 13.

turn that leads, ultimately, to the wrong conclusion. Meno's *aporia*, his awareness that he does not know, induced by Sokrates's questioning, is an achievement, but it is not secure. He lacks the epistemic courage to face the question which Sokrates insists is prior, namely, "What is virtue?" After the *aporia*, after the myth of recollection, and after the geometrical demonstration, Meno is poised on the verge of investigating the question but he fails. This failure is the turning point of the dialogue. According to Zwicky's diagnosis, Meno's courage "fails him"; in response to Sokrates's invitation to investigate what virtue is, Meno coyly and nervously reverts to his initial question ("Can virtue be taught?"); Sokrates, disappointed but not surprised, engages in a little rhetorical flirting.[39] We may also hear a colder and more ominous tone in Sokrates's response: "But because you do not even attempt to rule yourself, in order that you may be free, but you try to rule me and do so, I will agree with you—for what can I do? So we must, it appears, inquire into the qualities of something the nature of which we do not yet know."[40]

The diction of ruling echoes Meno's second attempted definition of virtue – the ability to rule over people.[41] It also echoes Sokrates's character sketch: "you are forever giving orders in a discussion, as spoiled people do, who behave like tyrants as long as they are young."[42] The connection between undisciplined eros and tyranny is also emphasized in *Republic*.[43] In the tyrant, the rule of reason has been undermined, and he is shoved around recklessly by a feverish eros. This image of Meno – as a tyrant who does not rule himself and yet tries to rule Sokrates – is disturbing. Meno is not only an undisciplined interlocutor but also a dangerous man. After the turning point, the tone of the dialogue shifts. As Zwicky observes: "throughout the remainder, Socrates aims the discussion and a good deal of irony well over Meno's head. It is almost as though he has abandoned the project of converting Meno to the philosophic life …"[44] Furthermore, it is due to Meno's initiative

39 Zwicky, *Plato as Artist*, 55–6 / AL, 180.

40 Plato, *Meno*, 86d–e.

41 Ibid., 73d.

42 Ibid., 76b. Scott also instructs us to take the reference to tyranny seriously, and to consider the sinister undertone (*Plato's "Meno,"* 63).

43 Plato, *Republic*, IX.572e–573d.

44 Zwicky, *Plato as Artist*, 58 / AL, 182.

that the dialogue reaches a conclusion which, according to the commitments of Platonic philosophy, can be regarded only as a travesty. To claim, with Scott, that the Sokratic education of Meno is to some degree successful strains the text.

Now consider Meno's other major error (2), his conflation of teaching with transmission. Sokrates does fail to transmit virtue to Meno – thus contributing yet another empirical datum to the argument from the absence of teachers. But what if virtue is not transmissible? In describing Sokrates's attempt to guide Meno, Zwicky employs suggestive imagery, and that imagery is designed to show something important. Repeatedly, her image for philosophical thinking is fire. Let us assemble four instances of this imagery, and the resonances will be apparent:

[1] Meno is such damp wood there is no teasing him into even a flicker of interest in reality.
[2] Socrates has sparked attention in a very unpromising subject.
[3] Socrates senses that the flame is still lit, but wavering …
[4] Meno is not ready. He has had a glimpse, the flame has riffled along the edge of his intelligence; but it has not caught.[45]

The selection of imagery is not coincidental; it echoes the imagery of the *Seventh Letter*.[46] The author of that letter, either Plato or a Platonist, writes: "There is no writing of mine about these matters, nor will there ever be one. For this knowledge is not something that can be put into words like other sciences; but after long-continued intercourse between teacher and pupil, in joint pursuit of the subject, suddenly, *like light flashing forth when a fire is kindled*, it is born in the soul and straightway nourishes itself."[47] What is important about this image is its suggestion that philosophical insight, like fire, is not transmitted through a unidirectional lecture but is kindled though a collaboration, through souls conversing "in good will and without envy."[48] The privileging of live

45 Ibid., 31, 44, 52, 56 / AL, 159, 170, 177, 180.

46 Zwicky twice refers to the "epistemological digression" of the *Letter* (ibid., 30, 89 / AL, 157, 206), but she conspicuously refrains from quoting the relevant passage.

47 Plato, *Letter VII*, 341c–d; emphasis added. The image of nourishment is also echoed by Zwicky (*Plato as Artist*, 42 / AL, 168), but following that lead would take us too far afield.

48 Plato, *Letter VII*, 344b.

intercourse over written discourse reflects one of the central themes of Plato's *Phaidros*. Furthermore, the *material* matters: some things just will not burn – "damp wood," for example.

§7.4. Zwicky's essay on Plato's *Phaidros* also employs suggestive imagery. Both essays (on *Meno* and *Phaidros*) read Plato's dialogues as works of philosophical and literary art. To read them as works of *art* is to read them not only for what they *say* but also for what they *show*. Furthermore, fully to appreciate the coherence of these works of art requires attending to aspects that are *shown* but *not said*. In the case of *Phaidros*, readers are witness to a deftly choreographed interaction between content and form. That interaction is an instance of resonance – not the pleasant chime that we might hear, for example, in a rhyming couplet, but resonance through "difference or reactivity."[49] In short, the dialogue's *form* is a *response* to certain arguments articulated in its *content*. On a cursory reading, *Phaidros* may appear to lack coherence: the first half appears to be about eros, the second, about rhetoric, and the dialogue thus appears disintegrated or "broken-backed"[50] across these two halves. The dialogue concludes with a written critique of writing. That critique consists of a number of distinct objections (Zwicky enumerates six).[51] But for our purposes we may concentrate these objections into one: according to Sokrates, philosophy occurs exclusively through living conversation, which is characterized by thoughtful questioning and responding. By contrast, writing cannot act as an interlocutor: it cannot respond to questions or defend what it says. It is, in other words, unphilosophically dogmatic, stupidly repetitive.

---

49 Cf. Zwicky, *Lyric Philosophy*, L202. Zwicky cites Kahn's reading of Herakleitos as a touchstone for her notion of resonance (cf. ibid., R23), but indicates that her notion is somewhat broader: in her sense, resonance "characterizes not only different expressions of similar ideas or themes but also similar (or overtly contrasting) expressions of different ideas or themes" ("Oracularity," 500, n. 23 / *AL*, 119). In Plato's account in *Phaidon*, recollection is not unlike a kind of resonance, which can be occasioned both by similarity and dissimilarity (74a).

50 Zwicky borrows the image from Ferrari, *Listening to the Cicadas* (New York: Cambridge University Press, 1987), 230.

51 Zwicky, "Plato's *Phaedrus*: Philosophy as Dialogue with the Dead," 24–7 / *AL*, 60–5.

Sokrates's complaint compares writing to painting: "The offsprings of painting stand there as if they are alive, but if anyone asks them anything, they remain most solemnly silent. The same is true of written words. You'd think they were speaking as if they had some understanding, but if you question anything that has been said because you want to learn more, it continues to signify just that very same thing forever."[52] We may hear an echo of a similar complaint made in Plato's *Protagoras*, where Sokrates compares orators or speech-makers to books and ringing bronze bowls: "But try asking one of [these orators] something, and they will be as unable to answer your question or to ask one of their own as a book would be. Question the least little thing in their speeches and they will go on like bronze bowls that keep ringing for a long time after they have been struck and prolong the sound indefinitely unless you dampen them. That's how these orators are: Ask them one little question and they're off on another long-distance speech."[53] The comparison of these metaphors from *Phaidros* and the *Protagoras* allows us to abstract the complaint: what is allegedly unphilosophical about both writing and speech-making is that they are *unresponsive*: they behave like pre-recorded monologues, like inanimate matter.[54]

The complaint sets up a test which any candidate for Sokratic (or Platonic) philosophy must face: it should be able *to respond* like a living thing. Can a piece of writing ever satisfy this test? The question is worth asking, and it is one that *Phaidros* invites us to ask: "the test of the integrity of a philosophical encounter is its livingness: the degree to which it provokes, in us, *erōs* — a movement toward meaning. A philosophical being's livingness, Plato suggests, is reflected in its ability to respond to questions"; and Zwicky suggests "that this may be understood as a written text's ability to make *us* respond, to provoke us to questions worth trying to answer."[55] Let us think about that movement toward meaning. Throughout Zwicky's essay, the image of a living thing, an ensouled thing, is the image of something *moving*. The dialogue, she writes, "does not *come to rest* with the notion that writing is simply the meek servant

52 Plato, *Phaidros*, 275d–e.

53 Plato, *Protagoras*, 329a–b.

54 The last image could be disputed, for example, by a Spinozist, a Stoic, or a Herakleitean. Indeed, it may be disputed by the author of the *Timaios*. What, exactly, is "inanimate" matter?

55 Zwicky, "Plato's *Phaedrus*," 46 / AL, 84.

of dialectic. Nor does it *come to rest* with its own writerly undoing of arguments against the legitimacy of writing. That is: it does not come to rest."[56]

Although she never explicitly refers to it, if we reflect, we can see that she is clearly alluding to the argument from motion for the immortality of the soul, the argument that occurs near the beginning of Sokrates's palinode for eros, after his diaeresis of the four kinds of divine madness.[57] What is relevant for our purposes is the role of the argument in the structure of Plato's *Phaidros*, its resonance in the context of a dialogue about eros and rhetoric. Why is it here, at the cusp of a discussion of the logic of desire, and the transcendental preconditions of the phenomenology of beauty, which phenomenology is located at the centre of a philosophical life? And what does any of that have to do with rhetoric?

The argument maintains that soul is always moving, and that what is always moving *moves itself.*[58] What Zwicky has seen, and what she shows but does not say, is something that Plato has shown but not said: here, nascent in the argument from motion, is a sketch of Sokrates's test of philosophical writing. Indeed, when Sokrates and Phaidros later describe (2) true philosophical intercourse, they echo (1) the earlier imagery. Compare:

(1) from the argument for the immortality of the soul: "whatever is always in motion is immortal, while what moves, and is moved by, something else stops living [παῦλαν ἔχει ζωῆς] when it stops moving"; "we should have no qualms about declaring that this [self-moving] is the very essence and principle of a soul [ψυχῆς οὐσίαν τε καὶ λόγον]";[59]

---

56 Ibid., 39 /AL, 78; cf. the images of motion at ibid., 44 /AL, 81.

57 Plato, *Phaidros*, 245c–e. In Zwicky's diaeresis, the four kinds are prophetic frenzy, purificational frenzy, poetic frenzy, and the passionate frenzy of the genuine lover (Zwicky, "Plato's *Phaedrus*," 32 / AL, 70).

58 When the argument from motion is extended (vicariously) to a certain kind of literary creation, one may hear an echo of Diotima's claim that those who are pregnant in soul give birth to immortal children, such as poetry and laws (Plato, *Symposium*, 208e–209e).

59 Plato, *Phaidros*, 245c, 245e.

(2) from the description of true philosophical intercourse: "It is a discourse [λόγον] that is written down, with knowledge, in the soul of the listener [ἐν τῇ τοῦ μανθάνοντος ψυχῇ]"; "the living, breathing [ζῶντα καὶ ἔμψυχον] discourse [λόγον] of the man who knows."[60]

A living thing moves itself – this feature is key. For writing and speech-making, like paintings and ringing bowls, appear to be in a sort of perpetual motion: they repeat themselves, over and over. But what distinguishes philosophical rhetoric from the unphilosophical kind – like profound paintings from shallow ones – is its ability to move spontaneously, and thus to move us, to stir us into restless thinking. (A dead thing can receive motion, through efficient causation; it can be shoved around. But it cannot do anything spontaneously, and so cannot surprise us.)

According to Zwicky, the dialogue of *Phaidros* may be seen as Plato's response to Sokrates's critique – an erotic response, one that records the force of the senior interlocutor's critique in respectful and loving detail. (And so we see how the themes of eros and rhetoric cohere.) But Plato records Sokrates's critique in the very medium that is the object of that critique, namely, writing, and he crafts that medium according to the form that Sokrates prefers, namely, dialogue. Plato *states* the objections, but he *shows* his response. Zwicky writes: "The momentum of the arguments [against the legitimacy of writing] is countered at every point by the brilliance of their written execution: this wrought counterplay of content and form is itself the *physis* of the work, content and form are themselves in dialogic relation, and their tension, instead of blowing the dialogue apart, *is* its torqued unity, the breathless updraft at its centre that pulls the questions from us."[61]

And that tension, between Sokrates's objections and the Platonic dialogue that encompasses them, is crucial. If we think that Plato emerges triumphant, we have missed the point. A Platonic dialogue is not like the Cartesian Objections and Replies, which are far more antiphonal than polyphonic; Descartes's detractors take their turn, and then he takes his, and tries to knock them out. If Descartes succeeds, then his detractors are defeated. But if Plato succeeds, then concepts such as triumph and defeat are without application. If Plato succeeds, then his characters – and their questions – continue to provoke us. Plato

---

60 Ibid., 276a.
61 Zwicky, "Plato's *Phaedrus*," 40 / AL, 78.

does have philosophical commitments, and he does argue for some of them, but the point is not that we should be persuaded of them, but that we should *think* about them. One important feature of the dialogic form is that it *preserves* disagreements; and it preserves them not as a museum preserves artifacts, but as stories are preserved in an oral culture. The analogy is exact: one of the ways in which an oral culture (an individual storyteller within that culture) preserves a traditional story is to innovate (theme and variation). To preserve, in this sense, is not to petrify but to revivify. The integrity of the Platonic dialogue is measured by its ability to keep these disagreements alive.

§7.5. Like Plato's *Phaidros*, his *Meno* aspires to be a kind of living, en-souled philosophy, and this aspiration is realized to the degree that the dialogue manages to provoke us, its readers, to ask its unspoken but implicit questions. In her study of *Meno*, Zwicky continues to emphasize the importance of the dialogic form, its integral role in provoking us to philosophical reflection. She writes:

There is much that is unvoiced in the writing; but it is latent, as a conclusion is latent in its premises. When we regard Plato not only as a purveyor of arguments but as a consummate philosophical artist, when we take every move, every sentence to be carefully and deliberately crafted to support the dialogue's thematic preoccupations, when we therefore regard every detail as worthy of our concentrated philosophical attention, the work's essential unity begins to emerge. When we focus on how the dialogue is *made*, we are led to ask the right questions. When we ask the right questions, its meaning springs to life.[62]

As with *Phaidros*, *Meno*'s vitality is a function of the synergistic relationship between reader and text, and it is because of the care with which it is built that the text is ready for that relationship. Plato refuses to supply PowerPoint® summaries, refuses to tell us precisely which answers to circle on the multiple-choice test. He expects us to work and to see for ourselves. The dialogue is thus crafted to act as a Sokratic interlocutor: it is, simultaneously, teacher and student. Teacher, because it asks genuine, open questions, which invite the reader to participate, to reflect, and to find the answers for herself. Student,

62 Zwicky, *Plato as Artist*, 17 / AL, 147–8.

because it contains latent ideas which can be elicited and sprung into focus by the reader's questions.

One characteristic of great works of art is that they are capable of *showing* more than they *say*. We have seen that Plato's *Meno* explicitly asks three questions ("Can virtue be taught?" "What is virtue?" "How can I learn what I do not already know?"); the dialogue seems concerned primarily with ethics and epistemology. However, let's remember the fourth question. As Zwicky observes, "the question 'What is teaching?', though philosophically central, is never explicitly asked ..."[63] The dialogue is also about education. Zwicky writes: "we notice that in Meno's original question there are, of course, two undefined concepts: human excellence [virtue] and teaching. And as soon as we notice that teaching is undefined, we realize that there is a difference between *imparting information* ('the Greek word for fish is spelled iota, chi, theta, upsilon, sigma') and *assisting someone towards understanding*."[64] The concept of teaching is indeed undefined in the dialogue, and Zwicky is proposing a dialectical division. Remember the hypothesis: if something is knowledge, then it can be taught. Zwicky is dividing the genus *things that can be known* into two species: *transmissible information* and *recollectable truths*. And there is, she claims, a crucial distinction between knowledge that is linguistically transmissible and knowledge that is recollectable.[65] The two kinds of knowledge are not necessarily mutually exclusive: the transmission of some information might play a role, for example, in assisting someone toward understanding. But transmission is not enough for recollection (that is, understanding). Sokrates might tell Meno that virtue is knowledge; Meno might be able to regurgitate with approval the claim, "Virtue is knowledge"; but still he might not *understand* what he has been told and is regurgitating.[66]

The first half of Zwicky's distinction, namely, transmissible information, is comparable to an image from another of Plato's works, *Symposium*; there, Sokrates suggests that, unlike water flowing along a twist of yarn, wisdom cannot be transmitted. Talking with the prize-winning tragedian, Sokrates says, "How wonderful it would be, dear Agathon, if the foolish were filled with wisdom simply by touching the wise. If only wisdom were

---

63 Ibid.
64 Ibid., 45–6 / AL, 171.
65 Ibid., 69–71 / AL, 190–1. Recall Cornford's distinction (from §7.3).
66 Cf. Zwicky, *Wisdom & Metaphor*, L24, L49, L90–1.

like water, which always flows from a full cup into an empty one when we connect them with a piece of yarn—well, then I would consider it the greatest prize to have the chance to lie down next to you. I would soon be overflowing with your wonderful wisdom."[67] The passage is doubly ironic: Sokrates does not really envy Agathon, who is a clever rhetorician but no sage. And, what is more important for our purposes, the analogy is self-consciously satirical: the wise are compared to full vessels, the ignorant, to empty ones, and wisdom is imagined as a substance that might be transmitted from the former to the latter.[68] The dynamic is not dis-analogous to the transmission of digital information by fibre-optic cables, and perhaps that more recent analogy makes the point more forcefully: the copying of such information is something that could be done by a machine, passively, and without understanding.

The dis-analogous image instructs us that wisdom should not be imagined as a substance that can be transmitted along yarn or cable. An analogy is drawn in Plato's *Protagoras* that similarly denies the sub-stantiality of wisdom; there, Sokrates advises that food nourishes the body, while teachings nourish the soul. Food can be stored in a container and shown to an expert before being consumed, but "you cannot carry teachings away in a separate container. You put down your money and take the teaching away in your soul having learned it, and off you go, either helped or injured."[69] Unlike food or water, wisdom is not some-thing that can be extracted and contained separately from its host. Meno's paradox also haunts this passage in *Protagoras*. Sokrates says: "So if you are a knowledgeable consumer, you can buy teachings safely from Protagoras or anyone else. But if you're not, please don't risk what is most dear to you on the roll of the dice."[70] If I am not a knowledgeable consumer, how can I ever become one? How can I know whom to trust to teach me? (Recall Annas's claim that the apprentice is held hostage by her own inexperience.)

---

67 Plato, *Symposium* 175d–e. Cf. Scott, *Plato's "Meno,"* 143.

68 Notice that, strictly followed out, the analogy would entail that the wise person is emptied of her wisdom (and thus rendered ignorant) as a consequence of the trans-mission. (Shades of one of the "Parmenidean" objections to the metaphysics of the Forms: how can one thing be in many places at once? Cf. Plato, *Parmenides*, 131a ff.)

69 Plato, *Protagoras*, 314b.

70 Ibid., 313e–314a.

To learn – to understand, to see – is to do something, to change one's soul. This pedagogy is represented in Plato's *Republic*. There, Sokrates says:

Education isn't what some people declare it to be, namely, putting knowledge into souls that lack it, like putting sight into blind eyes. ... But our present discussion, on the other hand, shows that the power to learn is present in everyone's soul and that the instrument with which each learns is like an eye that cannot be turned around from darkness to light without turning the whole body. ... Then education is the craft concerned with doing this very thing, this turning around [of the soul], and with how the soul can most easily and effectively be made to do it. It isn't the craft of putting sight into the soul. Education takes for granted that sight is there but that it isn't turned the right way or looking where it ought to look, and it tries to redirect it appropriately.[71]

There is no clearer representation of the aspirations of Sokratic (and Platonic) education. This representation, too, indirectly addresses Meno's skeptical question: if I cannot already see, how can sight be transmitted to me? Sokrates rejects the image of transmission in favour of the image of conversion. Sokratic education takes for granted – we might say that Sokrates has faith or hope – that we can already see. Starting with this hope, it offers an altered conception of the nature of the task: the question is not "How *can* I learn?" but "*How* can I learn?" It is not a skeptical question about the very possibility of learning, but a fully, already committed question about methodology.[72]

In her lectures from Roanne, Weil discusses this passage from *Republic*. "Education," she says, "is, according to the generally accepted view of it, nothing but the forcing of thoughts into the minds of children."[73] We know, from her "Reflections on the Right Use of School Studies" (discussed in Sections 2.2–2.3), that she thinks such a conception of education is misguided. Recall what she writes there: "Although people seem to be unaware of it today, the development of the faculty of

---

71　Plato, *Republic*, VII.518b–d.

72　On Sokrates's "psychagogic method" in *Republic*, see Lilburn, "Turning the Soul Around," *The Larger Conversation*, 125–42.

73　Weil, *Lectures on Philosophy*, 220 / 284.

attention forms the real object and almost the sole interest of studies."[74]
And again, she writes, more strongly: "Teaching should have no aim
but to prepare, by training the attention, for the possibility of [a certain
application of the full attention to the object]. // All the other advantages of instruction are without interest."[75] Those other advantages
include the transmission of data (e.g., the theorems of virtue). If we
follow Zwicky's distinction, then Weil is asserting that merely transmitting does not count; true education consists in assisting someone toward
understanding: "Education means turning the soul in the direction in
which it should look [viz., toward the unchanging patterns of things]."[76]

§7.6. In the third act of *Meno*, there is a scene that concerns a distinction between true belief and knowledge. Sokrates and Meno consider
the supposition that virtue might be true belief, on the ground that
such belief might be just as beneficial as knowledge. Suppose that
you have never been to the Kamloops Art Gallery, but have heard
second-hand, and believed, that it was on the corner of Fifth and
Victoria in downtown Kamloops. Having this (true) belief, would you
be a worse guide than someone who had actually been there and
knew where it was? If not, then what is the difference between true
belief and knowledge? Sokrates compares true beliefs to the fugitive
statues of Daidalos. The image is bizarre. If one is looking for an image of something that is not stationary, a statue is an unlikely candidate, but the point seems to be that true beliefs are insecure. They
must be rooted through the method of recollection, by ultimately
giving "an account of the reason why [αἴτιος λογισμός]."[77] On the
surface, this might look like "the standard analysis" of knowledge as
justified true belief; but we should hesitate before ascribing anachronistic notions of justification to Plato.[78]

   Zwicky's reading suggests, however, that Plato's distinction between
true belief and knowledge is not the distinction to which twentieth- and
twenty-first-century philosophers are accustomed: that is, Plato does not

---

74 Weil, "Reflections on the Right Use of School Studies," 57 / 85.
75 Weil, "Attention and Will," 120 / 137.
76 Weil, *Lectures on Philosophy*, 220 / 284.
77 Plato, *Meno*, 98a. Cf. Plato, *Theaitetos*, 201d.
78 Cf. Gettier's infamous little paper; Vlastos, "*Anamnesis* in the *Meno*," 96–7; and
Irwin, *Plato's Ethics*, 141–5.

think that *justification*, associated with "the provision of empirical evidence or argumentative reasoning,"[79] is what makes the difference between true belief and knowledge. Rather, knowledge involves "causal reasoning," which is a recollecting of the causes of the experiences of necessary truth, which causes are the forms. Zwicky is right in proposing that we can hear, in the phrase "αἴτιος λογισμός" (*aitios logismos*), an echo of the vocabulary of *Phaidon*.[80] It is difficult to render elegantly into English what Plato means by αἴτιος. The English word "cause" does not even adequately translate Aristotle's so-called four causes.[81] David Gallop's translation of αἴτιος as "reason" makes better sense of the relevant passages in *Phaidon*.[82]

Knowledge, for Plato, may require "the ability to *demonstrate* one's understanding through a dialectical, 'causal' account given in terms of Forms";[83] but we should not assume that together (1) having the true belief that x is the only thing that always follows y and (2) being able *to say* "x is the only thing that always follows y" are *sufficient* for knowledge. Believing and being able *to say* ("to justify") one's belief are nothing without *understanding* (although saying, when saying is possible, might be one application of one's understanding). Zwicky connects Plato's epistemology with the epistemology of the Eleusinian Mysteries.[84] Like that of the Mysteries, Plato's epistemology involves seeing. In *Phaidros*, the pre-incarnate soul sees the Forms; and in *Republic*, it is the soul's eye that is lifted out of the barbaric slime and turned toward the good. In *Meno*, too, the soul "has seen all things here and in the underworld."[85] These metaphors point to a salient feature of the phenomenology of necessary truth: as Zwicky writes, "since it *feels* like seeing, it *is* a kind of seeing, with the mind's eye, of non-physical Forms."[86]

The dialogue's well-known geometrical demonstration – in which Sokrates walks the slave through the doubling of the square – is set up as a demonstration of how learning-as-recollecting works. The structure

79 Zwicky, *Plato as Artist*, 84 / AL, 202.
80 Ibid., 82–3 / AL, 200–1; cf. Plato, *Phaidon*, 97b ff.
81 Cf. Wicksteed's commentary in his translation of Aristotle, *Physics*, 126–7.
82 See Gallop, "Explanatory Notes," in his translation of Plato, *Phaidon*, 93.
83 Zwicky, *Plato as Artist*, 69 / AL, 190.
84 See esp. ibid., 96 / AL, 210.
85 Plato, *Phaidros*, 247c ff; *Republic*, VII.518c, VII.533d; and *Meno*, 81c.
86 Zwicky, *Plato as Artist*, 48 / AL, 173.

of the demonstration mirrors the structure of Meno and Sokrates's investigation into virtue (indeed, Sokrates underlines the parallel).[87] And like Meno with respect to virtue, the slave does not begin with conscious knowledge of the solution, a line with a length of square-root eight. Furthermore, Sokrates repeatedly emphasizes that he is not teaching (that is, not transmitting), but only questioning; the slave is not being taught, but is only recollecting.[88] The method of recollection, according to Sokrates, has a proper order:[89] it proceeds through the questioning of the *elenkhos* to the *aporia*, at which point one is emptied of one's false beliefs. From the *aporia*, one is in a position to recover true beliefs, and, eventually, knowledge. Perhaps most important for our purposes is the following feature of the demonstration: during the *elenkhos*, the slave is led to recognize, *to see for himself*, when he is wrong; and after the *aporia*, when the diagonals are drawn, he understands, *he sees for himself*, the solution. (Concepts of seeing and thinking cross here.)[90]

The method by which the slave is assisted in his understanding includes at least two kinds of prompt: visual examples (presumably drawn on the ground) and Sokrates's questions. After the slave has arrived at the solution, Sokrates says "he will perform in the same way about all geometry, and all other knowledge."[91] The clear implication is that the method of recollection is entirely generalizable: geometrical understanding is analogous to ethical understanding: the same method that helped the slave to solve the geometry problem should be able to assist the slave, and anyone else, including Meno, to understand what virtue is. If one is shown clear paradigms, and asked apt questions, one could become a more virtuous person. Apparently, the slave did not know what he was looking for; how, then, did he recognize when he made a mistake? How did he recognize the solution when it was shown to him?

If we think deeply about these questions, we might begin to appreciate the complexity of the relationship between Meno's skeptical question

---

87 Plato, *Meno*, 84b–c.

88 Ibid., 82b, 82e, 84c–d, 85d.

89 Ibid., 82e.

90 Cf. Burns's suggestion that the phenomenon of seeing-as places pressure on the traditional dichotomy between seeing and thinking ("If a Lion Could Talk").

91 Plato, *Meno*, 85e.

and Sokrates's (and Plato's) hopeful response. Remember Meno's question, "How can I learn what I don't already know?" Is the solution to this question supplied by the myth of recollection and the supporting geometrical demonstration? Scott says the answer is "no," and he argues that the materials for the actual solution are offered much later in the dialogue, in Sokrates's distinction between true belief and knowledge.[92] We have seen that Weiss also denies that the myth and its demonstration solve Meno's question. As she sees it, Sokrates recommends the myth for pragmatic motives; in other words, it is a sophistical device deployed to trick Meno into continuing with the inquiry.[93] Furthermore, the geometrical demonstration is an example of straightforward teaching, namely transmission, disguised to appear to be an example of recollection; it, too, is a sophistical device. In Weiss's interpretation, technical subjects, for which there are objective criteria of correctness, can be straightforwardly taught, that is, transmitted. Geometry, she claims, is one example of such a technical subject. However, geometry and virtue are utterly dissimilar in this crucial respect: virtue is not governed by objective criteria.[94]

Weiss writes: "Socrates is able to teach the slave-boy because Socrates has the requisite knowledge; he has knowledge because someone has taught him; someone has been able to teach him because geometry is teachable; and geometry is teachable because the solutions to geometrical problems are objectively testable."[95] Definitions of virtue, on the other hand, are not objectively testable and therefore, in Weiss's view, are not teachable. So there is no analogy between geometry and virtue, and the geometrical demonstration cannot model the learning of virtue. The "one criterion" that determines whether or not one is teaching, according to Weiss, is whether or not one has knowledge. If one has knowledge, then one teaches, regardless of whether one leads by questions or uses declarative sentences; if one lacks knowledge, then one does not teach, regardless of whether one uses "elenchus or myth or speeches."[96]

92 Scott, *Plato's "Meno,"* 79.
93 Weiss, *Virtue in the Cave,* 64–5.
94 Cf. ibid., 62, 80–1.
95 Ibid., 84.
96 Ibid., 97–8.

This analysis, however, with its dismissal of the relevance of methodology, is an oversimplification of the concept of teaching. Considering the conclusion of the geometrical demonstration, and Sokrates's assessment of it, Weiss asks, rhetorically: "Having witnessed and participated in a proof that he certainly understands ... may he [the slave] not rightly be said now to *know*?"[97] The implication is that Sokrates has knowledge and has successfully transmitted that knowledge to the slave. But regardless of whether we interpret the demonstration as an example of transmission or recollection, Weiss's inference is too quick. Minimally, it would be premature, at this point, to ascribe knowledge to the slave. It is relevant to ask: "Can he go on? Faced with this geometrical problem again, or a variation on this problem, can he produce the solution? Let's wait and see." On the basis of this one lesson, Sokrates himself is not yet ready to ascribe knowledge: "These opinions have now just been stirred up like a dream." They can be transformed into knowledge, but it would require more practice: "if he were repeatedly asked these same questions in various ways, you know that in the end his knowledge about these things would be as accurate as anyone's."[98]

As we have seen, Weiss embraces the ostensible conclusion of the *Meno*: virtue is not knowledge, and cannot be taught; the best that we humans can do is foster beliefs. The cost of this interpretation is high. However, there are two peculiar bits of text to which any interpretation should be reconciled:

(1) At the conclusion of the myth of recollection, Sokrates says, "We must, therefore, not believe that debater's argument" – Meno's eristical skepticism – "for it would make us idle, and fainthearted men like to hear it, whereas my argument" – the myth of recollection – "makes them energetic and keen on the search."[99]

(2) At the conclusion of the geometrical demonstration, Sokrates repeats, "I do not insist that my argument is right in all other respects, but I would contend at all costs both in word and deed as far as I could that we will be better men, braver and less idle, if we believe that one must search for the

---

97 Ibid., 110.
98 Plato, *Meno*, 85c–d.
99 Ibid., 81d–e.

things one does not know, rather than if we believe that it is not possible to find out what we do not know and that we must not look for it."[100]

Weiss suggests that these two bits of text support her interpretation of the myth of recollection and its alleged demonstration: their truth-value is incidental; indeed, they are self-consciously fictional, and are motivated by exclusively pragmatic considerations.[101] But Zwicky's reading offers a more coherent way of integrating these two bits of text into the dialogue as a whole.

Of the myth of recollection, and (1) the first bit of text above, Zwicky writes, "First ... there is no irony or doubt: this is a profession of profound faith. Secondly, it is, overtly, a profession of faith, not a bad or weak argument. Thirdly, to the extent that justification is provided, it is phenomenological and aesthetic, and moral: the account, says Socrates, struck him as true and beautiful; and trusting it makes us better persons."[102] The myth, then, is not an argumentative solution to Meno's skeptical question; indeed, the repeatability of that question might make us wonder whether it can be defeated by argument. The myth is instead an alternative to the enervating parasite of skepticism: if we remain in a constant cycle of doubt about the teachability of virtue, we will be unable to move; but if we choose, *contra* skepticism, to trust that learning is possible, then at least we can attempt to learn about virtue and to become more virtuous.

Of the geometrical demonstration and (2) the second bit of text, Zwicky writes: "We *become* virtuous by believing what the mathematical demonstration suggests but does not prove; we awaken excellence, actually produce it in ourselves, by rejecting skepticism about it."[103] What does the demonstration suggest? Occurring where it does in the context of the dialogue, the demonstration is clearly designed "to serve as a model for the investigation of virtue."[104] It suggests that our experience of necessary truth, exemplified here by geometrical truth, is explained by the myth of recollection (we recognize such truth because

---

100 Ibid., 86b–c.

101 Cf. Weiss, *Virtue in the Cave*, 7, 64–5, 69. Cf. Scott, *Plato's "Meno,"* 122.

102 Zwicky, *Plato as Artist*, 41 / *AL*, 167. On the question of moral justification, cf. Zwicky, "Once Upon a Time in the West," 195, 198.

103 Zwicky, *Plato as Artist*, 53 / *AL*, 177–8.

104 Ibid., 48 / *AL*, 173.

it is not unfamiliar to us). And the demonstration suggests that there is a "phenomenological *similarity* between our experience of necessary truth and our apprehension of moral beauty."[105] The demonstration does not prove that there is an analogy between geometrical and ethical understanding; nor does the method of recollection guarantee that the student will learn virtue. (Consider Meno.) But the demonstration does witness an instance of genuine recognition; and it invites the reader to compare that instance with her own experiences of recognizing paradigms of virtue.

— "What's the alleged difference between Weiss's and Zwicky's strategies? Aren't they both interpreting the myth as a protreptic device?" — Some of Weil's remarks on Platonic pedagogy are relevant here. In the lectures from Roanne, she takes an egalitarian stance on education in *Republic*:

If anyone is not able to understand the unchanging patterns of things, that is not due to a lack of intelligence; it is due to a lack of moral stamina. ...

One must not say: 'I am incapable of understanding'; one should say: 'I can turn the eyes of the soul in such a way that I will understand.' This equality of minds is a duty, not a matter of fact.[106]

In emphasizing that the capacity for understanding is a matter of moral stamina and a duty, rather than a matter of contingent fact, Weil is pointing toward the efficacy of sincere eros. *Wanting* to understand, she suggests, can compensate for lack of natural talent; in the absence of immediate gratification, sustained wanting can also support hope. Weil's faith emerged after months of "inward darkness": "I suddenly had the everlasting conviction that any human being, even though practically devoid of natural faculties, can penetrate to the kingdom of truth reserved for genius, if only he longs for truth and perpetually concentrates all his attention upon its attainment."[107] Even when they result in no apparent fruit, real exercises of attention increase our aptitude for attending. "Certainties of this kind" – Weil's faith that "when one hungers for bread one does not receive stones"[108] – "are experimental.

105 Ibid., 50 / *AL*, 175.
106 Weil, *Lectures on Philosophy*, 220–1 / 284–5.
107 Weil, "Spiritual Autobiography," *Waiting for God*, 23 / 39.
108 Ibid., 24 / 39.

But if we do not believe in them before experiencing them, if at least we do not behave as though we believed in them, we shall never have the experience that leads to such certainties."[109]

This claim is crucial for understanding what Sokrates is offering Meno. He is asking Meno to take a truth on faith: learning is recollection. If Meno accepts this (as yet unproven) truth and rejects skepticism, then he will be enabled to learn; and if he does learn, then he will have an experience that may help to secure his belief in the truth. Here is one of the important differences between Weiss's and Zwicky's interpretations: Weiss argues that the myth is a sophistical device deployed to trick Meno, while Zwicky says that it is a profession of profound faith. Sokrates *has seen something*, and he is inviting Meno to share his vision.

Let us recollect some of what has been discussed. We have explored Zwicky's suggestion that reading Plato's *Meno* as a work of art is indispensable for appreciating its integrity, its deeper unity. Such an interpretive exercise requires attention to dramatic form and character. We started with three questions – "Can virtue be taught? What is virtue? How can I learn what I don't already know" – and, attending to Plato's artistry, we unearthed a fourth: "What is teaching?" Following Zwicky, we have noticed that at least two factors are centrally relevant to education: (1) the *character* of the student; and (2) the kind or *method* of teaching – that is, transmitting information or assisting understanding. Meno's character is responsible both for his failure to follow the Sokratic order of inquiry and for his failure to discern that there is more than one kind of teaching; and these failures explains the apparently despairing conclusion of the dialogue. We have seen that there are at least three ways of interpreting the third act of *Meno*. Weiss's interpretation accepts the ostensible conclusion that virtue is unteachable, while Cornford's interpretation insists that the true conclusion is masked. Zwicky's reading offers a third way: it emphasizes Plato's resolute hope that virtue is learnable, via the method of recollection, and it also explains why we must see this hope for ourselves. Significantly for our purposes, Zwicky's study makes a case for the interdependence of character and thought, and invites us to re-imagine what knowledge is.

109 Weil, "Reflections on the Right Use of School Studies," 58 / 87.

8

The Dance of Perception

We have within us the sparks of knowledge, as in a flint: philosophers extract them through reason, but poets force them out through the sharp blows of the imagination, so that they shine more brightly.

— René Descartes[1]

§8.1. WE HAVE REFLECTED ON PLATO'S own investigation of his thesis that virtue is knowledge, and we have seen that it is possible to salvage a version of that thesis from the apparently negative findings at the end of *Meno*. While Sokrates and Meno appear to reach the conclusion that virtue is not teachable knowledge but merely luckily true belief, that conclusion is the result of their having taken a wrong turn, and Meno is responsible for the error. The problem is that Meno's character is undisciplined and he has become addicted to the sophists' spectacular (but ethically vacuous) displays of rhetoric. He has come to assume that knowledge is nothing more than data or information, the sort of thing that a sophist could put into an impressive speech for the purposes of transmitting it. But if we read carefully, we can see that the dialogue affords us the resources for thinking about a different way of knowing, a way that is not transmissible but is still learnable. A teacher may offer opportunities or cues, as Sokrates does for Meno, but the educational process requires the student's full participation. If she wants to understand, she must attend; and her attending is not merely a stunt done by the brain – it also depends on her character. In Aristotelian terms, it requires an aspiration to integrate epistemic and characterological virtue. While Plato does not draw the same technical distinction between kinds of virtue, he *shows* us, in his dramatic work, how character affects thought: we see the result in the character of Meno, his lack of courage,

---

1 Descartes, "Private thoughts," in *The Philosophical Writings of Descartes*, vol. 1, AT X.217.

his short attention span, his hankering for facile gratification, his limited imagination. Again, these observations tell us something about what knowledge must be: it is not a "cognitive" faculty operating independently of "non-cognitive" desire-like impulses; it is a more holistic activity, a way of thinking whose clarity requires harmonious ways of feeling.

In this section, we continue to think about the integration of different aspects of the psyche. In Weil's early work, we find more than one detailed study of the integrative work done by what she calls the *imagination*. For Weil, the imagination plays an indispensable and fundamental role in knowing. In her dissertation at the École normale supérieure (1929–30) and her lectures on philosophy at the *lycée* in Roanne (1933–34), she describes perception as an interaction – a dance – between mind and world. She borrows from Descartes the idea that the mind, in imagining, contemplates the image of a bodily thing. And her definition of image is Spinozistic. But the role of the imagination in her epistemology is ultimately Kantian: the imagination is what integrates active understanding and passive sensibility. What is unique to her account is its physical dimension. As Robert Chenavier writes, "Kant was the first to reveal the link between understanding and intuition by making this apparent in its real exercise, but he should have brought in more perceptibly the important role of the body on the outward aspect of existence through work."[2] According to Weil, thinking is essentially activity, but the original action is a *re*action of the body to an external stimulus. Such reactions generalize across similar stimuli, resulting in meta-images (or general ideas) which are responsible for categorizing things and structuring perception. The imagination is Weil's answer to the question, "What are the transcendental preconditions of the possibility of my experience of the world?" The raw wash of sensations is needed, but is not enough, to answer this question; and similarly with the structured emptiness of concepts. The imagination is what takes the signet ring of the conceptual realm and presses it into the melting wax of sensation – and thus produces experience.

Peter Winch, in his monograph on Weil, argues that her thought undergoes a significant development from her dissertation "Science and Perception in Descartes" to her *Lectures on Philosophy*. He proposes that her dissertation confronts a dilemma that is not solved until the

---

2 Chenavier, *Simone Weil: Attention to the Real,* 27.

lectures: "order is the product of thought, but thought can only be exercised on what already exhibits order."[3] Weil herself articulates the dilemma in her late "Essay on the Notion of Reading": "It is in this way that at every moment of our life the meanings we ourselves read in appearances take hold of us as though from outside. We can therefore argue endlessly about the reality of the external world. Because what we call the world are the meanings we read — it isn't real. But it seizes us as though from outside — so it is real."[4] Recall that reading (*lecture*), for Weil, is a term of art: to read is to perceive appearances as meaning-ful.[5] The legacy of positivist science and philosophy has instructed us to shuck the value and seek the underlying fact. But Weil recommends meditating on the contradiction that she identifies in the passage above. On the one hand, the fact that we read *meanings* might imply that we are projecting them onto the blank (and otherwise meaningless) world; on the other hand, the fact that we are *seized* by these meanings suggests that we are the patient in this interaction, and that the agent is some-thing else – something that is independent of the perceiver.

Nevertheless, there remains a problem about the source of the order or structure necessary for thinking. For knowledge, my thinking does need structure, but it also needs to be answerable to something.[6] When we turn to defining that something, we face a dilemma: either it is made out of the same stuff as thought, or it isn't. In the first case, idealism swallows the world; in the second case, there is the risk of crude incom-mensurability (if the world is substantially different from thinking, then how could thinking be constrained by it?). Either horn is fraught with difficulties. Winch argues that Weil's response to the dilemma is "to abandon the thesis that all order is the product of thought. 'When we give birth to thought, it will be born into a world that is already ordered.'"[7] And it is ordered by the body.

---

3 Winch, *Simone Weil: "The Just Balance,"* 33.

4 Weil, "Essay on the Notion of Reading," 298 / 14; translation altered.

5 That formulation is misleading if it is taken to imply that there is another way to perceive appearances, i.e., as otherwise than meaningful – but such a view is not Weil's.

6 Cf. McDowell, *Mind and World.* The recognition of these two needs is one of the motivating themes of his investigation. Cf. Williams, *Problems of Knowledge,* 122.

7 Winch, *Simone Weil,* 33; he seems to be quoting his own translation of this passage (Weil, *Leçons de philosophie,* 24).

Briefly, Weil's solution is as follows: thought is intentional (it is *about* something) and it requires order. Assuming that thought is not only its own object, we look elsewhere; but the sensations of empiricism are not enough to supply the requisite order: "the 'material' on which thinking must work cannot be an inarticulate splurge of passive sensation."[8] However, the world is *already ordered* by the reactions of the body. At a proto-conceptual level, the body has a set of gestures – what Weil calls "congenital reactions" – which generalize across stimuli. For example, stimulated by various different foods – bread, apples, and so on – the human body salivates. This reaction serves to classify these stimuli under the general idea "food." Thus the world's welter of multitudinous particulars is limited (it is conceptually structured), and thought can get a grip.

Winch's characterization of Weil's solution is in some ways accurate and insightful, but let us consider two modest but important amendments. First, the solution that Winch locates in the lectures is already available in the dissertation. Second, the role of the imagination – which is consistent across the dissertation and the lectures, but which Winch does not discuss – is indispensable to the solution. For Weil, the imagination is an amphibious faculty: half mental, half physical, it mediates the relation between mind and body. In a striking image, Weil compares the imagination to an oracle:

I will go and ask oracles about things; I will not consult mute things, nor myself who am ignorant, but I will go to this third, ambiguous being that is a composite of myself and the world acting on each other. This seems to have been what the Greeks did at Delphi; they questioned this point of intersection between matter and a mind in the person of a woman whom they probably thought they had reduced to being no more than that. Since I wish to believe only in myself, I will consult this bond of action and reaction between the world and my thought in myself alone. I will name this bond the imagination ...[9]

---

8 Winch, *Simone Weil*, 18.

9 Weil, "Science and Perception in Descartes," 69 / 200. Cf. Zwicky: "Primary process thought is the point at which the mind emerges from the body, 'like a mushroom out of its mycelium' as Freud puts it; and the point at which the body coalesces

The imagination, so defined, is indispensable to the solution for two reasons: first, it is Weil's response to the interaction problem – that is, the problem, perhaps best articulated by Elisabeth of Bohemia, of explaining how mental and extended substances can interact.[10] Second, as indicated earlier, it is her answer to the question, "What are the transcendental preconditions of the possibility of my experience of the world?"

Roughly two millennia before Kant, Aristotle clearly articulated the problem: "Let us admit that the soul knows or perceives the elements out of which each of these composites is made up; but by what means will it know or perceive the composite whole ...? For each *is*, not merely the elements of which it is composed, but those elements combined in a determinate mode or ratio ... Nothing, therefore, will be gained by the presence of the elements in the soul, unless there be also present there the various formulae of proportion and the various compositions in accordance with them."[11] So, too, with experience: it is not merely sensations, but sensations structured by concepts; not merely raw material, but material in*form*ed. Sensations and concepts, considered individually, are each inadequate to generate experience. Something further is necessary to integrate the offerings of sensibility and understanding: and that is the imagination.[12]

§8.2. In the first part of her dissertation, Weil sketches a portrait of Descartes that is largely unfamiliar to the Anglo-American tradition. For the sake of concision, we shall omit most of the details of her account (despite its interest as an alternative reading of a fundamental thinker in the history of philosophy). For the purpose of the present investigation, however, there are two features that must be mentioned: in Weil's version of Descartes, he is a philosopher for whom

out of the mind" ("Dream Logic," 143 / *AL*, 101). The source for Freud's metaphor is *The Interpretation of Dreams*, trans. James Strachey (Harmondsworth: Penguin Books, 1976), §VII.A (p. 672).

10 Cf. Elisabeth's letter to Descartes, 6 May 1643, in *The Correspondence between Elisabeth of Bohemia and René Descartes*, AT III.661.

11 Aristotle, *On the Soul*, I.4.409b29–410a8.

12 Sensations and concepts may be needed, but why is a *third* thing needed? Thanks to Steven Burns for this crucial question, which I try to address in §8.8. The problem might be circumvented if we conceive of imagining as a process or activity rather than a thing.

the imagination is epistemically indispensable, and whose conception of geometry retains its link with the concrete earth.[13] He is not
a shallow, arch-rationalist dualist; while he does associate the imagination with the body, the body is not despised. On the contrary, it is
the way in which the mind makes direct contact with the world. And
one paradigm of making that contact is the imagination's engagement in geometry.

"The study of mathematics," writes Descartes to Princess Elizabeth, "chiefly
exercises the imagination" (3:692). Similarly, he writes in a passage from the
Rules: "Henceforth, we will do nothing without the aid of the imagination"
(10:443). It is in the imagination, he says again in the *Rules* (10:416) that
the idea of everything that can be related to the body must be found. Since
the mind engaged with geometry makes use of the imagination, it does not
handle empty ideas. It grasps something.[14]

This conception of the imagination accords with Weil's unorthodox
conception of Cartesian science: "Thus Cartesian science is far more
packed with matter than is ordinarily thought. It does not disdain geometrical figures, since Descartes explicitly says that 'the ideas of all things
can be fashioned' from them alone (10:450). It is so bound to the
imagination, so joined to the human body, so close to the most common
labors, that one may be initiated into it by studying the easiest and
simplest crafts; especially those that are the most subject to order, like
that of weavers, embroiderers, or lacemakers." In addition to being
"packed with matter," Cartesian science exhibits a characteristic method:
it "avails itself of the most familiar comparisons, drawn sometimes from
aspects of nature closest to us, such as eddies in rivers, but especially
from trades and tools, the slingshot, the pressing of grapes. We might
think that these comparisons are only methods of popularization; on
the contrary, they are the very substance of Cartesian physics."[15] These
comparisons (*comparaisons*) are essentially imagistic analogies: for example, the motion or structure of imperceptibly little things is compared

---

13 Sepper argues that in Descartes's early philosophy, the imagination "stood at
the center of cognitional activity by virtue of the analogical relationships among all
things" ("Descartes and the Eclipse of the Imagination," 380).

14 Weil, "Science and Perception," 50 / 179.

15 Ibid., 51 / 179–80.

to the motion or structure of perceptible things. Descartes declares that "comparisons are the most appropriate means of setting forth the truth about physical questions that the human mind can possess."[16]

Having unsettled an oversimplified picture of Descartes's project, Weil argues that imagination is inseparable from ordinary perception. She calls upon an image from the *Dioptrics* that will remain with her for the rest of her life: "the blind man who directly perceives the objects at the end of his stick, not the sensations that the pressure of the stick makes on his hand."[17] The lesson of that image is at once counterintuitive and intuitive. On the one hand, the man's perception is obviously mediated by the stick. On the other hand, the immediacy of the perception depicted in the image is familiar to anyone: think of the last time that you wrote a grocery list. It would require a special effort to transfer one's attention from the list on the paper to the pressure of the pencil in one's fingers. As Weil writes, "Right now I feel the paper at the end of my pen ... The pressure of the penholder on my hand—the only thing, it seems, I should feel—I must pay attention to in order to notice, just as I need to pay attention to see glazes of red or yellow pigment on the canvas that portrays the Gioconda, instead of seeing the skin of a woman."[18] The default focus is the whole perceived object (rather than the instrument of perception or the atomistic constituents of the object). Furthermore, in cases where an instrument is the only means of perception, then the instrument is *a condition of possibility* and *not* an intermediary. The lesson can be generalized: "for each of us the blind man's stick is simply his own body."[19] If our bodies and their sense organs can be considered instruments, then perception by means of them is not mediated: this is just what direct perception is like here.

Weil draws a further implication, and claims that Descartes constructs "a theory of sensations as signs, using the example of drawings in which

16 Descartes to Morin, 12 September 1638, AT II.368, quoted in Weil, "Science and Perception," 52 / 180. For the role of comparisons in Descartes's philosophy, see Galison, "Descartes's Comparisons: From the Invisible to the Visible."

17 Weil, "Science and Perception," 53 / 182. Cf. Descartes, *Dioptrics*, in *The Philosophical Writings of Descartes*, vol. 1, AT VI.84. The original of Descartes's metaphor seems to be found in the Stoics: cf. Diogenes Laertios (SVF 2.867) cited by Long and Sedley, *The Hellenistic philosophers*, §53.N (p. 316).

18 Weil, "Science and Perception," 79 / 210.

19 Ibid., 79 / 211.

we see not marks on paper but men and towns (6:113)."[20] This theory is Weil's own theory of reading, which receives its mature elaboration in her "Essay on the Notion of Reading" (which we discussed in Section 5). Indeed, the theory of the imagination that Weil develops in the dissertation and early lectures continues in her later work under the name of "reading."[21] When we look at a drawing, we perceive not its elements (the lines of graphite on paper), but the thing that the drawing depicts; similarly, when we read a letter, we perceive meanings, not pencilled letters. With effort, we can shift our perception to the lines and letters; but for a literate perceiver, the original perception is holistic, and the perception of a whole's parts is the result of a subsequent analysis. In the lectures, Weil explicitly connects this insight with gestalt psychology:

It is … the things as a whole that have an affect on our bodies, and not their particular aspects. … What we are saying now has to do with something very important – the theory of forms (Gestalt theory). German psychologists have made interesting experiments on this matter, which lead us to the conclusion that the body grasps relationships, and not the particular things. When one says that it is the relationships that make an impression on us, and that it is the things as a whole that do too, these two ideas are closely related one to the other. For example, someone makes a series of raps on the table: one can repeat the series without having counted them.[22]

The connection between the two ideas is presumably the fact that some wholes *are* patterned sets of relations. The series of raps, for example, is grasped not as a numerical sum but as a rhythm. And Weil is claiming that the perception of the pattern is prior to any quantitative analysis of parts.

Again, the lesson can be generalized: we perceive not blank sensations but meaningful states of affairs. We can abstract sensations or concepts from experience, but again that abstraction is secondary; in the default

20 Ibid., 53 / 182.

21 Weil makes this connection explicit: "In such cases we ordinarily talk about an effect of the imagination; but perhaps it is better to use the word 'reading'" ("Essay on the Notion of Reading," 229 / 15).

22 Weil, *Lectures on Philosophy*, 32 / 23. Cf. Zwicky "What Is Ineffable?," §1 (p. 200) / AL, 242.

case, our experience consists in sensations that are always already conceptually structured. "And so Descartes finds in perception," Weil concludes,
"a 'natural geometry' and 'an operation of thought that, although it is
only a simple act of imagination, nevertheless contains a form of reasoning
similar to that used by surveyors when, by standing in two different spots,
they measure inaccessible places' (6:138)."[23] This theory of perception,
and the role of geometry in it, is continuous from Weil's dissertation to
her lectures: "There is already ... an elementary geometry in perception,"
she says in the lectures. "Everything happens as if our bodies already knew
the geometrical theorems which our mind does not yet know."[24] To claim
that there is a natural or elementary geometry in perception is to claim
that we naturally perceive patterns rather than chaos.

§8.3. Having sketched an unconventional portrait of Descartes, and
having emphasized the centrality of imagination to it, Weil embarks,
in the second part of her dissertation, on her own meditation. By
thus imitating Descartes, Weil shows her understanding that the
Cartesian meditation must be inflected in the first person singular.
Let us retrace the relevant moves. As Winch observes, I begin in a
state of pure *passivity*, like someone "wallowing with eyes closed in a
warm bath."[25] However, like Descartes, I find that the activity of
doubting is revelatory. Let me assume that all the contents of my consciousness are illusory – for example, my perception that I am writing
at a chipboard desk, looking across the rooftops of the city to the
Salish Sea. Still, in this swirl of illusion, is there any indubitable resi-
due, anything that I can say that I know? When I try to doubt the existence of the desk, or when I turn that doubt on my own existence,
can I not say, with Descartes, that the act of doubt implies the existence of a doubting subject: namely, a thinking thing? Weil's innovation is to suggest that there is something more basic than doubting,
more basic than thought. But to formulate her insight in that way is
already to distort it. For what I find is not the existence of a *thing*.
Instead, I find that the *activity* of thinking is. And this activity is expressed, initially, in doubting. In believing, I may be passive; by ap-
pearing to me, things may elicit belief from me. Unsolicited, the desk

23 Weil, "Science and Perception," 53–4 / 182.
24 Weil, *Lectures on Philosophy*, 51 / 49.
25 Winch, *Simone Weil*, 8.

appears to me, it seizes my consciousness, it occupies my thoughts – but I can always suspend belief in that appearance. "And through this power of thinking—which so far is revealed to me only by the power of doubting—I know that I am. I can, therefore I am [*Je puis, donc je suis*]."[26] As Winch observes, what is important is "the way the formula characterizes thought itself — as *activity*."[27]

Having established that *acting is*, Weil next asks whether she is able to do anything in addition to doubting. For example, what about daydreaming? (In Weil's later work, "imagination" becomes a pejorative term more or less synonymous with "daydreaming" or "fancying" – that is, thinking about what isn't there. But in the dissertation, imagination is importantly distinct from fancying.)[28] Do I not express my power in daydreaming about whatever I want? Weil notices that there is a difference between believing and doubting: while I always retain the power to doubt, I cannot will myself to believe. "Even though I would like to, I can never arouse in myself the same belief in the existence of things in my daydreams as that inspired in me by what I call real things. Thus I recognize that my power over my belief is only a negative one; I can doubt, but I cannot believe."[29] My belief is elicited *involuntarily* by the appearance of real things – just as my assent is elicited by truth.

This involuntary quality is a clue: it implies that I neither control nor cause these appearances. Here, Weil is following Descartes in Meditation Six. My ideas of sensible things must be produced by "a certain active faculty"; but this faculty "cannot be in me, since it clearly presupposes no act of the understanding, and these ideas are produced without my cooperation and often even against my will."[30] If this active faculty is

---

26 Weil, "Science and Perception," 59 / 189; translation altered. McFarland and Van Ness translate "*je puis*" as "I have power." But that translation risks substantivizing what Weil characterizes as pure activity.

27 Winch, *Simone Weil,* 9. Cf. Weil, "Science and Perception," 73 / 204.

28 For this definition of the term "fancy," cf. Coleridge, *Biographia Literaria*, 206; and Zwicky, "Imagination and the Good Life," §I.11. See also this book, §3.1. There are a number of other early texts by Weil, in particular «Imagination et perception» (1925) and «Sur l'imagination» (1931–32), which would considerably enrich, but also complicate, the conception of imagination under discussion here. Weil's thinking in these texts does not seem fully consistent with her thinking in the dissertation and the lectures at Roanne. The apparent inconsistencies are deserving of separate study.

29 Weil, "Science and Perception," 60 / 190.

30 Descartes, *Meditations on First Philosophy*, AT VII.79.

not in me, then something other than me must exist. "It *is* true that events take me by surprise, even when they are desired; in what I perceive, even when it is pleasant, there is always something I have not desired, something that takes hold of me and imposes itself on me like an alien thing. This is what makes me almost invincibly convinced that, if my daydreams exist only for me, on the other hand this paper, this table, the heavens, the earth, Paris, all exist independently of me." But, Weil concludes, "this conviction is not a proof" of the existence of the external world. [31]

Nevertheless, we do learn something from these reflections: doubting is different from believing and perceiving. I am always free – always able – to doubt, and when I do, I act. But believing and perceiving are mixed activities: to some extent, I am passive when they occur. With perceiving, in particular, the content is a constraint: I cannot generate it *ex nihilo*. (We might say: matter is necessary for the specification of form.)[32] Like Descartes, Weil then makes a fresh start, returning to the axiom: "But who am I? A thing that exercises this power that I call thinking. ... So, in order to know myself, I must know the extent of this power." She contrasts what we might call "power over," which is limited, with "real power," which is infinite: "A power such as I would attribute to a king, which is a relation between one thing and another (for example, between the king's words and the actions of his subjects) can be measured. But my power is not this shadow of power."[33] In principle, she enjoys real, infinite power – at least insofar as she can doubt. But insofar as she needs *content* for her thinking – that is, insofar as her thinking is *intentional*, or *about* something other than itself – her power is limited.

From the fact of that limitation, she argues, in a few dense sentences, to the conclusion that external things exist:

My sovereignty over myself, which is absolute as long as I want only to suspend my thought, disappears as soon as it is a matter of giving myself something to think about. Freedom is the only power that I possess absolutely. Therefore, something other than myself exists. Since no power is limited by

31 Weil, "Science and Perception," 60–1 / 191.
32 Cf. Aristotle, *Metaphysics*, Z.8.1034a7.
33 Weil, "Science and Perception," 62 / 192–3. Cf. Descartes, *Meditations*, AT VII.56–7.

itself, it is enough for me to know that my power is not absolute to know that my existence is not the only existence.[34]

This conclusion invites some scrutiny. Why was the earlier argument – the one modelled on Descartes's argument from Meditation Six – not adequate to draw the conclusion that external things exist? Because the involuntariness of a phenomenon, while it is a clue, is not enough to establish the phenomenon's mind-independent existence. Weil observes that she gets angry "suddenly, often even when I want to remain calm."[35] That willing, on the one hand, and sensing or feeling, on the other, can come apart in this way is significant for two reasons. First, it indicates that, for all I know, I am the source of my feeling of frostbite, for example, and of the cold that putatively caused that frostbite, even if I suffer it unwillingly. Second, at this point in Weil's meditation, her only clear and distinct truth is that *acting is*; insofar as she is passive in feeling frostbite, such feeling, however involuntary, cannot be the ground of anything's existence. Weil's original argument for the external world departs from Descartes. I know that I am not alone because my acting is limited. And it is limited by another power. The world and I act on each other, and we suffer each other. On this account, knowing the world, even its most "inanimate" aspects, will turn out to be an inter-subjective achievement.[36] The medium through which the world and I encounter each other is the embodied imagination.

§8.4. We have spent some time discussing the frame and opening moves of Weil's dissertation because they are important to her characterization of the imagination: first, according to her unorthodox portrait of Descartes, imagining is an indispensable form of philosophical and scientific thinking; and second, it is the point of intersection between mind and world, the point at which the active and passive

---

34 Weil, "Science and Perception," 62 / 193.

35 Ibid., 61 / 191.

36 Cf. Code, "Taking Subjectivity into Account." In her Cartesian meditation, Weil does not encounter other humans, but she does enlarge her knowledge by interacting with other subjects. Some of them would be called "inanimate" by the European tradition, but other traditions have treated them differently. See Hallowell, "Ojibwa Ontology, Behavior, and World View"; and Bird-David, "'Animism' Revisited: Personhood, Environment, and Relational Epistemology."

aspects of the perceiver are integrated. Let us now outline some of the philosophical background for her account of the imagination.

Weil's conception of the imagination borrows from Descartes, Spinoza, and Kant, as well as Aristotle and the Stoics. She follows Descartes in associating the imagination with the body: Descartes states explicitly that when the mind imagines, "it turns toward the body,"[37] and imagining is "merely the contemplating of the shape or image of a corporeal thing."[38] But what, exactly, is an image? In the Roanne lectures, Weil paraphrases and abridges one of Spinoza's discussions of the imagination,[39] and in the course of doing so, she also offers a definition of "image"; that definition, while influenced by Spinoza, is her own. Here is Spinoza's definition:

Further, to retain the usual terminology, we will assign the word "images" to those affections of the human body the ideas of which set forth external bodies as if they were present to us, although they do not represent shapes. And when the mind regards bodies in this way, we shall say that it "imagines."[40]

And here is Weil's:

(Les «images» sont les traces des choses sur le corps, traces qui sont en réalité celles des réactions du corps à l'égard des choses.)

("Images" are the traces which things leave in the body, traces which in fact are the reactions of the body to things.)[41]

Images are proto-conceptual and spontaneous *modifications of the body* (in response to other bodies). Images are also *intentional*: they are *of* or *about* bodies. Not all images are veridical – sometimes we have an image when no corresponding body is present. But images themselves are blameless. Spinoza makes clear that the error is located not in the image, but in the mind's failure to have an idea that "excludes the existence"

---

37 Descartes, *Meditations*, AT VII.73.
38 Ibid., AT VII.28.
39 See Spinoza, *Ethics*, IIP40S1.
40 Ibid., IIP17S.
41 Weil, *Lectures on Philosophy*, 58 / 58.

of the imagined thing.[42] So, imagining is the mind's turning toward the body and contemplating its reactions to things. Those reactions, whether congenital or conditioned, are responsible for general ideas: such ideas are *meta-images*, that is, images of sets of similar images. (We shall elaborate on this point in Section 8.6.) Any thinking, then, which involves generalities or similarities – any thinking that does not have a proper name for each and every particular – depends on the imagination.

Furthermore, the duality of the imagination – its active and passive aspects – is crucial to Weil's project. The aim of this project is more or less Spinozistic (and ultimately Stoic):[43] understanding is active, and insofar as the agent understands, she becomes more free and converts passions (or reactions) into actions. As she suggests in her sketch of Spinoza's philosophy of the emotions, "One frees oneself from feelings in so far as one understands them."[44] An action is just an understood passion. Significantly, passivity cannot be eliminated: insofar as the world participates in my perceiving and thinking – insofar as I am part of nature, and my perceiving or thinking is *about* something other than itself – I am passive.[45] The aim is not to eliminate this content, but to understand it; and understanding consists in actively perceiving patterns. Knowledge will not free me from the causal nexus by making me immune to it. But if I *understand* my place in the nexus, then I am not merely shoved around by the world; instead, I take responsibility for what happens to me (and through me).[46]

It is through the imagination, "this knot of action and reaction that attaches me to the world that I must discover what is my portion and what it is that resists me. … The world is not outside my thought; it is above all what is not me in me."[47] Weil's characterization of the world is suggestive: rather than conceiving of the world as an object thrown against a subject in an oppositional relationship, we might conceive of the world as extending into the interior of the agent, like night air

42 Spinoza, *Ethics*, IIP17s. Cf. Descartes's error theory in Meditation Four.

43 For Spinoza's Stoicism, see James, "Spinoza the Stoic."

44 Weil, *Lectures on Philosophy*, 207 / 268. Cf. Spinoza, *Ethics*, IIIDef2–3.

45 Cf. Spinoza, *Ethics*, IVP3.

46 Weil's compatibilism fits Hume's account ("Of Liberty and Necessity," *Enquiry*, 53–69).

47 Weil, "Science and Perception," 70–1 / 201–2.

entering an open window. Or, to phrase the thought after John McDowell, we might conceive of the conceptual sphere being *open* to reality.[48] Ideally, this relation will be complementary: "Not only do I have a grasp on the world, but my thought is, as it were, a component part of the world, just as the world, in another way, is part of my thought."[49] For Weil, such a complementary relation is an achievement, however, rather than the default condition.

§8.5. In the dissertation, Weil reconstructs the world geometrically. My action is abstractly represented by straight-line motion,[50] that motion is analysable into a series of points, and that series is infinitely continuable.[51] Insofar as the world exhibits geometrical structure – insofar as it consists in interrelated polydimensional wholes – it can be understood. Furthermore, that structure is already present in the body's proto-conceptual reactions to the world. The body, itself a polydimensional structure, is primed to receive the images of the world. This theory of perception is traceable through Spinoza back to Aristotle, Plato, and Empedokles: "like is known only by like."[52] Aristotle reproaches Empedokles (and Plato in his *Timaios*) for allegedly assuming that the relevant similarity is elemental; instead, it is, he claims, formal: "By a 'sense' is meant what has the power of receiving into itself the sensible forms of things without the matter." In perceiving, the soul receives the form of the perceived thing "in the way in which a piece of wax takes on the impress of a signet-ring without the iron or gold."[53] Such impressions are not formless sense data; they are images, that is, complex structures or forms. And to perceive is to imagine: to imitate, in one's embodied soul, the form of the

48 See McDowell, *Mind and World*, §II.2 (p. 26).

49 Weil, "Science and Perception," 80 / 212.

50 Straight-line motion is a representation of what Spinoza, following Hobbes, calls *conatus*: the tendency of a thing to continue in its current state unless modified by another thing. Cf. Spinoza, *Ethics*, IIIP7; and Hobbes, *Leviathan*, I.II.1.

51 McFarland and Van Ness offer a helpful gloss on the reconstruction ("Introduction," 28–9). The project of reconstructing the world on the combination of geometrical units might sound analytic, but has precedent in Plato's *Timaios*, which in turn follows Pythagoras.

52 Cf. Aristotle, *On the Soul*, I.2.404b17–18, I.5.409b26–7.

53 Ibid., II.12.424a17–20. The original of Aristotle's metaphor seems to be Plato, *Theaitetos*, 191c–e.

perceived thing. Weil's geometrical reconstruction of the world, then, is a re-imagination of the world as a set of interrelated forms.

My relationship with the world is redefined, in this model, as the relationship between straight-line motion and an infinitely complex combination of straight-line motions. These motions are *co-modifying*. Weil writes: "I am always a dual being, on the one hand a passive being who is subject to the world, and on the other an active being who has a grasp on it ... I can unite [the two parts of myself] indirectly, since this and nothing else is what action consists of. ... Not the appearance of action ... but real action, indirect action, action conforming to geometry, or, to give it its true name, work."[54] Insofar as I suffer the world, sensibility and understanding are confusedly mixed, and the world is an opaque and alien force shoving me around. The aim is to transform the confused intermingling into an integrity in which the roles of the two faculties are clarified.

If I wish to know the world, I must re-imagine it: not as a baffling adversarial force, "a will foreign to mine,"[55] but as an "obstacle" (*l'obstacle*). For Weil, "obstacle" is a term of art: it is that aspect of the world to which one responds with "work" (*le travail*). Simone Pétrement, in her discussion of Weil's early essay "Concerning Perception," offers a helpful definition of work: "So work is essentially *indirect* action, action applied to the *means*."[56] Work, so defined, is an act of practical reason (rather than an aimless burst of force). While the passive spectator suffers the brutality of the world, the worker re-imagines the world as an obstacle, something which must be approached obliquely. Winch astutely invokes Weil's image of a sailboat tacking against the wind as an analogy for work.[57] In knowing, the mind does not blindly collide with the world; it turns away from the world, and returns to it indirectly. Such indirection can take the form of reflection – the worker is the one who thinks about how best to circumvent the obstacle – but it must return to the world.

Work, for Weil, offers the promise of reintegrating the two aspects of the imagination (passive sensibility and active understanding): "Only

---

54 Weil, "Science and Perception," 78 / 209.

55 Ibid., 71 / 202.

56 Pétrement, *Simone Weil: A Life*, 61. For a different interpretation of the role of work in Weil's early writings, cf. Chenavier, *Simone Weil: Attention to the Real*, 23–5.

57 Cf. Winch, *Simone Weil*, 56. Cf. Weil, "Science and Perception," 76, 80 / 207, 212.

through the intermediary of the world, the intermediary of work, do I reunite them; for if through work I do not reunite the two parts of myself, the one that undergoes and the one that acts, I at least cause the changes I undergo to be produced in me, so that what I am subject to is my own action."[58] This thought is Spinozistic (and Stoic): I am the patient of my own actions, I am the cause of the changes I undergo, insofar as I understand those changes. Whatever I do, I will be changed by the world. But when I work, turning away from the world in order to return to it more thoughtfully, I take responsibility for the changes in myself. I also use my body as a tool to learn about other bodies. The metaphor of body as tool is misleading if it is taken to imply an alienated and dualistic relation between mind and body. For Weil, on the contrary, when one uses one's own body as a tool – an ὄργανον (*organon*) – mind and body are most fully integrated: almost paradoxically, one's body is a medium through which the mind achieves *immediate* contact with the body of the world. (Recall this point from Section 8.2.)

My body is "the point of intersection" between my simple movement and the complex movement of the world: it moves and is moved.[59] The most obvious example of work is manual labour; Weil considers the particular example of a farmer using a scythe.[60] Because it affords immediate contact with the world, work is, for Weil, epistemically indispensable. Indeed, her defence of work is, in a sense, a repudiation of the Aristotelian distinction between characterological and epistemic virtues, and of the glorification of contemplation.[61] Contemplation is not the highest human activity; the various ways of making contact with reality all require a bodily element.[62]

§8.6. At the climax of the dissertation, Weil offers the following definition of perception:

58 Weil, "Science and Perception," 78 / 209. For a subtle and nuanced account of the connexions among attention, imagination, and work in Weil's dissertation, see Janiaud, «L'étendue sans mystère,» *Simone Weil: L'attention et l'action*, 11–18.

59 Weil, "Science and Perception," 79 / 210.

60 Ibid., 81 / 212.

61 Aristotle, *Nicomachean Ethics*, I.13.1103a3–10, and X.7–8.

62 For help with rephrasing this point, thanks to Steven Burns.

La perception, c'est la géométrie prenant possession en quelque sorte des passions mêmes, par le moyen du travail.

Perception is geometry taking as it were possession of the passions themselves, by means of work.[63]

We have considered the suggestion that the theory of perception presented in the dissertation already anticipates the theory outlined in the lectures. The aphorism above, which defines perception in terms of geometry, is key to seeing the connection. The lectures pursue an ascetic regime of thinking, starting with a paring back of ambitions to the barest materialism, and then attempting to find the mind in that apparently barren landscape.

The very first lecture begins, auspiciously enough, with *action*: "*Study of the ways in which thought in other people shows itself* (objective psychology). Actions: reflex (from an external point of view everything is at the level of reflexes), custom, habit, voluntary actions."[64] One of the questions that Weil's theory is designed to address is: "What is the origin of general ideas?" Earlier we saw that her response is broadly Spinozistic: general ideas are *meta-images*, abstractions from a surfeit of similar images, which in turn are the body's reactions to other bodies. (They are meta-images in the sense that they are *images of collections of images*.) The ground of general ideas is, then, the imagination; and since the imagination belongs to the body, the mind finds its roots in the material world.

Furthermore, as the original thought is an image, so the original action is a *re*action. Weil writes, "It is, then, reflexes that the body gives us, that is to say reactions which are brought about by known stimuli." She then draws a distinction between "congenital" and "acquired or conditioned" reflexes. As examples of the former, she offers "secretion of digestive juices, movement of the leg when someone strikes it."[65] These reflexes do not involve any will or effort; they are autonomic and genealogically prior to theoretical reflection (although such reflection might also be understood as a species of conditioned reflex). Later in the lectures, Weil suggests that congenital reflexes are synonymous with

63 Weil, "Science and Perception," 79 / 210.
64 Weil, *Lectures on Philosophy*, 27 / 17.
65 Ibid., 30 / 21.

what she calls "spontaneous language": "it is something *animal* (and so human too). It is what conveys affections. It is natural in the sense that it is made up of natural reactions of muscles, glands and lungs."[66] It is important that these reactions are also general:

If we examine the relation between reactions and stimuli, we see that the latter are limitless in number, while the former are limited. The salivary gland, for example, always secretes saliva, whatever the food is. It is as if it were able to discern the general character of food throughout the infinite variety of foods. ...

So, by means of our reactions we generalise stimuli.[67]

Already, before bringing in Spinoza, and relying instead on behaviourist psychology, Weil begins to sketch her theory of general ideas. And, again, it is her ascetic or minimalist method that indicates this starting place: she is trying to see whether she can discover the mind – its conditions of possibility – while making only materialist assumptions: "It is by studying matter that we shall find mind."[68] Through its correlation with unlimited stimuli which are similar in way Σ, a single reaction ρ serves to sort those stimuli into kind Σ: "It is in this way that the body classifies things in the world before there is any thought. ... So, from the very fact that we have a body, the world is ordered for it; it is arranged in order in relation to the body's reactions."[69] These reactions – these meta-images – do the work in Weil's epistemology that is done by the categories in Kant's: they *organize* sensations into experience. There are important differences, however: meta-images belong to us, not insofar as we are rational agents, but insofar as we are imagining bodies. Furthermore, meta-images cannot belong uniquely to humans; following Aristotle, we can say that the capacity to imagine is shared by any animal soul.[70] For an animist such as Spinoza, the capacity will be distributed even more widely. What's more, a glance around us reveals organisms whose survival suggests that their meta-images have managed

66 Ibid., 65 / 66. Cf. Wittgenstein, *On Certainty*, §475. Analogously, Weil conceives of "language proper" as a kind of "conditioned reflex."

67 Weil, *Lectures on Philosophy*, 30 / 21–2.

68 Ibid., 40 / 34.

69 Ibid., 31 / 22.

70 Cf. Aristotle, *On the Soul*, III.10.433b27–30.

to track reality. "For how," asks Plato (according to Diogenes Laertios), "could animals have survived unless they had apprehended the idea and had been endowed by Nature with intelligence to that end? As it is, they remember similarities and what their food is like, which shows that animals have the innate power of discerning what is similar."[71]

"Acquired," or "conditioned," reflexes are developed through a repetitive process of association and transference: reflex P is a congenital response to stimulus Σ; stimulus Σ is repeatedly presented to the patient in association with stimulus T; if the conditioning is successful, then stimulus T (no less than stimulus T) will eventually elicit response P. "The training of animals," Weil writes, "consists in their acquiring conditioned reflexes, by means of an association of ideas."[72] Insofar as humans are animals, our training also consists in acquiring conditioned reflexes. Aristotle calls this process ἔθος (*ethos*/habit), and in her late «Notes sur caractère,» Weil tells an Aristotelian story about the formation of character (as we saw in Section 5).

That story is already latent here in the lectures (and in some early fragments such as «L'habitude»). She says that education, "for the most part, consists in providing children with conditioned reflexes." But she does not confine such conditioning to the education of children; she writes: "we shall have to look into the question of whether all the moral ideas we have are nothing but conditioned reflexes."[73] When she returns to this question, she adds: "Conditioned reflexes play a big part in our life ... One can ask oneself: aren't essentially moral ideas, like that of a lie, reflexes?"[74] — "But she's making a big leap from a stimulus-response mechanism to moral ideas," an interlocutor might object. "What does it even mean to claim that the idea of a lie is a 'reflex'? Furthermore, for Aristotle, becoming moral isn't just brainless robotic conditioning: it requires doing things *for the right reason*, and that requirement isn't satisfied by mere conditioning. Following Murdoch, some of us believe that virtue ethics offers an antidote to the plague of behaviourism."

---

71 Diogenes Laertios, *Lives of Eminent Philosophers*, III.15. Cf. Konrad Lorenz, quoted in Zwicky, *Wisdom & Metaphor*, R26. Cf. Zwicky, "Imagination and the Good Life,"§I.5.

72 Weil, *Lectures on Philosophy*, 31 / 22.

73 Ibid., 32 / 24.

74 Ibid., 37 / 29. Cf. ibid., 64 / 65–6.

— Let's address the first part of the objection first. A moral idea is a reflex insofar as it is a disposition to react in a particular way in the presence of a "morally relevant" stimulus. If one feels ashamed of lying and blushes when one tries to lie, this disposition is not something that one can choose, instantaneously, to override. And if we are responsible for the moral education of children, and we wish them to be honest, then we might try, over time, to encourage such an attitude of shame about lying; or we might try to encourage a feeling of admiration toward exemplars of honesty. The second part of the objection opens an expansive vista concerning what counts as a *reason* for virtuous action. Here, let us say only a few words: the virtuous agent acts differently from the enkratic (or continent) agent. The enkratic agent perceives a "moral" reason[75] in competition with other reasons, and must struggle to act morally; but it is a mark of the virtuous agent that she does not struggle – she simply does the right thing. One way of characterizing the effortlessness with which she acts is to call it a *reaction*. For those of us living in a historical period after the advent of free will, a reaction might seem too humble to deserve praise, and we might look instead with respect upon the agony of the enkratic hero. But another way of thinking about the aretaic reaction is to see it as an admirable kind of innocence, a kind that we might want to revive.

§8.7. The upshot of Weil's theory is that reactions are understood as the transcendental ground of the possibility of coherent experience:

Both congenital and acquired reflexes establish a classification among things in the world. ...

So, when we are on the point of giving birth to thought, it comes to birth in a world that is already ordered.[76]

We can experience the world because it is coherently structured, and to say that it is structured is to say that it consists in wholes standing in relations with each other. Alternatively, it is to say, with Weil, that there is "an elementary geometry" in perception. As we saw (in Section 8.6),

---

75 "Moral" is in scare quotes (like "morally relevant" above) because the "moral" is not a species of some genus which would also include a species of "non-moral" things. For a student of virtue ethics, what isn't "morally relevant"?

76 Weil, *Lectures on Philosophy*, 32 / 23–5.

the recognition of that elementary geometry is the key to seeing the continuity between the dissertation and the lectures. Weil writes: "Everything happens as if our bodies already knew the geometrical theorems which our mind does not yet know. ... // It is the same cause really (imagination) which enables us to perceive the most ordinary things, and do geometry."[77] The thesis that the same imagination is at work in ordinary perception and geometry is straight out of the dissertation: to repeat the climax: "Now I recognize that the two kinds of imagination, which are found separately in the emotions and in geometry, are united in the things I perceive. Perception is geometry taking as it were possession of the passions themselves, by means of work."[78] Let us elaborate this thought.

In the lectures, Weil argues that the imagination is responsible for our experience of spatio-temporal objects. "What is in the foreground of consciousness?" she asks. "Is it what is imagined or what is sensed?"[79] We can recognize that the disjunction is rhetorical, since Weil has argued (in the dissertation) that sensations do not come to us independently of their meanings. When we see a cube, for example, we do not merely lie back and let sensations wash over us. Our experience of three-dimensional things requires our active participation. "Cubic space consists essentially in the *gesture* of grasping the object."[80] In this respect, seeing a real cube is analogous to seeing a drawing of a cube. When we look at the drawing, we do not merely see some lines on a plane – we see a cube. Similarly, when we look at a real sugar cube, for example, we do not merely see an assemblage of warped quadrilaterals – we see a solid that can be grasped between finger and thumb. The point of the analogy is not that our minds reconstruct three-dimensional objects out of flat sense-data. The point is that imagination responds to the call of reality.

The body's living archive of meta-images is continuously working. And its work is not fanciful or false: on the contrary, imagining is governed by laws and limited by materials: "So, space, depth, shapes are given to us by our imagination. We must not forget, in this case, that 'imagination' should not be taken as something completely synonymous

77 Ibid., 51 / 49–50.
78 Weil, "Science and Perception," 79 / 210.
79 Weil, *Lectures on Philosophy*, 48 / 45; translation altered.
80 Ibid., 49 / 46; translation altered.

with fantasy or as something arbitrary: when we see two points we are not free to see anything except a straight line."[81] In other words, imagination does make an indispensable contribution to perception, but that contribution is not capricious; it is responsive to structure independent of itself. As such, it satisfies one of the requirements for knowledge: recall that knowledge is not possible in the absence of some kind of mind-independent constraint.

And so we reach the climax of the first set of lectures:

C'est le rapport essentiel entre nous et l'extérieur, rapport qui consiste en une *réaction*, un *réflexe*, qui constitue pour nous la *perception* du monde extérieur. *La simple perception de la nature est une sorte de danse*; c'est cette danse qui nous fait percevoir.[82]

Our *perception* of the external world constitutes the essential relation between us and what is outside us, a relation which consists in a *reaction*, a reflex. The elementary perception of nature is a sort of dance; this dance is the source of our perceiving.[83]

But what exactly does it mean to say that perception is a dance? As Winch suggests, a dance is indeed "a *pattern* of movements,"[84] but Weil does not restrict the sense modality to vision. For a spectator, a dance might be experienced via visual images; but for a dancer, the same dance might be experienced via kinaesthetic images. Even in dances where one partner leads, each partner must be responsive to the movements of the other; and in a solitary dance, the dancer must nevertheless be responsive to the "geometry of the emotions" that music is.[85]

The key idea is that a dance is a pattern of movements – what Weil might call an "elementary geometry" – to which our body responds with patterns of its own (whether that response takes the shape of visual or kinaesthetic images). More precisely, our body perceives patterns by imitating them. Furthermore, a dance is not only physical but

81 Ibid., 51 / 49.
82 Weil, *Leçons de philosophie*, 50.
83 Weil trans. Winch, *Simone Weil*, 41.
84 Winch, *Simone Weil*, 41.
85 The quoted phrase is from Zwicky, "Practising Bach," *Forge*, 26.

also *inter*active, or *co*-responsive.[86] Perception is a dance because it is a pattern of movements in which both our body and the body of the world participate. The agent who perceives clearly is not merely bruised by the random force of the world. When we understand what we perceive, our imagination focuses the images given to our body by the world and discerns their interrelations – and thus transforms a passion into an action. (For example, I realize that her loudness is not, as I initially surmised, an expression of brashness, but rather an attempt to compensate for incapacitating shyness, and thus my irritation dissolves into empathy. Or I gradually recognize that my flash of anger is not caused, but only occasioned, by the jar that exploded on the kitchen floor, and as I turn to the work of sweeping up the glass, my attitude of blame dissipates.)

§8.8. We have found that, for Weil, the imagination is an amphibious faculty. It mediates (and makes possible) the relation between mind and body. This duality leads to a couple of references to two imaginations,[87] which we might interpret as imagination under the aspect of (active) understanding and imagination under the aspect of (passive) sensibility. Recall the passage (from Section 8.1) in which Weil characterizes imagination as an oracle, "this bond of action and reaction between the world and my thought in myself alone." That passage continues: "I will name this bond the imagination, as opposed to the understanding, the name of the 'I' who thinks, and the sensibility, my name insofar as I am acted upon."[88] And so Weil shows her Kantian hand. Consider the famous passage in the first *Critique* in which Kant draws the same distinction: "If the receptivity of our mind, its power of receiving representations in so far as it is in any wise affected, is to be entitled sensibility, then the mind's power of producing representations from itself, the spontaneity of knowledge,

---

86 Cf. Zwicky on the collaborative experience of meaning (*Lyric Philosophy*, L250). Corbí's notion of "passive receptivity" – a notion inspired by Weil's work – is also helpful here ("First Person Authority and Self-Knowledge as an Achievement," §10.1 [pp. 345–7]). Like Weil, Corbí uses the metaphor of dancing to illustrate what he means. Cf. Abram, who describes perception as "this silent or wordless dance ... this improvised duet between my animal body and the fluid, breathing landscape that it inhabits" (*Spell of the Sensuous*, 53).

87 See Weil, "Science and Perception," 71, 79 / 202, 210.

88 Ibid., 69 / 200.

should be called the understanding … Without sensibility no object would be given to us. Without understanding no object would be thought. Thoughts without content are empty, intuitions without concepts are blind."[89]

Is imagination, then, a third faculty, in addition to understanding and sensibility? A crucial question. We have considered the suggestion that imagination is the *integrity* of understanding and sensibility. Weil offers a couple of metaphors that go some distance toward making sense of that suggestion:

If I were only understanding and sensibility, I would know that I see a flash of lightning or hear thunder almost in the same way I know that the words I see in silent film titles are uttered by the voice of a man or a woman. … I would be always like a spectator at a badly staged play in which the storm, riot, or battle is represented in a ludicrous way.[90]

Here, understanding and sensibility are not *integrated with* but *added to* each other, in the way that words might be appended to the picture in a silent film. Analogously, I would have a sense impression of lightning, to which would be added the concept "lightning," impression and concept each retaining its independence and being merely externally related to the other. Sensibility and understanding would thus run on parallel but separate tracks. Like the spectator at the badly staged play, I would be able to label what I perceive (for example, "that performer is attempting to depict anger") without being moved by it. But this is not the way things are:

But this supposition is absurd, so contrary is it to reality, for the only way sense impressions reach my mind is by causing a disturbance in it, and, far from being an understanding to which senses have been added like telephone operators to a staff headquarters, I am first and foremost nothing but imagination. From the fact that thunder crashes it follows, not that I become

---

89 Kant, *Critique of Pure Reason*, B75 / A51. Kant is not the inventor of this distinction, which is traceable at least as far back as Aristotle's distinction between the passive and active intellect: see Aristotle, *On the Soul*, Bk III, Ch. 5. Regarding Kant's productive imagination, see Strawson, "Imagination and Perception"; Warnock, "Imagination and Perception"; and Kearney, "The Transcendental Imagination."

90 Weil, "Science and Perception," 69–70 / 200–1.

aware of a sound, but that my thinking is disturbed at its source ... The world and my mind are so thoroughly intermingled ... The slightest disturbance of the senses hurls me into the world.[91]

I am first and foremost nothing but imagination. For Weil, as for Aristotle and Spinoza, the original form of thinking is imagination – and it will be at the root of all further thinking.[92] The contributions of understanding and sensibility can be analysed out, but it does not follow that they made their contributions atomically (any more than the possibility of analytically distinguishing skeleton from muscle shows that skeleton and muscle began separately and were then combined into an organism). The senses do not merely relay neutral information to HQ, which then interprets that information; again, Weil's metaphor is designed to illustrate a merely external relation. But in fact I have no experience of meaning-free sense data. On the contrary, to perceive the flash of lightning is to read its meaning. For example, if I am swimming in a lake, and I perceive lightning, then I perceive something bright but also threatening. On the other hand, if I am safely sheltered in a cabin, watching lightning fracture the sky over the lake, then I perceive something bright and perhaps also sublime. Afterward, I might be able to analyse out the brightness and distinguish it from its valence – but that is not how it comes to me. In perceiving, what comes first is the complex whole of conceptually structured sensation: experience *means* something to me.

— "But you're making some highly questionable assumptions! Can't we imagine someone else, swimming in the same lake, who perceives the lightning as a bright and thrilling risk? Sure, such a person would be reckless, but the different 'readings' of these two swimmers show that what you are calling 'meaning' is not perceived but projected. Both swimmers perceive the same meteorological phenomenon, but that phenomenon, objectively considered, is neither threatening nor thrilling – it's just 'a natural electrical discharge of short duration and high voltage.' It could kill you, but it isn't 'threatening' because it's intentionless." — But notice that in objecting you have offered a reading of your own: to claim that it's "*just* a natural electrical discharge" is to read the

---

91 Ibid., 70 / 201. Cf. Weil, *First and Last Notebooks*, 24, quoted in Winch, *Simone Weil*, 14.

92 Cf. Aristotle, *On the Soul*, III.7.431a14–17 and 431b2; Ross, *Aristotle*, 152; Spinoza, *Ethics*, IIP40S2; and James, Lloyd, and Gatens, "The Power of Spinoza," 53.

phenomenon through the spectacles of positivism. Heidegger's critique remains insightful: positivism, no less than the "pseudo-science" it purports to expose, is a metaphysical position.[93] The lightning *is* a natural electrical discharge – but it is not *only* that. From the possibility of reading the lightning in more than one way, it does not follow that all readings are equal.[94] Some readings are more accurate than others. Indeed, some readings are *corrections* of mistaken readings.

Weil offers an example of imagining that she repeats, over a decade later, in the "Essay on the Notion of Reading." Compare the following passages:

Thus at times something at a bend in the road frightens me; what is it? Not a sense impression; impressions have no more access to my thought than do the strange designs formed by the letters when I am reading. What frightens me is the idea, formed by the imagination out of what I see, of a hostile and powerful will that threatens me. A few moments later my imagination forms another idea: that of some harmless being, a tree.[95]

If at night, on a deserted road, instead of a tree I think I see a man lying in wait, a threatening human presence forces itself on me, and, as in the case of the letter, makes me tremble even before I know what it's all about; I draw near, and suddenly everything is different, I no longer tremble, I read a tree and not a man. There is not an appearance and an interpretation ...[96]

When Weil writes that the idea of a threat is "formed by the imagination out of what I see," we must understand that act of forming as occurring transcendentally. It is not as if I first receive the sense impressions, and they are subsequently processed and shaped by the imagination: "There is *not* an appearance *and* an interpretation" (emphases added). The point of the comparison with (literal) reading is again the insight from gestalt psychology: perception of wholes is prior to perception of their components. The fact that components can (sometimes) be discerned retrospectively through analysis does not establish their epistemic or ontological priority – it does not mean that the wholes were constructed

93 See Heidegger, "What Is Metaphysics?," *Basic Writings*, 93–110.
94 Cf. Zwicky, *Wisdom & Metaphor*, §§97–8.
95 Weil, "Science and Perception," 71–2 / 202–3.
96 Weil, "Essay on the Notion of Reading," 299 / 15.

out of separate components. Weil is arguing that the imagination is always already at work in experience, and it *must* be at work if there is to be experience.

But Weil does not leave us there, at the mercy of these faculties. Her project, in her study of the imagination, is not only descriptive; it has a normative dimension.[97] We have glimpsed the possibility of *integrating* sensibility and understanding by way of the imagination. Since imagination, for Weil, is a condition of the possibility of experience, we cannot stop imagining any more than we can stop experiencing. We can, however, aspire to understand the images that appear to us. To understand, according to this (Spinozistic-Stoic) epistemology, is not to master or control; it is to see clearly how any given image is interrelated with other images. That may sound like a meagre achievement, especially when measured by the yardstick of the free market, since it does not multiply our choices. But it is real freedom for the Stoics, and Descartes, and Spinoza. Recall Descartes's re-conception of freedom (from Section 3.5): "In order to be free I need not be capable of being moved in each direction; on the contrary, the more I am inclined toward one direction—either because I clearly understand that there is in it an aspect of the good and the true, or because God has thus disposed the inner recesses of my thought—the more freely do I choose that direction."[98] The more clearly I perceive truth, the less I vacillate in its presence, the less I wrench against the harness of necessity.[99] According to this view, understanding is not the value-free grasp of the basic facts; it is appreciating *why* an image has the meaning it does. Sometimes an act of understanding situates an image in a causal sequence; sometimes it notices similarities between this image and other images. Truth is liberatory, not because it gives power over, but because it gives peace.

---

97 For the normative dimension of imagination, see Murdoch, "Ethics and the Imagination"; Church, "Seeing Reasons"; and Zwicky, "Imagination and the Good Life."

98 Descartes, *Meditations*, AT VII.57–8.

99 Recall the infamous Stoic metaphor of the dog tied to the cart: SVF 2.975 (Long and Sedley, eds., *The Hellenistic philosophers*, §62.A).

9

Integrative and Disintegrative Perspectives

§9.1. LET US REVIEW, VERY BRIEFLY, our findings from the previous section. In Simone Weil's dissertation, the imagination is amphibious, mediating between mind and body, understanding and sensibility. In her lectures, this account is embellished and fleshed out: the workings of imagining are explained in terms of reactions, which limit and generalize phenomena. In a sense, Peter Winch is right to see the account in the lectures as more articulate – but it makes articulate what was already latent in the dissertation. What the lectures share with the dissertation is the idea that there is an elementary or natural geometry in perception. In both texts, it is the imagination that is responsible for that elementary geometry. It is the transcendental precondition of the possibility of experiencing. And the fact that we have coherent experience, rather than a chaotic blur of sense-data, implies, for Weil, that the deliverances of our sensibility are already structured by the understanding. According to this epistemology, the imagination is simply that collaborative relation between those two different epistemic faculties. But the imagination has a further responsibility. An image is a complex whole that consists in relations with other images. By arranging multiple images into patterns, the imagination can clarify the interrelations among them. To perceive, clearly, how an image fits into a set of relations with other images is to know. And to know is to be free (in the Stoic sense of freedom). We have been thinking about imagination as the integration of epistemic organs; we turn now to thinking about the ethical dimension of integrity.

In "Moral Integrity," Winch's inaugural lecture as chair of philosophy at King's College, he warns that he will not be attempting an *analysis* of the concept of integrity;[1] his method, he implies, is closer to that of Kierkegaard, who "does not attempt to *say* what purity of heart is; he *shows* what it is by portraying various cases."[2] Winch's subject "is the relation of a man to his acts."[3] And in the course of his investigation, he offers a number of object lessons or case studies which illustrate two different kinds of relation. When we are trying to understand the ethical character of an agent, says Winch, we must notice not only *what he (or she) decides to do,* but also "*what he considers the alternatives to be* and ... what are the reasons he considers it relevant to deploy in deciding between them." These latter considerations, and the possibility of different descriptive framings of a situation, can be comprehended by the notion of *perspective:* "a situation, the issues which it raises and the kind of reason which is appropriate to a discussion of those issues, involve a certain perspective"; and "the agent *is* this perspective."[4]

To distinguish between the two kinds of relation investigated by Winch, let us call them the *disintegrative* and the *integrative perspectives.* The adjective "disintegrative" is not meant to be pejorative; as we shall see, it marks the gap that can open between an agent and his context, and the concomitantly felt need to articulate reasons to bridge the gap. Intermittent recourse to the disintegrative perspective is characteristic of an ethically responsible agent; occasionally, we need to bring reasons to the surface of consciousness in order to criticize them. The theoretical error consists in assuming that it is incumbent upon the agent *ceaselessly* to occupy that perspective, and that the integrative perspective is, by comparison, ethically and rationally deficient.

Winch begins with a sketch, which he admits is a "caricature," of the agent belonging to the disintegrative perspective. This agent is pictured primarily as an actor, that is, a *world-changer,* and a *spectator* of "a world which includes his own body."[5] It is the agent's will that effects changes in the world, and the job of moral philosophy is to provide guidance for the exercise of the will. The preceding caricature involves a very specialized picture of agency and action. It is not unlike looking over

1 Winch, "Moral Integrity," 171.
2 Ibid., 180. Cf. Wittgenstein, *Tractatus,* prop. 4.1212.
3 Winch, "Moral Integrity," 171.
4 Ibid., 178.
5 Ibid., 171–2.

a chessboard, with one's hand hovering above one's king, and deliberating about the relative merits of several available moves. The deliberating agent is *separate* from the piece that he will eventually choose to move; his deliberations are instrumental and goal-directed; he evaluates the merits of the available moves by comparing them, *weighing* one against another. This specialized picture of action "separates the agent from the world in which he acts, and to make action intelligible, this gap has first to be bridged."[6] And the gap is bridged – the agent is shoehorned back into the world – by the provision of reasons. These reasons serve *to mediate* the relation between the agent and his actions.

This disintegrative perspective is not unfamiliar, and largely innocuous. If it is not already operative in a given situation, the slightest doubt can be sufficient to trigger its operation. And that is the risk of this perspective: unlike the integrative perspective, it is to this disintegrative perspective that the Glaukonian question is addressed, and from this perspective that the question is intelligible; that is, "What advantage does morality bring? And the form of the question suggests that we must look *outside* morality for something on which morality can be based."[7] The question expresses a hankering for a foundationalist justification for morality, and the disintegrative perspective is vulnerable because it is capable of surveying so-called moral reasons as *some* reasons *among others*. With the possibility of conflict between "moral" and "non-moral" reasons comes the intelligibility of the question, "Why should I act morally?"

Winch canvasses some of the ways in which theorists might try to engineer the mediation, including, for example, the utilitarian principle of the greatest happiness of the greatest number, and the Kantian principle of acting for the sake of duty.[8] We can picture a disintegrated agent in a moral dilemma, asking himself how he should act, and consulting one of these general principles in order to settle the question. In dissidence, Winch contends that "there is *no* general kind of behaviour" – neither maximizing happiness, for instance, nor acting for the sake of duty – "of which we have to say that it is good without qualification. … All we can do, I am arguing, is to look at particular examples and see what we *do* want to say about them; there are no general rules which

6 Ibid., 174.
7 Ibid., 175. Cf. Plato, *Republic*, II.357a–361d.
8 Winch, "Moral Integrity," 173–4, and 178–80.

can determine in advance what we *must* say about them." What is crowded out by the generalist thesis that one acts in a morally valuable way only if one's action is rationally mediated by principles? The problem with the generalist position is not only that it "forces us to accept as 'good without qualification' kinds of behaviour which we may quite legitimately think are not," but also that it "prevents us from recognizing as 'good without qualification' kinds of behaviour which we may quite legitimately think are."[9] There is a range of actions whose value is invisible from the generalist position but available to the alternative, integrative perspective. This perspective is thrown into relief by some contrasting cases.

§9.2. Winch asks us to consider his version of Mrs Solness (from Ibsen's *Master Builder*): she is "someone who is obsessed with the Kantian idea of 'acting for the sake of duty'. She does not appear, though, as a paragon of moral purity but rather as a paradigm of a certain sort of moral corruption. No doubt her constant appeal to duty is a defence against the dangerous and evil resentments she harbours within her."[10] Winch contrasts Mrs Solness with Weil's example of a father playing with his child – "not out of a sense of duty but out of pure joy and pleasure."[11] It is this image of unmediated, spontaneous, joyous activity which exemplifies (but does not exhaust) the *integrative* perspective. The activity is also autonomous, in a way that would be recognizable to Spinoza. Kant, by contrast, would seem obliged to diagnose this case as an instance of heteronomy of the will.[12] Winch is careful to explain that he is not trying to replace Kantian *acting for the sake of duty* with *acting spontaneously*. The point is that if we are committed exclusively to the Kantian principle (or to

9 Ibid., 181.

10 Ibid., 180. Winch's characterization of Aline Solness does not seem entirely fair. It is true that she appeals to duty whenever she is on stage: cf. Ibsen, *The Master Builder*, 143, 163, 169, 183, 190, 202. On the other hand, her resentments are arguably justified: she has lost two of her children as a result of a house fire, and her guest has arrived under questionable pretences having to do with her husband. Thus I refer not to Ibsen's but to Winch's version of the character. For advocating on behalf of Ibsen's text, thanks to Letitia Meynell and Laura Zebuhr.

11 Winch, "Moral Integrity," 181. Cf. Weil, *Notebooks*, I.46 / *OC*, VI.1.323.

12 Cf. Spinoza, *Ethics*, ID7, IIID2, IIIP11S, IIIP13S; and Kant, *Grounding*, Ak. 440–1.

some other generalist principle), we will fail to recognize the ethical value of instances of spontaneous activity. "We might speak of the father in this example," writes Winch, "as 'absorbed in' what he is doing and my suggestion is that we do not always need to think of a man's action as performed by him in accordance with some principle ('maxim') in order to think of it as unequivocally his act and to attach moral value to it."[13]

Returning to the case of Mrs Solness, Winch reiterates the distinction: "When Hilda Wangel arrives at the Solnesses' house as a guest, Mrs Solness, in splendid Kantian tones, says, 'I'll do my best for you. That's no more than my duty.' How very different we should have regarded her if she had said: 'Do come and see your room. I hope you will be comfortable there and enjoy your stay.'"[14] There is a difference between the strictures of etiquette and unprompted generosity. By contrast, we can picture Winch's Mrs Solness, in the former scenario, looking over the shoulder of her guest at the moral law, and forcing her will into conformity with it, meanwhile gritting her teeth and curbing resentful inclinations to slam the door in her guest's face. Similarly, we can picture a different father, or the same father overworked and worn out, "who finds himself unable to enjoy himself spontaneously with his child; though he goes out of his way to entertain the child out of a sense of his duty as a father."[15] We need not pass judgement on these cases of disintegrated agency. We might find much to commend in a host who dutifully provides shelter to an inconvenient guest, or a tired and disaffected father who remains mindful of his parenting responsibilities. And as a matter of fact agents just do occasionally come apart from their contexts in these ways. When this happens, there is dissonance between the situational demands and the affective, characterological state of the agent. And then moral principles can be invoked to direct the agent.

This thought is distilled in an aphorism that serves as one of Williams's epigraphs to *Ethics and the Limits of Philosophy*: «Quand on n'a pas de caractère, il faut bien se donner une méthode.»[16] When the needed

---

13 Winch, "Moral Integrity," 184.

14 Ibid., 183. Cf. Ibsen, *The Master Builder*, 143.

15 Winch, "Moral Integrity," 181.

16 Albert Camus, *La Chute*, quoted in Williams, *Ethics and the Limits of Philosophy*, xiii. (Cf. Zwicky, *Lyric Philosophy*, L184.) The quote's original context conveys a sinister overtone: "I live in the Jewish quarter or what was called so until our Hitlerian

motivation does not follow from the interaction between character and context, a moral system can serve as a kind of abstracted and external-ized character – a mechanism to which one submits oneself, and which then requires one to obey its directives. But a moral system cannot *replace* character, for it lacks the flexibility required for responsivity to context. This responsivity is not something that can be systematized in advance of particular contexts. The mistake is to assume or insist that moral principles must always be operating – even where it appears otherwise – if action is to be ethical. In some cases, one might think, I don't *want* to do this thing, but I *should* do it – and that second clause indicates a distinct component in one's motivation. ("It is only where moral emo-tion is comparatively weak," writes George Eliot, "that the contemplation of a rule or theory habitually mingles with its action.")[17] Insofar as one succeeds in acting as one should, one is enkratic. But there are other cases – and not all of them are morally worthless – in which one *does* want to act in that way, and in these cases the "should" is superfluous.

Finally, compare the following cases:

[1] "If I don't repay this money I shall be sent to prison."
[2] "I must repay this money in order to fulfil my duty."
[3] "He lent me this money and I must repay it."[18]

Case (1) may coincide with duty, but the speaker is motivated by a medi-ate inclination (that is, a desire to avoid incarceration). Case (2) would seem to satisfy the Kantian criterion for moral worth: the repayment is made, not from any inclination (mediate or immediate), but from duty.[19] Case (3) is neither necessarily reducible to a case like case (1), nor necessarily convertible (for example, through the explication of alleg-edly "tacit" premises), into a case resembling case (2). What the Kantian analysis omits – indeed, precludes – is the possibility that case (3), if not

---

brethren made room. What a cleanup! Seventy-five thousand Jews deported or assas-sinated; that's real vacuum-cleaning. I admire that diligence, that methodical patience. When you don't have character, you'd better give yourself a method. Here it did wonders incontrovertibly, and I am living on the site of one of the greatest crimes in history" (Camus, *The Fall*, trans. J. O'Brien [New York: Vintage Books, 1956], 11; translation altered).

17 Eliot, "Worldliness and Other-Worldliness," 206–7.
18 Winch, "Moral Integrity," 183. Cf. Kant, *Grounding*, Ak. 397.
19 Cf. Kant, *Grounding*, Ak. 398.

converted into case (2), could be morally valuable. Weil suggests a different way of thinking about case (3): "A man tempted not to return something entrusted to him will not refrain simply because he has read the *Critique of Practical Reason;* he will restrain himself, perhaps, as it may seem to him, even in spite of himself, if the very appearance of the thing entrusted to him seems to cry out that it must be returned."[20] If we could learn to read the meanings of particulars, we would not need to rely on the epicycles of general principles. And it is this possibility – that a father might be moved, spontaneously, and ethically, by his daughter; that a host might respond similarly to her guest – that Winch is concerned to defend. Aristotle, no less than Kant, suffers from this blind spot: he claims that the nutritive psychological faculty, due to its autonomic character, is irrelevant to ethics.[21] Photosynthesis, as we know, is the process by which green plants and some other organisms use sunlight to synthesize nutrients from carbon dioxide and water. By analogy, imagination is an agent's educable capacity autonomically to use whatever motivational energy is available in the ecological community.[22]

It is possible for an agent to act ethically (that is, in an ethically responsible way), without an explanatory gap having first opened between the agent and her action, and without her needing to engage in Humean or Kantian deliberations in order to traverse the gap. In each case, the presence of a daughter, a guest, a lender can be enough to motivate ethical action. And the following sort of retrospective, reason-giving exchange can be complete (that is, not requiring further analysis or supplementation): – "Why did you return the money?" – "Because he lent it to me." It is not impossible to follow up this initial inquiry, to ask for further explanations, or to switch to an analytic strategy. We can imagine elaborating the context in various ways which would motivate explanatory sequels. (For example, – "But he doesn't remember having lent it to you, nor does he miss it"; or – "But for him it's petty cash, and for your family it's a month's worth of groceries"; and so forth.)[23] It is misguided, however, to regard the first explanation as superficial or

---

20 Weil, "Essay on the Notion of Reading," 302 / 18–19.

21 Aristotle, *Nicomachean Ethics*, I.13.1102a32–b12.

22 Cf. Weil's remarks on chlorophyll as a capacity for feeding on light (*Gravity and Grace*, 3 / 10).

23 Cf. the "default and challenge" model of justification, as developed by Williams, *Problems of Knowledge*, Chapter 13.

insufficient. And to require, a priori, that all explanations conform to a single paradigm is to diminish ethics.

§9.3. Let us consider Winch's closing example, a brief study of Tolstoy's story "Father Sergy." In the course of the story, Sergy vacillates between the integrative and disintegrative perspectives, and Winch's characterization of them is strikingly analogous to John McDowell's characterization of Aristotelian *aretē* and enkrateia/akrasia, respectively. The analogy makes a further case for thinking of integrity as a virtue, and also faintly suggests its niche in the psychological ecology. Winch introduces the story of Sergy to illustrate the claim that "one's own moral perfection is not a possible end of one's conduct at all and, *a fortiori*, not a possible moral end."[24] The claim in the first clause might be too strong; however, it seems right to suggest that fully virtuous action is not primarily motivated by a reflexive concern for the agent's own virtue. The apprentice could glance (out of the corner of his eye, so to speak), while acting, at his own characterological state to check its growth, asking himself whether he is having the right feelings at the right times about the right things, and so on – much as an athlete, while training, might check his pulse or breathing. But the virtue of the expert is second nature; insofar as it is the excellence of the integrative perspective out of which she acts, it is not available to disintegrative reflexivity.

Sergy is motivated, in his vocation as a monk, both by "sincere religious feeling" and by a "desire for pre-eminence," that is, by a desire to be regarded with admiration; and these motivations correspond, roughly, to integrative and disintegrative perspectives on the same life. The disintegrative perspective views this life from "sideways on."[25] That is, the religious life, regarded externally, seems to be an object of admiration. But if one does not already appreciate, internally, what is worthwhile or admirable about that life, and regards it as one object among rivals, demanding that it justify itself in that arena, one cannot provoke that appreciation. Winch discusses two separate episodes in which Sergy

24 Winch, "Moral Integrity," 187.
25 Cf. McDowell, "Non-Cognitivism and Rule-Following," 207, 214; and McDowell, *Mind and World*, 34. For drawing my attention to this metaphor, thanks to Carolyn Richardson. On the theme of shifting between perspectives, I have learned a great deal from her "Talk About Talk."

faces sexual temptation: in the first episode, when "a young society woman" tries to seduce him, Sergy resists by chopping off one of his fingers. (A man who responds to temptation by amputating his finger is arguably not a man whose psyche hangs in untroubled equilibrium. The example seems to illustrate not the virtue of sophrosyne but enkrateia. A better example of sophrosyne would be a different Sergy, who acts as Sokrates does in his reportedly placid indifference to the advances of Alkibiades.[26] More on this point shortly.)

In the second episode, "an intellectually feeble young girl," Marya, succeeds in seducing him, asking the Glaukonian question, "What does it matter?" In the first episode, Sergy has the power to resist because "the problem presented to him by his lust was understood by him from the perspective of genuine religious feeling. That is to say it was not then a case of setting the satisfaction of his desire alongside the demands of his religion and choosing between them."[27] From the integrative perspective, the religious demands present themselves as what we have called a *silencing reason* (in Section 4.2). Sergy perceives these demands as salient, and other features of the situation (for example, the attractiveness of this person), which might otherwise serve as reasons, do not spark on the radar of consideration. There is, in a sense, no conflict, and no choice.

By contrast, when Sergy confronts Marya's question, he does so from a perspective that is disintegrated with respect to his religious duties. As Winch sees it, her question "invited a judgment explaining why religious purity is more important than satisfaction of lust, a comparison, as it were, between two different objects. And no such judgment was possible. I do not mean that earlier, at the time of his strength, Sergius *could* have answered the question; the point is that, from that earlier perspective, the question did not arise for him."[28] These remarks return us to Winch's initial suggestion that our understanding of an agent's character must take into account "*what he considers the alternatives to be and … the reasons he considers it relevant to deploy in deciding between them.*"[29] What is intriguing is that a consideration's irrelevance, its

26 Cf. Plato, *Symposium*, 217a–219d.

27 Winch, "Moral Integrity," 188–9.

28 Winch, "Moral Integrity," 189. Cf. McDowell, "Are Moral Requirements Hypothetical Imperatives?," §6 (p. 22); and Weil, *Notebooks*, I.110 / *OC*, VI.2.105.

29 Winch, "Moral Integrity," 178.

inaudibility, from a certain perspective, can be a sign of that perspective's strength. (Grateful as we might be when our immune system valiantly attacks an infection, we might feel better served, and healthier, if we were spared the infection altogether.)

Winch leaves Sergy there, in Marya's embrace. But we might follow him for a few more moments. After his fall from grace, Sergy flees to a river, where he has a vision of his cousin, Pashenka (Praskovya), whom he and his childhood friends had disdained and ridiculed. He remembers that she married a man who squandered her fortune and beat her, and that one of her two children, her son, died while still young. She now lives in poverty, caring for her daughter's family. Sergy walks over three hundred kilometres to her home. When he arrives, he is not initially recognized, but taken to be a wanderer:

Praskovya Mikhaylovna rubbed her thin arms against one another, wiped her hands on her apron and went upstairs to get a five-kopek piece out of her purse for him, but remembering that she had nothing less than a ten-kopek piece she decided to give him some bread instead. She returned to the cupboard, but suddenly blushed at the thought of having begrudged the ten-kopek piece, and telling Lukerya to cut a slice of bread, went upstairs to fetch it. 'It serves you right,' she said to herself. 'You must now give twice over.'

She gave both the bread and the money to the wanderer, and when doing so, far from being proud of her generosity, she excused herself for giving so little.[30]

What are we to make of this scene? Notice that Praskovya is free from the ring of Gyges. No-one is watching her when she blushes about the ten-kopek piece; no-one would have scolded her if she had given only bread. Still, she engages in ethical reasoning; indeed, it appears to be a case of enkrateia, except it is an unusual kind, because the conflict she experiences is not between being generous or ungenerous, but between different degrees of generosity: either give a ten-kopek piece or some bread. And her response to that conflict is to choose both options. In doing so, she transcends the constraints of the enkratic structure.

Sergy spends the evening speaking with Pashenka, and learns that she works tirelessly to support her daughter, her "neurasthenic" son-in-law,

30 Tolstoy, "Father Sergy," 272.

and her five grandchildren. While she sends the children to church, she herself does not attend, because she is ashamed "for my daughter's sake and the children's, to go there in tattered clothes." She prays at home; but, she confesses, "I lack real religious feeling. The only thing is that I know how vile I am."[31] We are invited to consider the hypothesis that such knowledge *is* real religious feeling, without ceremony or ostentation. In the course of their conversation, Pashenka is interrupted three times by the needs of her family, to which she responds without complaint, while also giving her attention to Sergy (a costly act in more than one way, since she forfeits paid work in order to be present with him).

The portrait that Tolstoy draws is clearly intended to be one of a self-lessly virtuous person. It is complicated by the fact that it is gendered. We might worry that, in her attentiveness, Pashenka is suffering the very exploitation against which Peta Bowden and Hilde Nelson warn (see Section 3.6). This worry is legitimate and worth registering. But in the context of the story, Pashenka seems to be presented not as an exemplar for women in general to emulate, but for Sergy in particular, someone whose attention has been aimed in the wrong direction. Leaving the conversation, Sergy thinks about what he learned: "I lived for men on the pretext of living for God, while she lives for God imagining that she lives for men. Yes, one good deed, a cup of water given without thought of reward, is worth more than any benefit I imagined I was bestowing on people."[32]

Sergy had been unable to manage the purity of giving a cup of water because his desire to serve God had been "soiled and overgrown by desire for human fame."[33] It should now be clear that the amputation of the finger was not an act of integrity (*pace* Winch), but a complicated act of self-control. The sexual temptation was defeated, but the motive that prevailed was itself strife-riven. By contrast, in the closing scene of the story, Sergy does act with integrity. Having become a poor wanderer, he is walking with two old women and a soldier when they are stopped by a party of nobles on horseback and in a gig. The party regards Sergy and his companions as a quaint spectacle, and patronizingly gives them some "*petite monnaie.*" In the past, such an interaction would have humiliated Sergy. But now he functions as a Weilian conduit: "he had

31 Ibid., 276.
32 Ibid., 277.
33 Ibid.

disregarded the opinion of men and had done the simplest, easiest thing, humbly accepted twenty kopeks and given them to his comrade, a blind beggar."[34] In serving as a medium, Sergy also purifies the money as it passes through his hands: the noble had given it to him in a patronizing way, telling him to spend it on tea instead of church candles, and patting him on the shoulder "with his gloved hand"; by contrast, Sergy's redirecting the money is like giving the cup of water to the one who needs it. He is no longer an enkratic hero, but "an intermediary ... between the starving beggar and the beggar who has been fed."[35]

§9.4. As we have seen, the stages of Sergy's development illustrate McDowell's characterization of the distinction between Aristotelian *aretē* and enkrateia/akrasia.[36] Aristotle's account of enkrateia and akrasia is an engagement with the Platonic thesis that virtue is knowledge. For the akratic agent looks like a counter-example to that thesis: someone who *knows* that he *shouldn't* do something, but *does* it anyway. We can try to save the thesis by explaining away the akratic agent, but that seems to sacrifice recognizable phenomena for the sake of theory. Aristotle's innovation is to qualify the theory and explore the phenomenon in an effort to save both. McDowell's study nicely explicates the following set of distinctions: while both the aretaic state and the enkratic state can produce the same outcome, the two states are *formally different*; and while the enkratic state and the akratic state can produce different outcomes, they are *formally similar*.

These various formal distinctions are designed to address the puzzle: how can the perspective of a virtuous agent be matched, perfectly, by that of another agent, and yet that agent act unvirtuously? The formal distinctions suggest that the match is approximate, but not, in fact, perfect.[37] The imperfect fit, McDowell suggests along with Aristotle, is the result of the interference of inappropriate feeling in the perception of enkratic and akratic agents. Their perceptions are thus *aggregates* (of belief and desire) in a way that aretaic perception is not. (Here it

---

34 Ibid., 279.

35 Weil, "Necessity and Obedience," 46 / 57. Cf. this book, §3.5.

36 See, esp., McDowell, "Aristotle's Moral Psychology," §14; McDowell, "Virtue and Reason," §3; and McDowell, "Are Moral Requirements Hypothetical Imperatives?," §§9–10.

37 Cf. McDowell, "Aristotle's Moral Psychology," §14 (p. 47).

might be helpful to consider the analogy of out-of-tune *vs* perfectly tuned chords. There is a sense in which the out-of-tune chord breaks down into its component tones, while the perfectly tuned or integrated chord resonates as a whole.) Following Julia Annas's suggestion (from Section 7.2), we need the phenomenon of the enkratic agent to address the paradox of the learning of virtue: if virtue is learned by the performance of virtuous actions; and if virtuous actions issue from a state of virtue; and if an agent lacks this state – then it seems that he can never acquire it.[38] There seems to be no way of transitioning from the unknowing apprentice to the knowing expert. The enkratic agent is the scalar middle term that gives us traction here: someone whose state of knowing approximates – without perfectly matching – the expert's, and who manages to rehearse the motions of "virtuous" action (and we use the term "virtuous" here to mark the aspiration rather than the achievement).

McDowell notes that, "for Aristotle, continence is distinct from virtue, and just as problematic as incontinence. If someone needs to overcome an inclination to act otherwise, in getting himself to act as, say, temperance or courage demand, then he shows not virtue but (mere) continence."[39] The crucial distinction is between *silencing* and *overriding*, and it is a distinction between attending to a unified focus, and dispersing attention across a multiplicity of (potentially competing) foci. According to McDowell, "the dictates of virtue, if properly appreciated, are not weighed with other reasons at all, not even on a scale which always tips on their side"; given the clear perception of a situational requirement, other considerations, which might have constituted reasons for acting otherwise, are not overridden but silent.[40] By contrast, the enkratic agent, who also perceives the requirement, but less clearly, further perceives these other considerations as competing reasons, and ultimately succeeds in overriding them in favour of the requirement.

Since *aretē* is associated with the integrative perspective, and enkrateia and akrasia with the disintegrative perspective, it is important to note that periodic recourse to the disintegrative perspective remains indispensable *even for the virtuous agent*. The reason for this indispensability

---

38 Recall the paradox from Plato's *Meno* (80d) and Aristotle's *Nicomachean Ethics* (II.4.1105a17–21).

39 McDowell, "Virtue and Reason," §3 (p. 334).

40 McDowell, "Are Moral Requirements Hypothetical Imperatives?," §9 (p. 26).

should be apparent: "the singleness of motivational focus"[41] character-istic of the integrative perspective is not good without qualification, in the same way that spontaneity is not good without qualification. Periodically shifting to the disintegrative perspective, which permits the comparison of a plurality of foci, allows the agent to practise flexibility and avoid bad habits of attention. McDowell makes a hint in this direction (in the context of a different argument) when he acknowledges the potential for conflict between the requirements of, for example, kindness and fairness. If one's sensitivity to others' feelings is developed to the exclusion of sensitivity to rights, and if one finds oneself in a situation whose "morally important fact ... is not that A will be upset by a projected action (though he will), but, say, that B has a right,"[42] then one will likely act gently with A while neglecting B. In a *different* context, one's acting gently (kindly) would be acting rightly; but *here* that narrowness of motivational focus is blameworthy.

Moreover, such narrowness can become pernicious. Under socio-cultural conditions of oppression, attention may be travel along grooves.[43] A white person may be habituated to attending to other whites, perceiving them as "patients" of kindness. He autonomically perceives their needs as salient. In some contexts, autonomic perception will be appropriate and praiseworthy. But when it becomes exclusive, it is a kind of negligence. And his settled state, inside his integrative perspective, from which he is consistently, reflexively kind – but only to other whites – is a state of complacency and a way of participating in systems of oppression. In other words, his obliviousness, even if it is not intentional, is racist. As Peggy DesAutels observes: "Feminists have long been aware that stereotypes associated with race, class, and gender can be so entrenched that we may be oblivious to the needs (and may even harm) many of those with whom we interact on a day-to-day basis."[44]

The agent who is responsibly committed to continuous ethical learning is under an obligation periodically to shift into the disintegrative perspective (or to take advantage of life's inevitable shifts), and to turn

41 McDowell, "Aristotle's Moral Psychology," §14 (p. 47).

42 McDowell, "Virtue and Reason," §2 (p. 333). Cf. Annas, "The phenomenology of virtue," 32–3.

43 Thanks to Meredith Schwartz whose important questions helped me to understand this point.

44 DesAutels, "Moral Mindfulness," 74.

elenctic attention, reflexively and critically, on her own psyche.[45] The dynamic might be imagined like that which obtains in an automobile with manual transmission. For the vehicle to drive, the gearbox must be engaged with the engine (this situation is analogous to the integrative perspective). But if one wishes to change gears (read: critique and revise one's moral psychology), then it is necessary to depress the clutch pedal (this situation is analogous to the disintegrative perspective). And just as one can reflect while acting, so one can move while changing gears – but the nature of this motion (action) is different: it is coasting. Furthermore, downshifting gears can be a method of braking; similarly, triggering the disintegrative perspective can be a way of inhibiting spontaneous activity. (If we infer that the psyche is a machine, the metaphor is misunderstood.)

The disintegrative perspective opens up a splendid vista of reasons. Again, there is nothing intrinsically wrong with such a vista; and occasionally opening it up will be needed for self-reflexive moral critique. But it does not follow that it has to be kept permanently open. In many circumstances, its invocation will be illicit and will constitute a kind of sabotage of the most spontaneously appropriate gesture. Consider the case of performance anxiety, analysed by Abigail Lipson and Michael Lipson.[46] Self-reflexivity, they say, is a defining characteristic of performance anxiety, and such anxiety can be alleviated by the performer shifting her focus away from herself and onto the audience. Redirecting her focus might precipitate a shift from the disintegrative to the integrative perspective. And yet, from the disintegrative perspective, the agent can survey herself as one among many, and her reasons as some among many. All deliberation is, in this sense, disintegrative. But action is the end of deliberation: the vista contracts to a point.

§9.5. Winch's work on integrity has been upstaged by Bernard Williams, who has written a number of influential essays about this character trait. In his well-known essay "A critique of utilitarianism," Williams argues that utilitarianism threatens integrity. As a moral system founded on a principle of impartiality, it can require agents to sacrifice their deepest personal commitments. In one of Williams's

45 Cf. Zwicky, "Alcibiades' Love," 96–7 / *AL*, 296–7.
46 Lipson and Lipson, "Psychotherapy and the Ethics of Attention," 20–1.

examples, twenty protestors face unjust execution by a firing squad.[47] The situation is incredibly rigged in such a way that Jim, a bystander, can rescue nineteen of the protestors by killing one of them; otherwise, another man (whom Williams calls "Pedro")[48] will kill all twenty of them. According to Williams, the utilitarian analysis of the situation involves a special application of the principle of impartiality, namely the doctrine of "negative responsibility": if Jim refuses to kill one person, then he is responsible for the deaths of twenty people. Furthermore, he might be guilty of indulging in what Williams calls "squeamishness"[49] and Cheshire Calhoun calls a "clean-hands" picture of integrity: "A person has integrity when there are some things she will not do regardless of the consequences of this refusal. In bottom-line situations, she places the importance of principle and the purity of her own agency above consequentialist concerns."[50] This picture of integrity might seem to undermine Williams's critique: when twenty lives are at stake, surely concern with keeping one's own hands clean is outweighed. And yet, as Williams argues, to regard the situation in this way is to concede to the utilitarian analysis.

In a later essay, Williams returns to the question of whether someone in Jim's position – an agent with integrity who refused to do a detestable action – might be charged with "moral self-indulgence." A defining feature of such self-indulgence would be a second-order "*reflexive* concern" with one's own character and agency.[51] Williams's contrast between first- and second-order motivations can be illustrated by contrasting their objects: returning to Weil's example, one might be moved, immediately, by the thirsting man, to give him a drink of water. Or, on the other hand, one might be moved to give him water by the image of oneself acting charitably. The latter sort of motivation would warrant the charge of moral self-indulgence. One would be attending, not to the man in need, but to oneself. "This sort of reflexivity," writes Williams, "involves a reversal at a line which I take to be fundamental to any

---

47 See Williams, "Critique," §3 (pp. 98–100).

48 The racialization of the conflict – a stalwart British botanist confronting a squadron of nefarious South Americans – is redolent of colonial pulp fiction, and invites critical discussion.

49 Williams, "Critique," §4 (p. 102).

50 Calhoun, "Standing for Something," §III (p. 246).

51 Williams, "Utilitarianism and moral self-indulgence," 45.

morality or indeed sane life at all, between self-concern and other-concern; it involves a misdirection not just of attention, though that is true too, but genuinely of concern."[52] If Jim refuses merely because he is disinclined to get his hands dirty, then he could be charged with self-indulgence. Williams objects that Jim's aversion to killing is not just some quantity of disutility but a vital expression of his character, the perspective which, in Winch's sense, constitutes his agency.[53] Still, one might protest that this entire orientation toward the situation is corrupt; that what is wrong with the situation is not that Jim's integrity will be hurt, but that an innocent person will be murdered.

Williams is trying to share a significant insight, but its significance is distorted by his way of discussing it. In some moods, Williams is basically a Romantic existentialist fascinated by the adventure of the free individual.[54] One of the central themes of his "Critique," for example, is the conflict between the integrity of an individual and the demands of a collectivist moral system. And Calhoun has rightly criticized Williams's vision of integrity for being too individualistic.[55] However, to see what remains significant about it, we need to shift our perspective: rather than describe Jim from the outside, in the third person, we need to try to see the situation from his point of view, in the first person. If we do so, we will stop talking about his integrity; instead, his integrity, itself unmentioned, will structure our perception of the situation. From the integrative point of view, some actions otherwise available to the omniscient third-person perspective will not be audible. "It could be a feature of man's moral outlook that he considered certain courses of action as unthinkable, in the sense that he would not entertain the idea of doing them; and the witness to that might, in many cases, be that they simply would not come into his head."[56] The more significant distinction is not the conflict between Jim's integrity and the utilitarian imperative, but the distinction between the integrative and the disintegrative perspective.

---

52 Ibid., 47.

53 Williams, "Critique," §4 (pp. 103–4).

54 See, for example, his Romanticization of Gauguin in his "Moral luck," *Moral Luck*, 20–39.

55 See Calhoun, "Standing for Something," §IV.

56 Williams, "Critique," §2 (p. 92). Cf. Annas, "The phenomenology of virtue," 27.

From the integrative perspective, some aspects of a situation are salient, whereas others are silent. And those that are silent might nevertheless be perceptible through a disintegrative perspective on the same situation. The integrative perspective is preoccupied with its focus; and that focus is enough to motivate the agent, without the interference of extra thoughts or desires.[57] Furthermore, Williams agrees with Annas, McDowell, Winch, and Zwicky that a defining characteristic of the integrative perspective is its unselfconsciousness.[58] By contrast, in the disintegrative perspective, self-regarding thoughts might intrude, and, as Annas suggests, they may be symptomatic of the agent's apprenticeship status.[59] To act with full integrity is not to be moved by thoughts of one's own integrity, but to be wholly focused on something else – an injustice, an ideal, a particular being. The indeterminateness of that focus leads Williams to observe that, "while it is an admirable human property, [integrity] is not related to motivation as the virtues are. It is not a disposition which itself yields motivations, as generosity and benevolence do; nor is it a virtue of that type, sometimes called 'executive' virtues, which do not themselves yield a characteristic motive, but are necessary for the relation to oneself and the world which enables one to act from desirable motives in desirable ways — the type that includes courage and self-control."[60]

– But why not identify integrity as an "executive" virtue? Indeed, assuming that "self-control" mistranslates σωφροσύνη, why not identify integrity with this virtue? Consider this tantalizing remark from Aristotle: phronesis, he says, "is a true and reasoned state of capacity to act with regard to the things that are good or bad for man …

This is why we call temperance [σωφροσύνην] by this name; we imply that it preserves one's practical wisdom [σῴζουσαν τὴν φρόνησιν]."[61]

---

57 On the extra thought, see Williams, "Persons, character and morality," *Moral Luck*, 18.

58 Cf. Annas, "The phenomenology of virtue," 24; McDowell, "Virtue and Reason," §2 (p. 332); Winch, "Moral Integrity," 187; and Zwicky, "Alcibiades' Love," 91 / *AL*, 291.

59 Annas, "The phenomenology of virtue," 22–3.

60 Williams, "Utilitarianism and moral self-indulgence," 49.

61 Aristotle, *Nicomachean Ethics*, VI.5.1140b4–6, b11–12. Cf. Plato: "Moderation (*sōphrosunē*) is the saviour (*sōteria*) of the wisdom (*phronēsis*) we just looked at" (*Kratylos*, 411e).

As Terence Irwin notes, the etymology is "fanciful," but it "indicates the special connection of [*phronēsis*]—as opposed to some other virtues of thought—to character."[62] Aristotle articulates that special connection in the following way: "it is not possible to be good in the strict sense without practical wisdom, or practically wise without moral virtue. ... for with the presence of the one quality, practical wisdom, will be given all the virtues."[63] Phronesis and sophrosyne need each other. Sophrosyne is an "executive" virtue, in Williams's terms, because it enables the agent to exercise phronesis. Conversely, an agent who lacks sophrosyne also suffers from a deficiency of phronesis: "the man who has been ruined by pleasure or pain forthwith fails to see any such originating cause" (that is, the "end" of "the things that are done"),[64] and phronesis is responsible for clarity in such seeing. Here is one of the reasons that "sound-mindedness" is better than "self-control" as a translation of σωφροσύνη: it points to the special connection of sophrosyne (a virtue of character) with phronesis (a virtue of thought). As Irwin writes, "a more probable etymology than Aristotle's derives the term [*sōphrosunē*] from 'sound (*sōs*) mind (*phronein*).'"[65]

– But doesn't the distinction between virtues of character and thought represent a concession to the dualists? We have already dissented from Anscombe's Thomistic interpretation of Aristotle, which traces the Humean distinction between belief and desire back to the *Nicomachean Ethics*. In Book IV of *Republic*, Plato does associate particular virtues with particular components of the soul, but he is ultimately committed to a unity of virtues and a psychological unity. Adapting the Platonic psychology, Aristotle might seem to drive the wedge deeper, to insist on a more categorical distinction between "moral" and "intellectual" virtues, insofar as they correspond to categorically different parts of the soul. However, Aristotle's distinction between desire and reason is not Hume's. Aristotelian desire and reason share the same profile and are distinguished like convexity and concavity in the same curve. Phronesis is, in fact, included in the early, general definition of virtue of character: "Virtue, then, is a state of character concerned with choice, lying in a

---

62 Irwin, "Notes," *Nicomachean Ethics*, 242.

63 Aristotle, *Nicomachean Ethics*, VI.13.1144b30–1145a2. Cf. ibid., II.6.1106b36–1107a2, X.8.1178a16–19. Cf. Ross, *Aristotle*, 226.

64 Aristotle, *Nicomachean Ethics*, VI.5.1140b16–18.

65 Irwin, "Notes," *Nicomachean Ethics*, 350.

mean, i.e. the mean relative to us, this being determined by reason, and by that reason by which the man of practical wisdom would determine it."[66] We are now considering the suggestion that if one comes at it from the other side, one will appreciate not only that phronesis is necessary to virtues of character, but also that sophrosyne is necessary to virtues of thought. In other words, phronesis and sophrosyne are internally related. As Zwicky suggests: "Becoming an excellent human being requires one to adopt a moral ecology; and ecologies aren't modular constructions. They don't consist of separate bricks that are snapped together (or unsnapped) like pieces of Lego. Moral ecologies, like biological ones, are organic wholes, whose distinguishable aspects — the virtues — stand in internal relations to one another."[67]

Sophrosyne, according to Aristotle, is the mean "with regard to pleasures,"[68] between the excess of self-indulgence on the one hand, and the deficiency of insensibility on the other. More specifically, it is concerned with the kinds of pleasures we share with other animals, particularly touch and taste, and especially enjoyment through touch, "both in the case of food and in that of drink and in that of sexual intercourse. This is why a certain gourmand prayed that his throat might become longer than a crane's, implying that it was the contact that he took pleasure in."[69] However, we should not assume that sophrosyne is puritanical. As Helen North writes, Aristotle "is careful to correct the current view that sophrosyne itself is abstinence from pleasure. The *sôphrôn* person enjoys pleasure in moderation."[70] McDowell's characterization of the temperate person (that is, the person with the virtue of sophrosyne) is pertinent as well:

The temperate person need be no less prone to enjoy physical pleasure than anyone else. In suitable circumstances it will be true that he would enjoy some intemperate action which is available to him. In the absence of a requirement, the prospective enjoyment would constitute a reason for going

---

66 Aristotle, *Nicomachean Ethics*, II.6.1106b36–1107a2.

67 Zwicky, "A Ship from Delos," *Learning to Die*, 69–70. Incidentally, I think that Zwicky's metaphor dissolves the puzzle about the unity of virtue in Plato, *Protagoras*, 329d.

68 Aristotle, *Nicomachean Ethics*, III.10.1117b25.

69 Ibid., III.10.1118a31–1118b1.

70 North, *Sophrosyne*, 201.

ahead. But his clear perception of the requirement insulates the prospective enjoyment—of which, for a satisfying conception of the virtue, we should want him to have a vivid appreciation—from engaging his inclinations at all. Here and now, it does not count for him as any reason for acting in that way.[71]

The temperate person must be distinguished from the insensible person, the merely enkratic (or continent), and the self-indulgent. The enkratic is tempted by an intemperate action, but forces himself to obey a contrary requirement; the insensible person is simply left cold by intemperate actions; and the self-indulgent … indulges.

— "But what does any of this have to do with integrity? Surely temperance is a minor virtue – resisting the urge to gobble too many grapes? And even supposing that we take Aristotle's pun seriously, what could it mean to say that sophrosyne 'preserves' phronesis?" — Just as phronesis determines each individual mean with which the respective virtues of character are concerned, so sophrosyne exemplifies the mean. As North writes, "The fact that Aristotle uses the Mean to arrive at his own definition of sophrosyne should not blind us to the presence of sophrosyne, in a larger sense, as the very foundation of the Mean."[72] On this reading, sophrosyne is a kind of meta-virtue; like the other virtues, it is a mean between extremes; but it is also a paradigm of the mean itself. Virtue, says Aristotle, "is concerned with pleasures and pains." The human "who abstains from bodily pleasures and delights in this very fact is temperate."[73] Truly virtuous action is well oiled with pleasure; it is freed from characterological friction or resistance. The agent is able clearly to perceive the appropriate action because it is not obscured by pain. When one's character is integrated by sophrosyne, it attains an untroubled equilibrium. As Zwicky puts it, the agent with integrity is free to experience her feelings: she does not need to fear that they will shove her around.[74]

But if we listen to Aristotle, then we shall not call this freedom "enkrateia." According to North, Book VII of the *Nicomachean Ethics* "makes the first rigorous distinction in Greek thought between sophrosyne

---

71 McDowell, "Are Moral Requirements Hypothetical Imperatives?," §10 (p. 27).
72 North, *Sophrosyne*, 200.
73 Aristotle, *Nicomachean Ethics*, II.3.1104b5–9.
74 Zwicky, "Alcibiades' Love," 94 / *AL*, 294.

and *enkrateia.*[75] And Aristotle makes that distinction in order to save his teacher's thesis that virtue is knowledge. Aryeh Kosman eloquently describes the contrast between enkrateia and sophrosyne:

> The σωφροσύνη that Plato and Aristotle alike wish to endorse is the virtue that just transcends ἐγκράτεια; it lies just beyond this mode of strong-willed containment and is linked to the wisdom by which the σώφρων is freed from the need for restraint.

The distinction that I am here invoking between a just lesser and an ideal form of self-mastery is a recognizable topos in many "wisdom traditions," but I believe that we are familiar with it in broader outline from ordinary contexts. Think of the skill by which a beginning artisan, as the result of intense effort, achieves control and mastery over his intractable material, and then contrast to that difficult control the ease and virtual nonchalance with which the master craftsman works. Or contrast to the equestrian skill of a novice able to control his horse only with effort and struggle the apparent effortlessness of an experienced rider. Her control doesn't even look like control, but if we have ridden we know that to hold the reins that lightly is a consummate achievement.[76]

Recall Aristotle's analysis of the difference: unlike *aretē*, enkrateia is marked by internal conflict. The presence of conflict implies that the soul is in a disintegrative state: there is a civil war among its parts. By contrast, the agent who embodies sophrosyne is freed from this conflict. As Zwicky writes: "this freedom allows our useful bits and pieces to settle naturally into place – the result of a kind of chiropractic of the soul. The muscle unclenches, space opens in the joint, and a single, unbroken, continuous motion becomes possible. This is integrity in action."[77]

Let us say, for the sake of argument, that integrity might be helpfully understood as the characterological virtue of sophrosyne. As an executive virtue which enables or unifies the other virtues, sophrosyne would lack a distinctive content. But recall that attention also lacks a distinctive content (as we discussed in Section 3.3). Recall further McDowell's claim (from Section 6.7) that a virtue of character, "strictly so called,

75 North, *Sophrosyne,* 203.
76 Kosman, "Self-Knowledge and Self-Control in Plato's *Charmides,*" §4 (p. 240). For discussions of Kosman's *Virtues of Thought,* thanks to Steven Burns.
77 Zwicky, "Alcibiades' Love," 92 / *AL,* 291.

involves [an intimate] harmony of intellect and motivation … Practical wisdom *is* the properly moulded state of the motivational propensities, in a reflectively adjusted form; the sense in which it is a state of the intellect does not interfere with its also being a state of the desiderative element."[78] North agrees: "Sophrosyne is the effortless, because habitual, harmony of appetite and reason."[79] There are some real things which are perceptible only if our characters have been appropriately shaped. Phronesis and sophrosyne converge at the waist of the soul's hourglass where thought pours into character and character effloresces as thought. Regarded as a phronetic capacity to perceive salience, the integrative perspective may be called "epistemic"; but regarded as the well-regulated character which grounds and enables this capacity, integrity may be called "characterological." That is, phronesis (attention) and sophrosyne (integrity) are aspects of the same virtue, viewed from different angles. The integrated agent is one for whom attentiveness is second nature.

78 McDowell, "Aristotle's Moral Psychology," §11 (p. 40).
79 North, *Sophrosyne*, 202–3.

1 0

Lyric Details and Ecological Integrity

οὐ ξυνιᾶσιν ὅκως διαφερόμενον ἑωυτῷ ὁμολογέει · παλίντροπος ἁρμονίη ὅκωσπερ τόξου καὶ λύρης.

– Herakleitos[1]

§10.1. THE PROBLEM OF FINDING AN ACCOUNT of ecological integrity which preserves (and ideally explains) individual integrity is a version of the ancient problem of the one and the many. It is, among other things, a coordination problem, a problem with political as well as epistemological and ontological dimensions. Perhaps its most familiar recent iteration, in political philosophy, is the one we have inherited from Hobbes. (Given a plurality of rational, self-interested agents, how can a legitimate social organization be constructed? Why would such agents ever cooperate, and what could possibly justify a limitation on their natural freedom?) On either side of Hobbes, both Plato and Spinoza were thwarted in their endeavours to solve the problem; in different ways, each of these two succumbed to the temptation of holism. The problem might be insoluble; and this section is not a contribution to the project of trying to solve it. Nevertheless, we may look for clues among the ruins.

Let us think about some images of integrity. Recall some of the distinct uses of the concept: sometimes we use it to indicate the uprightness or intactness of an individual ethical agent; at other times we use it to indicate the connectedness of components in a complex structure (such as an ecology or an artwork). Sometimes the first use implies a *contrast* between an individual and the collective which threatens her and against

---

1 Herakleitos, DK 22B51. In a draft, Weil translates: «ILS NE COMPRENNENT PAS COMMENT CE QUI S'OPPOSE | *CONVIENT* | S'ACCORDE DANS UNE IDENTITÉ. L'HARMONIE EST CHANGEMENT DE CÔTÉ (ACTE DE TOURNER) ΠΑΛΙΝΤΡΟΠΟΣ, COMME POUR L'ARC ET LA LYRE. // (Cf. Lao Tseu sur l'arc.)» (*OC*, IV.2.136). Her editors refer the reader to Laozi, *Daodejing*, chap. 77.

which she takes a stand; whereas the second use can imply the appropriate *subordination* of components to the overarching structure. And so the two uses may seem to be at odds with each other. However, our working hypothesis is that these two uses, while distinct, are not disjoint; and that we can learn something about each by juxtaposing them. Consider: a structure whose components are integrated is better able to resist antagonistic influence, to adapt to changing circumstances, and to act in a concerted way; in other words, a structure which has integrity in the second sense (above) is better able also to exhibit integrity in the first sense. The thought is Spinoza's: individual integrity *derives from* ecological integrity. An individual *is* insofar as it is an integrated ecology of other individuals, that is, "an unvarying relation of movement" among them.[2] But the derivation is not straightforward: what, on one plane of description, are individuals, will turn out, on another plane, to be complex structures.

In the previous section, we glanced at Bernard Williams's image of individual integrity, and we now proceed to discuss Jan Zwicky's image of ecological integrity. If we keep these two distinct images in our mind's eye, set beside each other as objects of comparison, we may be able to see connections between them.[3] The ordering of the images is provisional, and it should not be taken to imply that ecological integrity *evolves* from individual integrity. While both Hobbes and Spinoza are prone to picturing society as a kind of super-individual, we will not learn about the distinct character of ecological integrity by starting from the individual and inflating it. Here it is helpful to attend to Wittgenstein's cautionary remark about his method of comparison: "one might illustrate an internal relation of a circle to an ellipse by gradually converting an ellipse into a circle; *but not in order to assert that a certain ellipse actually, historically, had originated from a circle* (evolutionary hypothesis), but only in order to sharpen our eye for a formal connection."[4] (Plato is looking for such a "formal connection" when he analogizes the καλλίπολις [*kallipolis*] with the soul in *Republic*.) Analogical relations are not narrative, temporally inflected relations. In this spirit, let us not imagine that the ecological image is merely a

2 Spinoza, *Ethics*, IID7, IIP13L3A2.

3 Cf. Wittgenstein, *Philosophical Investigations*, §§122, 130, and "Remarks on Frazer's *Golden Bough*," 131–3.

4 Wittgenstein, "Remarks on Frazer's *Golden Bough*," 133.

macro-scale projection of Williams's individualistic image (if it were such a projection, we should be on guard for distortion); instead, let us try to sharpen our eye for the *formal* connection between individual and ecological integrity. In the context of Zwicky's work, the individual that interests us may be called a *lyric detail.* In order to understand what a lyric detail is, as well as its relationship to ecological integrity, we need to begin by thinking about lyric philosophy.

§10.2. What is lyric philosophy? The clearest response is Zwicky's *Lyric Philosophy*, a book-length meditation that incorporates the philosophical forms of aphorism and dialogue, as well as the musical form of polyphony, in an integrative effort to *show* its meaning. Significantly, Zwicky stipulates no criteria for the concept of lyric philosophy, and refraining from doing so is central to the very nature of her investigation. "Lyric meaning," she writes, "can underlie and inform linguistic meaning but it is, at the same time, broader in scope. Its root is gestural."[5] Appreciating the centrality of this issue – the gestural root of lyric meaning – is indispensable for appreciating the book's other themes and its unorthodox format. Conversely, understanding *how* the format enacts the book's central issue cannot be dissevered from an understanding of the nature of lyric meaning itself. "Form and content are inextricably bound up with one another—how you say is what you mean."[6]

The book's opening epigraph, from Ludwig Wittgenstein, anticipates the theme of the ineffability of musical gestures: "It is impossible for me to say one word in my book about all that music has meant in my life; how then can I possibly make myself understood?"[7] This epigraph speaks to those of us who have had the experience of finding some music deeply meaningful and yet failing to fit any words to it. Such an experience might be shelved as a mere curiosity if music's resistance to linguistic articulation were trivial or unique. But it isn't: a few moments of reflection suggest that it shares this feature with many other phenomena. Consider loving someone; being in the presence of beauty; bearing witness to atrocity. Pausing on a gravel road at twilight, caught

5 Zwicky, "What Is Lyric Philosophy?," §3. Cf. Zwicky, *Lyric Philosophy*, 1st ed., L251.

6 Zwicky, "What Is Lyric Philosophy?," §14.

7 Wittgenstein, quoted in Zwicky, *Lyric Philosophy*, n.p.

in the gaze of a deer. Sitting down at the kitchen table, after a death, and trying to write an adequate letter of sympathy. Trying accurately to describe something relatively common, but specific, like the sound of a clarinet, or the aroma of coffee. *Why* can it not be done?

In one sense, it is this question that motivates Zwicky's entire investigation. Let us set the question beside her revision of Wittgenstein's well-known aphorism: some things, she suggests, "can be more clearly shown than said."[8] And the way that music means is a clue: "it doesn't mean the same way as language does. Music's meaning is a function of resonance and resonance involves a kind of integrity."[9] Discussing these characteristics – resonance and integrity – will assist us in fleshing out the nature of lyric philosophy. Let us think about the book's format.

Each two-page spread is composed as a structural unit, which has been called a "duon."[10] On the left hand, one finds text authored by Zwicky (which is not itself monologic, since it moves around and splits, questions itself, impersonates a variety of interlocutors with different tones of voice, some impatient, others sympathetic, for example); on the right hand, one finds excerpts from texts by analytic, continental, and lyric philosophers, musical scores, paintings, photographs, and so forth. Zwicky writes: "The right-hand text is a scrapbook; a way of paying intellectual debts; a series of suggestions for further reading; a chorus of *agents provocateurs*; the vocal score for a conceptual opera; a homage. ... // The relation of the two texts to one another is somewhere between counterpoint and harmony, somewhere between a double helix and the allemande of the earth and moon."[11] In a study of the book's structure, Dennis Lee writes: "It's hard to believe, when printed books have been around for almost six hundred years in the West, that someone could look at their physical structure and construe its logic differently. But that is what Zwicky has done. ... to see that a work of philosophy can proceed both contrapuntally (left/right on each duon) *and* sequentially (page one to the end) – that appears to be something new."[12]

8 Zwicky, "Bringhurst's Presocratics: Lyric and Ecology," 65 / AL, 19. Cf. Wittgenstein, *Tractatus*, prop. 4.1212.

9 Zwicky, "The Details," 92.

10 Lee credits this term to Susan Haley, the editor of *Wisdom & Metaphor* (Lee, "The Music of Thinking," 39).

11 Zwicky, *Lyric Philosophy*, foreword.

12 Lee, "The Music of Thinking," 38.

Lee's insight is significant and on the right track, but let us notice that the book exhibits more *kinds* of motion than the "double momentum" that he stresses. Within the counterpoint of any given duon, for instance, in the left or right entry, there may be an *intra-*textual dialogue: the left-hand text may be questioning itself, or members of the right-hand chorus may be harmonizing or disagreeing with one another. Equally important, some of the echoes between disparately placed entries move along an axis *at a different angle than* either the contrapuntal or the sequential axes. (For example, the eighth Oxherding Picture rhymes with the single page of silence; as the reader's mind comes to rest, it also arcs backward, and across the intervening pages the two moments are instantaneously associated.)[13]

Let us focus on one particular duon, which addresses the following ancient question: what is philosophy? Zwicky offers a response:

Philosophy is thinking in love with clarity.[14]

Beside her definition Zwicky sets Robert Bringhurst's "Poem about Crystal."[15] The poem's intensely concentrated single sentence is both a meditation on the clarity with which philosophical thinking is in love and an illustration of such thinking. The world, writes Zwicky, "finds voice in the music of Bringhurst's work as carbon becomes articulate in diamond."[16] Reflecting on Zwicky's left-hand entry, we might notice, among other things, the generosity of the suggested definition. As she emphasizes elsewhere, it can include "the thought of Herakleitos, as well as that of the best Anglo-American analysts."[17] (This inclusivity is important. Zwicky repeatedly cautions that she is not attempting to supplant analysis with lyric,[18] and her work might be read as a reminder to philosophy of its own complexity and diversity.) The accuracy of the definition can be tested by its ability to save the phenomena, to save

---

13 Zwicky, *Lyric Philosophy*, R150 and R249.

14 Ibid., L18.

15 I do not attempt to analyse Bringhurst's poem here. Zwicky has offered a meticulous and detailed map in *The Experience of Meaning* (Montreal & Kingston: McGill-Queen's University Press, 2019), 153–5.

16 Zwicky, quoted on the back cover of Bringhurst, *The Calling* (Toronto: McClelland & Stewart, 1995).

17 Zwicky, "What Is Lyric Philosophy?," §8.

18 Zwicky, *Lyric Philosophy*, L75.

what we already recognize as philosophy while also inviting us to extend recognition to cases that have been neglected or marginalized. And we might notice something else about the definition: it is sonorously composed; listen: it rings, not unlike a tintinnabulum. Such sonority is another test of truth in a lyric context.

This pair of texts – Zwicky's aphoristic definition of philosophy on the left-hand page and Bringhurst's poem on the right-hand page – also shows us one of the forms clarity can assume: resonance.[19] A contrasting form of clarity, with which many twenty-first-century anglophone philosophers are more comfortable, is, of course, analysis. For our purposes, it will be helpful to focus on two of its characteristic features that Zwicky identifies: (1) "a methodology that, for the most part, appears ... to proceed on the assumption that understanding is a function of breaking a whole into its component parts, and that such parts are metaphysically independent of and prior to the wholes into which they are combined"; and (2) "an insistence on the generic superiority of the rational intellect to emotions, desires, and sensations."[20]

We may call the first feature (1) "analytic method," and the second feature (2) "hierarchical dualism." Both receive a definitive modern formulation in the work of Descartes. Cartesian mind-body dualism is familiar from the *Meditations* (especially Meditations Two and Six). For a prototype of the analytic method, two key texts are his *Rules for the Direction of the Mind* and *Discourse on Method*. The method is most succinctly articulated in the second and third rules of the second part of the *Discourse*: "The second was to divide each of the difficulties which I encountered into as many parts as possible, and as might be required for an easier solution. // The third was to think in an orderly fashion 'when concerned with the search for truth', beginning with the things which were simplest and easiest to understand, and gradually and by degrees reaching toward more complex knowledge, even treating, as though ordered, materials which were not necessarily so."[21] In this method, clarity is achieved by analysing what we want to understand into its simplest parts and then ordering those parts systematically – even when this ordering is unnatural.

19 Zwicky, *Lyric Philosophy*, L48.
20 Zwicky, "What Is Lyric Philosophy?," §23.
21 Descartes, *Discourse*, AT VI.18–19, quoted in Zwicky, *Lyric Philosophy*, R13.

These different forms of clarity are responsive to different sorts of structure. An old-fashioned pocket watch is a good physical analogue of an analytic structure. When the hairspring wears out, a technician can take the watch apart, remove the expired spring, replace it with a fresh one, and reassemble the watch. The character of each part is independent of its relations with the other parts. — "But that's an exaggeration: the hairspring *is* a hairspring because of its mechanical role in regulating another part, the balance wheel!" — What I mean is that the technician, during the surgery, can select more or less arbitrarily among the things in the drawer labelled "hairsprings." Logico-analytic arguments should work in this way, too: we should be able to abstract from any stylistic particulars and paraphrase the thing purely, in unornamented prose, for example, or in symbols. And such representations can be very useful for achieving a clarifying overview of some argumentative structures.

Resonant structures, by contrast, resist such analysis. To analyse them would be to disintegrate them and thus to damage their meaning. "Resonance is a function of the integration of various components in a whole."[22] When they stand in an appropriate relationship – when they are integrated, or attuned – distinct components can transmit vibrations to each other. And to permit of integration, the whole itself needs to be complex or "polydimensional."[23] Here it is worth remembering, as one model of polydimensionality, the many different axes of motion exemplified by Zwicky's book: contrapuntal *and* sequential *and* dialogic *and* echoic, et cetera. (For the sake of contrast, we might ask: is "integration" imaginable for a unidimensional object? Would it make sense to claim that the conclusion of a valid argument "resonates" with its premises?)

Another illustration of gestural integrity is a photograph by Ansel Adams.[24] For the sake of discussion, we might discern at least three distinct components in the photograph (while noting that it is possible to discern more or less than three, or to study the photograph along different axes): the tall aspen trunks in the background, the medium aspen tree in the left foreground, and the smaller one in the right

22 Zwicky, *Lyric Philosophy*, L34.
23 Ibid., L5.
24 Adams, *Aspens, Northern New Mexico*, 1958, shown in Zwicky, *Lyric Philosophy*, R259.

10.1 Ansel Adams, *Aspens, Northern New Mexico,* 1958

foreground. (Alternatively, one could say that the trunks in the background keep a steady beat, which is punctuated by the trochee of the
two trees in the foreground.) Regarding the aspen on the left, it would
not be hyperbolic to call it "luminous." However, it would be a mistake
to become absorbed solely with this particular aspen. For we fail to
appreciate the photograph when we fail to appreciate that it is not
restricted to a single focal point. Indeed, it is not symmetrically composed, but balanced: the brightly leafed trees in the foreground balanced
against the darkly slender trunks at the back; the blazing aspen on the
left, against the flickering one on the right.

The balancing, or integration, of these several dimensions, and the
resonances among them, lend the photograph *depth* (reminiscent of
the composition of Jean Renoir's shots – their deep focus and depth of

field – in *La Règle du jeu*).[25] We can see, especially from the sparsely leafed branches of the smaller aspen, that it is autumn; yet the two trees in the foreground are comparatively young. The overwhelming impression conveyed by the photograph is of something fiercely alive and simultaneously on the very cusp of snuffing out. (What Zwicky calls "the preciousness and losability" of things.)[26] Like Bringhurst's poem, Adams's photograph makes a resonantly integrated gesture.

Zwicky's metaphors – polydimensionality, integrity, and resonance – seem abstract. (For the usefulness of the first and last metaphors, look also at Charles H. Kahn's two fundamental principles for reading the philosophy of Herakleitos: "density" and "resonance.")[27] And the concept of a "resonance-body" – a resonantly integrated, polydimensional whole – can range widely, from ontological structures (ecological communities, for example) to works of art in diverse media (Zwicky's examples include Vermeer's interiors, the gacelas and casidas of García Lorca, the string quartets of Mozart, and Woolf's novels, among many others). But the roots of these metaphors are not esoteric; they are *physical.* When the concept of resonance is introduced in *Lyric Philosophy*, via an entry from *The Oxford Companion to Music*, what is remarkable is the deference to physics.[28]

Elsewhere, Zwicky writes that stringed instruments are "good physical analogues" of some kinds of "lyric structures."[29] Indeed, the Greek etymology of "lyric" might remind us of a specific stringed instrument featured in an aphorism by Herakleitos: "They do not comprehend: quarrelling with itself the logos accords: it is a back-turning attunement, like the bow and the lyre."[30] For the purposes of the analogy, let us imagine the lyre's distinct strings, and its two curved horns, as the

25 See Zwicky, *Lyric Philosophy*, R258.

26 Ibid., L243.

27 Kahn, *The art and thought of Heraclitus*, 89, quoted in Zwicky, *Lyric Philosophy*, R23.

28 Zwicky, *Lyric Philosophy*, R5.

29 Zwicky, "Being, Polyphony, Lyric: An Open Letter to Robert Bringhurst," 183.

30 Herakleitos, DK 22B51; translated after Kahn, *The art and thought of Heraclitus*, 64–5, 195–200. Kahn's argument for *palintropos*, which includes *palintonos* as an overtone, is decisive because it increases the density of Herakleitos's word. The original of Herakleitos's metaphor of the bow and the lyre seems to be Homer, *Odyssey*, 21.404–11.

relevant components of the whole. The horns, back-turning and pulling the yoke in opposite directions, sustain the tension of the strings, permitting them to be tuned in relation to each other. When the complex structure is in tune – integrated – it is capable of resonance.

— "But how is the lyre different from the pocket watch? When one component, such as the hairspring, goes 'out of tune' – when it wears out, goes slack – the complex malfunctions. (And don't the strings of the lyre, like the parts of the watch, need occasionally to be replaced?) Isn't the pocket watch, then, also a 'resonantly integrated, polydimensional whole'?" — Let us shift the analogy slightly, to another of Zwicky's examples: one could say that a chord *is* its component tones; and there is no hierarchy of importance among these tones: each makes an indispensable contribution, in collaboration with its brothers and sisters, to the identity of *this* chord. (Compare – while also noting the differences – a chord, an organism, a family, an ecological community.)

Can one say the same of the pocket watch and its parts? Does it depend, perhaps, on whether one is approaching the watch primarily as a time-telling mechanism or as a fragile artifact? We speak of understanding something in the sense in which it can be replaced by another which means the same; but also in the sense in which it cannot be replaced by any other. (According to legend, when Charlie Parker arrived at a gig at Massey Hall in Toronto in 1953, he had pawned his saxophone. Somehow, in the nick of time, a cream-coloured acrylic alto was found for him. One might say that Parker's saxophone could, and could not, be replaced.) We are not trying, here, to establish a categorical difference between lyric structures and analytic ones; for the moment, let us only contemplate the suggestion that some thinking – lyric thinking – is more chord-like than device-like, and that different forms of clarity are appropriate in response to different contexts. Some things – whose way of meaning is *like* the way that music means – can be more clearly shown through resonant gestures than through those that foreclose on resonance.

Philosophy, then, may assume lyric form when thought whose eros is clarity is driven also by profound intuitions of coherence. When it is also an attempt to arrive at an integrated perception or understanding of how something might affect us as beings with bodies and emotions as well as the ability to think logically.

When philosophy attempts to give voice to an ecology of experience.[31]

There is more than one path through the woods of the book. As Zwicky hints in the foreword, it is also a book about time; it is a new sort of overview of Wittgenstein's work; it is a respectful quarrel with anglophone philosophy's recently exclusive commitment to systematic analysis. And, what was not appreciated by the book's first commentators but has since been emphasized by many of Zwicky's ensuing essays and a few more recent commentaries, the book is also a contribution to ecological ethics. "The coherence that lyric awareness intuits, and that lyric thought attempts to render, is ecological in form."[32]

§10.3. Let us reflect on an image of integrity. Wynton Marsalis says:

In American life, you have all of these different agendas, you have conflict all the time, and we're attempting to achieve harmony through conflict. Which seems strange to say that, but it's like an argument that you have with the intent to work something out, not an argument that you have with the intent to argue. And that's what jazz music is. You have musicians, and they're all standing on the bandstand, and each one has their personality and their agenda. And invariably they're going to play something that you would not play. So, you have to learn when to say a little something, when to get out of the way. So you have that question of the integrity, the intent, the will to play together. That's what jazz music is. So you have yourself, your individual expression, and then you have how you negotiate that expression in the context of that group.[33]

Marsalis uses the concept of "integrity" ambiguously, and the ambiguity is both unsettling and helpful: is integrity an *individual* virtue, or a relational, *collective* one? The ambiguity is most concentrated here: "So you have that question of the integrity, the intent, the will to play together." On the one hand, there is the personal integrity of each

31 Zwicky, "What Is Lyric Philosophy," §11. Cf. Zwicky, *Lyric Philosophy*, L68.
32 Zwicky, "What Is Lyric Philosophy?,"§13.
33 Marsalis, "A Masterpiece by Midnight." "Harmony through conflict" – this conception of integrity is lyric. The instrument of Herakleitos is a paradigm of lyric form: "Being drawn apart, it is brought together with itself" (Zwicky, "Lyric and Ecology," §2.21).

individual musician: "each one has their personality and their agenda." And their integrity consists, *inter alia* but importantly, in non-interchangeability: "they're going to play something that you would not play." On the other hand, the collective integrity of this group requires *both* the integrity of each individual musician *and* their negotiated expression. If the expression is not negotiated, then there is no cohesion: one ends up, perhaps, with a heap of random solos, but not jazz music. If the individual musicians are totally subordinated to and dissolved in a group agenda, then perhaps the product is homophony, but again, not jazz. The dynamic of influence is reciprocal: each solo contributes to the character of the group, while the context of the group characterizes each solo.[34] As Marsalis says of Count Basie's piano solos, "one note can swing." The single note swings, not in isolation, but in a momentary silence contextualized by other notes.

There is a familiar, ordinary sense in which integrity is a virtue of *individuals*; but there is also a sense in which integrity is a virtue of *complex structures* or *collectives*. This latter usage of "integrity," no less familiar or ordinary than the individualistic usage, derives especially from aesthetic and ecological contexts. We may say of a work of art, Tallis's *Spem in alium* or Eliot's *Middlemarch*, for example, that "it has integrity." And Aldo Leopold's original talk of the integrity of biotic communities has become normal in ecological discourse.[35] In these usages, we are saying something about the relation between components and whole, something about how the whole hangs together.

Consider Zwicky's remark, which may apply equally to aesthetic or ecological structures:

Integrity is an ecological concept. It names a particular kind of wholeness: one in which every "detail" contributes to the stability of the whole, and to the well-being of every other component part. Integrity stands to the parts that it integrates as a gestalt stands to the elements it embraces: it is

34 On the need to respect both particularity and complexity, cf. Hagberg, "Jazz Improvisations and Ethical Interaction: A Sketch of the Connections."

35 Cf. Leopold, *Sand County Almanac*, 210, 224; *Canada National Parks Act*, article 2.(1), definition of "ecological integrity"; and Westra, "From Aldo Leopold to the Wildlands Project: The Ethics of Integrity."

ontologically dependent on them and yet the full meanings of those elements are indiscernible, apart from the whole in which they live.[36]

At first glance, one of Zwicky's claims might seem too strong: that in an integrated whole, "every 'detail' contributes ... to the well-being of every other component part." From an ecological perspective, it is correct to say that every part contributes (in some sense) to the larger whole, but it is not obvious that every other part is thereby benefited: for general stability sometimes comes at the price of a part. (Indeed, it is a version of this insight which consequentialism enshrines.) Consider the case of predation: a predator-species does contribute to the overall stability of a biotic community; but does every individual predator contribute to the well-being of every other member of the community – for example, does *this wolf* contribute to the well-being of *this deer* who is killed and eaten? There is more than one way of answering this objection; one way is to acknowledge that ecological causation is complex (as we shall see in Section 10.7). In his well-known parable "Thinking Like a Mountain," Leopold illustrates the mistake of assuming that such causation is simple or linear. He recounts a day when he and some others shot a wolf and her pups:

We reached the old wolf in time to watch a fierce green fire dying in her eyes. I realized then, and have known ever since, that there was something new to me in those eyes—something known only to her and to the mountain. I was young then, and full of trigger-itch; I thought that because fewer wolves meant more deer, that no wolves would mean hunters' paradise. But after seeing the green fire die, I sensed that neither the wolf nor the mountain agreed with such a view.[37]

From experience, Leopold learns that no wolves eventually means no deer: in the absence of wolves, the deer population irrupts and

36 Zwicky, "Integrity and Ornament," 210–11. Cf. Ames on the Chinese culinary art of the stewing pot as a metaphor for aesthetic integrity: "The combination and blending of these particular ingredients—*this* cabbage and *this* piece of pork—is undertaken in such a manner as to integrate them in mutual benefit and enhancement without allowing them to lose their unique and particular identities" ("Taoism and the Nature of Nature," 325).

37 Leopold, "Thinking Like a Mountain," *A Sand County Almanac*, 130. Cf. Ripple and Beschta, "Linking Wolves and Plants: Aldo Leopold on Trophic Cascades."

overgrazes – and then starves to death. The wolves play an indispensable role in the ecological community. If we wish to understand how this wolf could contribute to the well-being of this deer, then we need to take the perspective of the mountain: the wolf contributes to ecological stability, and that stability lets the deer flourish for however long it lives.[38] I confess that I am not entirely at peace with this response. Leopold's own parable bears witness to the epiphany of an irreplaceable particular, the mother wolf with fire-green eyes. But we shall return to this tension in Section 11. For now, let us focus on Zwicky's characterization of integrity as an ecological concept. According to this characterization, integrity is *not fusion*; it is a kind of wholeness which preserves the *distinctness* and *particularity* of its component details (unlike, for example, systematic consistency or homogeny); and insofar as this structure is integrated, it is capable of resonance.[39]

Zwicky stresses the centrality of details in integrated structures: "we say Vermeer's paintings (or Wittgenstein's *Tractatus*) are lyric because every detail counts. Every thing in them is resonant, like tones in a chord. There is no real distinction between details and centres in such compositions; they are, we might say, radically coherent."[40] Reflecting on Martha Nussbaum's study of ethical attention in literature, Bethany Hindmarsh echoes this idea: "Poetic meaning is vulnerable: we cannot change its shape and have it retain its meaning. In a well-composed poem, everything is relevant. Everything demands attention. Everything is sculpted to create the greatest possible resonance."[41]

— "Oh, sure," the critic will claim, "in aesthetic contexts, we do sometimes exclaim that every comma or every brush-stroke counts. But that's just an exaggeration, meant to emphasize our assessment that the work is well crafted. I know that Shakespeare scholars have fretted anxiously for centuries over these minuscule lexical cruxes in *Henry IV*, for

---

38 A more complex illustration may be found in Yellowstone: the reintroduction of wolves might have initiated a trophic cascade, benefiting other members of the ecological community, including bison, beavers, willows, cottonwoods, and aspens. Other predators such as cougars and humans, as well as climate change, may also be factors. See Morell, "Lessons from the Wild Lab." Thanks to Jan Zwicky for drawing my attention to this example and for discussion of the passage from her "Integrity and Ornament."

39 Zwicky, *Lyric Philosophy*, L34, L67, L181.

40 Zwicky, "The Details," 93.

41 Hindmarsh, "Tasks of Love," 3–4.

example, but out here in the real world, who can take seriously the idea that moving around a couple of punctuation marks will destroy the play's integrity? And if this idea – that every detail counts – seems absurd in aesthetic contexts, its blurring into environmental contexts only serves to inspire those embarrassing clichés of a butterfly flapping its wings in Ecuador and causing a tornado in New Brunswick." — This objection is not trivial. It must be addressed if we are to grasp the significance of Zwicky's notion for ecological or aesthetic contexts. It is to consideration of this objection that we now turn.

§10.4. Why does attention to detail matter? In a preface to "Bringhurst's Presocratics: Lyric and Ecology," Zwicky writes:

The argument is as lengthy as it is because of its insistence on detail—an insistence that stems from an attempt to take seriously the notion of an *ecology* of thought. My aim is indeed as it will frequently appear: to spend hours crawling around on my hands and knees in the linguistic undergrowth, rather than chartering a helicopter in hopes of a contest-winning wide-angle vista. Just as an ecologist attends not … to the real-estate potential … of a stretch of glittering sea and sand, but to the millions of organisms, microorganisms, and nonorganic beings and processes that make the beach the living entity that it is, so the serious reader of integrated thought must pay attention to the microcomponents that produce that thought's stability and integrity.[42]

Zwicky's analogy may be elaborated: ecological thinking is like an ecological community insofar as both are integrated polydimensional structures; in both cases, appreciation of integrity on a macro-structural scale requires attending to the micro-components – the details – which constitute the structure. These details are not logical atoms with merely external relations: each detail (not unlike a Tractarian object) might permit of internal complexification and relation with other details. Yet each one is distinct. Consider a less abstract example: consider someone you love. She is not a mere sum of her parts. Nevertheless, if you *know* her, then you also know *details* about her: the way she wears her hat, the way she sips her tea. The English word "detail" is related to the French for cutting or tailoring: your tailored shirt – the one that your

---

42 Zwicky, "Bringhurst's Presocratics: Lyric and Ecology (Part 1)," *Terra Nova* 1, no. 1 (1995), 43.

grandmother made for you by hand – is one that *fits you, specifically.*
Similarly, a detail is non-interchangeable. In Kantian terms, a detail is
"priceless"; it cannot be replaced by anything else. In Marxist terms, a
detail has no "exchange-value"; it cannot be commodified.[43]

Perhaps we may draw one further connection: in Book 6 of Plato's
Republic, we encounter something called "dialectic," the most advanced
level of knowing on the divided line. In Plato's other works, we learn
that dialectic is the method of collection and division: the practice of
specifying differences and gathering together similarities. And this
practice promotes and demonstrates understanding. You show that you
understand something by describing it so specifically that we could
identify it in a crowd. Contrast these two instructions: (1) "when you
pick my friend up at the train station, look for somebody with a suitcase";
(2) "when you pick my friend up at the train station, look for a hazel-
haired woman with a burgundy-coloured birthmark on her throat; her
eyes are sparks of lazuli, and when she says the word 'sure' her lip curls
to the left." One reason that attending to detail matters is that it is a test
of understanding.

But what, exactly, is a detail?

Elsewhere, Zwicky offers a clue. Her imagined interlocutor asks (with
some impatience): "What is meant by 'detail' here? Each syllable and
punctuation mark? Each word?" And Zwicky responds: "Ideally, for
verbal lyric, each phonic, rhythmic, and semantic counter, each idea,
each image and the relations — including discontinuous relations —
among them. (What the dog did in the night-time.)"[44] — And *what,*
one might ask, is a "discontinuous relation," and how could it be taken
into account? What *did* the dog do in the night-time? — Nothing. And
this silence (this discontinuous relation) itself becomes a salient detail
when set in the larger context of a mystery story (which context includes,
for example, the clue that dogs bark at those they do not recognize).[45]
Here is what is crucial: these kinds of details – however esoteric they
might seem to those of us who are untrained in this sort of reading – are
not only relevant, they are *indispensable* to the meaning of a work of lyric

43 Cf. Kant, *Grounding,* Ak. 434–5; and Marx, *Selected Writings,* 220–43.
44 Zwicky, *Lyric Philosophy,* L112. Cf. Zwicky, "Lyric and Ecology," §3.1; and
"Oracularity," 496 / *AL,* 115–16.
45 Cf. Zwicky, "Oracularity," 503 / *AL,* 123.

art ("*even the dust has its place*").[46] If we ignore them, we don't only miss something (as we miss something when we read Aquinas in English translation). We miss everything.

— "Another exaggeration. That last claim is straightforwardly false – even on your own terms it is false. Here's why: if neglect of 'lyric details' meant that we missed *everything*, we would never be able to learn how to read poetry. Because at first we don't know how to parse such details; but we still pick up on *content*. And content is something that I can get, even at the apprenticeship stage. When I first read Hamlet's 'To be or not to be, et cetera,' maybe I can't name the metre; but I do grasp that he's contemplating suicide. So the details can't be 'indispensable' in any non-rhetorical sense, because I can dispense with them and still understand the poem. At best the details are a kind of 'enrichment,' no more important than ornaments are. All this enthusing over details is a wasteful distraction. It's the same with your enviro-analogy: if I am an ecosystem manager, I don't need to count the number of quills on the back of Ralph the porcupine. What I do need is a sort of statistical overview of large-scale group relations; and at that level of analysis, the details over which you're rhapsodizing are irrelevant."

— Let us call a witness for the claim that details are indispensable. The Italian film director Sergio Leone remembers when he was sixteen, volunteering as a gofer for Vittorio de Sica:

Another thing I remember about *Bicycle Thieves* is one of the first script sessions; I was there almost by chance. Amidei and Zavattini were there, then of course later on the collaboration fell apart and Amidei left. But what really struck me in the twenty-some minutes I was with them was when Zavattini, with his Northern accent, said: "I think that the protagonist should come out with a mortadella sandwich wrapped in a Communist Party newspaper." There was a dead silence in the room. De Sica was at the window with his back turned to us, looking outside. Amidei and Zavattini were sitting at a desk, and I was in my little corner, ready to bring cigarettes to the first person who asked for them. After a moment, Amidei exploded and shouted: "Goddamn it, what the fuck does the Communist Party have to do with it? If anything, we can put just a glimpse of the newspaper!" After this there was another long silence, and then we heard De Sica's voice: "My good friends,

---

46 Wittgenstein, quoted in Zwicky, *Wisdom & Metaphor*, R83.

in my opinion we need an apple, a red apple, one of those multicolored ones, half red and half shaded, and he leaves the house biting on this apple!" Well, I was shocked by this, and I started to wonder: "Oh my God, we're in trouble. If in writing a screenplay you have to deal with these kinds of details, it must be a crazy business!"[47]

Leone's account is helpful, not only due to his respectful sense of humour, but due to his apprenticeship perspective. For the whole ceremony and controversy does seem esoteric (not to mention laughable) from the outside. But Leone makes the point that, *as a matter of empirical fact, working artists do attend to details* – details that might seem utterly unremarkable to the rest of us. And Leone's account extends our understanding: for he testifies to the fact that it is possible to have serious, even explosive, disagreement over these details. Should the sandwich be wrapped in a Communist party newspaper, or not? Should it be a mortadella sandwich or an apple? The intensity of the disagreement points to a sense that the decision regarding this detail could affect the whole film. (Wittgenstein, quoting Longfellow: "In the elder days of art, / Builders wrought with greatest care / Each minute and unseen part, / For the gods are everywhere.")[48]

— "So what? The mere appearance of disagreement proves nothing. If Drinker #1 swears that he sees Monica Vitti's unclothed shoulder in the gradually melting ice-cube, and Drinker #2 declares that he's darn sure it's the shoulder of Claudia Cardinale, and they roll up their plaid sleeves and settle it with an arm-wrestling match, it does not follow, from any of this subjectivist-emotivist grunting, however vehement, that a disagreement has transpired. You're just begging the question: what you need to prove is that it is possible to have a meaningful disagreement where no justification can be given for either position."

§10.5. Let's also consider John McDowell's discussion of this issue.[49] Suppose that Krzysztof Kieślowski is arguing with Tom Tykwer (who directed one of Kieślowski's last scripts) over the timing of a shot of a

47 Leone, "The Smallest Detail," 63.

48 Wittgenstein, *Culture and Value*, 34e. The quotation is not exact; in Longfellow's original, the punctuation differs and the final line of this stanza reads: "For the Gods see everywhere."

49 McDowell, "Virtue and Reason," §4 (pp. 336–42).

sugar cube soaking up coffee: Tykwer is insisting, against the senior director's expertise, that it should last eight seconds instead of five. In exasperation, Kieślowski stands up, knocking over the card table on which they've been working, and complains, "But don't you see?" Here is the form of the dilemma which haunts this scene and others like it: in putative hard cases over normative matters (aesthetic, ethical, et cetera), either (1) one of the interlocutors can, ultimately, articulate the general principle that will resolve the disagreement – for example, Kieślowski might declare: "Listen, you aren't experienced enough to know it, but it is a universal rule of film-making that eight-second close-ups are too long for the audience" – and thus the case isn't really hard after all; or (2) neither of the interlocutors can articulate a general principle and thus the appearance of disagreement must be illusory. But McDowell suggests that it is an underlying rationalist "prejudice" which forces the dilemma. The prejudice is the idea that, to explain or to justify an action (or an aesthetic decision), a reason must be the sort of thing that is susceptible to articulation as a general principle. If the action is explicable, then there will be an articulable principle; and if there is no such principle, then the action is not explicable. QED.

McDowell's approach to this question is characteristically subtle. While he resists the demand for codifiability, he does not advocate for dogmatic obscurantism. For example, his approach "casts no doubt on the possibility of putting explanations of particular moves ... in a syllogistic form." *In some cases* "we can formulate the explanation so as to confer on the judgment explained the compellingness possessed by the conclusion of a proof." The prejudice consists in assuming that *all* reasonable actions (as reasonable) *must* conform to this rationalist paradigm; and, further, it consists in assuming that "the explanation lays bare the inexorable workings of a machine: something whose operations, with our understanding of them, would not depend on the deliverances, in particular cases, of (for instance, and centrally) that shared sense of what is similar to what else."[50] This shared sensitivity is not mechanical; it belongs to the "whirl of organism" (the form of life) in which we are immersed.[51] McDowell suggests that this sensitivity to "what is similar

---

50 Ibid., §4 (p. 339).
51 McDowell borrows the phrase "whirl of organism" from Stanley Cavell, *Must We Mean What We Say?* (New York: Charles Scribner's Sons, 1969), 52.

to what else" is inextricably implicated in both kinds of cases: *both* those which are assimilable to the rationalist paradigm, *and* those (the ones we are considering) which resist assimilation. If we are willing to countenance this suggestion, then we ought not be alarmed by the resistant cases. For our confidence in deductive proofs is not guaranteed by the machinery of rationality, either. "The cure for the vertigo" – vertigo induced by contemplating the precariousness of our capacity to appreciate reasons – "is to give up the idea that philosophical thought, about the sorts of practice in question, should be undertaken at some external standpoint, outside our immersion in our familiar forms of life."[52] To say that a sensitivity to similarity arises within a form of life is not to say "it's all relative." Instead, it is to say that some real things cannot be perceived clearly without patience and imagination.

Suppose that we do give up the prejudice; where does it leave us? In Kieślowski's quarrel with Tykwer over the timing of the shot, it frees them from the dilemma: assuming that the disagreement is not illusory, they are not forced to concede that articulable general principles must be lurking just out of the reach of their inarticulate minds and tongues. But neither are they forced to default to dogmatism. A field of reasons becomes perceptible, which field may appear peripheral from the vantage point of the rationalist paradigm, but which does not ordinarily disappoint our faith. To show Tykwer that the five-second shot is apt, Kieślowski might offer some of the following reasons: "Consider the rhythm of this shot: it counterbalances the preceding shots by a proportion of *a* to *b*." Or: "A longer shot would imply that our protagonist is obsessive; but we know, from other details of the script, that she is not obsessive, but rather resolutely loyal." Or Kieślowski might set up some objects of comparison: "Recall that passage from Wittgenstein's notebooks, in which he is transfixed by the stove: *this* moment is *like* that one."[53] None of these reasons is helpfully formulable as a general principle (such as might be applied, mechanically, to other shots in other films); but any one of them might be helpful to Tykwer or to us eavesdroppers.[54]

---

52 McDowell, "Virtue and Reason," §4 (p. 341).

53 Cf. Wittgenstein, *Notebooks 1914–1916*, 83e.

54 Cf. Zwicky, *Lyric Philosophy*, §§203–4. On this methodology, cf. Wittgenstein, quoted in Moore, "Wittgenstein's Lectures 1930–33," 106; Wittgenstein, "Remarks on Frazer's *Golden Bough*," 133, and *Philosophical Investigations*, §§122, 127, 130; and

10.2 Édouard Manet, *Argenteuil, les canotiers,* 1874

§10.6. Let us turn to a more momentous exhibit for the defence: Édouard Manet's *Argenteuil, les canotiers,* 1874. I have always found Monet's work more beautiful than Manet's. To my layperson's eye, Manet's style is too splotchy, too unclear – and not "impressionistically" so. The drab light feels smeared onto the canvas in irregular, inert chunks. By contrast, Monet's light actually deserves the adjective "dappled" (however trite that adjective is); on his canvas, the light dances. I cite my long-held preferences only to explain that they are unfounded.

Zwicky, "What Is Lyric Philosophy?," §§33–4. Cf. this book, §4.6.

Consider Manet's *Canotiers*: it depicts a couple, disconcertingly off-centre, apparently holidaying in the suburbs, against the backdrop of a marina. The dun-coloured man, with a parasol tucked under his arm, is half-turned toward the woman, who regards us from under a grotesque meringue-like hat. Their faces are featureless smudges, the wrinkled and blurred stripes on their clothing clash at right angles, and their combined bulk crowds out most of what passes for the landscape – except for the horizon, which is buttressed by a wall and sporadically broken by smokestacks. If one does not adopt the pretence of an art critic or the discourse of civility, one could call the painting "ugly." Or one could resort to the unkind words of Manet's contemporary: "Monsieur Manet is deliberately out to choose the flattest sites, the grossest types. He shows us a butcher's boy, with ruddy arms and pug nose, out boating on a river of indigo, and turning with the air of an amorous marine towards a trollop seated by his side, decked out in horrible finery, and looking horribly sullen."[55] Contrast this scene with Monet's pretty representations of the same region of Argenteuil: here one may find relief in the pure landscapes, uncluttered by tourists and unpolluted by industry.[56] The light rushes through them, unobstructed.

But if one suffers from this reaction (which was mine), then one needs to be taught *how* to look at Manet's painting.[57] T.J. Clark acknowledges what I have been complaining about: the painting is awkward, dissonant, flat.[58] The woman's face, in particular, "is scarred and shadowed and abbreviated, hairless and doll-like, animate but opaque. ... The woman resists the critics' descriptions: she is not quite vulgar, not quite 'ennuyé,' not quite even sullen."[59] Not surprisingly, these difficulties belong to the artwork's meaning. Manet is painting "the look of a new form of life"[60] – a peculiarly modern one, coagulating in the environs of Paris in the late nineteenth century, where the middle class, something like

55 Chaumelin, quoted in Clark, *The Painting of Modern Life*, 168. For drawing my attention to Clark's book, thanks to David Howard.

56 Even in Manet's painting of Monet (*Claude Monet et sa femme*, 1874), the latter is "turned away from the evidence of industry" (Clark, *The Painting of Modern Life*, 179).

57 My reading of Manet's *Argenteuil, les canotiers* is indebted to Howard, "Sex, Alcohol, and Blood: Impressionism, Prostitution, and the Paris Commune of 1871."

58 Clark, *The Painting of Modern Life*, 165–6.

59 Ibid., 168.

60 Ibid., 172.

countryside, and industry converge uneasily.[61] This form of life is characterized by "dislocation and uncertainty, and the sense of the scene [is] suggested best by a kind of composition—perfected here [by Manet and Seurat, for example]—in which everything was left looking edgy, ill-fitting, or otherwise unfinished."[62] It is a painting of ostensible leisure which actually confronts the viewer with discomfort.

Let us now focus on a particular detail: the colour of the river. Consider this longer passage by Clark:

It has the look of an icon, this picture, does it not? ... Yet it is no icon: it is too casual, too uncomposed, too untidy. The river is full of the signs of *canotage*: rigging and bits of boats and rolled-up canvas, the whole thing patchy and provisional. It is the lack of order which must have been striking in 1875, for here was a subject which lent itself normally to simple rhythms and sharp effects ... Manet's regatta was not like this ... *Canotage* was a litter of ropes and masts and pennants, its casualness confirmed by the invading slab of blue which so perplexed the critics. The blue was the foil for this patchwork, this debris; it was the consistency of nature, they might have said, as opposed to the random signs of manufacture; it was what survived of landscape.[63]

The blue, one may be tempted to say, is the elemental purity reverenced by Monet, piercing vividly through Manet's jumble. But things are not as they seem (or, more accurately, when we see them as they are, they will seem differently). The clue is given by a wood-engraved satire of Manet's *Canotiers* in *L'Eclipse* (30 May 1875). The cartoonist Paul Hadol "imagined the man's (now phallic) hat floating in the Seine beside its flowery partner, in front of a building labelled 'Fabrique d'Indigo.' He added the caption, 'The Seine at the Sewer of Saint-Denis.' And thus the blue of the river was explained—by the great chemical-dye factories a few miles upstream from Argenteuil, pouring their indigo waste into the water."[64] The socio-historical facts can be fleshed out more graphically: "Government studies in 1874 estimated that 450,000 kilograms of waste was flushed into the river every day. ... The Seine [at the points of flushing] was, according to these reports 'a cauldron of bacteria,

---

61 Ibid., 164.
62 Ibid., 147.
63 Ibid., 166–7.
64 Ibid., 169–70.

infection and disease.'"[65] Furthermore, by the time "that the waste and indigo dye had passed downstream to Argenteuil, pleasure-seekers could both see and smell the effects of modernization. In the heat of the summer, and judging from the shadows in Manet's painting, it's at the height of such a day, a foetid stench rose from the fields at Gennevilliers, and from the stinking waters of the Seine (not to mention the solid waste [littering the banks of the river])."[66]

It is possible not only to read this detail – namely, the indigo – wrongly (or to fail to read it), but, having done so, to read the entire painting wrongly. The river is not really (naturally) indigo-coloured; it is, however, contaminated with indigo dye. Manet's decision to use this pigment cannot be explained on straightforwardly "representational" grounds. The indigo pigment, for a literate audience, evokes the dye-factory and the pollution of the Seine. If one reads this detail ignorantly, as I did initially, the painting remains bolted closed. But read accurately, the detail works like a key, realigning the painting's other details like tumblers inside a lock: the rise of the middle class, the encroachment and expansion of the industrial factory system, the strangulation of the wild margins of cityscapes, the pervasive uneasiness and imperfection of the scene, and more. The painting is not a bland and static scene of an urbane husband and wife vacationing in the countryside; it is a fierce act of witness to the emergence of modernity in a particular ecological community.[67]

§10.7. What does this discussion of details have to do with the concept of ecological integrity? – An ecology is a complex structure whose components – call them "details"– stand in multiple relations with each other. If we wish to understand the structure constituted by those details, then not one of them is negligible. Echoing Wittgenstein, Zwicky writes:

We can imagine any given detail — any identifiable part of a lyric composition — as a set of possibilities of resonance, some of which are actuated by situating the detail in the context of the composition.

65 Tucker, quoted in Frascina et al., *Modernity and Modernism: French Painting in the Nineteenth Century*, 121.

66 Frascina et al, *Modernity and Modernism*, 121. Nor are these facts esoteric: "All of this would have been known by many Parisians who flocked to the Salon" (ibid.).

67 Cf. the ecological literacy endorsed by Leopold in his discussion of the marshland habitat of the sandhill cranes in his "Marshland Elegy," *A Sand County Almanac*, 95–101; and more programmatically by Callicott in "The Land Aesthetic."

The set of actuated possibilities of resonance is the resonant structure of the composition, its gestural architecture.

What is expressed by the purposive arrangement of possibilities of resonance is a lyric thought.[68]

To compose – that is, purposively to arrange these details – is to think. And the structure is not given in advance. By situating multiple details in relation to each other, one actuates some of their possible resonances (that is, associative, non-linear relations). Other possible resonances would be actuated by other situations. But it is important to recognize that a given detail does not fit, indifferently, with just any other detail. "In lyric, nothing is accidental: if a detail fits into a composition, the possibility of this fitting must be written into the detail itself."[69] Some relations will be more appropriate, within a particular context, than others. Here it is difficult to keep our heads above water: for we must also recognize that the context – the network of relations – is itself a function of the interrelated details.

Much of this discussion is allusive and abstract, and it may be helpful to remember that a detail is a particular image, a particular sound. For example, we may think of *Antigone*; in that play, Sophokles repeatedly presents the image of a yoke. Kreon introduces the image, complaining that some of his citizens pull out of "the yoke of justice"; but later, after tragedy has struck, it is Kreon himself who is yoked by a god.[70] The image is most intense in the choral ode to humanity:

So, as you see, by his sly
inventions he masters
his betters: the deep-throated
goats of the mountain,
and horses. His yokes ride the necks
of the tireless bulls who once haunted these hills.[71]

68 Zwicky, "What Is Lyric Philosophy?," §16. Cf. Zwicky, *Lyric Philosophy*, R111, L114; and Wittgenstein, *Tractatus*, props. 2.0123, 2.032, 2.15, 3.

69 Zwicky, "What Is Lyric Philosophy?," §15. Cf. Zwicky, *Lyric Philosophy*, L114; and Wittgenstein, *Tractatus*, prop. 2.012.

70 Sophokles, *Antigone*, ll. 292, 1273–5.

71 Sophokles (translated by Bringhurst), "Of the Snaring of Birds," 53.

Consider the yoke as a detail, a set of possibilities of resonance. By repeating that detail, with slight variations, Sophokles actuates one of its resonances. The introductory image of the yoke charges it with meaning, and that charge arcs across the spaces each time the image recurs. One thing we learn, by attending to this detail, is the cost of the human ambition to tame and control the world.

– Again, what does any of this have to do with integrity, ecological or otherwise? – Perhaps the investigation feels upside-down; we want the big picture, and I keep grabbing a magnifying glass and peering at specimens. But that is the point: integrity depends on detail. Let us consider some last objects of comparison. Once every fifty years, in Northeastern India, Bangladesh, and Burma (Myanmar), the bamboo forests flower, releasing eighty tonnes per hectare of pear-sized seeds. These seeds serve as food for the local rats, whose populations consequently explode. When that population inevitably outpaces the food supply, the rats turn, in hordes, to the neighbouring farmers' rice crops, which they decimate. The outcome is famine. In 1959 "the misery touched off a rebellion in what is now India's Mizoram State."[72]

This story might be set instructively beside Aldo Leopold's discussion of "an ecological interpretation of history":

Many historical events, hitherto explained solely in terms of human enterprise, were actually biotic *interactions* between people and land. …

Consider, for example, the settlement of the Mississippi valley. In the years following the Revolution, three groups were contending for its control: the native Indian, the French and English traders, and the American settlers. Historians wonder what would have happened if the English at Detroit had thrown a little more weight into the Indian side of those tipsy scales which decided the outcome of the colonial migration into the cane-lands of Kentucky. It is time now to ponder the fact that the cane-lands, when subjected to the particular mixture of forces represented by the cow, plow, fire, and axe of the pioneer, became bluegrass. What if the plant succession inherent in this dark and bloody ground had, under the impact of these forces, given us some worthless sedge, shrub, or weed?[73]

---

72 Normile, "Holding Back a Torrent of Rats," 806.
73 Leopold, "The Land Ethic," 205; emphasis added.

— "This is ridiculous: you aren't seriously suggesting that the bamboo forest was the cause of the 1959 rebellion, or that bluegrass decided the settlement of Kentucky? (Shades of the Ecuadorean butterfly.) There is a straightforward distinction to be drawn between individual *agents* and the environmental *conditions* under which they act. You would agree, wouldn't you, that Aristotle's 'material cause' is misnamed: the block of marble (the material) upon which Michelangelo imposes the efficient cause of his will is not itself a cause, but a condition (and a recalcitrant one). The conditions themselves cannot be said to be 'the cause' of *anything!* – they merely make things more or less practically difficult for the causal agent (where 'impossible' and 'necessary' are the limiting cases of the degree of difficulty). I cannot drive my car without gas, but gas does not drive my car; and refusal to recognize this straightforward distinction is obtuse."

— Heidegger has a point when he suggests that Aristotle's theory of αἰτία (*aitia*) was distorted, not only linguistically but also conceptually, by its Latinization.[74] Indeed, the reduction, in our philosophical imagination, of all four αἰτίαι (*aitiai*) to the *causa efficiens* is a significant loss in the history of ideas. The primary sense of αἰτία is "responsibility": and Aristotle's theory, properly understood, is not a theory of causality (as we moderns are accustomed to thinking of it), but of *responsibility*; and some of the components of that theory would be better called "reasons." I am not suggesting that the bamboo forest was "the cause" of the rebellion; I am suggesting that the question, "What is *the* cause of war?," is malformed. It is not always enlightening to isolate an individually blameworthy agent. Our culture (including our culture of philosophy) prefers the tidier sort of history which singles out the lone gunman. However, in simplifying and managing the wild phenomena, we are prone to miss things.

Consider R.C. Lewontin's discussion of the cause of tuberculosis:

Any textbook of medicine will tell us that the cause of tuberculosis is the tubercle bacillus, which gives us the disease when it infects us. ...

It is certainly true that one cannot get tuberculosis without a tubercle bacillus. ... But that is not the same as saying that *the* cause of tuberculosis

---

74 See Aristotle, *Physics*, II.3.194b16 ff. and Wicksteed's commentary in his translation, 126–7; Aquinas, *Summa Theologica*, II.ii, q. 27, a. 3; and Heidegger, "The Question Concerning Technology," 313–18.

is *the* tubercle bacillus. ... Suppose we note that tuberculosis was a disease extremely common in the sweatshops and miserable factories of the nineteenth century, whereas tuberculosis rates were much lower among country people and in the upper classes. Then we might be justified in claiming that *the* cause of tuberculosis is unregulated industrial capitalism, and if we did away with that system of social organization, we would not need to worry about the tubercle bacillus.[75]

While it is true that the bacillus makes a necessary contribution to tuberculosis, Lewontin suggests that a less atomistic explanation – and a more contextualist conception of aetiology – is available if one widens the lens to include "environmental" and "social" factors. The social factors (which Lewontin calls "social causes") are one special form of the ecological agency to which we have alluded above. Lewontin is drawing on Marx's theory of the fetishism of the commodity when he claims that the "transfer of causal power from social relations" – in this case, those of industrial capitalism – "into inanimate agents ... is one of the major mystifications of science and its ideologies."[76] His suggestion is a helpful tonic for those of us habituated to identifying and fixating upon an individual scapegoat. However, again the question, "What is *the* cause?" is malformed, and the emphasis in Lewontin's answer is misplaced; like many revolutionary critics, he overcompensates. We do not need to decide – or, minimally, we should not decide hastily – about where to place blame: that is, to assign it *either* to the tubercle bacillus *or* to unregulated industrial capitalism. What Lewontin's example – his widened lens – helps to illustrate is the insight that causality (or, again, responsibility) is not a simple thing. Responsibility can occur, simultaneously, on more than one plane in a polydimensional world. This observation is crucial in coming to understand aetiology and agency in complex ecological contexts.

§10.8. The epistemology of lyric attention implies a shift away from a more traditional conception of agency. In the shifted conception, agency is not the exclusive property of the attender; it is rather a

---

75 Lewontin, *Biology as Ideology*, 41–2.
76 Ibid., 46. Cf. Marx, *Capital*, Vol. One, Chap. 1, §4 (in *Selected Writings*, 230–43).

function of a larger, interactive context, which minimally includes the "attender," the "object" or focus of attention, the relations between them, and their (relevant) relations to other things. ("Attender" and "object" are in scare-quotes because those names sound inappropriate in the larger context. It would be better to call some of the components "co-responders."[77] Furthermore, the question of which relations are relevant to a given situation cannot be settled in advance, and will need to be negotiated, by the co-responders, on a case-specific basis.) At the same time, and notwithstanding the importance of this ecological context, among the phenomena that we need to save are individuals.

We have been preoccupied with addressing the objection that attending to specific details – that is, concern with particular individuals in an ecological context – is pointless or misguided. We have been preoccupied with this objection because attending to such details, concern for individuals, is fundamental to an epistemology that is necessary to understanding of ecological wholes. Furthermore, each of these details might be said, individually, to display integrity. The task is to offer an account of *ecological* integrity that does not do conceptual violence to the recognizable integrity of *individuals*, and which nevertheless acknowledges their relational constitution; an account in which we are not alienated from our ground-level experiences of living as and relating to individuals, *as well as* functioning as participants in political and ecological communities; an account in which individuals do not vanish in holistic talk of "knots in the biospherical net," vortices in a stream of flowing water, or local perturbations "in an energy flux or 'field.'"[78] We need to imagine a macro-structural sort of integrity which can accommodate these individuals and their interrelations without effacing them. As Zwicky writes, "Integration is not fusion."[79] At the same time, the account needs to reflect the intuition that each participant, "each detail is informed by the whole."[80] Zwicky's conception of lyric makes an

77 For this notion of "co-response," cf. Heidegger, "The Thing," 179; and Zwicky, *Lyric Philosophy*, L181.

78 Naess, "The Shallow and the Deep, Long-Range Ecology Movement," §2.1 (p. 95); and Callicott, "Metaphysical Implications of Ecology," §IV (pp. 309–10).

79 Zwicky, *Lyric Philosophy*, L181.

80 Zwicky, "What Is Lyric Philosophy?," §15.

important contribution to ecological ethics because it asks us to rethink the connections between participants and complex wholes. In its insistence on the interrelations among participants, it avoids the desolate fiction of atomism; and in recognizing the distinctness of each participant, it avoids the totalizing blur of holism. Her image of integrity asks us to attend to each detail, *and* to the resonances among them.

Exodos

§ THE PROBLEM OF THE CRITERION

THOMAS H. BIRCH: Although I didn't consciously realize it at the time, in retrospect, I think that I was stunned in such a way that my normal manner of considering the rock was stopped, and having been cleared and cleansed of it, and, now empty, I was opened to seeing the rock as a being in its own right—and because I had been compelled to extend such complete attention to it, *had* to reconsider it, or *had* to consider it ethically for the first time.[1]

Since the 1970s, when environmental ethics became a distinct academic subdiscipline, many professional anglophone philosophers have assumed that its problems should be solved through the deployment of a system – either an old system, refurbished for this purpose, or a new one, unanticipated in the history of ideas.

To rehearse a few of the familiar representatives: Peter Singer finds inspiration in Bentham, Tom Regan and Paul Taylor in Kant, and Arne Naess in Spinoza, while J. Baird Callicott declares that he aspires "to create something new under the philosophical sun ... 'a new, an environmental ethic,' such as Richard Routley had warranted in 1973. ... one that is unprecedented in the

---

1 Birch, "Moral Considerability and Universal Consideration," 325.

Western canon of moral philosophy, an environmental ethic that is both holistic and non-anthropocentric."[2]

The representatives can be schematically arranged as a set of concentric circles – in Val Plumwood and Richard Sylvan's metaphor, successive accretions around the heartwood of a tree.[3]

This list comprises nothing more than a sample from one discursive strand of environmental ethics; consider, by contrast, ecofeminism, ecophenomenology, environmental pragmatism, and others. We are concerned for the moment, however, not with the entire field of environmental ethics, but only with this one strand: namely, the meta-ethical problem of demarcating the boundaries of what Kenneth Goodpaster has called "moral considerability."

— What things are morally considerable?

KENNETH GOODPASTER: However the question gets formulated, the thrust is in the direction of necessary and sufficient conditions on X in

(1) For all *A*, *X* deserves moral consideration from *A*.

where *A* ranges over rational moral agents and moral 'consideration' is construed broadly to include the most basic forms of practical respect (and so is not restricted to "possession of rights" by *X*).[4]

> It is assumed that the problem should be solved by articulating a criterion. — What do we mean by *criterion*? — Roughly, a decision procedure, a compact set of instructions or an explication of the necessary and sufficient conditions which determines whether any

---

2 Callicott, "An Introductory Palinode," n.p.

3 Cf. Callicott, "Conceptual Foundations of the Land Ethic," 217, n. 41. As Midgley argues, the lived situation is not so linear or neat ("Duties Concerning Islands," 40).

4 Goodpaster, "On Being Morally Considerable," 309.

given thing is a member of the class of the "morally considerable."[5]

It is usually assumed that the paradigmatic member of this class is humanity; but that the criterial property, possession of which secures membership, has been arbitrarily stipulated as rationality, or language-use, and so forth.

ALDO LEOPOLD: ... the problem we face is the extension of the social conscience from people to land.[6]

The problem, which has achieved calcified textbook status, has been called "moral extensionism."[7] It is hoped that the redrawn boundaries can be fixed and legitimated by a *single* criterion. (The trance of monism.)

CHRISTOPHER STONE: It suggests that moral considerateness is a matter of either-or; that is, the single viewpoint is presumably built upon a single salient moral property, such as, typically, sentience, intelligence, being the subject of a conscious life, etc. Various entities (depending on whether they are blessed with the one salient property) are *either* morally relevant (each in the same way, according to the same rules) *or* utterly inconsiderate, out in the moral cold.[8]

This categorical moral distinction between persons (who deserve respect) and things (which don't) seems to have been codified by Kant.[9]

The structure of this reasoning resembles the oppressive conceptual framework criticized by Karen Warren. Instead of the hierarchical dualisms *mind/body, reason/emotion, male/female,* et cetera, we have *considerable/inconsiderable.*

5 Cf. Zwicky, *Lyric Philosophy,* §§41–4.
6 Leopold, "The Land Ethic," 209; cf. ibid., 202–3.
7 Stone, "Moral Pluralism," 144. (Stone notes that the term was suggested by Holmes Rolston.)
8 Ibid., 143.
9 Cf. Kant, *Grounding,* Ak. 428. Cf. Midgley, "Is a Dolphin a Person?," 136.

But there is an important difference here: Warren
suggests that an oppressive framework is ultimately
grounded in a logic of domination. (Roughly, some
version of the normative claim: "For any X and Y, if X
is superior to Y, then X is justified in subordinating
Y.")[10] However flawed and appalling such a framework
is, it is nevertheless susceptible, in Warren's account, to
rational critique: there is a sense in which the so-called
"inferior" disjunct of the hierarchical dualism is still morally recognizable, and thus advocates of justice can get
some argumentative leverage.

(But what if the oppressor doesn't care about reasonable practices like justification?)

In the dualism *considerable/inconsiderable*, it is
hypothesized that there is an entire class of things
which may be excluded from our moral thinking.

PETER SINGER: One should always be wary of talking of "the last
remaining form of discrimination". If we have learnt anything from
the liberation movements, we should have learnt how difficult it is
to be aware of latent prejudices in our attitudes to particular groups
until this prejudice is forcefully pointed out.[11]

THOMAS H. BIRCH: Historically, environmental consciousness and
concern have thrown the moral considerability question wide open.
From the historical perspective, we see that whenever we have
closed off the question with the institution of some practical criterion, we have later found ourselves in error … The lesson of history
is that we must open up the question of moral considerability and
keep it open.[12]

> — *But in practice we make plenty of discriminations,*
> *some of them involuntary and unavoidable. To focus*
> *IS to discriminate. When we attend to something, when*

10 See Warren, "The Power and the Promise of Ecological Feminism," 126–32.
11 Singer, "All Animals Are Equal," 103.
12 Birch, "Universal Consideration," 321.

*it becomes salient and leaps out of the manifold, other
things recede into the background.*

— But such perception of salience is *dynamic*. By
contrast, the extension of moral considerability is
theoretically fixed in advance of all particular cases.

ROBERT BRINGHURST: For simple-minded animists like me, there
is no hope of escape from the moral realm, and I think that, for
saintlier animists, there is no stable hierarchy either. I am far from
saintly myself, but when I think about these things, it is clear to me
that I owe some respect not just to my closest relatives and friends
but to all the material and immaterial things I see or touch, and to
all the objects and creatures I encounter.[13]

*— But that sounds like the abandonment of moral
criteria altogether! And how could one possibly opera-
tionalize such an indiscriminate respect? Wouldn't it
be paralysing?*

— These objections assume that the purpose of morality
is to supply practical guidance in the solution of
problems.

PETER SINGER: ... the capacity for suffering [is] the vital characteristic that gives a being the right to equal consideration. ... The
capacity for suffering and enjoying things is a pre-requisite for
having interests at all, a condition that must be satisfied before we
can speak of interests in any meaningful way. It would be nonsense
to say that it was not in the interests of a stone to be kicked along
the road by a schoolboy. A stone does not have interests because
it cannot suffer. Nothing that we can do to it could possibly make
any difference to its welfare.[14]

In Unama'kik (Cape Breton), on Kluskap's Mountain,
there is a cave sacred to the Mi'kmaq. In 1989, the

13 Bringhurst, "Boats Is Saintlier than Captains," §V.
14 Singer, "All Animals Are Equal," 107.

mining corporation Kelly Rock Limited proposed
"a 'glory hole' method for extracting 5.4 million tons
of granite a year for the next 20 to 40 years to provide
aggregate for roads in the eastern US." The corporation's
discourse reconstructs the mountain as a quantifiable
and exploitable "natural resource." The epistemological
distortion is strikingly illustrated in the reduction of
Kluskap's Cave: in the idiolect of Kelly Rock Limited's
EIA (Environmental Impact Assessment), Mi'kmaq artifacts, ceremonial materials, and petroglyphs are reduced
to a tag: "VEC [Valued Ecosystem Component]-11
Lifestyle—Mic mac site."[15]

ALF HORNBORG: This [bureaucratic] approach immediately
defines the proper relationship to the mountain as one of analysis,
fragmentation and objectification, rather than holism and participation. Turning a mountain into gravel is facilitated by first breaking
it down conceptually.[16]

> — *But how can we* KNOW *that the Mi'kmaq perspective
> on the mountain is any more accurate than the dis-
> course of the mining companies? If you are charging the
> latter discourse with constructivism, doesn't that charge
> generalize? What if the mountain is just a big lump of
> amorphous rock? What if it isn't even an individual
> thing? Where does the "ground" end and the "mountain"
> begin? What standard will you use to adjudicate among
> these competing stories?*
>
> — To paraphrase Jan Zwicky: the distinction between
> "organically linked" myth and the technocratic myth
> of Kelly Rock Limited is a distinction between myth that
> maintains and is maintained by an integrated form of

---

15 Nolan, Davis, and Associates, quoted in Mackenzie and Dalby, "Moving
Mountains," 314. Kluskap's Mountain continues to be threatened by the mining
industry: see "Between a rock and a sacred place on Kellys Mountain," *Cape Breton
Post*, 19 November 2017.

16 Hornborg, "Environmentalism, ethnicity and sacred places," 250–1.

life, and one that maintains and is maintained by a
disintegrated form of life.[17]

*— This is nothing more than a shell-game! You've
surreptitiously introduced a new criterion: instead of
sentience, or being subject-of-a-life, or whatever, you're
just proposing that we check for integrity.*

ALDO LEOPOLD: A thing is right when it tends to preserve the
integrity, stability, and beauty of the biotic community. It is wrong
when it tends otherwise.[18]

Callicott calls this famous and frequently quoted line the
"summary moral maxim," "the categorical imperative or
principal precept"[19] of the land ethic. According to this
tack of interpretation, Leopold's "maxim" is "a unified
and coherent practical principle and thus a decision
procedure at the practical level." It "locates ultimate
value in the 'biotic community' and assigns differential
moral value to the constitutive individuals relatively
to that standard."[20] Callicott insists that the land ethic
is holistic in contrast to the alleged individualism of
animal liberation theory.

However, despite surface dissimilarities, the deeper
structures of both theories are the same.

Like animal liberation, the land ethic is extensionist;
and it, too, deploys a criterion to sift the considerable
from the inconsiderable. "In every case," writes Callicott,
"the effect upon ecological systems is the decisive factor
in the determination of the ethical quality of actions."[21]
Perceptive undergraduates have little trouble observing

17 Cf. Zwicky, "Integrity and Ornament," 210.
18 Leopold, "The Land Ethic," 224–5.
19 Callicott, "Conceptual Foundations," 196; Callicott, "Animal Liberation: A
Triangular Affair," 320.
20 Callicott, "Animal Liberation: A Triangular Affair," 337–8.
21 Ibid., 320.

that Callicott's theory is another species of
consequentialism.

§ INTUITION & IMAGINATION

Here is what the animal liberation or animal rights theorists get right: we do cherish individuals. And such cher-
ishing makes some actions impossible for us, and others
possible. And here is what Leopold, Callicott, and Naess
get right: we can contextualize individuals in relation to
others within a collective structure, such as an ecological
community.

But neither an individualistic nor a holistic system is
adequate.

JAN ZWICKY: If we think of nature as ecology, its "individuals" are
really nothing more than nodes in a huge network—imagine the
mathematical points of intersection that define a geodesic dome.
Remove any one of these nodes, or pull it out of place, and everything
else in the system shifts to accommodate the change. A remarkable
interdependence. But the odd thing is, as the analogy with mathematical points makes clear, it leaves the individuals—the mountains,
the rivers, the swallows and frogs—ontologically dimensionless.
Once again, they turn out to be nothing more than *sets of relata*. But
what we love when we love a mountain, or a river, or an animal, is
nothing so abstract, much less is it the whole system that, in a sense,
expresses itself as the series of relations that define a given node.
What we *love*, what love reveals and is disciplined by, is a *this*— a
particular and *irreplaceable* entity, that stands out, haloed, against the
chaotic backdrop of "everything else." And surely, on another view,
nature just is the collection of these distinct—loved or feared, rafter-
skimming or pond-delving—*things*. Or, rather, it is this also.[22]

The strength of a criterion-driven moral system is that
one's decisions can be justified or explained. And also
criticized.

22 Zwicky, "Lyric Realism," 90–1. Cf. Zwicky, "What Is Ineffable?," §4 (p. 208 / *AL*,
255).

A practice of attending risks the relinquishment of prefabricated criteria in favour of a living, flexible sensitivity. On this alternative model, the discipline of the ethical agent is not primarily managerial but epistemological; she aspires not to control but to know. However, the epistemology of attending does not enjoy the conventional security of justification.

SIMONE PÉTREMENT: Finally, she unquestionably owed something to Spinoza: his definition of the "third kind of knowledge," the knowledge at once intuitive and rational that was in her opinion the perfect knowledge. ... She endeavored as much as possible through the mind alone to perceive each thing by apprehending all the rational relationships that form it and could be called its essence. She speaks later on in her *Notebooks* of this "ultra-Spinozist form of meditation" that she practiced while at Henri IV and that consisted of "contemplating an object fixedly with the mind, asking myself, 'What is it?' without thinking of any other object or relating it to anything else, for hours on end."[23]

Pétrement rightly identifies Spinoza's influence on Weil. However, *perceiving each thing by apprehending all the rational relationships that form it* is not the same as *contemplating a thing without relating it to anything else*. In Pétrement's commentary, two different forms of attending are conflated.

There are more than two forms of attention, but let us reflect on two: *elemental attention* or *intuition*, which we may define, following Aristotle and Spinoza, as focusing on a particular, and *lyric attention* or *imagination*, which Zwicky defines as a sensitivity to resonance.[24]

The world is polydimensional and appears in more than one way. Under one aspect, it is a complex set of

23 Pétrement, *Simone Weil: A Life*, 39–40. Pétrement is quoting Weil, *Notebooks*, II.446/*OC*, VI.3.134.

24 See Aristotle, *Nicomachean Ethics*, VI.11; Spinoza, *Ethics*, IIP40S2, VP36S; Zwicky, *Wisdom & Metaphor*, L60, and "Imagination and the Good Life," §II.40.

resonances; under another aspect, it is a collection of distinct things.

For this reason, no single form of attending is enough.

In environmental ethics, the relationship between the particular and the whole is often fraught. Seeking to make sense of how ecologies hang together, holists such as Naess and Callicott emphasize the internal relations between things.

ARNE NAESS: Organisms as knots in the biospherical net or field of intrinsic relations. An intrinsic relation between two things A and B is such that the relation belongs to the definitions or basic constitutions of A and B, so that without the relation, A and B are no longer the same things.[25]

J. BAIRD CALLICOTT: An individual organism, like an elementary particle is, as it were, a momentary configuration, a local perturbation in an energy flux or "field." [26]

DAVID GEORGE HASKELL: Virginia Woolf wrote that "real life" was the common life, not the "little separate lives which we live as individuals." Her sketch of this reality included trees and the sky, alongside human sisters and brothers. What we now know of the nature of trees affirms her idea ... Like the union of leaf-cutter ants, fungi, and bacteria below the ceibo, a tree's root/fungus/bacteria complex cannot be divided into little separate lives. In the forest, Woolf's common life is the only life.[27]

One truth: organisms, and things in general, are constituted by their internal relations. Another way of expressing this truth is to say that things have needs.

---

25 Naess, "The Shallow and the Deep, Long-Range Ecology Movement," §2.1 (p. 95).

26 Callicott, "The Metaphysical Implications of Ecology," 310.

27 Haskell, *The Songs of Trees*, 39. He is quoting Woolf, *A Room of One's Own* (London: Hogarth Press, 1929).

Defined negatively, a need is a state of lack. Defined positively, a need is a genitive relation to the energy of others.

BENEDICT DE SPINOZA: A human body needs for its preservation a great many other bodies, by which, as it were, it is continually regenerated.[28]

> That a living body depends on other bodies is a basic ecological truth. (Spinoza specifies that the body is human, but there is nothing uniquely human about that truth.)
>
> According to Plato, the fact that we are needy beings explains the human ecology of the polis. If the polis embodies sophrosyne, then vital needs are coordinated and relieved, and the political body is healthy; but if the polis seeks more than it needs, then it contracts a fever.
>
> For organisms on earth, the origin of energy is the sun.

ALDO LEOPOLD: Plants absorb energy from the sun. This energy flows through a circuit called the biota, which may be represented by a pyramid consisting of layers. ...

The pyramid is a tangle of chains so complex as to seem disorderly, yet the stability of the system proves it to be a highly organized structure. Its functioning depends on the co-operation and competition of its diverse parts. ...

Land, then, is not merely soil; it is a fountain of energy flowing through a circuit of soils, plants, and animals.[29]

> Leopold offers the image of the fountain as a source of ethical motivation; it is meant to inspire our love. The image is beautiful, but abstract. It can be imagined, but not seen by the naked eye. Some literacy is required to perceive it.

28 Spinoza, *Ethics*, IIP13Post4.
29 Leopold, "The Land Ethic," 215–16.

ELIZABETH COSTELLO: In the ecological vision, the salmon and the river-weeds and the water-insects interact in a great, complex dance with the earth and the weather. The whole is greater than the sum of the parts. In the dance, each organism has a role: it is these multiple roles, rather than the particular beings who play them, that participate in the dance. As for actual role-players, as long as they are self-renewing, as long as they keep coming forward, we need pay them no heed.

I called this Platonic and I do so again. Our eye is on the creature itself but our mind is on the system of interactions of which it is the earthly, material embodiment.[30]

> The world is an unfathomably complex biotic pyramid, a fountain of solar energy. In Zwicky's metaphor, it is a shifting geodesic sphere, a wholly resonant structure.[31] This structure needs to continue being the structure that it is.
>
> Insofar as this need is met, the structure is integrated, beautiful, and stable. Insofar as it is not met, the structure disintegrates.
>
> The structure is elastic and resilient, but mortal.
>
> The limiting case of disintegration is death. It is the end of individuality.

GUSTAVE THIBON: I saw her for the last time at the beginning of 1942. At the station she gave me a portfolio crammed with papers, asking me to read them and to take care of them during her exile. As I parted from her I said jokingly, in an attempt to hide my feelings: 'Goodbye till we meet again in this world or the next!' She suddenly became serious and said: 'In the next there will be no meeting again.'[32]

---

30 Coetzee, "The Lives of Animals," 150.

31 Cf. Zwicky, "Lyric Realism," 90–1, and "What Is Ineffable?," 208 / AL, 255 (cited above).

32 Thibon, "Introduction," in Weil, *Gravity and Grace*, xii.

Holists such as Callicott have been accused of environmental fascism – because preserving the integrity of the whole may require sacrificing some parts.

Without denying the reality of wholes, we may acknowledge, with Spinoza and Wittgenstein, the following truth: what is a whole at one level of analysis, may be a part at another level.

BENEDICT DE SPINOZA: Now let us imagine, if you please, a tiny worm living in the blood, capable of distinguishing by sight the particles of the blood—lymph, etc.—and of intelligently observing how each particle, on colliding with another, either rebounds or communicates some degree of its motion, and so forth. That worm would be living in the blood as we are living in our part of the universe, and it would regard each individual particle as a whole, not a part.[33]

LUDWIG WITTGENSTEIN: But what are the simple constituent parts of which reality is composed?—What are the constituent parts of a chair?—The bits of wood of which it is made? Or the molecules, or the atoms?—"Simple" means: not composite. And here the point is: in what sense 'composite'? It makes no sense at all to speak absolutely of the 'simple parts of a chair'.[34]

Acknowledging this truth helps to explain why integrity, like sentience, et cetera, cannot serve as a monistic criterion for ethical decision-making, and why we must keep the question of moral considerability open.

Ecological ethics cannot be exhausted by the management of wildlife and "natural resources." We must not become transfixed by the macro-ecological structure, forgetting the preciousness and losability of each particular.

KARYN L. LAI: Based on the discussion of *de* in this section, two important features of *de* may be detected: (a) there is a strong suggestion of an intrinsic relatedness between individuals within the framework of the *dao*. Relations are intrinsic rather than extrinsic

33 Spinoza, "Letter 32" (to Oldenburg), *Ethics*, 281.
34 Wittgenstein, *Philosophical Investigations*, §47.

in that individuals are determined in part by their respective places in the *dao*. ...

A corollary to the theme of intrinsic relatedness is that of *interdependence* of individuals. ...

(b) Associated with the deeper notion of environment articulated in (a), *de* seems to provide the specifications for an individual's *integrity* in the context of its relations with other individuals. Within an environment where interdependence is emphasized, the integrity of individuals is important as it is necessary to prevent the obliteration of individual distinctiveness, interests and needs, which might too easily be subsumed under the rubric of the whole.

These two features—interdependence and integrity—are held in a finely tuned balance.[35]

> The North Treaty and South Teigen Creeks in northwest British Columbia, home to chinook, sockeye, coho, steelhead, Dolly Varden, bull trout, rainbow trout, and mountain whitefish, have been listed under Schedule Two of the Metal Mining Effluent Regulations of the *Fisheries Act*. That is, the federal government has reclassified the creeks as "tailings impoundment areas"; and a mining corporation, Seabridge Gold Inc., proposes to dump 2.3 billion tonnes of toxic tailings into them.[36] The Gitanyow Hereditary Chiefs Office has stated that this project "represents the biggest threat to the Gitanyow way of life to date."[37]

---

35 Lai, "Conceptual Foundations for Environmental Ethics: A Daoist Perspective," 252–3.

36 See Judith Lavoie, "Mining Company Gets Federal Approval to Use B.C. Fish-Bearing Streams to Dump Tailings," *The Narwhal*, 11 July 2017, thenarwhal.ca/mining-company-gets-federal-approval-use-b-c-fish-bearing-streams-dump-tailings.

37 "KSM Mine Project," Gitanyow Hereditary Chiefs Office, 26 April 2014, www.gitanyowchiefs.com/images/uploads/maps/Gitanyow_KSM_Presentation_2014_04_26.pdf.

§ IMAGINATION AS SENSITIVITY

JAN ZWICKY: Imagination as a way of knowing or perceiving is a sensitivity to resonance, to inner structural relations.[38]

JOHN MCDOWELL: … we use the concepts of the particular virtues to mark similarities and dissimilarities among the manifestations of a single sensitivity which is what virtue, in general, is: an ability to recognize requirements which situations impose on one's behaviour.[39]

> Some internal relations are requirements. When imagination is rendered excellent through discipline and practice, it perceives these requirements.

LUDWIG WITTGENSTEIN: A property is internal if it is unthinkable that its object should not possess it.
(This shade of blue and that one stand, eo ipso, in the internal relation of lighter to darker. It is unthinkable that *these* two objects should not stand in this relation.)[40]

RICHARD RORTY: For if among the properties that are essential to a thing (for example, the state of Maine) are relational properties, properties whose characterization essentially involves reference to some other thing (for example, the property of being north of Boston), then we say that the relations in question (for example, the relation between Maine and Boston) are *internal* to that thing (Maine).[41]

> But does it require imagination to perceive that one shade of blue is lighter than another, or that Maine is north of Boston? To understand that these characteristics are essential to these things? How could such perceptions be relevant to ethics?

38 Zwicky, "Imagination and the Good Life," §II.40.
39 McDowell, "Virtue and Reason," §2 (p. 333).
40 Wittgenstein, *Tractatus Logico-Philosophicus*, prop. 4.123.
41 Rorty, "Relations, Internal and External," *Encyclopedia of Philosophy*, vol. 8, 335.

(— Furthermore, isn't imagination merely a faculty
for confecting unicorns on a whim? A minor epistemological curiosity? — No. Imagination is distinct from
what Coleridge calls "fancy": the wilful manipulation of
impressions of absent things.[42] By contrast, imagination
is, as Zwicky says, "thinking in images as a way of
understanding the real.")[43]

The fact that imagination is needed to perceive
internal relations does not mean that they are unreal.
It means that reality is complex. And some of the complexity of reality is reflected in the complexity of our
organs of perception.

EDUARDO VIVEIROS DE CASTRO: But if saying that crickets are
the fish of the dead or that mud is the hammock of tapirs is like
saying that my sister Isabel's son, Miguel, is my nephew, then there
is no relativism involved. Isabel is not a mother "for" Miguel, from
Miguel's "point of view" in the usual, relativist-subjectivist sense of
the expression. Isabel is the mother *of* Miguel, she is really and objectively Miguel's mother, just as I am really Miguel's uncle. This is
a genitive, internal relation.[44]

When imagination is exercised ethically, it is sensitive to
a species of internal relations. Not primarily the relations
between shades or cities, but the relations between need
and what is needed, and between the needs of others
and our own.

§ NEEDS

Clearly to perceive a real need is to be moved to relieve it.

SIMONE WEIL: The poet produces the beautiful through attention
focussed on the real. Same with the act of love. Knowing that this

---

42 Coleridge, *Biographia Literaria*, 206.

43 Zwicky, "Imagination and the Good Life," §I.12.

44 Viveiros de Castro, "Exchanging Perspectives: The Transformation of Objects
into Subjects in Amerindian Ontologies," 473.

man, who is hungry and thirsty, truly exists as much as I do—that's enough, the rest follows of itself.[45]

There are cases where a thing is necessary from the mere fact that it is possible. Thus to eat when we are hungry, to give a wounded man, dying of thirst, something to drink when there is water quite near. Neither a ruffian nor a saint would refrain from doing so. [46]

Necessity. Seeing the relations among things, and oneself, including the ends that one carries within, as one of the terms. Action follows naturally.[47]

> Weil's thesis is a variation on the Platonic thesis that virtue is knowledge. In this case, what one knows is not a Platonic form, but rather the reality of this thirsting person. According to Weil, such knowledge is enough to motivate right action: by implication, to relieve the vital need of this being.
>
> *— But Weil's claim is naive and unjustified! Knowing that someone is thirsty doesn't compel any action. Most of us are aware that there's a huge welter of hunger and thirst in the world and yet we do nothing about it. We see human beings hungering in the streets and walk past them. We know that the meat bleeding on the styrofoam comes from a tortured animal. We know that the electronic devices that decorate our lives were torn violently out of the earth and assembled by de facto slaves in factories, that they will be thrown back into mass graves. Our inaction isn't vicious or immoral; it simply proves that Plato is wrong and mere knowledge is feeble.*

MURLIDHAR DEVIDAS AMTE: The physical signs of leprosy are hypo-pigmented patches [of skin] and loss of sensation. Then later, there is thickening of the nerves. Now in so-called healthy society,

---

45 Weil, "Attention and Will," *Gravity and Grace*, 119 / 137; translation altered.
46 Weil, "Necessity and Obedience," *Gravity and Grace*, 44 / 55.
47 Ibid., 48 / 60; translation altered.

you can see a lot of injustice and poverty, yet you are not moved.
You have lost your sensation, your feeling. You suffer from psychological anesthesia. The mind is so dull; the heart so unfeeling,
thick-skinned like a hippopotamus. That's mental leprosy.[48]

> *To traverse the gap from perception to action, we need*
> *to add in another mental state, called "desire." For*
> *example, if I've been conditioned by morality and I*
> *desire to relieve the suffering of others, then that desire*
> *will engage with the perception of suffering – like a car's*
> *engine engaging with the transmission – to motivate the*
> *offering of relief. But if I'm an experimenter trying to*
> *induce suffering in a test subject, then the suffering*
> *means something very different to me. The perception,*
> *by itself, is inert. The active ingredient in motivation*
> *is a desire, analysed as a teleological propositional*
> *attitude.*[49]

— But this objection fails to understand the nature of
need.

   A vital need is internally related to what will relieve it.

   Ontologically, a vital need is an organic state of lack
that must be relieved. If it is not relieved, then the whole
to which the state belongs will, eventually, disintegrate.

   To perceive such an organic state is (normally) to be
moved to relieve it. (Yes, the relation between perception and motivation can be defeated; but let us not
become distracted by that fact.)

   The perception of a vital need is internally related to
the motivation to relieve it.

   The relation between the perception and the motivation is assumed to be obvious in the subjective case –
I am (immediately) motivated by my own vital needs –

---

   48 Amte, quoted in "BIOGRAPHY of Murlidhar Devidas Amte," Ramon Magsaysay
Award Foundation, September 1985, web.archive.org/web/20041028174300/
http://rmaf.org.ph:80/Awardees/Biography/BiographyAmteMur.htm.
   49 Cf. Smith, "The Humean Theory of Motivation."

BENEDICT DE SPINOZA: Each thing, in so far as it is in itself, endeavors to persist in its own being.[50]

> – but dubious when the perceiver considers the needs of "other minds."
> However, when I see that her vital needs (the internal relations that constitute them) are analogous to mine, I also see that the identity of the one in need is irrelevant to the nature of the need.

BERNARD WILLIAMS: The strong doctrine of negative responsibility [the doctrine that I must be just as much responsible for things that I allow or fail to prevent, as I am for things that I myself, in the more everyday restricted sense, bring about] can be seen also as a special application of something that is favoured in many moral outlooks not themselves consequentialist — something which, indeed, some thinkers have been disposed to regard as the essence of morality itself: a principle of impartiality. Such a principle will claim that there can be no relevant difference from a moral point of view which consists just in a fact, not explicable in general terms, that benefits or harms accrue to one person rather than another — 'it's me' can never in itself be a morally comprehensible reason.[51]

> Williams thinks that impartiality is a threat to personal integrity. If I am a pacifist, and facing a situation calling for violence – to avert greater violence, for example – then my commitment to non-violence is not morally irrelevant. It matters who does what.
> But a need is a need. The need for water can be expressed by anyone. The origin alters nothing about the need.

SIMONE WEIL: All human beings are absolutely identical in so far as they can be thought of as consisting of a centre, which is an

---

50 Spinoza, *Ethics*, IIIP6.
51 Williams, "A critique of utilitarianism," 96.

unquenchable desire for good, surrounded by an accretion of psychical and bodily matter.[52]

> Perceiving her vital needs as analogous to mine is imagining. Perceiving her vital needs as internal relations is also imagining.
> Perceiving clearly what a vital need really is – who perceives? who suffers? it doesn't matter – is being moved to relieve it.

§ ANALOGICAL THINKING

Weil thinks that these two tercets of practical reasoning are analogous.

A1. I need food.	B1. He needs water.
A2. Here's food.	B2. Here's water.
∴ I eat the food.[53]	∴ I give the water to him.

The Humean theorist thinks that they are not.

To observe that the conclusion can be defeated in various ways is to miss the point of Weil's example. Both moral character and level of intelligence, according to her, are irrelevant to the motivational power of a need.[54]

As a Humean agent, I am alone, surrounded by a colourless and soundless wasteland. (It is the wasteland known by early modern empiricism.) Photosynthesis has failed, and my environment is devoid of energy. Instead, I must peer into the interior of my mind, where I may find the batteries of potential energy called "desires."

It is true that energy is needed to synthesize – to integrate – thought and passion into motivation. But it is a grave error to assume that energy is the private property of the agent.

---

52 Weil, "Draft for a Statement of Human Obligations," 223 / 76. Cf. Weil, "Human Personality," 71 / 13.

53 Cf. Aristotle, *Movement of Animals*, Ch. 7.

54 Cf. Weil, *Notebooks*, I.224 / *oc*, VI.2.322.

SIMONE WEIL: The source of man's moral energy lies outside him, as does that of his physical energy (food, respiration). He generally finds it, and that is why he has the illusion—as on the physical plane—that his being carries the principle of preservation within itself. Privation alone makes him feel his need. And, in the event of privation, he cannot help turning to *anything whatever* which is edible.

There is only one remedy for that: a chlorophyll conferring the faculty of feeding on light.[55]

> Weil re-imagines ethical agency. In her view, the agent is not a free-willed efficient cause but a conductor. Energy enters this conductor through attention and is expressed in action.
>
> It is a distortion to represent needs as mere preferences. Preferences are idiosyncratic and, for this reason, arbitrary (even when they happen to be shared). A reasonable person can see around the edges of her preferences; she is able to see things from other angles and to admit that her preferences need not be normative for others.
>
> In North American culture, preferences are emblematic of freedom. They fill up a space that has been evacuated of moral constraints. I am free to prefer Android™ phones or iPhones®, and so are you. I am free to take pleasure in the elderly cedar trees on my property or to procure more light in my kitchen by killing them. I am free to purchase a second car or to give to charity. The "good" is indeterminate.
>
> Needs are fundamentally different from preferences.

LUISA COLL: No, you know, I don't see it as being very courageous, because I don't feel that. I don't stop to think about that. I see it as something that I am called to do and I need to do. It's not anything to do with courage or fear. It's … I guess it has more to do with obedience. Obeying the call that I hear, and doing what I hear I am asked to do.[56]

---

55 Ibid., I.222–3 / *OC*, VI.2.320. Cf. Weil, *Gravity and Grace*, 3, 31, 45.
56 Coll, quoted in Colby and Damon, *Some Do Care*, 73.

MURRAY SINCLAIR: I'd always told students when I lectured at law schools, that our obligation is this: If you can, you must. And so, I took up my own challenge: I could, so I did.[57]

> Weil wants to say, in both cases, my own and the other's, the need is the same. If anything is a reason for action, a need is. Needs are deeper than rights and also deeper than desires.
>
> As both Hobbes and Weil recognize, the assertion of a right is agonistic, and it is meaningless unless it relies on force in the background to punish violations.

SIMONE WEIL: The first characteristic which distinguishes needs from desires, fancies or vices, and foods from gluttonous repasts or poisons, is that needs are limited, in exactly the same way as are the foods corresponding to them. A miser never has enough gold, but the time comes when any man provided with an unlimited supply of bread finds that he has had enough. Food brings satiety. The same applies to the soul's foods.[58]

> It is this limitation that distinguishes Sokrates's healthy city from Glaukon's feverish city. In the healthy city, the citizens meet each other's vital needs. In the feverish city, everyone wants more than he needs.

EPIKTETOS: The measure of possessions for each person is the body, as the foot is of the shoe. So if you hold to this principle you will preserve the measure; but if you step beyond it, you will in the end be carried as if over a cliff.[59]

SOKRATES: It isn't merely the origin of a city that we're considering, it seems, but the origin of a *luxurious* city. And that may not be

---

57 Sinclair, interviewed by Todd Lamirande, "Murray Sinclair warns of violent rebellion if Indigenous rights continue to be oppressed," *Nation to Nation*, APTN, 2 May 2019.

58 Weil, *The Need for Roots*, 12 / 20–1. For a survey of some of the literature on needs, see Wolfe, "Together in Need," §§1–2.

59 Epiktetos, *Enkheiridion*, §39.

a bad idea, for by examining it, we might very well see how justice and injustice grow up in cities. Yet the true city, in my opinion, is the one we've described, the healthy one, as it were. But let's study a city with a fever, if that's what you want.[60]

> Need is the ontological ground of the modal category of necessity.
> If I believe that her vital needs are not normative for me, then I am not reasonable, because I have failed to understand a crucial feature of the space of reasons. That space is structured, and needs lie at the substratum: they are the limiting case of norms. Someone aspiring to practical wisdom strives to perceive the real structure of that space.

SIMONE WEIL: Kant: 'The light dove, when in her free flight she cleaves the air and feels its resistance, might imagine that she would fly even better in the void.'

So, we must *struggle* against the world as the swimmer does against the water, as the dove struggles against the air, but we must *love* it as the swimmer loves the water that bears him up, etc. The Stoics have made a synthesis of these two sentiments and it is the second which seems more important – that of *the love of the world*.[61]

> Being free *is* being determined. Fully integrated character interacts with circumstances to facilitate clear understanding, and action follows.

§ A COUNTER-EXAMPLE

> If the Platonic theory of motivation is accurate, then the following case should be impossible: two psychologists, Stephen Suomi and Harry Harlow, designed an apparatus for producing psychopathology in rhesus monkeys.

---

60 Plato, *Republic*, II.372e–373a.
61 Weil, *Lectures on Philosophy*, 179–80 / 229; translation altered. Weil is quoting Kant, *Critique of Pure Reason*, A5 / B8.

SUOMI AND HARLOW: Depressed human beings report that they are in the depths of despair or sunk in a well of loneliness and hopelessness. Therefore we built an instrument that would meet these criteria and euphemistically called it the pit.[62]

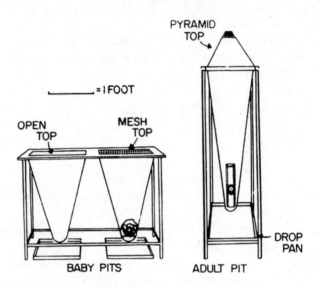

11.1 Suomi and Harlow, "Baby and adult pits"

Infant monkeys were taken away from their mothers and incarcerated in the pit for a month. The apparatus was a success: "Clearly, chamber confinement early in life rapidly and effectively produces profound and persistent deficits of a depressive nature in young monkeys."[63]

If we know anything, then we know that a sentient organism needs not to be tortured. And if anything is wrong, then violating this need is wrong.

---

62 Suomi and Harlow, "Apparatus conceptualization for psychopathological research in monkeys," 247.

63 Suomi and Harlow, "Depressive Behavior in Young Monkeys Subjected to Vertical Chamber Confinement," 17.

Someone might object that in the '60s and '70s, experimenters were not burdened by the conscience awakened by the animal liberation movement. But the question we are considering is not historical; it is conceptual. We are not asking, "How was it possible to torture monkeys in North America in 1969?" We are asking, "How is it possible for someone knowingly to torture someone else?"

(Moral philosophy has become fascinated with a version of this question. It is typical for textbooks and introductory courses in ethics to begin with it; the moral skeptic defines the field, and the rest of the textbook or the course is then dedicated to playing defence. If we start with the skeptic, then of course the attentive person will seem strange and inexplicable.)

§ SETTING APART

If imagination is a sensitivity to resonance, to internal relations, then what Weil calls "the ring of Gyges" is the failure or refusal of imagination: the failure to be sensitive to real, mind-independent internal relations.

SIMONE WEIL: The ring of Gyges who has become invisible—this is precisely the act of setting apart: setting oneself apart from the crime one commits; not establishing the connexion between the two. ...

Gyges: 'I have become king, and the other king has been assassinated.' No connexion whatever between these two things. There we have the ring.

The owner of a factory: 'I enjoy this and that expensive luxury and my workmen are miserably poor.' He may be very sincerely sorry for his workmen and yet not form the connexion.[64]

---

64 Weil, "The Ring of Gyges," *Gravity and Grace,* 138–9/156–7; translation altered.

There is a real ethical and causal relation between Gyges
assassinating the other king and his becoming king;
he has become king because he assassinated the other
king. Similarly, there is a real ethical and causal relation
between the factory owner enjoying expensive luxuries
and his workers being miserably poor.

— Are all ethical relations causal in this way? — No.
We can be responsible for things that we have not
directly caused. For example, the Samaritan is responsible for the afflicted flesh left in the ditch. Accepting
such responsibility is what Margaret Urban Walker calls
integrity.[65]

Imagination perceives real internal relations. It is
necessary for being responsible.

SIMONE WEIL: Justice consists in all cases that are analogous of
establishing identical relations between homothetical terms.
Similitude of triangles. 'Geometry, o Callicles, has great power
among gods and among men.'[66]

In Weil's account of the psychology of what she calls
mettre à part, there is a disintegration of knowing
and willing.

SIMONE WEIL: We set things apart without knowing we are doing
so; that is precisely where the danger lies. Or, which is still worse, we
set them apart by an act of will, but by an act of will that is furtive in
relation to ourselves.[67]

By contrast, in the psychology of the virtuous agent, the
will waits until it is determined by knowledge.

---

65 Cf. Walker, "Picking Up Pieces: Lives, Stories, and Integrity."
66 Weil, *Notebooks*, II.346 / *OC*, VI.2.471; translation altered. Weil is quoting
Plato, *Gorgias*, 508a.
67 Weil, "The Ring of Gyges," 138 / 156; translation altered.

*— You're claiming that the factory owner "sets apart"
his workers' misery from his own luxury. Maybe there is
a factory owner who does that; but surely there are other
factory owners who are fully aware of the connection
and who simply don't care? Others who believe that they
deserve luxuries while their workers do not? Others who
take pleasure in the indentureship of their workers? In
short, isn't human psychology far more variegated and
ugly than Weil imagines?*

*Furthermore, "setting apart" is too individualistic
to explain political harms such as exploitation and
oppression. To understand the causes of those harms,
we should be examining systemic ideologies and
practices, not psychoanalysing private minds.*

— But setting apart *is* an ideology. Because ignorance
of certain internal relations is the default for those of
us who are privileged, we tend not to understand that
being ignorant is a political act.

CHARLES W. MILLS: It could be said that, if there are things one
needs to know, then there are also things one needs not to know,
and an interesting socio-psychological account could probably be
constructed of mechanisms of societal blocking of unwanted information that would be the Marxist equivalent of the Freudian repression of unhappy memories.[68]

SIMONE WEIL: We do not want to know it, and, by dint of not wanting to know it, we reach the point of not being able to know it.[69]

It is such ignorance that Aristotle regards as blameworthy. It is like the man who deliberately becomes
drunk so that he will have an "excuse" for cheating on
his partner. If the state was knowingly and voluntarily
induced, then the one who gets himself into that state

68 Mills, "Alternative Epistemologies," §2 (p. 247).
69 Weil, "The Ring of Gyges," 138 / 156.

is responsible for what follows from him, despite his
protestations to the contrary.[70]

Weil also marks a transition: from voluntarily inducing
a state to its non-voluntary persistence. Having entered
by choice and closed the door, one finds that the key no
longer fits the lock.

ARISTOTLE: But if *without* being ignorant a man does the things
which will make him unjust, he will be unjust voluntarily. Yet it does
not follow that if he wishes he will cease to be unjust and will be just.
For neither does the man who is ill become well on those terms.[71]

Accepting responsibility is more difficult than it sounds.
It requires honesty and courage. Few things are more
unpleasant than acknowledging that we are morally
wrong. Self-consciousness of one's own aspiration to
virtue is an obstacle to such acknowledgement.

Humility is a kind of honesty.

Weil's notion of setting apart is ultimately hopeful.
What is set apart, imagination may reconnect.

— *But the torturer, no less than the bleeding heart,
relies on imagination! In order to devise effective
methods, the torturer must imagine what it would be like
to be subjected to them. Isn't Suomi and Harlow's pit an
ingenious product of the imagination?*

— No. If one really imagines what it would be like,
then one sees that such a thing must never be built.

It is exactly analogous to seeing that the diagonal of
a given square must be the base of the square double
in area.

70 Cf. Aristotle, *Nicomachean Ethics*, III.5.1113b32–3.
71 Ibid., III.5.1114a12–15.

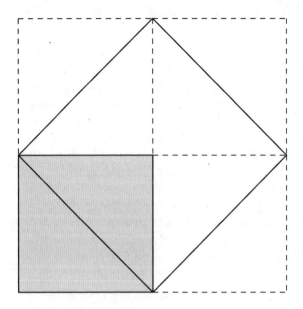

11.2 Doubling the square

§ PARTICULARS & RELATIONS

In Weil's example of the thirsting human being, attending is complex: it involves attending to this particular
being; attending to the internal relation between a vital
need and the thing that relieves it (thirst and water);
and attending to the analogy between one's own needs
and the needs of others. We have called the first form
of attention *intuition*. The second and third forms are
imagination. Intuition focuses on a particular.
Imagination thinks about relations: internal relations
(between need and relief) and analogical relations
(between sets of internal relations).

JAN ZWICKY: A metaphor can appear to be a gesture of healing —
it pulls a stitch through the rift that our capacity for language opens
between us and the world. A metaphor is an explicit refusal of
the idea that the distinctness of things is their most fundamental
ontological characteristic.

But their distinctness is *one* of their most fundamental ontological characteristics (the other being their interpenetration and connectedness). In this sense, a metaphor heals nothing — there is nothing to be healed.[72]

> We need an ontology that is neither monistic nor dualistic.
>
> Because the world is polydimensional, we need more than one form of attention. We need to attend to particular things, to the relations among things, and to the analogies among the relations. Excessive emphasis on only one form of knowing results in a skewed epistemology, one that is unfit for finding truth.
>
> Ecologies are holistic structures. In order to do justice to them, we need imagination; we need to perceive the sets of relations that constitute them.
>
> Organisms, and more generally things, are also holistic structures; but they are not only structures. *Pace* Callicott and Naess, they are not only sets of relations, even when the intersection of those relations defines a unique point in the overall network.
>
> An enumeration of the relations will never explain why we love the thing.

JAN ZWICKY: Ontological attention is a response to particularity: *this* kingfisher, *this* lagoon, *this* slant-wise smoky West Coast rain. It is impossible to pay such attention and to regard that to which one attends as a 'resource.' In perceiving *this*ness, we respond to having been addressed. (In fact we are addressed all the time, but we don't always notice this.)[73]

> Birch testifies to what he calls "deontic experience": the experience that one must (or must not) do something. (Sokrates calls this experience his δαίμων [*daimōn*].) If one attends to this lake, one finds that one *must not* use it as a dumping ground for tailings. One may attend to the lake as a precious and losable particular; and one

72 Zwicky, *Wisdom & Metaphor*, L59.

73 Zwicky, "Imagination and the Good Life," §II.33. Cf. Zwicky, *Wisdom & Metaphor*, L52.

may also attend to it as a set of relations, a biotic community, a home to numerous organisms.

SUE SINCLAIR: James Joyce, in an early draft of *Portrait of the Artist as a Young Man*, describes the epiphany before an object as a moment in which "its soul, its whatness, leaps to us from the vestment of its appearance. The soul of the commonest object ... seems to us radiant." It seems to me that it's impossible to think of a radiant, soulful object as [what Heidegger calls] standing reserve, as something that exists only for me to make use of as I will. I can't clearcut an acre of forest in which I recognize its whatness, its radiance.[74]

— But is it true? For as long as literature has witnessed the radiance of things, we have been wrecking it.

[SÎN-LEQI-UNNINNI (?)]

6   ... They were gazing at the Cedar Mountain,
7   dwelling of gods, throne-dais of goddesses:
8   [on the] face of the land the cedar was proffering its abundance,
9   sweet was its shade, full of delight.
10   [All] tangled was the thorny undergrowth, the forest a thick canopy,
11   cedars (and) *ballukku*-trees were [so entangled,] it had no ways in.
12   For one league on all sides cedars [sent forth] saplings,
13   cypresses [...] for two-thirds of a league.
14   The cedar was scabbed with lumps (of resin) [for] sixty (cubits')
           height,
15   resin [oozed] forth, drizzling down like rain,
16   [flowing freely(?)] for ravines to bear away.
17   [Through] all the forest a bird began to sing:
18   [...] were answering one another, a constant din was the noise,
19   [A solitary(?)] tree-cricket set off a noisy chorus,
20   [...] were singing a song, making the ... pipe loud.
21   A wood pigeon was moaning, a turtle dove calling in answer.
22   [At the call of] the stork, the forest exults,
23   [at the cry of] the francolin, the forest exults in plenty.

74 Sinclair, "The Integrated Life: On Epiphany and Ecology," 44. The passage from which Sinclair quotes may be found in James Joyce, *Stephen Hero*, ed. Theodore Spencer et al. (New York: New Directions, 1955), 213.

24   [Monkey mothers] sing aloud, a youngster monkey shrieks:
25   [like a band(?)] of musicians and drummers(?),
26   daily they bash out a rhythm in the presence of Ḫumbaba. ...
          ...
302   [Enkidu] opened his mouth to speak, saying to Gilgameš:
303   "[My friend,] we have reduced the forest [to] a wasteland,
304   [how] shall we answer Enlil in Nippur?
305   '[In] your might you slew the guardian,
306   what was this wrath of yours that you went trampling the forest?'"[75]

> Here is a home of cedars, *ballukku*-trees, cypresses, tree
> crickets, wood pigeons, turtle doves, storks, francolins,
> monkeys. It is one of the oldest images in world litera-
> ture of an ecological community. How is it possible to
> stand at the threshold of this home, to smell the incense
> and listen to the music, to see the radiance, and to
> destroy it?
>
> It is an old image, and utterly contemporary. For it is
> the same threshold on which we stand today. How is it
> possible to perceive the hummingbird in the arms of the
> arbutus, the seahorse in the branches of coral, really to
> see the preciousness and losability of these things, and
> to destroy them?
>
> (— The western tanager that makes your soul leap to the
> window of your body, and press its face against the glass.)
>
> *— It's true: perception is an input for motivation. If our*
> *heroes were to perceive the forest differently, maybe they*
> *would act differently. But talking about "radiance" is just*
> *hocus-pocus; in fact, the forest is simply an assemblage of*
> *organic matter. The monkeys see it as a "home" (or they*
> *would, if they could operate with the concept of home),*
> *the loggers see it as a natural resource. Why assume that*
> *the monkeys' rights outweigh those of the citizens of Uruk,*
> *who want the timber? Moreover, it's entirely natural to*
> *privilege the interests of one's own species.*

75 [Sîn-leqi-unninni (?)] translated by Al-Rawi and George, "Back to the Cedar
Forest," 77, 83.

11.3 *Dick Marrie's Moose*, 1973

As Weil argues, analysing such cases as conflicts among rights-claims obscures the deeper needs that are at stake.

Here is one possibility: the protagonists engage in setting apart. They set the cutting of cedar apart from the destruction of someone's home. Indeed, they set the harvesting of timber apart from the destruction of each cedar tree.

— Life for life. That is the law. Even trees feed on meat. If you wish to annihilate yourself by practising asceticism, that's your business, but stop proselytizing.

Here is another possibility: the protagonists are afflicted with a sickness of insensitivity. As a result, they are undeterred by the suffering that they inflict.

— Here is another possibility: they don't care! They don't care about trees and birds and monkeys, and why should they?

— To this question, there is no good answer.

Caring about others cannot be rationalized, without distortion, in terms of self-interest.

The interlocutor who sincerely asks, "Why should I care about others?," does not need an argumentative response. He needs retraining.

— Then you are forfeiting philosophy! "Why should I care about others?" is one of the most profound and fundamental questions in moral philosophy. It would not be too much to say that a moral theory stands or falls with its effort to answer this question. Blankly to refuse to address it is to embrace dogmatism.

The openness defended by Birch is the opposite of dogmatism.

There is no thing that cannot be a focus of attention.

TIM LILBURN: But what is contemplative attention? It is what happens to you when you are knocked to the ground by some astonishment. You go very still at some point in yourself and become entirely eye.

You fall apart before some arresting thing, some terrible beauty, and you empty. If you stay low, this thing may come toward you like an animal from the forest.[76]

JORGE LUIS BORGES: We, in a glance, perceive three wine glasses on the table; [Ireneo] Funes saw all the shoots, clusters, and grapes of the vine. He remembered the shapes of the clouds in the south at dawn on the 30th of April 1882, and he could compare them in his recollection with the marbled grain in the design of a leather-bound book which he had seen only once, and with the lines in the spray which an oar raised in the Rio Negro on the eve of the battle of the Quebracho. These recollections were not simple; each visual image was linked to muscular sensations, thermal sensations, etc. ...

A circumference on a blackboard, a rectangular triangle, a rhomb, are forms which we can fully intuit; the same held true with Ireneo for the tempestuous mane of a stallion, a herd of cattle in a pass, the ever-changing flame or the innumerable ash, the many faces of a dead man during the course of a protracted wake. He could perceive I do not know how many stars in the sky.[77]

JAN ZWICKY: Ontological attention is a form of love.

When we love a thing, we can experience our responsibility toward it as limitless (the size of the world). Responsibility is the trace, in us, of the pressure of the world that is focussed in a *this*. That is *how much* it is possible to attend; that is how large complete attention would be.[78]

> There is a form of poetry which has been called *the thing poem* (Rilke) and *the elemental ode* (Neruda). It is practised by Lorna Crozier, Ted Hughes, Don McKay,

76 Lilburn, "Poetry's Practice of Philosophy," 37, 39.

77 Borges, "Funes, the Memorious," 112–13.

78 Zwicky, *Wisdom & Metaphor*, L57. Cf. Zwicky, *Contemplation and Resistance*, 9, and "Imagination and the Good Life," §III.50.

Mary Oliver, Sue Sinclair, Souvankham Thammavongsa, and Jan Zwicky, among many others.

The elemental ode is paradoxical. It focuses on a particular. But it thinks in images linking the particular with other things. For these reasons, the elemental ode may be described as a hybrid genre, one that flickers back and forth between intuition and imagination.

Its primary method of understanding is metaphorical: Sinclair's red pepper is seen as a heart, Neruda's hand-knit socks are seen as sharks, Crozier's clothes hanger is seen as a question mark, Rilke's broken statue is seen as a gaslamp turned down low.

In one of Oliver's odes, the spring azure is seen as a ribbon of flame, a blue bobbin, an epiphany that appears to William Blake, who turns from it to "a life of the imagination." By thinking about the spring azure, Oliver thinks about Blake's vocation, the vision to which he is devoted.

The turning that Oliver witnesses in her poem is not a turning away from reality. It is a turning away from "the dark city," "the factories, the personal strivings,"[79] a turning away from the industrialized European culture which has spread like a disease through the world. The life of the imagination to which Blake turns is not fanciful; like Oliver herself, Blake is aspiring to see more of reality, not less.

LES MURRAY: The non-living things in a poem are as alive as the living things, and the animals are as alive as the people, and everything's got a kind of equality about it.[80]

The spring azure (*Celastrina ladon*) may be seen as a mundane bug, one of thousands, something to be brushed aside. Or it may be seen as an infinitely specific individual, precious and losable, the only one in the universe.

79 Oliver, "Spring Azures," *New and Selected Poems*, 8–9.
80 Murray interviewed in "Escape," *To the Best of Our Knowledge*, Wisconsin Public Radio, April 2014.

SOUVANKHAM THAMMAVONGSA

A FIREFLY

casts its body

into the night

arguing

against darkness and its taking

It is a small argument

lending itself to silence,

a small argument

the sun will never come to hear

Darkness,

unable to hold against

such tiny elegant speeches,

opens its palm

to set free a fire

its body could not put down[81]

---

81 Thammavongsa, "A Firefly," *Small Arguments,* 41.

The title of Thammavongsa's first book, *Small Arguments*, tells us that the poem (like the firefly) is an argument.

It utters *light*, over and over, not as noun but as imperative.

Like Rilke under the inspiration of Rodin, like Neruda with his columns, his "slim stalks of celery," Thammavongsa sculpts her poems as though they were *things*. And they *are* things. The physicality of the poem matters, the exact placement of each letter on the graph.

Fifty-six words shaped into three unstopped sentences. The rest is empty space. In its spareness, the poem is a spark in the void.

The volta marks the moment when darkness lets go. The poem's most important rhyme – *argument/darkness* – forges a lyric harmony between the firefly and the massive force it resists.

The poem makes an argument for attending to the smallest things. It argues not by debating, but by bearing witness.

GEORGE ELIOT: How Cowper's exquisite mind falls with the mild warmth of morning sunlight on the commonest objects, at once disclosing every detail, and investing every detail with beauty! No object is too small to prompt his song — not the sooty film on the bars, or the spoutless teapot holding a bit of mignonette that serves to cheer the dingy town-lodging with a 'hint that Nature lives'; and yet his song is never trivial, for he is alive to small objects, not because his mind is narrow, but because his glance is clear and his heart is large.[82]

The connection between thing and relation, intuition and imagination, is illustrated by an obituary for Murlidhar Devidas Amte. Amte was a successful criminal lawyer, but "when the scavengers came to him with grievances one week, he decided to try their work, scraping out latrines for nine hours a day." While doing

---

82 Eliot, "Worldliness and Other-Worldliness," 209. For drawing my attention to this essay, thanks to Bethany Hindmarsh.

that work, he encountered a dying leper, and "shaking with terror and nausea," he ran away.

THE ECONOMIST, 1 March 2008 (quoted by Zwicky): Where there was fear, he told himself, there was no love ... Deliberately, he went back to the gutter to feed the leper and to *learn his name*, Tulshiram. He then carried him home to care for him until he died, and began — once he had had training in Calcutta — to work in leper clinics all around the town. ...

[He subsequently founded his own ashram for the disabled and lepers, which focussed not on charity, but on self-sufficiency through work and creativity. He was] a Gandhian of the pure, old style, who believed that economic development had to be person by person and village by village, by means as small as handwoven threads and finger-fuls of salt. ... In his last three decades, ... his focus shifted to the preservation of rivers and the well-being of the tribes who lived in the unexploited forest.[83]

> Amte perceives *this* person – not as an anonymous representative of the genus "leper," but as an irreplaceable particular with a proper name: Tulshiram. Notice the movement of the obituary, how Amte's attention ramifies: from focusing on Tulshiram, to attending to a human community, and finally to imagining a larger biotic community including humans, other animals, rivers, and trees. Imagination is required to perceive the larger community, but once it is perceived, it can become a focus for intuition. We can begin to attend to its needs.
>
> An ecology needs to continue being the structure that it is. Since it is constituted by its inhabitants and the relations among those inhabitants, it needs them. The inhabitant of an ecology needs to continue being the individual that it is. Since it is constituted by the ecology and its relations with other inhabitants, the inhabitant needs the ecology.
>
> An ecology is the home of its inhabitants.

---

83 *The Economist*, quoted in Zwicky, "Imagination and the Good Life," §III.50.

JANE GOODALL

one was just when I'd been following
  a little group of chimpanzees and I was very wet
and they climbed in the evening up into this
  tree which had new
    shoots of beautiful
      lime green and the sun behind them was making
     them shine and the
    trunks of the trees were still wet
and the chimpanzccs' coats were
  black ebony shot with little gleams of chestnut
and the smell
  of ripe figs was strong in the air
and then this beautiful
  male bushbuck appeared with his coat dark with the rain
   and his spiralled horns gleaming and just stood there
and it seemed I could hear the insects
  really loud and clear
it was just
  incredibly vivid
being at
  one with
    that beautiful world[84]

> A myth that redescribes the site of a sacred cave as
> a "glory hole" is not a good myth.
> A law that reclassifies a home as a "tailings
> impoundment area" is not a just law.
> One of the deepest needs is the need for roots.
> Anyone who has ever been arrested by radiance
> knows that what humans are doing is unspeakable.
> The strain of trying to comprehend it shatters the
> imagination.

---

84 Goodall, interviewed in "Eye-To-Eye Animal Encounters," *To the Best of Our Knowledge*, Wisconsin Public Radio, 8 February 2020.

And yet there have always been a handful of radicals and protesters. (*Radical*, from Latin for *root*; *protest*, for *witness*.)

Those who have offered their own bodies to defend the body of the earth.

Those who have not been able *not* to attend to the smallest things.

Those who have tried to live, now, in the *kallipolis*, the beautiful polis, even if no such polis has ever existed or ever will exist.

SIMONE WEIL: The human soul needs above all to be rooted in several natural environments and to make contact with the universe through them.[85]

GWAAGANAD: In those early years the first lesson in my life that I remember is respect. I was taught to respect the land. I was taught to respect the food that comes from the land. I was taught that everything had a meaning. Every insect had a meaning and none of those things were to be held lightly. ...

So I want to stress that it's the land that helps us maintain our culture. It is an important, important part of our culture. Without that land, I fear very much for the future of the Haida nation. Like I said before, I don't want my children to inherit stumps.[86]

85 Weil, "Draft for a Statement of Human Obligations," 229 / 83. Cf. Weil, "The Colonial Question and the Destiny of the French People," 110.

86 GwaaGanad, "Speaking for the Earth: The Haida Way," 77, 79. For drawing my attention to this testimony, thanks to Jan Zwicky.

ANSEL ADAMS

Acknowledgements

This book was written on the ancestral and unceded homelands of the Mi'kmaq and the Snuneymuxw.

*

For financial assistance in the form of scholarships, the author would like to thank the Social Sciences and Humanities Research Council of Canada and the Killam Trusts. For financial assistance in the form of grants, the publisher and author would like to thank the Awards to Scholarly Publications Program at the Federation for the Humanities and Social Sciences and the Vancouver Island University Research Awards Committee.

The author's royalties will be donated to the RAVEN legal defence fund for the Wet'suwet'en Nation.

*

Mary Pratt, *Dick Marrie's Moose*, 1973. Oil on Masonite, 91.4 x 61 cm. Collection of Blackwood Gallery, University of Toronto Mississauga. Reprinted with permission of Blackwood Gallery.

Stephen J. Suomi and Harry F. Harlow, "Baby and adult pits." Reprinted by permission from Springer Nature Customer Service Centre GmbH: Springer Nature *Behavior Research Methods & Instrumentation* "Apparatus conceptualization for psychopathological research in monkeys," Suomi and Harlow, 1969.

Thammavongsa, Souvankham, "A Firefly," *Small Arguments* (Toronto: Pedlar Press, 2003). Reprinted with kind permission from Pedlar Press.

"History," by Jan Zwicky. *Robinson's Crossing*. London: Brick Books, 2004. Reprinted with permission of Brick Books.

An excerpt from Zwicky, Jan. "Bringhurst's Presocratics: Lyric and Ecology" in *Terra Nova: Nature and Culture*, vol. 1, no. 1 (1995), pp. 42–58, p. 43, reprinted courtesy of the MIT Press.

Excerpts from *Lyric Philosophy* by Jan Zwicky. Copyright © Jan Zwicky, 1992, 2011, 2014. Reproduced by permission of Brush Education.

Excerpts from *Wisdom & Metaphor* by Jan Zwicky. Copyright © Jan Zwicky, 2003, 2008, 2014. Reproduced by permission of Brush Education.

The author and McGill-Queen's University Press apologize for any errors or omissions in the preceding list and would be grateful to be notified of corrections that should be incorporated into any subsequent edition of this volume.

The author and publisher also wish to thank the following individuals:

Farouk N.H. Al-Rawi and Andrew George for their permission to reprint excerpts from their translation of the fifth tablet of the *Epic of Gilgameš* from their article "Back to the Cedar Forest," in *Journal of Cuneiform Studies*.

Robert Bringhurst for his permission to reprint an excerpt from his "Of the Snaring of Birds" from *Selected Poems* and an excerpt from his "Boats Is Saintlier than Captains" from *Everywhere Being Is Dancing*.

GwaaGanad for her permission to reprint excerpts from her testimony to the BC Supreme Court, published as "Speaking for the Earth: The Haida Way" in *Healing the Wounds: The Promise of Ecofeminism*.

Bethany Hindmarsh for her permission to reprint an excerpt from her "Tasks of Love: On Awareness & Responsibility in Moral & Poetic Contexts."

Alice MacLachlan for her permission to reprint an excerpt from an email communication.

Kevin Koch on behalf of the Gitanyow Hereditary Chiefs for permission to quote from a presentation on the KSM project.

Tim Lilburn for his permission to reprint an excerpt of his "Poetry's Practice of Philosophy" from *Prairie Fire.*

Sue Sinclair for her permission to reprint an excerpt of her "Integrated Life: On Epiphany and Ecology" from *CV2.*

Souvankham Thammavongsa for her permission to reprint her "A Firefly" from *Small Arguments;* and Beth Follett, publisher of Pedlar, for her additional permission.

Jan Zwicky for her permission to reprint her "History" (after Joseph Haydn, Op. 24, No. 2, Adagio) from *Robinson's Crossing,* as well as her permission to reprint excerpts from her "Integrity and Ornament," "Just the World," "Lyric Realism," *Alkibiades' Love, Lyric Philosophy,* and *Wisdom & Metaphor.*

(For details of publication, please see the bibliography.)

*

Versions of some of the book's sections have been published in the following places:

A version of Section 5 was published as "Reading and Character: Weil and McDowell on Naïve Realism and Second Nature." *Philosophical Investigations* 41, no. 3 (July 2018): 267–90.

A version of Section 8 was published as "The Dance of Perception: The Rôle of the Imagination in Simone Weil's Early Epistemology." In *Imagination and Art,* edited by Keith Moser and Ananta Ch. Sukla, 304–31. Leiden: Brill, 2020.

A version of part of Section 10 was published as "What Is Lyric Philosophy?" *Philosophy and Literature* 39, no. 1 (April 2015): 188–201.

A version of another part of Section 10 was published as "Lyric Details and Ecological Integrity." *Ethics & the Environment* 22, no. 1 (Spring 2017): 89–109.

A version of part of Section 11 was published as "Second Glance at *Small Arguments.*" *Canadian Literature* 242 (February 2021).

*

Writing philosophy is, for me, a communal activity.

For early encouragement, thanks to Brian Oliver and Sean McGrath.

For support, thanks to Matthew Heiti, Stephen Heiti, and Sara Warren.

For critical and insightful engagement with an early draft of the manuscript, thanks to Steven Burns, Sue Campbell, Michael Hymers, Duncan MacIntosh, Alice MacLachlan, and Letitia Meynell.

Early drafts of some sections of this book were read at meetings of the Canadian Philosophical Association. For their comments on those drafts, thanks to Kaveh Boveiri, David Checkland, Karim Dharamsi, Sheila Mason, and Belinda Piercy.

For inspiration, thanks to the students of the Lyric Philosophy seminar and to the members of the Attention Reading Collective at the University of King's College.

For thoughtful and sympathetic engagement with the manuscript, thanks to three anonymous readers for McGill-Queen's University Press. For taking good care of the manuscript at the Press, thanks to Mark Abley. Thanks also to Jane McWhinney for rescuing the final draft of the manuscript from numerous errors; for those which remain, I am of course responsible.

Special thanks to Carolyn Richardson, for her editorial brilliance, and to Steven Burns, for his generosity and wisdom.

For the dialogue without which this book would not have been possible, thanks to Lucy Alford, Darren Bifford, Steven Burns, JanaLee Cherneski, Clare Goulet, Bethany Hindmarsh, Danielle Janess, Amanda Jernigan, Tim Lilburn, Carolyn Richardson, Sue Sinclair, Saša Stanković, Katie Wolfe, Laura Zebuhr, and Jan Zwicky.

Bibliography

Abram, David. *The Spell of the Sensuous*. New York: Vintage Books, 1997.

Aesara of Lucania [Aisara of Leukania]. "On Human Nature." Translated by Vicki Lynn Harper. In *Pythagorean Women*, by Sarah B. Pomeroy, 100–1. Baltimore: Johns Hopkins University, 2013.

Alford, Lucy. "Out of Nothing: Imagination as a Mode of Poetic Attention." Paper presented at the meeting of the Canadian Philosophical Association, Ryerson University, Toronto, Ontario, 28 May 2017.

– "Problems in Post-Foundational Ethics: Contingency, Responsibility, Attention." PhD dissertation, University of Aberdeen, 2011.

Allen, Diogenes. "The concept of reading and 'The Book of Nature.'" In *Simone Weil's Philosophy of Culture*, edited by Richard H. Bell, 93–115. Cambridge: Cambridge University Press, 1994.

Al-Rawi, F.N.H., and A.R. George. "Back to the Cedar Forest: The Beginning and End of Tablet V of the Standard Babylonian Epic of Gilgameš." *Journal of Cuneiform Studies* 66 (2014): 69–90.

Ames, Roger T. "Taoism and the Nature of Nature." *Environmental Ethics* 8, no. 4 (Winter 1986): 317–50.

Annas, Julia. "Being Virtuous and Doing the Right Thing." *Proceedings and Addresses of the American Philosophical Association* 78, no. 2 (November 2004): 61–75. [Reprinted in *Ethical Theory*, edited by Russ Shafer-Landau, 735–45. Malden: Blackwell Publishing, 2007.]

– *An Introduction to Plato's "Republic."* Oxford: Clarendon Press, 1982.

– "Moral Knowledge as Practical Knowledge." In *Moral Knowledge*, edited by Ellen Frankel Paul, Fred D. Miller, Jr, and Jeffrey Paul, 236–56. Cambridge: Cambridge University Press, 2001.

Anscombe, G.E.M. *Intention*. 2nd ed. Oxford: Basil Blackwell, 1963.

– "Modern Moral Philosophy." *The Journal of the Royal Institute of Philosophy* XXXIII, no. 124 (January 1958): 1–19.

– "Thought and Action in Aristotle: What Is 'Practical Truth'?" In *New Essays on Plato and Aristotle*, edited by Renford Bambrough, 143–58. London: Routledge & Kegan Paul, 1965.

Aquinas, Thomas. *Basic Writings.* 2 vols. Edited by Anton C. Pegis. New York: Random House, 1945.

– *Summa Theologica.* Part II (First Part), First Number. Translated by the Fathers of the English Dominican Province. London: Burns Oates & Washbourne Ltd., 1927.

Arendt, Hannah. *The Life of the Mind: Willing.* New York: Harcourt Brace Jovanovich, 1978.

– "Some Questions of Moral Philosophy." In *Responsibility and Judgment*, 49–146. New York: Schocken Books, 2003.

Aristotle. *The Basic Works.* Edited by Richard McKeon. New York: The Modern Library, 2001.

– *The Complete Works: The Revised Oxford Translation.* 2 vols. Edited by Jonathan Barnes. Princeton: Princeton University Press, 1995.

– *Metaphysics.* Translated by W.D. Ross. In Aristotle, *The Basic Works*, 681–926.

– *Movement of Animals.* Translated by Martha Nussbaum. In *A New Aristotle Reader*, edited by J.L. Ackrill, 233–40. Princeton: Princeton University Press, 1987.

– *Nicomachean Ethics.* 2nd ed. Translated by Terence Irwin. Indianapolis: Hackett Publishing Company, 1999.

– *Nicomachean Ethics.* Translated by H. Rackham. Cambridge: Harvard University Press, 1975.

– *Nicomachean Ethics.* Translated by David Ross, revised by Lesley Brown. Oxford: Oxford University Press, 2009.

– *Nicomachean Ethics: Book Six.* Translated by L.H.G. Greenwood. Cambridge at the University Press, 1909.

– *On the Soul.* Translated by W.S. Hett. Cambridge: Harvard University Press, 1964.

– *On the Soul.* Translated by J.A. Smith. In Aristotle, *The Basic Works*, 533–603.

– *Physics.* 2 vols. Translated by Philip H. Wicksteed and Francis M. Cornford. London: William Heinemann Ltd, 1929.

– *Poetics.* Translated by I. Bywater. In Aristotle, *The Complete Works*, vol. 2, 2316–40.

Ayer, A.J. *Language, Truth and Logic.* Harmondsworth: Pelican Books, 1971.

Bazin, André. *What Is Cinema?* Vol. 2. Translated by Hugh Gray. Berkeley: University of California Press, 1971.

Birch, Thomas H. "Moral Considerability and Universal Consideration." *Environmental Ethics* 15, no. 4 (Winter 1993): 313–32.

Bird-David, Nurit. "'Animism' Revisited: Personhood, Environment, and Relational Epistemology." *Current Anthropology* 40, no. S1 (February 1999): S67–S79.

Borchert, Donald M., ed. *Encyclopedia of Philosophy*. 2nd ed. 10 vols. Detroit: Thomson Gale, 2006.

Borges, Jorge Luis. "Funes, the Memorious." Translated by Anthony Kerrigan. In *Ficciones*, 107–15. New York: Grove Press, 1962.

Bourgault, Sophie. "Attentive Listening and Care in a Neoliberal Era: Weilian Insights for Hurried Times." *Etica & Politica / Ethics & Politics* XVIII, no. 3 (2016): 311–37.

– "Beyond the Saint and the Red Virgin: Simone Weil as Feminist Theorist of Care." *Frontiers: A Journal of Women Studies* 35, no. 2 (2014): 1–27.

– "Simone Weil's Politics of Silence and Attention." *Les Cahiers Simone Weil* XXXV, no. 4 (December 2012): 487–512.

– "Weil and Rancière on Attention and Emancipation." In *Simone Weil and Continental Philosophy*, edited by A. Rebecca Rozelle-Stone, 223–40. London: Rowman & Littlefield International, 2017.

Bowden, Peta. "Ethical Attention: Accumulating Understandings." *European Journal of Philosophy* 6, no. 1 (April 1998): 59–77.

Bringhurst, Robert. "Boats Is Saintlier than Captains: Thirteen Ways of Looking at Morality, Language and Design." In *Everywhere Being Is Dancing: Twenty Pieces of Thinking*, 187–200. Kentville: Gaspereau Press, 2007.

Brink, David. "Externalist Moral Realism." *The Southern Journal of Philosophy* XXIV, no. 5 (January 1986): 23–41.

Broackes, Justin, ed. *Iris Murdoch, Philosopher: A Collection of Essays*. Oxford: Oxford University Press, 2012.

Burns, Steven. "If a Lion Could Talk." *Wittgenstein Studien* 1, no. 1 (1994). http://sammelpunkt.philo.at/396/1/09-1-94.TXT.

– "Justice and Impersonality: Simone Weil on Rights and Obligations." *Laval théologique et philosophique* 49, no. 3 (October 1993): 477–86.

– "The Place of Art in a Reasonable Education." In *Reason in Teaching and Education: Essays in Philosophy of Education*, edited by William Hare, 23–40. Halifax: Dalhousie University, 1988.

– "Virtue and Necessity." *Laval théologique et philosophique* XXXII, no. 3 (1976): 261–75.

Burns, Steven, and Alice MacLachlan. "Getting It: On jokes and art." *Canadian Aesthetics Journal* 10 (Fall 2004). www.uqtr.uquebec.ca/AE/Vol_10/wittgenstein/burns.htm.

Calhoun, Cheshire. "Standing for Something." *Journal of Philosophy* 92, no. 5 (May 1995): 235–60.

Callicott, J. Baird. "Animal Liberation: A Triangular Affair." *Environmental Ethics* 2, no. 4 (Winter 1980): 311–38.

– "The Conceptual Foundations of the Land Ethic." In *Companion to a Sand County Almanac,* edited by Callicott, 186–217. Madison: University of Wisconsin Press, 1987.

– ["An Introductory Palinode"] "Uma Palinódia Introtório." In *Os Animais têm Direitos?,* edited by Pedro Galvão, 121–31. Lisbon: Dinalivros, 2011. jbcallicott. weebly.com/introductory-palinode.html.

– "The Land Aesthetic." In *Ecological Prospects: Scientific, Religious, and Aesthetic Perspectives,* edited by Christopher Key Chapple, 169–83. State University of New York Press, 1994.

– "The Metaphysical Implications of Ecology." *Environmental Ethics* 8, no. 4 (Winter 1986): 301–16.

Campbell, Sue. "Empathy and Egoism." In *Engaged Philosophy,* edited by Susan Sherwin and Peter K. Schotch, 221–47. Toronto: University of Toronto Press, 2007.

– *Interpreting the Personal.* Ithaca: Cornell University Press, 1997.

Camus, Albert. *Le mythe de Sisyphe.* Paris: Éditions Gallimard, 1942.

Carr, Nicholas. "Is Google Making Us Stupid? What the Internet is doing to our brains." *The Atlantic,* July/August 2008. www.theatlantic.com/magazine/ archive/2008/07/is-google-making-us-stupid/306868.

Chenavier, Robert. *Simone Weil: Attention to the Real.* Translated by Bernard E. Doering. Notre Dame: University of Notre Dame Press, 2012.

Church, Jennifer. "Seeing Reasons." *Philosophy and Phenomenological Research* LXXX, no. 3 (May 2010): 638–70.

Citton, Yves. *The Ecology of Attention.* Translated by Barnaby Norman. Cambridge: Polity Press, 2017.

Clark, T.J. *The Painting of Modern Life.* Rev. ed. Princeton: Princeton University Press, 1999.

Code, Lorraine. "Taking Subjectivity into Account." In *Feminist Epistemologies,* edited by Linda Alcoff and Elizabeth Potter, 15–48. New York: Routledge, 1993.

Coetzee, J.M. "The Lives of Animals." In *The Tanner Lectures on Human Values,* vol. 20, edited by Grethe B. Petersen, 113–66. University of Utah Press, 1999.

Colby, Anne, and William Damon. *Some Do Care: Contemporary Lives of Moral Commitment.* New York: The Free Press, 1992.

Coleridge, Samuel Taylor. *Biographia Literaria.* Edited by Adam Roberts. Edinburgh: Edinburgh University Press, 2014.

Collins, Arthur W. "The Psychological Reality of Reasons." *Ratio* X, no. 2 (September 1997): 108–23.

Corbí, Josep. "First Person Authority and Self-Knowledge as an Achievement." *European Journal of Philosophy* 18, no. 3 (2009): 325–62.

Cornford, F.M. "*Anamnesis.*" In *Principium Sapientiae: The Origins of Greek Philosophical Thought*, edited by W.K.C. Guthrie, 45–61. Cambridge at the University Press, 1952.

Csikszentmihalyi, Mihaly. "Attention and the Holistic Approach to Behavior." In *Flow and the Foundations of Positive Psychology*, 1–20. Dordrecht: Springer, 2014.

– *Flow: The Psychology of Optimal Experience*. New York: Harper Perennial Modern Classics, 2008.

Dancy, Jonathan. *Moral Reasons*. Oxford: Blackwell, 1993.

– *Practical Reality*. Oxford: Oxford University Press, 2000.

Day, Jane M., ed. *Plato's "Meno" in Focus*. London: Routledge, 1994.

De Sica, Vittorio, director. *Bicycle Thieves/ Ladri di biciclette*. 1948. Criterion Collection, 2007.

– *Umberto D.* 1952. Criterion Collection, 2003.

DesAutels, Peggy. "Moral Mindfulness." In *Moral Psychology*, edited by DesAutels and Walker, 69–81.

DesAutels, Peggy, and Margaret Urban Walker, eds. *Moral Psychology: Feminist Ethics and Social Theory*. Lanham: Rowman & Littlefield Publishers, Inc., 2004.

Descartes, René. *Discourse on Method*. Translated by Donald Cress. In Descartes, *Philosophical Essays and Correspondence*, 46–82.

– *Meditations on First Philosophy*. 3rd ed. Translated by Donald A. Cress. Indianapolis: Hackett Publishing Company, 1993.

– *Optics*. Translated by Robert Stoothoff. In Descartes, *The Philosophical Writings*, 152–75.

– *Philosophical Essays and Correspondence*. Edited by Roger Ariew. Indianapolis: Hackett Publishing Company, 2000.

– *The Philosophical Writings of Descartes*. Vol. 1. Translated by John Cottingham, Robert Stoothoff, and Dugald Murdoch. Cambridge: Cambridge University Press, 1985.

– *Principles of Philosophy*. Translated by John Cottingham. In Descartes, *The Philosophical Writings*, 177–291.

Diogenes Laertios. *Lives of Eminent Philosophers*. Vol. 1. Translated by R.D. Hicks. London: William Heinemann Ltd., 1966.

Dostoevsky, Fyodor. *Notes from Underground*. Translated by Ronald Wilks. London: Penguin Books, 2009.

Dworkin, Gerald. "Unprincipled Ethics." *Midwest Studies in Philosophy* XX, no. 1 (September 1995): 224–39.

Eliot, George. *Middlemarch*. Peterborough: Broadview Press, 2004.

– "Worldliness and Other-Worldliness: The Poet Young." In *Selected Essays, Poems and Other Writings*, edited by A.S. Byatt and Nicholas Warren, 164–213. London: Penguin Books, 1990.

Elisabeth of Bohemia. *The Correspondence between Elisabeth of Bohemia and René Descartes*. Translated by Lisa Shapiro. Chicago: University of Chicago Press, 2007.

Epictetus [Epiktetos]. *Encheiridion*. Translated by Nicholas P. White. Indianapolis: Hackett Publishing Company, 1983.

Foot, Philippa. "The Problem of Abortion and the Doctrine of the Double Effect." *Oxford Review* 5 (1967): 5–15.

Frascina, Francis, et al. *Modernity and Modernism: French Painting in the Nineteenth Century*. New Haven: Yale University Press, 1993.

Freud, Sigmund. *Civilization and Its Discontents*. Translated and edited by James Strachey. New York: W.W. Norton and Company, 2010.

– *An Outline of Psychoanalysis*. Translated by Helena Ragg-Kirby. London: Penguin Books, 2003.

Fricker, Miranda. "Epistemic Injustice and a Role for Virtue in the Politics of Knowing." *Metaphilosophy* 34, nos. 1/2 (January 2003): 154–73.

– "Silence and Institutional Prejudice." In *Out from the Shadows: Analytical Feminist Contributions to Traditional Philosophy*, edited by Sharon L. Crasnow and Anita M. Superson, 287–304. Oxford: Oxford University Press, 2012.

Galilei, Galileo. *The Assayer*. Translated by A.C. Danto. In *Readings in Modern Philosophy*, Vol. 1, *Descartes, Spinoza, Leibniz, and Associated Texts*, edited by Roger Ariew and Eric Watkins, 8–11. Indianapolis: Hackett Publishing Company, 2000.

Galison, Peter. "Descartes's Comparisons: From the Invisible to the Visible." *Isis* 75, no. 2 (June 1984): 311–26.

Gibson, James J. "The Theory of Affordances." In *The Ecological Approach to Visual Perception*, 127–43. Boston: Houghton Mifflin Company, 1979.

Goodpaster, Kenneth. "On Being Morally Considerable." *Journal of Philosophy* 75, no. 6 (June 1978): 308–25.

Groarke, Louis. "Following in the Footsteps of Aristotle: The Chicago School, the Glue-Stick, and the Razor." *The Journal of Speculative Philosophy* VI, no. 3 (January 1992): 190–205.

Gwaganad [GwaaGanad]. "Speaking for the Earth: The Haida Way." *Healing the Wounds: The Promise of Ecofeminism*, edited by Judith Plant, 76–9. Toronto: Between the Lines, 1989.

Hagberg, Garry L. "Jazz Improvisations and Ethical Interaction: A Sketch of the Connections." In *Art and Ethical Criticism*, edited by Hagberg, 259–85. Malden: Blackwell Publishing, 2008.

Hallowell, A. Irving. "Ojibwa Ontology, Behavior, and World View." In *Culture in History*, edited by Stanley Diamond, 19–52. New York: Columbia University Press, 1960.

Haskell, David George. *The Songs of Trees: Stories from Nature's Great Connectors.* New York: Penguin Books, 2017.

Heidegger, Martin. *Basic Writings.* Edited by David Farrell Krell. New York: HarperCollins Publishers, 1993.

– "The Question Concerning Technology." Translated by William Lovitt. In Heidegger, *Basic Writings*, 311–41.

– "The Thing." In *Poetry, Language, Thought*, translated by Albert Hofstadter, 163–80. New York: HarperCollins, 2001.

– "What Is Metaphysics?" Translated by David Farrell Krell. In Heidegger, *Basic Writings*, 93–110.

Herakleitos. *The art and thought of Heraclitus.* Translated by Charles H. Kahn. Cambridge: Cambridge University Press, 1979.

Hindmarsh, Bethany. "Attention & Imagination: On the Moral Epistemologies of Simone Weil and Hannah Arendt." Paper presented at the meeting of the Canadian Philosophical Association, University of Ottawa, Ottawa, Ontario, 1 June 2015.

– "Tasks of Love: On Awareness & Responsibility in Moral & Poetic Contexts." Paper presented at the Dalhousie Arts and Social Sciences Conference, Dalhousie University, Halifax, Nova Scotia, 7 March 2015.

Hobbes, Thomas. *Leviathan.* Edited by A.P. Martinich and Brian Battiste. Peterborough: Broadview Press, 2011.

Homer. *The Odyssey.* Translated by Robert Fitzgerald. New York: Farrar, Straus and Giroux, 1998.

– *The Odyssey.* 2 vols. Translated by A.T. Murray. London: William Heinemann Ltd., 1946.

Hooker, Brad, and Margaret Olivia Little, eds. *Moral Particularism.* Oxford: Clarendon Press, 2000.

Hopkins, Gerard Manley. *Poems and Prose.* Edited by W.H. Gardner. Harmondsworth: Penguin Books, 1963.

Hornborg, Alf. "Environmentalism, ethnicity and sacred places." *Canadian Review of Sociology and Anthropology* 31, no. 3 (August 1994): 245–67.

Houle, Karen. "Making Strange: Deconstruction and Feminist Standpoint Theory." *Frontiers: A Journal of Women Studies* 30, no. 1 (January 2009): 172–93.

Howard, David. "Sex, Alcohol, and Blood: Impressionism, Prostitution, and the Paris Commune of 1871." Lecture presented at the University of King's College, Halifax, Nova Scotia, 6 March 2013.

Hume, David. *An Enquiry Concerning Human Understanding*. Edited by Eric Steinberg. 2nd ed. Indianapolis: Hackett Publishing Company, 1993.

– *An Enquiry Concerning the Principles of Morals*. In Hume, *Moral Philosophy*, 185–296.

– *Moral Philosophy*. Edited by Geoffrey Sayre-McCord. Indianapolis: Hackett Publishing Company, 2006.

– *A Treatise of Human Nature*, Books II–III. In Hume, *Moral Philosophy*, 12–184.

Hyman, Arthur, and James J. Walsh, eds. *Philosophy in the Middle Ages*. 2nd ed. Indianapolis: Hackett Publishing Company, 1983.

Ibsen, Henrik. *The Master Builder*. Translated by Una Ellis-Fermor. Harmondsworth: Penguin Books, 1958.

Irwin, T.H. "Ethics as an Inexact Science." In Hooker and Little, eds., *Moral Particularism*, 100–29.

– *Plato's Ethics*. New York: Oxford University Press, 1995.

James, Susan. "Spinoza the Stoic." In *The Rise of Modern Philosophy*, edited by Tom Sorrell, 289–316. Oxford: Oxford University Press, 1993.

James, Susan, Genevieve Lloyd, and Moira Gatens. "The Power of Spinoza: Feminist Conjunctions." *Hypatia* 15, no. 2 (Spring 2000): 40–58.

James, William. "Attention." In *The Principles of Psychology*, vol. 1, 402–58. New York: Dover Publications, 1950.

Janiaud, Joël. *Simone Weil: L'attention et l'action*. Paris: Presses Universitaires de France, 2002.

Jenni, Kathie. "Vices of Inattention." *Journal of Applied Philosophy* 20, no. 3 (2003): 279–95.

Joyce, James. "The Dead." In *Dubliners*, 183–236. New York: Signet Classic, 1991.

Kahn, Charles H. "Discovering the will: From Aristotle to Augustine." In *The Question of "Eclecticism": Studies in Later Greek Philosophy*, edited by J.M. Dillon and A.A. Long, 234–59. Berkeley: University of California Press, 1988.

Kant, Immanuel. *Critique of Pure Reason*. Translated by Norman Kemp Smith. New York: Palgrave Macmillan, 2007.

– *Grounding for the Metaphysics of Morals*. 3rd ed. Translated by James Ellington. Indianapolis: Hackett Publishing Company, 1993.

– "On a Supposed Right to Lie." In Kant, *Grounding*, 63–7.

Kearney, Richard. "The Transcendental Imagination." In *The Wake of Imagination*, 155–77. London: Routledge, 2003.

Kosman, Aryeh. "The Faces of Justice: Difference, Equality, and Integrity in Plato's *Republic*." In *Proceedings of the Boston Area Colloquium in Ancient Philosophy* XXI, edited by John J. Cleary and Gary M. Gurtler, 153–68. Leiden: Brill, 2005.

– "Self-Knowledge and Self-Control in the *Charmides*." In *Virtues of Thought: Essays on Plato and Aristotle*, 227–45. Cambridge: Harvard University Press, 2014.

Lafayette, Marie-Madeleine Pioche de. *The Princesse de Clèves*. Translated by Terence Cave. Oxford: Oxford University Press, 2008.

Lai, Karyn L. "Conceptual Foundations for Environmental Ethics: A Daoist Perspective." *Environmental Ethics* 25 (Fall 2003): 247–66.

Lao-Tzu [Laozi]. *Tao Te Ching* [*Daodejing*]. Translated by Stephen Addiss and Stanley Lombardo. Indianapolis: Hackett Publishing Company, 1993.

Lee, Dennis. "The Music of Thinking: The Structural Logic of *Lyric Philosophy*." In *Lyric Ecology*, edited by Mark Dickinson and Clare Goulet, 19–39. Toronto: Cormorant Books, 2010.

Le Guin, Ursula K. *The Dispossessed*. New York: Harper Perennial Modern Classics, 2014.

Leone, Sergio. "The Smallest Detail." In *Bicycle Thieves*, 62–3. Criterion Collection, 2007.

Leopold, Aldo. "The Land Ethic." In Leopold, *A Sand County Almanac*, 201–26.

– *A Sand County Almanac*. New York: Oxford University Press, 1949.

– "Thinking Like a Mountain." In Leopold, *A Sand County Almanac*, 129–33.

Lévinas, Emmanuel. *Totality and Infinity*. Translated by Alphonso Lingis. Pittsburgh: Duquesne University Press, 1969.

Lewontin, R.C. *Biology as Ideology*. Toronto: House of Anansi Press, 1991.

Liezi. *The Book of Lieh-tzŭ*. Translated by A.C. Graham. London: John Murray, 1960.

Lilburn, Tim. *The Larger Conversation: Contemplation and Place*. Edmonton: University of Alberta Press, 2017.

– "Poetry's Practice of Philosophy." *Prairie Fire* 23, no. 3 (Autumn 2002): 33–40. [Reprinted in *Measures of Astonishment*, presented by the League of Canadian Poets, 1–10. Regina: University of Regina Press, 2019.]

Lipson, Abigail, and Michael Lipson. "Psychotherapy and the Ethics of Attention." *The Hastings Center Report* 26, no. 1 (January–February 1996): 17–22.

Little, Margaret Olivia. "Seeing and Caring: The Role of Affect in Feminist Moral Epistemology." *Hypatia* 10, no. 3 (Summer 1995): 117–37.

Locke, John. *An Essay Concerning Human Understanding*. Edited by Kenneth P. Winkler. Indianapolis: Hackett Publishing Company, 1996.

Long, A.A., and D.N. Sedley. *The Hellenistic philosophers*. Vol. 1, *Translations of the principal sources with philosophical commentary*. Cambridge: Cambridge University Press, 1987.

Lorde, Audre. "The Uses of Anger." *Women's Studies Quarterly* 25, no. 1/2 (1997): 278–85.

Lovibond, Sabina. *Realism and Imagination in Ethics*. Minneapolis: University of Minneapolis Press, 1983.

– "The Simone Weil factor." In *Iris Murdoch, Gender and Philosophy*, 28–44. New York: Routledge, 2011.

Lugones, María. "Playfulness, 'World'-Travelling, and Loving Perception." *Hypatia* 2, no. 2 (Summer 1987): 3–19.

Mackenzie, A. Fiona D., and Simon Dalby. "Moving Mountains: Community and Resistance in the Isle of Harris, Scotland, and Cape Breton, Canada." *Antipode* 35, no. 2 (March 2003): 309–33.

Mackie, J.L. *Ethics: Inventing Right and Wrong*. Harmondsworth: Penguins Books, 1977.

– *Problems from Locke*. Oxford: Clarendon Press, 1976.

Marsalis, Wynton. Interview. In *Jazz*, episode 10, "A Masterpiece by Midnight," directed by Ken Burns. PBS Home Video, 2000.

Marx, Karl. *Selected Writings*. Edited by Lawrence H. Simon. Indianapolis: Hackett Publishing Company, 1994.

Mason, Sheila. "The Role of Epiphanies in Moral Reflection and Narrative Thinking." *Interchange* 38, no. 4 (December 2007): 351–66.

Maurer, Armand. "Ockham's Razor and Chatton's Anti-Razor." *Mediaeval Studies* 46 (1984): 463–75.

McDowell, John. "Aesthetic Value, Objectivity, and the Fabric of the World." In McDowell, *Mind, Value, & Reality*, 112–30.

– "Are Moral Requirements Hypothetical Imperatives?" *Proceedings of the Aristotelian Society, Supplementary Volumes* 52, no. 1 (January 1978): 13–29. [Reprinted in McDowell, *Mind, Value, & Reality*, 77–94.]

– "Might There Be External Reasons?" In McDowell, *Mind, Value, & Reality*, 95–111.

– *Mind, Value, & Reality*. Cambridge: Harvard University Press, 1998.

– *Mind and World*. Cambridge: Harvard University Press, 1996.

– "Non-Cognitivism and Rule-Following." In McDowell, *Mind, Value, & Reality*, 198–218.

– "Some Issues in Aristotle's Moral Psychology." In McDowell, *Mind, Value, & Reality*, 23–49.

– "Two Sorts of Naturalism." In McDowell, *Mind, Value, & Reality*, 167–97.

– "Values and Secondary Qualities." In McDowell, *Mind, Value, & Reality*, 131–50.

– "Virtue and Reason." *The Monist* 62, no. 3 (July 1979): 331–50. [Reprinted in McDowell, *Mind, Value, & Reality*, 50–73.]

McEvilley, Thomas. "The Ethics of Imperturbability." In *The Shape of Ancient Thought: Comparative Studies in Greek and Indian Philosophies*, 595–633. New York: Allworth Press, 2002.

McNaughton, David. *Moral Vision*. Oxford: Basil Blackwell, 1988.

Midgley, Mary. "Duties Concerning Islands." *Encounter* LX, no. 2 (February 1983): 36–43.

– "Is a Dolphin a Person?" In *The Essential Mary Midgley*, edited by David Midgley, 132–42. London: Routledge, 2005.

Mill, J.S. *Utilitarianism*. Peterborough: Broadview Press, 2000.

Mills, Charles W. "Alternative Epistemologies." *Social Theory and Practice* 14, no. 3 (Fall 1988): 237–63.

– "White Ignorance." In *Race and Epistemologies of Ignorance*, edited by Shannon Sullivan and Nancy Tuana, 11–38. Albany: State University of New York Press, 2007.

Mole, Christopher. *Attention Is Cognitive Unison*. New York: Oxford University Press, 2011.

– "Attention, Self and *The Sovereignty of Good*." In *Iris Murdoch: A Reassessment*, edited by Anne Rowe, 72–84. Basingstoke: Palgrave Macmillan, 2006.

– "The Metaphysics of Attention." In *Attention: Philosophical and Psychological Essays*, edited by Mole, Declan Smithies, and Wayne Wu, 60–77. New York: Oxford University Press, 2011.

Moore, G.E. "Wittgenstein's Lectures in 1930–33." *Mind* LXIV, no. 253 (January 1955): 1–27. [Reprinted in Wittgenstein, *Philosophical Occasions*, 87–114.]

Moran, Richard. "Anscombe on 'Practical Knowledge.'" *Royal Institute of Philosophy Supplements* 55 (September 2004): 43–68.

Morell, Virginia. "Lessons from the Wild Lab: Yellowstone Park is a real-world laboratory of predator-prey relations." *Science* 347, no. 6228 (20 March 2015): 1302–7.

Mullett, Sheila. "Shifting Perspectives: A New Approach to Ethics." In *Feminist Perspectives: Philosophical Essays on Method and Morals*, edited by Lorraine Code, Sheila Mullett, and Christine Overall, 109–26. Toronto: University of Toronto Press, 1988.

Murdoch, Iris. "Ethics and the Imagination." *Irish Theological Quarterly* 52, no. 1–2 (March 1986): 81–95.

– "Knowing the Void." *The Spectator* (2 November 1956): 613–14.

– *The Sovereignty of Good.* London: Routledge, 1970. [This book collects the three essays, "The Idea of Perfection," "On 'God' and 'Good,'" and "The Sovereignty of Good Over Other Concepts."]

Naess, Arne. "The Shallow and the Deep, Long-Range Ecology Movement. A Summary." *Inquiry: An Interdisciplinary Journal of Philosophy* 16, no. 1 (1973): 95–100.

Nelson, Hilde. "Against Caring." *The Journal of Clinical Ethics* 3, no. 1 (Spring 1992): 8–15.

Nietzsche, Friedrich. *On the Genealogy of Morals.* Translated by Walter Kaufmann. New York: Vintage Books, 1989.

Normile, Dennis. "Holding Back a Torrent of Rats." *Science* 327, no. 5967 (12 February 2010): 806–7.

North, Helen. *Sophrosyne: Self-Knowledge and Self-Restraint in Greek Literature.* Ithaca: Cornell University Press, 1966.

Nussbaum, Martha. "The Discernment of Perception: an Aristotelian Conception of Private and Public Rationality." *Proceedings of the Boston Area Colloquium in Ancient Philosophy* 1, no. 1 (January 1985): 151–201.

– "'Finely Aware and Richly Responsible': Moral Attention and the Moral Task of Literature." *Journal of Philosophy* 82, no. 10 (Oct. 1985): 516–29.

– *The Fragility of Goodness.* Rev. ed. New York: Cambridge University Press, 2001.

– *Upheavals of Thought: The Intelligence of Emotions.* New York: Cambridge University Press, 2003.

– "Why Practice Needs Ethical Theory: Particularism, Principle, and Bad Behaviour." In Hooker and Little, eds., *Moral Particularism*, 227–55.

Oliver, Mary. *New and Selected Poems.* Vol. 1. Boston: Beacon Press, 1992.

Pakaluk, Michael. *Aristotle's "Nicomachean Ethics."* Cambridge: Cambridge University Press, 2005.

Pasternak, Boris. *Doctor Zhivago.* Translated by Max Hayward and Manya Harari. New York: Pantheon Books, 1991.

Paton, Alan. *Too Late the Phalarope.* London: Penguin Books, 1971.

Pétrement, Simone. *Simone Weil: A Life.* Translated by Raymond Rosenthal. New York: Schocken Books, 1976.

Plato. *Complete Works.* Edited by John M. Cooper. Indianapolis: Hackett Publishing Company, 1997.

– *Cratylus* [*Kratylos*]. Translated by C.D.C. Reeve. In Plato, *Complete Works*, 101–56.

– *Gorgias.* Translated by Donald J. Zeyl. In Plato, *Complete Works*, 791–869.

– *Laches, Protagoras, Meno, Euthydemus.* Translated by W.R.M. Lamb. Cambridge: Harvard University Press, 1962.

– *Letter VII.* Translated by Glenn R. Morrow. In Plato, *Complete Works*, 1646–67.
– *Lysis, Symposium, Gorgias.* Translated by W.R.M. Lamb. Cambridge: Harvard University Press, 1961.
– *Meno.* Translated by G.M.A. Grube. In Plato, *Complete Works*, 870–97.
– *Phaedo* [*Phaidon*]. Translated by David Gallop. Oxford: Oxford University Press, 2009.
– *Phaedrus* [*Phaidros*]. Translated by Alexander Nehamas and Paul Woodruff. In Plato, *Complete Works*, 506–56.
– *Protagoras.* Translated by Stanley Lombardo and Karen Bell. In Plato, *Complete Works*, 746–790.
– *Republic.* Translated by G.M.A. Grube, revised by C.D.C. Reeve. In Plato, *Complete Works*, 971–1223.
– *Republic.* 2 vols. Translated by Paul Shorey. Cambridge: Harvard University Press, 1969.
– *Symposium.* Translated by Alexander Nehamas and Paul Woodruff. In Plato, *Complete Works*, 457–505.
– *Timaeus* [*Timaios*]. Translated by Donald J. Zeyl. In Plato, *Complete Works*, 1224–91.
Platts, Mark. *Ways of Meaning.* 2nd ed. Cambridge: MIT Press, 1997.
Pseudo-Dionysus. *The Complete Works.* Translated by Colm Luibheid. New York: Paulist Press, 1987.
Richardson, Carolyn. "Talk About Talk." In *Lyric Ecology*, edited by Mark Dickinson and Clare Goulet, 40–9. Toronto: Cormorant Books, 2010.
Ripple, William J., and Robert L. Beschta. "Linking Wolves and Plants: Aldo Leopold on Trophic Cascades." *BioScience* 55, no. 7 (July 2005): 613–21.
Ross, David. *Aristotle.* 6th ed. London: Routledge, 1995.
Rousseau, Jean-Jacques. *Discourse on the Origin of Inequality.* Translated by Franklin Philip. Oxford: Oxford University Press, 2009.
Rozelle-Stone, A. Rebecca. "*Le Déracinement* of Attention: Simone Weil on the Institutionalization of Distractedness." *Philosophy Today* 53, no. 1 (Spring 2009): 100–8.
Schwenkler, John. "Understanding 'Practical Knowledge.'" *Philosophers' Imprint* 15, no. 15 (June 2015): 1–32.
Scott, Dominic. *Plato's "Meno."* New York: Cambridge University Press, 2006.
Sepper, Dennis L. "Descartes and the Eclipse of the Imagination, 1618–1630." *Journal of the History of Philosophy* 27, no. 3 (July 1989): 379–403.
Shanker, Stuart. "Emotion Regulation through the Ages." In *Moving Ourselves, Moving Others*, edited by A. Foolen, U.M. Ludtke, T.P. Racine, and J. Zlatev, 105–38. Amsterdam: John Benjamins, 2012.

- "Self-Regulation: Calm, Alert, and Learning." *Education Canada* 50, no. 3 (Summer 2010): 4–7.

Shiner, Roger. "Ethical Perception in Aristotle." *Apeiron* 13, no. 2 (December 1979): 79–85.
- "On Giving Works of Art a Face." *Philosophy* 53, no. 205 (July 1978): 307–24.

Sinclair, Sue. "The Integrated Life: On Epiphany and Ecology." *CV2* 32, no. 1 (Summer 2009): 42–6.

Singer, Peter. "All Animals Are Equal." *Philosophic Exchange* 1, no. 5 (1974): 103–16.
- "Famine, Affluence, and Morality." *Philosophy & Public Affairs* 1, no. 3 (Spring 1972): 229–43.

Smith, Michael. "The Humean Theory of Motivation." *Mind*, New Series 96, no. 381 (January 1987): 36–61. [Reprinted in Smith, *The Moral Problem*, 92–129.]
- *The Moral Problem*. Oxford: Blackwell, 1994.

Sophocles [Sophokles]. *Antigone*. Translated by Paul Woodruff. Indianapolis: Hackett Publishing Company, 2001.
- "Of the Snaring of Birds." In *Selected Poems*, by Robert Bringhurst, 52–3. Kentville: Gaspereau Press, 2009.

Spinoza, Benedict de. *Ethics*. Translated by Samuel Shirley. Indianapolis: Hackett Publishing Company, 1992.

Steinbeck, John. *The Log from the Sea of Cortez*. New York: Penguin Books, 1986.

Stohr, Karen E. "Moral Cacophony: When Continence Is a Virtue." *Journal of Ethics* 7, no. 4 (January 2003): 339–63.

Stone, Christopher. "Moral Pluralism and the Course of Environmental Ethics." *Environmental Ethics* 10, no. 2 (Summer 1988): 139–54.

Strawson, Peter. "Imagination and Perception." In *Experience & Theory*, edited by Lawrence Foster and J.W. Swanson, 31–54. Amherst: University of Massachusetts Press, 1970.

Suomi, Stephen J., and Harry F. Harlow. "Apparatus conceptualization for psychopathological research in monkeys." *Behavior Research Methods & Instrumentation* 1, no. 7 (1969): 247–50.
- "Depressive Behavior in Young Monkeys Subjected to Vertical Chamber Confinement." *Journal of Comparative and Physiological Psychology* 180, no. 1 (1972): 11–18.

Thammavongsa, Souvankham. *Small Arguments*. Toronto: Pedlar Press, 2003.

Thomas, Laurence. "Moral Deference." In *Theorizing Multiculturalism*, edited by Cynthia Willett, 359–81. Malden: Blackwell Publishers, 1998.

Tolstoy, Leo. "Father Sergy." In *The Devil and Other Stories*, translated by Louise and Aylmer Maude, 237–79. Oxford: Oxford University Press, 2009.

Varah, Chad. "The Samaritans: Befriending the Suicidal." In *Comprehending Suicide: Landmarks in 20th-Century Suicidology*, edited by Edwin S. Shneidman, 171–7. Washington: American Psychological Association, 2001.

Viveiros de Castro, Eduardo. "Exchanging Perspectives: The Transformation of Objects into Subjects in Amerindian Ontologies." *Common Knowledge* 10, no. 3 (Fall 2004): 463–84.

Vlastos, Gregory. "*Anamnesis* in the *Meno*." *Dialogue* 4, no. 2 (September 1965): 143–67. [Reprinted with amendments and additional references in Day, ed., *Plato's "Meno,"* 88–111.]

Von der Ruhr, Mario. *Simone Weil: An Apprenticeship in Attention*. London: Continuum, 2006.

Waismann, Friedrich. "Notes on Talks with Wittgenstein." *The Philosophical Review* 74, no. 1 (January 1965): 12–16.

Walker, Margaret Urban. "Feminism, Ethics, and the Question of Theory." *Hypatia* 7, no. 3 (Summer 1992): 23–38.

– "Moral Psychology." In *Feminist Philosophy*, edited by Linda Martín Alcoff and Eva Feder Kittay, 102–15. Oxford: Blackwell Publishing, 2007.

– "Picking Up Pieces: Lives, Stories, and Integrity." In *Moral Understandings: A Feminist Study in Ethics*, 103–29. New York: Routledge, 1998.

Warnock, Mary. "Imagination and Perception." In *Imagination*, 13–34. Berkeley: University of California Press, 1976.

Warren, Karen J. "The Power and the Promise of Ecological Feminism." *Environmental Ethics* 12, no. 2 (Summer 1990): 125–46.

Watzl, Sebastian. "The Nature of Attention." *Philosophy Compass* 6, no. 11 (November 2011): 842–53.

Weber, Max. "Science as a Vocation." In *The Vocation Lectures*, translated by Rodney Livingstone, 1–31. Indianapolis: Hackett Publishing Company, 2004.

Weil, Simone. *An Anthology*. Edited by Siân Miles. London: Penguin Books, 2005.

– *Attente de Dieu*. Paris: Éditions Fayard, 1966.

– "Attention and Will." In Weil, *Gravity and Grace*, 116–22.

– "The Colonial Question and the Destiny of the French People." In *Simone Weil on Colonialism: An Ethic of the Other*, edited and translated by J.P. Little, 105–19. Lanham: Rowman & Littlefield Publishers, 2003.

– *La connaissance surnaturelle*. Paris: Éditions Gallimard, 1950.

– "Draft for a Statement of Human Obligations." In Weil, *An Anthology*, 221–30.

– *Écrits de Londres et dernières lettres*. Paris: Éditions Gallimard, 1957.

– *L'enracinement: Prélude à une déclaration des devoirs envers l'être humain*. Paris: Éditions Gallimard, 1949.

- "Essay on the Notion of Reading." Translated by Rebecca Fine Rose and Timothy Tessin. *Philosophical Investigations* 13, no. 4 (October 1990): 297–303.
- «Essai sur la notion de lecture.» *Les Études philosophiques,* nouvelle série, 1ère année, no. 1 (January/March 1946): 13–19.
- «Étude pour une déclaration des obligations envers l'être humain.» In Weil, *Écrits de Londres,* 74–84.
- "Factory Journal." In Weil, *Formative Writings,* 155–226.
- *First and Last Notebooks.* Translated by Richard Rees. London: Oxford University Press, 1970.
- *Formative Writings 1929–1941.* Edited and translated by Dorothy Tuck McFarland and Wilhelmina Van Ness. Amherst: University of Massachusetts Press, 1988.
- *Gravity and Grace.* Translated by Emma Crawford and Mario von der Ruhr. London: Routledge Classics, 2002.
- «L'habitude.» In Weil, *Œuvres complètes,* tome I, 275–7.
- "Human Personality." In Weil, *An Anthology,* 69–98.
- «Imagination et perception.» In Weil, *Œuvres complètes,* tome I, 297–8.
- *Intimations of Christianity among the Ancient Greeks.* Translated by Elisabeth Chase Geissbuhler. London: Routledge, 1957.
- «Journal d'usine.» In *La Condition ouvrière,* edited by Robert Chenavier, 77–204. Paris: Éditions Gallimard, 2002.
- *Late Philosophical Writings.* Translated by Eric O. Springsted and Lawrence E. Schmidt. Notre Dame: University of Notre Dame Press, 2015.
- *Leçons de philosophie.* Transcribed by Anne Reynaud-Guérithault. Paris: Union Générale d'Éditions, 1959.
- *Lectures on Philosophy.* Transcribed by Anne Reynaud-Guérithault, translated by Hugh Price. Cambridge: Cambridge University Press, 1978.
- "Necessity and Obedience." In Weil, *Gravity and Grace,* 43–50.
- *The Need for Roots.* Translated by Arthur Wills. London: Routledge Classics, 2002.
- *The Notebooks of Simone Weil.* Vol. 1. Translated by Arthur Wills. London: Routledge & Kegan Paul, 1976.
- *The Notebooks of Simone Weil.* Vol. 2. Translated by Arthur Wills. London: Routledge & Kegan Paul, 1956.
- «Notes sur le caractère.» In Weil, *Œuvres complètes,* tome IV, vol. 1, 80–9.
- *Œuvres complètes.* 7 tomes. Edited by Robert Chenavier, André A. Devaux, and Florence de Lussy. Paris: Éditions Gallimard, 1988–.
- *Œuvres complètes.* Tome I, *Premiers écrits philosophiques,* edited by Gilbert Kahn and Rolf Kühn. Paris: Éditions Gallimard, 1988.

‒ *Œuvres complètes.* Tome IV, vol. 1, *Écrits de Marseille,* edited by Monique Broc-Lapeyre, Marie-Annette Fourneyron, Pierre Kaplan, Florence de Lussy, and Jean Riaud. Paris: Éditions Gallimard, 2008.

‒ *Oppression and Liberty.* Translated by Arthur Wills and John Petrie. New York: Routledge Classics, 2006.

‒ *Pensées sans ordre concernant l'amour de Dieu.* Paris: Éditions Gallimard, 1962.

‒ «La personne et le sacré.» In Weil, *Écrits de Londres,* 11–44.

‒ *La pesanteur et la grâce.* Paris: Librairie Plon, [1947] 1988.

‒ «La philosophie.» *Cahiers du Sud,* no. 235 (May 1941) : 288–94. [Published under the pseudonym Emile Novis.]

‒ "Philosophy." In Weil, *Formative Writings,* 283–9.

‒ «Quelques réflexions autour de la notion de valeur.» In Weil, *Œuvres complètes,* tome IV, vol. 1, 53–61.

‒ "Reflections on the Right Use of School Studies." In Weil, *Waiting for God,* 57–65.

‒ "Science and Perception in Descartes." In Weil, *Formative Writings,* 31–88.

‒ «Science et perception dans Descartes.» In Weil, *Œuvres complètes,* tome I, 161–221.

‒ "Some Reflections around the Concept of Value." Translated by Eric O. Springsted. *Philosophical Investigations* 37, no. 2 (April 2014): 105–12. [Reprinted in Weil, *Late Philosophical Writings,* 29–36.]

‒ «Sur l'imagination.» Transcribed by Elisabeth Bigot-Chanel and Yvette Argaud, edited by Gilbert Kahn. *Cahiers Simone Weil* 8, no. 2 (June 1985): 121–6.

‒ *Waiting for God.* Translated by Emma Craufurd. New York: HarperCollins, 2001.

Weiss, Roslyn. "Learning without Teaching." *Interpretation* 34, no. 1 (Fall/Winter 2006): 3–21.

‒ *Virtue in the Cave: Moral Inquiry in Plato's "Meno."* New York: Oxford University Press, 2001.

Westra, Laura. "From Aldo Leopold to the Wildlands Project: The Ethics of Integrity." *Environmental Ethics* 23, no. 3 (Fall 2001): 261–74.

Williams, Bernard. "A critique of utilitarianism." In *Utilitarianism: for and against,* 77–150. Cambridge at the University Press, 1973.

‒ *Ethics and the Limits of Philosophy.* Cambridge: Harvard University Press, 1985.

‒ *Moral Luck.* Cambridge: Cambridge University Press, 1981.

‒ "Persons, character and morality." In Williams, *Moral Luck,* 1–19.

‒ "Utilitarianism and moral self-indulgence." In Williams, *Moral Luck,* 40–53.

Williams, J. Mark G. "Mindfulness, Depression and Modes of Mind." *Cognitive Therapy and Research* 32, no. 6 (December 2008): 721–33.

Williams, Mark, and Danny Penman. *Mindfulness.* New York: Rodale, 2012.

Williams, Michael. *Problems of Knowledge.* Oxford: Oxford University Press, 2001.

Winch, Peter. "Moral Integrity." In *Ethics and Action,* 171–92. London: Routledge & Kegan Paul, 1972.

– *Simone Weil: "The Just Balance."* Cambridge: Cambridge University Press, 1989.

Wittgenstein, Ludwig. "Cause and Effect: Intuitive Awareness." In Wittgenstein, *Philosophical Occasions,* 368–405.

– *Culture and Value.* Edited by G.H. von Wright, translated by Peter Winch. Chicago: University of Chicago Press, 1984.

– "A Lecture on Ethics." *The Philosophical Review* 74, no. 1 (January 1965): 3–12.

– *Notebooks 1914–1916.* Translated by G.E.M. Anscombe. New York: Harper Torchbooks, 1969.

– *On Certainty.* Translated by Denis Paul and G.E.M. Anscombe. Oxford: Basil Blackwell, 1979.

– *Philosophical Investigations.* 3rd ed. Translated by G.E.M. Anscombe. Malden: Blackwell, 2001.

– *Philosophical Occasions: 1912–1951.* Edited by James Klagge and Alfred Nordmann. Indianapolis: Hackett Publishing Company, 1993.

– *Philosophical Remarks.* Edited by Rush Rhees, translated by Raymond Hargreaves and Roger White. Oxford: Basil Blackwell, 1990.

– "Remarks on Frazer's *Golden Bough.*" In Wittgenstein, *Philosophical Occasions,* 115–55.

– *Tractatus Logico-Philosophicus.* Translated by D.F. Pears and B.F. McGuinness. London: Routledge Classics, 2001.

Wolfe, Katharine. "Together in Need: Relational Selfhood, Vulnerability to Harm, and Enriching Attachments." *The Southern Journal of Philosophy* 54, no. 1 (March 2016): 129–48.

Wollheim, Richard. *Painting as an Art.* Princeton: Princeton University Press, 1987.

Wu, Wayne. *Attention.* London: Routledge, 2014.

– "Attention as Selection for Action." In *Attention: Philosophical and Psychological Essays,* edited by Christopher Mole, Declan Smithies, and Wu, 97–116. New York: Oxford University Press, 2011.

Xenophon. *Anabasis. Xenophon in Seven Volumes.* Vol. 3. Translated by Carleton L. Brownson. Cambridge: Harvard University Press, 1922.

Zavattini, Cesare. "Some Ideas on the Cinema." Translated by Pier Luigi Lanza. In *Vittorio De Sica: Contemporary Perspectives,* edited by Howard Curle and Stephen Snyder, 50–61. Toronto: University of Toronto Press, 2000.

Zwicky, Jan. "Alcibiades' Love." In *Philosophy as a Way of Life: Ancients and Moderns,* edited by Michael Chase, Stephen R.L. Clark, and Michael McGhee, 84–98.

Chichester: John Wiley & Sons, 2013. [Reprinted in Zwicky, *Alkibiades' Love*, 283–97.]

– *Alkibiades' Love: Essays in Philosophy.* Montreal & Kingston: McGill-Queen's University Press, 2015.

– "Being, Polyphony, Lyric: An Open Letter to Robert Bringhurst." *Canadian Literature* 156 (Spring 1998): 181–4.

– "Bringhurst's Presocratics: Lyric and Ecology." *Terra Nova: Nature and Culture* 1, no. 1 (1995): 42–58, and no. 2 (1996): 77–98.

– "Bringhurst's Presocratics: Lyric and Ecology." In *Poetry and Knowing: Speculative Essays & Interviews*, edited by Tim Lilburn, 65–117. Kingston: Quarry Press, 1995. [Reprinted in Zwicky, *Alkibiades' Love*, 19–58.]

– *Chamber Music.* Edited by Darren Bifford and Warren Heiti. Waterloo: Wilfrid Laurier University Press, 2015.

– "Dream Logic and the Politics of Interpretation." In *Thinking and Singing: Poetry & the Practice of Philosophy*, edited by Tim Lilburn, 121–51. Toronto: Cormorant Books, 2002. [Reprinted in Zwicky, *Alkibiades' Love*, 85–106.]

– "The Experience of Meaning." In *Simplicity: Ideals of Practice in Mathematics and the Arts*, edited by Roman Kossak and Philip Ording, 85–103. Cham: Springer, 2017.

– *Forge.* Kentville: Gaspereau Press, 2011.

– "Imagination and the Good Life." *Common Knowledge* 20, no. 1 (Winter 2014): 28–45. [Reprinted in Zwicky, *Alkibiades' Love*, 262–82.]

– "Integrity and Ornament." In *Crime and Ornament: The Arts and Popular Culture in the Shadow of Adolf Loos*, edited by Bernie Miller and Melony Ward, 205–16. Toronto: YYZ Books, 2002.

– "Just the World." In *Bush Dweller*, edited by Donald B. Ward, 35–7. Muenster: St Peter's Press, 2010.

– *Lyric Philosophy.* Toronto: University of Toronto Press, 1992.

– *Lyric Philosophy.* 2nd ed. Kentville: Gaspereau Press, 2011.

– "Lyric Realism: Nature Poetry, Silence, and Ontology." *The Malahat Review* 165 (December 2008): 85–91.

– "Once Upon a Time in the West: Heidegger and the Poets." In *Thinking and Singing: Poetry & the Practice of Philosophy*, edited by Tim Lilburn, 187–99. Toronto: Cormorant Books, 2002.

– "Oracularity." *Metaphilosophy* 34, no. 4 (July 2003): 488–509. [Reprinted in Zwicky, *Alkibiades' Love*, 107–29.]

– *Plato as Artist.* Kentville: Gaspereau Press, 2009. [Reprinted in Zwicky, *Alkibiades' Love*, 144–210.]

– "Plato's *Phaedrus*: Philosophy as Dialogue with the Dead." *Apeiron* 30, no. 1 (March 1997): 19–48. [Reprinted in Zwicky, *Alkibiades' Love*, 59–84.]
– *Robinson's Crossing*. London: Brick Books, 2004.
– "A Ship from Delos." In *Learning to Die: Wisdom in the Age of Climate Crisis*, by Zwicky and Robert Bringhurst, 41–71. Regina: University of Regina Press, 2018.
– "What Is Ineffable?" *International Studies in the Philosophy of Science* 26, no. 2 (June 2012): 197–217. [Reprinted in Zwicky, *Alkibiades' Love*, 237–61.]
– "What Is Lyric Philosophy?" *Common Knowledge* 20, no. 1 (Winter 2014): 14–27. [Reprinted in Zwicky, *Alkibiades' Love*, 3–18.]
– *Wisdom & Metaphor*. 2nd ed. Kentville: Gaspereau Press, 2008.
Zwicky, Jan, and Tim Lilburn. *Contemplation and Resistance: A Conversation*. LaRonge: JackPine Press, 2003.
Zwicky, Jan, and Jay Ruzesky. "The Details: An Interview with Jan Zwicky." *The Malahat Review: The Green Imagination* 165 (December 2008): 92–7.

Index